Case Studies
in Advanced Financial F

Case Studies in Advanced Financial Reporting

John Casey and Clare Kearney

Published by
Chartered Accountants Ireland
Chartered Accountants House
47 – 49 Pearse Street
Dublin 2
www.charteredaccountants.ie

ISBN: 978-1-907214-93-6

Typeset by Datapage
Printed and bound by GRAFO, S.A.

JC:

To my Dad, thanks for everything

CK:

To Bernard, with love and thanks

Table of Contents

Introduction

This book is written for students of advanced financial reporting modules of masters in accounting programmes and for students studying for the later stages of the financial reporting examinations of the professional accounting bodies.

The case studies are not intended to be sample exam questions. Instead, they should be used to practice both technical knowledge and answering case study style questions. Often, the time taken to answer these case studies is beyond the length of time that you may have in an exam. This should not be a source of concern.

While the case studies are deliberately complex, they do not address obscure reporting issues. It is the number of different issues that make these case studies challenging. Each individual issue on its own should be relatively manageable once you have studied the relevant standard(s). Combining all of the issues together is sometimes where the difficulty lies.

How to use this book

This book is a series of case studies on 'close-to-real-life' companies. Each case study follows a similar format:

- The **details** of the case study
  - The background to the company is set out, which is often important as it provides an insight into the type of financial reporting issues that subsequently arise.
  - Then the various issues are elaborated upon and, usually, a draft of the financial statements is provided.
  - This is followed by the requirements and allocation of marks.
- The **guidance** section
  - The purpose of the guidance section is to provide some tips on how to begin to answer the requirements of the case study. This section is structured along the lines of the requirements. Sometimes it is easy to get blind-sided by all of the information that is provided in the text of the case study. Hopefully, the guidance will eliminate this by ensuring that attention is focused on the main issues involved.
  - The intention is not to provide the answer, but to direct the reader towards the solution. This is often done by suggesting the appropriate paragraphs of the relevant standard.
  - The guidance section also provides some suggestions on examination technique that may be relevant to the case study under consideration.
- The **solution**
  - The solution provided is comprehensive. The intention is to explain how the solution was arrived at and not to present a series of journal entries without any commentary.
  - However, this approach results in very lengthy solutions – much more than what could reasonably be expected in an exam scenario. With that in mind, the *key* elements of each solution are presented in grey shading, showing the bare detail of what might be required for an exam.

Apart from the first three case studies, the order that the case studies appear in this book is not significant. The first three case studies (Armada, Knightstown and Derrynane) address standards that usually appear on the syllabus of an intermediate financial reporting subject, e.g. the second year of an accounting degree course. While, you may not have approached the standards from a case study perspective, it should be possible to answer these cases based on your previous studies.

Exam Technique: The Case Study Technique

These case studies are essentially a series of financial reporting problems that framed within the context of a particular company. In many instances, the sector in which the company operates is not of great significance, as your solution should rely on the relevant financial reporting standard. These standards do not tend to be industry specific, so if you can identify the broader principle from the information provided then you have made the first step in answering that particular issue.

In this book, each individual issue is clearly delineated. This is intentional: the case method itself is an abstraction of reality. In real life it is different, as there can be many conflicting sources of information present – a lot of 'noise'. It is often best to deal with each issue in turn, make an informed decision, set out the journal entry (if necessary) and then move on. You need to be ruthless with your time in an exam.

Another unique aspect of this book is how group financial reporting is treated. In many of the case studies (Case Study 4, Stay Inn, is an example) various financial reporting issues are described. Then you are asked to redraft the financial statements (as an intermediate step) before going on to complete the consolidated financial statements. In an examination, the intermediate step (redrafting the financial statements prior to the process of consolidation) is not a normal requirement and this stage is skipped. The reason it is included in these case studies is for clarity purposes, otherwise the solutions may be too difficult to follow. In addition, by splitting many cases in two (the general reporting problems and the consolidation related issues) it means that it is possible to part answer them without having all of the material/syllabus covered as part of your study.

Exam Technique: Time Management

While these case studies are not intended to be sample exam questions, it is important to keep an eye on the clock as you attempt the requirements. Bear in mind that as you start your course, these cases may take considerable time to answer. However, as you get closer to the exam you should notice that it takes less time to complete them. (As noted earlier, these cases are considerably longer than what might be expected to appear as an exam question.)

Try not to get bogged down in any one issue. Remember: you do not have to get 100% to pass an exam. However, if you spend too long on one issue to the detriment of the remainder of the case study then you will jeopardise your chances of passing the exam. Marks are usually allocated to all elements of the case study so trying for perfection is not a good exam strategy. In any case study it is important to complete the answer. A large number of students make the mistake of producing the workings but then failing to produce the financial statements detailed in the requirements.

The number of marks allocated to each requirement gives an indication of the relative length of time that it should take to complete your answer. It is important that you begin to appreciate the discipline of time management as you work through the cases.

You will notice that the requirements can either be technical or discursive. It is possible to get consumed by the technical requirements (resolving the issues, preparing the financial statements). Often, the discursive requirements can take considerably less time to answer and attract relatively 'easy' marks. As you become more practised, try to get a feel for this distinction – don't leave the discursive marks behind by not answering that requirement, sometimes it may be beneficial to answer the discursive question out of sequence.

Benefits of this Book

We believe this book has many potential benefits, both for students and instructors:

For the Student

The first three case studies are based on typical intermediate level accounting standards. Often the knowledge acquired on an intermediate financial reporting programme is re-examinable on an advanced programme. This serves a number of purposes: first, it will aid the revision and application of the intermediate level material. Secondly, it acts as a useful introduction to the case study method as students should already have the basic knowledge to answer these cases. Thus, you will not be grappling with new material, which can often obscure your thinking.

With regard to the benefits for students of all the cases:

(a) The cases are technical and cover practically all of the international reporting standards. Through applied learning, students gain exposure to all aspects of a typical advanced financial reporting syllabus.

(b) Advanced financial reporting examination candidates are required to consider the appropriate accounting treatment of a number of (often) multi-layered financial issues. These case studies are structured in a multi-layered format so that students learn to identify the pertinent issues in each case and present answers that are both acurate and complete.

(c) The cases simulate 'real life'. Many of the issues included in these case studies are derived from our observations of business practice. Studies show that an extremely effective tool in learning is to simulate real life. Accounting standards do not exist in individual blocks in practice and any instruction should reflect this.

(d) The case studies have an inherent structure. This is an abstraction from real life and, while it could be argued that it unduly simplifies the scenario, learning at this level is a process and students cannot be expected to jump immediately into a full case study where the information is provided in an unstructured format. This could be too difficult and may have the undesired effect of creating a sense of overload.

(e) A guidance note is provided with each case study. Students can choose to refer to this as they attempt the requirements of the case study or can answer the case study 'blind' (similar to exam conditions). The guidance notes are designed to help students through the case studies. However, they do not provide students with the answer. In our experience students find the quantity of information on an advanced financial reporting course quite intimidating. The guidance notes provide students with focus and direction, while at the same time ensuring that judgement and knowledge are used to arrive at a solution. The intention is to help students in the transition from knowledge acquisition to knowledge application.

(f) A grievance that many students have is that solutions provided to sample questions and case studies are overly comprehensive and cannot be replicated in a time constrained examination. We provide two versions of the solution to each case study: a comprehensive version and a 'key elements' version. The intention behind the 'key elements' version is to provide students with an indication of an 'examination acceptable' correct solution without the explanation and detail of the comprehensive solution. The key elements in each solution are highlighted in greyscale shading.

(g) Considerable discussion of and advice on exam technique is also provided. It has been our experience that many students do not perform to their knowledge and ability in exams because of poor exam technique. Rather than include a chapter on exam technique, we decided to intersperse the advice throughout the book as part of the 'guidance note'. By grounding the advice in the context of each case study it is hoped to increase its impact and relevance.

For the instructor:

(a) This book provides the instructor with a block of cases to use in lectures to illustrate the application of accounting standards. The structure of the case studies allows one to either dip in and out of individual cases to illustrate particular aspects, or work through a case study in its entirety.

(b) While it is intended that this book can be used in conjunction with any advanced financial reporting textbook, each case study is referenced in detail to Ciaran Connolly, *International Financial Accounting and Reporting*, 3rd Edition, (Chartered Accountants Ireland. 2011) Furthermore, a table referencing the case studies back to the financial reporting standards is provided below. This should make the teaching task less onerous and save the instructor time and effort in linking the case notes back to their original source.

(c) While one complete solution is provided, the 'key elements' of the solution are separately highlighted. The intention is that the 'key elements' are short, concise and covers only the necessary journal entries and/or adjustments to the draft statements. The short form can be used in class to review answers in an expedient fashion while students can review the long from answers in their own time to ensure they understand the basis of all answers. This will save the instructor time and should keep instruction focused and concise.

(d) The solution is referenced back to the original sources.

(e) The guidance notes provide direction and advice on each case study. This note summarises what the case is about, outlines what sections of the accounting standards candidates may wish to review before they begin the case and gives advice on time management and professional presentation. This note should save the instructor time and effort when preparing the lecture.

Summary of the Cases

The table below provides a list of the standards that are addressed in each case study. The number of tick marks gives an indication of the depth of knowledge required of the particular standard in order to be able to attempt that case study (three tick marks indicating a greater level of knowledge required than one tick mark).

Standards	Armada	Knightstown	Derrynane	Stay Inn	Pickle	Howard	Doherty	Dove Air	Led	Elite	IWTL	Rochfort
IFRS 1 *First Time Adoption of IFRS*												
IFRS 2 *Share Based Payments*												
IFRS 3 *Business Combinations*	√√√	√√√		√√√	√√√				√√√		√√√	
IFRS 5 *Non Current Assets Held for Sale and Discontinued Operations*				√√√			√√√			√√√	√√√	
IFRS 7 *Financial Instruments: Disclosures*						√√				√√√	√√	
IFRS 8 *Operating segments*												√√√
IFRS 9 *Financial Instruments*					√	√√√					√√	
IFRS 10 *Consolidated Financial Statements*	√√√	√√√		√√√	√√√				√√√		√√√	
IFRS 11 *Joint Arrangements*												

Standards	Armada	Knightstown	Derrynane	Stay Inn	Pickle	Howard	Doherty	Dove Air	Led	Elite	IWTL	Rochfort
IFRS 12 *Disclosure of Interests in Other Entities*												
IFRS 13 *Fair Value Measurement*	√				√√	√√						
IAS 1 *Presentation of Financial Statements*	√√√	√√√	√√√	√√√	√√√	√√√	√√√		√√√		√√√	
IAS 2 *Inventories*	√√√	√√√					√√√		√√√			
IAS 7 *Cash Flow Statements*								√√√		√√√		
IAS 8 *Accounting Policies, Changes in Estimates & Errors*			√√√	√√√	√√√							
IAS 10 *Events after the Reporting Period*	√√√	√√	√√√	√√			√√			√√		
IAS 11 *Construction Contracts*		√√√					√√					
IAS 12 *Taxation*						√√√	√√√					
IAS 16 *PPE*	√√√	√√√	√√√	√√√	√√√	√√				√√		

Standards	Armada	Knightstown	Derrynane	Stay Inn	Pickle	Howard	Doherty	Dove Air	Led	Elite	IWTL	Rochfort
IAS 17 *Leases*			√√√			√√√		√√√		√√√		
IAS 18 *Revenue Recognition*				√√√		√√√	√√√		√√			
IAS 19 *Employee Benefits*				√√√	√√√							
IAS 20 *Accounting for Government Grants*				√√								√√
IAS 21 *The Effects of Changes in Foreign Exchange Rates*				√√√							√√√	
IAS 23 *Borrowing Costs*					√√√	√√√						
IAS 24 *Related Party transactions*									√√√		√√	√√√
IAS 28 *Investments in Associates*						√√					√√√	
IAS 32 *Financial Instruments – Presentation*						√√						√

Standards	Armada	Knightstown	Derrynane	Stay Inn	Pickle	Howard	Doherty	Dove Air	Led	Elite	IWTL	Rochfort
IAS 33 *Earnings per Share*							√√√		√√			√√√
IAS 34 *Interim Financial Reporting*												√√
IAS 36 *Impairment of Assets*				√			√√√					
IAS 37 *Provisions, Contingent assets and Contingent Liabilities*				√	√√√	√√	√√		√√	√√√		√√√
IAS 38 *Intangible Assets*				√√		√√	√√		√√√			
IAS 39 *Financial Instruments: Recognition and Measurement*											√√	
IAS 40 *Investment Properties*				√√√		√√√	√√		√√			
IAS 41 *Agriculture*												

Acknowledgements

We are both indebted to Michael Diviney, Director of Publishing, who saw the merit of this project in its initial, raw state. We are also sincerely grateful to Becky McIndoe at Chartered Accountants Ireland, who had the unenviable task of editing the original manuscript, displaying considerable patience with our inability to meet deadlines. If she was in any way annoyed with us, she certainly didn't show it. Any remaining errors and omissions are entirely our own.

As part of the process of developing this book, a number of reviewers read early drafts. The comments we received back were extremely helpful and contributed greatly to ensuring that the cases were realistic and (hopefully) error free. We are very grateful to those anonymous reviewers who generously gave their time to this project.

To all our colleagues at Waterford Institute of Technology, who encouraged and supported us while we developed the cases. If either of us has appeared distracted at times, you now know why.

A special note of gratitude to the students on the MBS in Accounting at WIT: you have been unwitting guinea pigs in the development of these cases.

Individually, …

John Casey: I would like to acknowledge the support of my family: Bríd, Liam and Eimear, my mother and father (Lilian and Denis), my sisters (Edel, Lisa and Pony) and, in the interests of harmony over the Christmas dinner, my own in-laws (Mary, Michael, Nuala, Aodan, Colman) as well as those in-laws that I can thank my sisters for (Eamon, Kieran and Cian).

Clare Kearney: Thank you to my nearest and dearest: to Bernard, Anna, John and Stephen, thank you for your constant support and patience. To Nora and Paddy, my parents, thank you for the encouragement and all the homemade brown bread(!). And to the rest of my family (siblings, inlaws and 'out'laws) thanks for the kind, practical and often humorous advice; it made it all worthwhile.

Case 1

Armada Group

This case study is based on a manufacturing and distribution company. The accounting standards IAS 1, IAS 2, IAS 10, IAS 16, IFRS 3, IFRS 10 and IFRS 13 are addressed in this case.

Background – The Armada Group

You are the financial accountant to Armada Plc. Armada Plc is a diversified manufacturing and distribution company. It was founded in 1999 by Heather Connolly and Tony O'Brien who set up the business following redundancy from their previous employments. Both founders had a wealth of experience when embarking on their new business. They raised finance in 1998 and began to trade on the 1 January 1999. Armada's financial year-end is 31 December. It is now January 2013. You are preparing the financial statements for the year ended 31 December 2012.

You are based in head office and have just finished the first draft of the financial statements of the parent company. There are a number of outstanding issues that you need to discuss with the finance director (see below: 'Outstanding Issues').

Once these are resolved, you hope to move on to preparing the consolidated financial statements. The company has just one subsidiary, Gem Limited. The subsidiary company has submitted their financial statements to you (see below: 'Consolidating the Results of Gem with Armada').

The 2012 draft financial statements of Armada Plc, the parent company, are as follows:

Armada Plc
DRAFT STATEMENT OF FINANCIAL POSITION
as at 31 December 2012

Non-current Assets	**€000**
Property, plant and equipment	7,500
Long-term investments (Gem)	7,500
Loan to Gem	1,500
Intangible assets (all development expenditure)	11,000
	27,500
Current Assets	
Inventories	4,500
Trade receivables	2,000
Cash and cash equivalents	8,000
	14,500
Total Net Assets	**42,000**
Equity	
Ordinary share capital (€1 each)	10,000
Share premium	3,000
Retained earnings	19,500
Revaluation surplus	450
	32,950
Non-current Liabilities	
Bank loans	1,000
Bonds	2,500
Provisions	300
Retirement benefit obligations	1,200
Non-current trade payables	200
Deferred tax	500
	5,700
Current Liabilities	
Payables	300
Intragroup payable (to Gem)	2,500
Bank loans	300
Current tax	250
	3,350
Total Equity and Liabilities	**42,000**

Armada Plc
STATEMENT OF COMPREHENSIVE INCOME
for the year ended 31 December 2012

	€000
Revenue	**50,000**
Cost of sales	(32,000)
Gross Profit	**18,000**
Other operating income	500
Selling and distribution costs	(11,000)
Administration costs	(2,500)
Profit from Operations	5,000
Finance costs	(250)
Profit Before Tax	**4,750**
Taxation	(500)
Profit for the Year	**4,250**
Other Comprehensive Income	
Gain on property revaluation	250
	250
Total Comprehensive Income	**4,500**

Armada Plc
STATEMENT OF CHANGES IN EQUITY
for year ended 31 December 2012

	Share Capital	Share Premium	Retained Earnings	Revaluation Surplus	Total
	€000	€000	€000	€000	€000
Opening Balance	**10,000**	**3,000**	**16,250**	**200**	**29,450**
Comprehensive Income			4,250	250	4,500
Dividend			(1,000)		(1,000)
Closing Balance	**10,000**	**3,000**	**19,500**	**450**	**32,950**

Outstanding Issues in Respect of the Parent Company's Financial Statements

Outstanding Issue 1

Armada constructed a showroom that was ready for its intended use on 31 October 2012. The costs incurred in construction and then capitalised were as follows:

	€
Land at cost	600,000
Building cost	1,600,000
Labour costs	1,000,000
Architect's fees	170,000
Solicitor's fees	100,000
General overhead allocated	30,000
Site identification fees	100,000
	€3,600,000

The company paid €100,000 to a consultant; this is included under 'site identification fees'. The consultant was hired to identify a suitable site; however, he was unsuccessful. In the end, the building was constructed on land identified by one of the company's accountants for whom no separate fees were allocated.

Labour costs include overtime of €180,000. This overtime was not included in the original projections. The overtime occurred because additional work had to be carried out on the roof of the building. A large section of roof tiles were damaged during a severe storm. It was discovered that the tiles were not properly secured in the first place. If they had been properly secured, the tiles would have weathered the storm.

Included in the building cost above is the annual insurance premium of €90,000. The insurance cover runs from the 1 November 2012 to 31 October 2013.

A government grant, of €300,000 towards the cost of construction, was received in December 2012. This was credited, in full, to 'Other operating income' in the Statement of Comprehensive Income. It is the company's policy to deduct capital grants from the cost of the relevant assets in accordance with IAS16 Property, Plant and Equipment, paragraph 28 and IAS 20 *Accounting for Government Grants and Disclosure of Government Assistance*. (Although IAS 20 permits two methods for presenting government grants relating to assets, the current legal position in ROI is that the immediate deduction approach is prohibited. For the purpose of this case study the legal position has been set aside to allow the provisions of the accounting standards to be demonstrated).

No depreciation has yet been charged on the showroom. The group's policy is to charge depreciation monthly at a rate of 5% per annum (straight line).

Outstanding Issue 2

Armada Plc measures its land and buildings at re-valued amounts. Revaluation reviews are conducted on a regular basis. In January 2012, a review was carried out and a surplus of €250,000 was recorded at that time. (See the Statement of Changes in Equity in the draft financial statements.)

Although the review was correctly recorded in the financial statements in January 2012, it is now clear that a further review of the company's property portfolio is necessary. There are indications that two other properties held by the company have significantly changed in value since the beginning of the year and their carrying values may need to be revised.

The first of these properties is Property Z, which was originally acquired on 1 January 2002 for €500,000 and was being written off over 50 years (straight-line method). It was re-valued upwards by €200,000 at the end of 2007 and this revaluation balance is still outstanding. The remaining useful life, at the time (end of 2007), was revised to 40 years. An auctioneer has now valued this property at €407,000.

The second property, Site X, was acquired in 2006 for €265,000. Site X, a five-acre plot of land, was not depreciated as it was considered to have an indefinite economic life. In 2009 the site was reduced in value by €50,000 and a charge for this amount was made to the income statement. In 2012, planning permission was granted to build a private hospital in the area. As a result, property prices there have risen. Property X is now valued at €305,000.

Outstanding Issue 3

A new accounting clerk joined Armada Plc towards the end of the financial year. She was given responsibility for valuing part of the year-end inventory that is stored in a warehouse located in Cork. She has calculated the value of this inventory using different valuation techniques as follows:

- Last In First Out (LIFO) €100,000;
- First In First Out (FIFO) €120,000; and
- Net Realisable Value (NRV) €140,000.

This inventory has been included in the overall inventory figure in the draft financial statements at the lowest value of €100,000.

Additionally, included in 'Finished Goods', in the group inventory is a small amount of product which the company no longer manufactures. Since the year-end, the company has managed to secure a customer for the discontinued product. The agreed selling price is €154,000. To modify the product to customer specifications, the company will incur additional costs of €16,000. This inventory is included in the overall inventory at a cost of €152,000.

Finally, inventory to the value of €1.3 million has been pledged as security on the group's borrowings.

Outstanding Issue 4

The financial director is unsure how to include the following transaction in the financial statements and nothing has been entered so far. He is unsure whether this transaction should be accrued, disclosed or omitted from the financial statements altogether.

The background to this transaction is that in January 2013 one of Armada's principal customers, Howlett Ltd, closed down. A fire at their premises in the UK on 18 January 2013 destroyed the company's factory and all of its inventory. A news report states that the company is unable to continue trading.

The closure of Howlett is likely to have a material impact on Armada Plc. Armada has been selling goods to Howlett Ltd for several years. Sales to Howlett Ltd constitute about 5% of Armada's annual sales.

The CEO of Armada, although very concerned about the situation, has proposed that no reference be made about this event in the 2012 financial statements. He is of the opinion that, as the event took place in 2013, it should be treated in the financial statements of that year. He proposes that a full disclosure be made in the 2013 financial statements and nothing until then.

An amount of €670,000 is outstanding from Howlett Limited at 31 December 2012 and this is included in trade receivables in the draft financial statements above.

Consolidating the Results of Gem with Armada

Having resolved outstanding issues one to four, your next task is to prepare the consolidated financial statements. There is one subsidiary in the group. The draft results for the subsidiary, Gem Ltd, are shown below.

Gem Ltd
DRAFT STATEMENT OF FINANCIAL POSITION
for the Year Ended 31 December 2012

	€000
Non-current Assets	
Property, plant and equipment	1,000
Intangible assets (all development expenditure)	1,000
	2,000
Current Assets	
Inventories	500
Trade receivables	750
Intragroup receivable (from Armada)	4,000
Cash and cash equivalents	2,500
	7,750
Total Net Assets	9,750

Equity	
Ordinary share capital (€1 each)	1,000
Retained earnings	3,000
	4,000
Non–current Liabilities	
Bank loans	2,000
Loan from Armada	1,500
Provisions	500
Retirement benefit obligations	200
Non-current trade payables	200
Deferred tax	100
	4,500
Current Liabilities	
Payables	800
Bank loans	250
Current tax	200
	1,250
Total Equity and Liabilities	9,750

Gem Ltd

DRAFT STATEMENT OF COMPREHENSIVE INCOME
for the Year Ended 31 December 2012

	€000
Revenue	10,000
Cost of sales	(5,500)
Gross profit	4,500
Other income	250
Selling and distribution costs	(2,500)
Administration costs	(1,200)
Finance costs	(100)
Profit before tax	950
Taxation	(200)
Profit for the year	750
Other comprehensive income	0
Total comprehensive income	750

Gem Ltd

DRAFT STATEMENT OF CHANGES IN EQUITY

For the Year Ended 31 December 2012

	Ordinary Share Capital €000	Retained Earnings €000	Total €000
Opening balance	1,000	2,250	3,250
Comprehensive income		750	750
Dividend		0	0
Closing balance	1,000	3,000	4,000

You have been provided with the following additional information regarding Gem Ltd which will be of assistance in the preparation of the consolidated financial statements:

Note 1: Purchase of Investment in Gem. On 29 May 2000 Armada purchased 80% of Gem for €7,500,000 when its retained earnings were €2,000,000 and ordinary share capital was €1,000,000. There were no fair value issues at acquisition.

Note 2: Intragroup Trading. On the acquisition of Gem, the group put in place procedures to leverage some of the benefits of the takeover. Gem now sells product to Armada. In the period Gem sold €5,000,000 worth of product to Armada at a mark up on cost of 25%. One quarter of this remained in the inventory of Armada at year end.

Although there is an agreement that intragroup payables be paid at year end, it does not always occur. In practice, Armada pays for the products purchased on an intermittent basis, see 'intragroup receivable' and 'intragroup payable'.

Just before year end Armada paid €1.5 million of the amount owed to Gem. However, due to the Christmas postal delay, the cheque was not received by Gem until after the year end.

Note 3: Intragroup Financing. In 2008, Gem underwent a major revamp of its production facility. Rather than approach a bank for the finance, the parent company gave a loan to Gem. The amount of the loan was €1.5 million. An interest rate of 4% was applied to the loan. The interest has been accounted for as other income by Armada and finance costs by Gem. There was no interest payable or receivable at year end.

Note 4: Valuation of Non-controlling Interests. The group values non-controlling interests (minority interest) based on the proportionate share of net assets, i.e. the traditional approach.

Requirements

(**Note**: Unless you are specifically required to consider deferred taxation, you can assume that it is not applicable.)

(a) You are required to re-draft the financial statements of Armada Plc (the parent) for the year ended 31 December 2012 (this incorporates Outstanding Issues numbers 1 to 4).

Your answer should include detailed workings for each of the issues and you should support your workings by reference to the relevant accounting rules.

(40 Marks)

(b) Prepare the Consolidated Financial Statements of the Armada Group of Companies as at 31 December 2012.

(50 Marks)

(c) Briefly comment on the following observation made by a shareholder of the Armada Group:

"The financial statements include many different valuation techniques. Property is valued at re-valued amounts, while other items of property, plant and equipment are at historical cost and inventory is measured at either cost or Net Realisable Value.

I wonder why so many different techniques are used in the one set of financial statements and is there one valuation technique that represents the true value of the business?"

(10 Marks)

Guidance Notes – Armada Group

Exam Technique

Read the case carefully; then read the requirements.

This case is written at an introductory level and incorporates some of the more basic accounting standards. This is the first of three case studies written at this level. The others are Knightstown and Derrynane. These cases can be used as revision as well as providing an introduction to more advanced aspects of financial reporting and the accounting standards.

The Armada case is divided into three sections:
1. Revision of the financial statements of the parent company, Armada Plc (see **requirement (a)**).
2. Completion of the consolidated accounts of the Armada Group (**requirement (b)**).
3. Commentary on the valuation techniques used in preparing financial statements (**requirement (c)**).

You should approach this case study by answering **requirement (a)** *before* you attempt the consolidation issues. **Requirement (a)** relates to the parent company only. In this section you are required to consider what adjustments should be made, if any, to the financial statements of Armada Plc (the parent). There are four separate issues to consider. Some issues will test you on a single international accounting standard while other issues will relate to more than one standard. This is purposely done. It is extremely important that you begin to take an integrated approach to accounting standards. A single event may have multiple reporting effects and you need to be familiar with many accounting standards to produce professional and complete answers.

This 'integrated' approach is introduced gently in these introductory case studies and is developed further later in the series.

When you have completed your recommended accounting treatment for the four issues you should then proceed to re-draft the parent's financial statements.

Once you have completed your answer to **requirement (a)**, you can then move on to the consolidation issues (**requirement (b)**). In answering consolidation style questions, it is important to have an approach that you can draw upon. In a consolidation question most of the marks are often awarded for:

- goodwill
- retained earnings
- non-controlling interests; and
- how you deal with each of the adjustments/additional information items.

Usually, there are only very few marks awarded to items that require just limited effort, e.g. if the group payables figure is just a matter of adding the parent's payables with those of the subsidiary then this will not attract very many marks (if any). However, if the group property plant and equipment (PPE) figure requires you to add the parent and the subsidiary's PPE and make a number of adjustments then the correct figure will be rewarded.

When you have completed the Consolidated Financial Statements of the Armada Group, you can then move on to the final section of the case study, **requirement (c)**. Here, you must prepare a brief memorandum addressing the observations made by a shareholder. Your answer need not be long but will require some careful thought on your behalf. Answer clearly and succinctly.

Finally, manage your time. You should establish, before commencing the case study, how much time you should allocate to each section. This should be done based on the marks allocated to each section; remember to allow some time at the beginning for reading the case study.

You will score better marks if you *attempt* all parts of the case rather than completing some sections and not answering others at all.

Answering the Case Study

Requirement (a) – Guidance

Outstanding Issue 1 – Construction of the Showroom This issue examines the accounting standard IAS 16 *Property, Plant and Equipment.*

To answer this requirement you will need to be reasonably familiar with what may, or may not, be included in the cost of an item of PPE. This is outlined in IAS 16, paragraphs 16–22.

If there are items that need to be excluded from the cost of PPE, you need to consider what journal entries are necessary to make the appropriate adjustments. You need also to be familiar with the point at which capitalisation begins and ends (IAS 16, para 16).

Armada received a government grant towards the cost of construction, which is currently included in 'other income' in the statement of comprehensive income. You will need to consider if this is acceptable treatment. IAS16, paragraph 28 will provide you with the relevant guidance. (The accounting treatment for the receipt of government grants is outlined in detail in

IAS20 *Accounting for Government Grants and Disclosure of Government Assistance*. It is not the intention of this case study to examine IAS20 other than to highlight the cross-reference with IAS 16.)

Finally, the inclusion of a depreciation charge must be considered. The calculation of depreciation is relatively straightforward and you should have no difficulty in approaching this calculation. The issue here is **when** to commence depreciation. IAS 16, paragraph 55, outlines when depreciation should commence and when it should cease.

Outstanding Issue 2 – Revaluation This issue tests your understanding of how the revaluation of assets should be treated in the financial statements. The rules of revaluation are laid down in IAS 16, paragraphs 31–42. Armada Plc measures its land and buildings at re-valued amounts. At the end of the financial year 2012, a revaluation review is required as there are indications that two of the company's properties have significantly changed in value.

The first of these properties, Property Z, has fallen in value. This property was previously re-valued at the end of 2007. You must decide how to record this latest change in value. Should the reduction be charged as a depreciation expense in profit or loss or should it be deducted from the outstanding revaluation surplus on this property?

Property X, a five-acre site, has increased in value. This site, acquired in 2006, was devalued in 2009 and a charge was made in the financial statements at that time. You must now decide how to record this latest increase. Should it be credited in full to the income statement or should it be added to the revaluation surplus?

The answer to these questions is outlined in IAS 16, paragraphs 31–42.

Outstanding Issue 3 – Inventories There are three separate inventory issues to consider. The first issue examines how inventory should be measured in the financial statements. Three separate values are given: €100,000 (LIFO), €120,000 (FIFO) and €140,000 (NRV). You need to consider which is the most appropriate measure to use. To answer this, you will need to familiarise yourself with the rules for measuring inventories. Review IAS 2, paragraphs 9–33.

The second inventory issue also considers how inventory is measured. In this issue you are presented with the cost of the inventory, but must determine the net realisable value (NRV). IAS 2, paragraphs 28–33, gives guidance on how NRV is determined.

Once you have established the NRV, you must then consider whether to measure inventory at cost or NRV. IAS 2, paragraph 9 will give the appropriate guidance.

The third inventory issue relates to inventory that has been pledged as security on a loan. This is a disclosure issue only. There are no adjustments required. IAS 2, paragraph 36(h), covers this point.

Outstanding Issue 4 – Events after the reporting period. This issue requires you to consider the reporting implications of an event that has occurred after the end of the reporting period. An important customer of Armada Plc has been forced to shut down its business due to a fire that destroyed its premises and inventory. The fire occurred in January 2013. You must consider whether this event is relevant to the 2012 financial statements. The CEO of Armada has proposed that no mention be made of this event in the 2012 financial statements. You must consider if this is an appropriate and ethical position to take on this matter.

To answer this requirement, you should refer to the accounting guidance in IAS 10 *Events after the Reporting Period.*

Prepare the Revised Financial Statements The final element of **requirement (a)** is to redraft the financial statements of Armada Plc, the parent company, incorporating any changes you propose to make. The revised financial statements will form the basis of the next requirement – the consolidated financial statements.

Requirement (b) – Guidance

In this requirement you will have to take the revised financial statements of Armada and consolidate these with the financial statements of Gem. You will need to include the effect of the additional information on the acquisition of Gem and the intragroup transactions. This information is provided following the draft financial statements of Gem Ltd. This can be a time-consuming exercise; however, deal with each item in turn, make your decision and then move on to the next item.

In this instance, you are asked to prepare a full set of consolidated financial statements. This is unusual; normally, the requirement is to prepare either a consolidated statement of financial position or a consolidated statement of comprehensive income. As a result, arriving at a solution will be more time-consuming. However, it is not double the work – the 'thinking time' on the additional information items need only occur once.

You will have to decide which statement to do first (the statement of financial position or the statement of comprehensive income). The solution given in this text begins with the statement of financial position. It does not matter which one you start with, the final outcome will be the same.

1. Consolidated Statement of Financial Position To assist in the preparation of the consolidated statement of financial position it is often beneficial to have a process to follow. This will allow you to spend extra time addressing the more complex issues. In addition, it may also prevent some basic errors that may arise from failing to identify the effect of the standard items of information. A four-step process is presented here. There are other approaches but it is important that you have your own system that you can rely on.

- **Step 1 – Set out the group structure** Usually, this is not difficult. The information for this is found in the additional information in note 1.
- **Step 2 – Deal with the 'additional information'**
  - Note 2 – Intragroup Trading: IFRS 10, paragraph B86, gives the regulatory guidance here. There are a number of items to consider. First, you will need to decide what to do with the total sales made by Gem and the purchases made by Armada. Then deal with the profit element that is included in the inventory of Armada. The next step will be to consider the payment made by Armada that is 'in transit' and has not been recorded by Gem. Finally, deal with any intragroup payable and receivable that is still outstanding.

- Note 3 – Intragroup Financing: This is similar to the preceding item – the effect of intragroup transactions will need to be eliminated. There are two elements to this arrangement. First, eliminate the intragroup interest expense in one company with the intragroup interest income in the other company. Then the 'loan asset' in one company will need to be eliminated against the 'loan liability' in the other.

- **Step 3 – Prepare the Consolidation Table** (i.e. calculate the goodwill, non-controlling interests and retained earnings figures) These are key figures in a consolidated statement of financial position (see **exam technique guidance**).

  Using the adjustments from Step 2, you should now be in a position to calculate the goodwill on acquisition of Gem, non-controlling interests and retained earnings. A template for this is presented below:

SPECIMEN CONSOLIDATION TABLE[1]

	Goodwill 80%	**Non-controlling Interests 20%**	**Retained Earnings**
	€	**€**	**€**
Cost of Acquisition (all in Goodwill column)	XX		
Ordinary Share Capital of Subsidiary, Gem (split 80:20)	XX	XX	
Retained Earnings of Subsidiary, Gem – pre-acquisition (split 80:20)	XX	XX	
Retained Earnings of Subsidiary Gem – post-acquisition (split 20:80)		XX	XX
Retained Earnings – Parent, Armada			XX
Adjustment 1	?	?	?
Adjustment 2	?	?	?
Adjustment 3	?	?	?
Adjustment X	?	?	?
Adjustment X	?	?	?
	XX	XX	XX

- **Step 4** – Bring Step 2 and Step 3 together to prepare the consolidated statement of financial position. This should be a relatively mechanical exercise, as all the thinking has been done. Take the revised financial statements of Armada and those of Gem. Just make sure that you correctly include all the adjustments that you have identified. Be sure to show the calculation of each of the figures in the statement of financial position. (**Note**: If you fail to do this, and some of the figures are incorrect, it will not be possible for the examiner to award any marks for those elements of the answer that are correct.)

Once you have prepared the statement of financial position, you should then move onto the statement of comprehensive income.

[1] The 'Consolidation Table' is just one approach to arriving at these figures. Other approaches may involve the use of 'T' accounts which can be more time-consuming.

2. Consolidated Statement of Comprehensive Income At this stage you will already be aware of the group structure and how the additional information should be dealt with. Thus, you should be able to start with the template for preparing the consolidated statement of comprehensive income. This is presented below – note that it looks very like the individual companies' statements of comprehensive income, except for the non-controlling interests items at the end.

SPECIMEN CONSOLIDATED STATEMENT OF COMPREHENSIVE INCOME
for the Year Ended 31 December 2012

	Armada Revised €000	**Gem €000**	**Adjust 1**	**Adjust 2**	**Adjust 3**	**Adjust X**	**Total €000**
Revenue	50,000	10,000					
Cost of sales	(31,994)	(5,500)					
Gross profit	18,006	4,500					
Other income	200	250					
Selling and distribution costs	(11,000)	(2,500)					
Administration costs	(2,794)	(1,200)					
Finance costs	(250)	(100)					
Profit before tax	4,162	950					
Taxation	(500)	(200)					
Profit for the year	3,662	750					
Other comprehensive income							
Gain on property revaluation	137	0					
	137	0					
Total comprehensive income	3,799	750					
Profit for the Year Attributable to							
Ordinary shareholders							
Non-controlling interests							
Total Comprehensive Income Attributable to							
Ordinary shareholders							
Non-controlling interests							

Consider each adjustment in turn and evaluate the impact that it has on items in the consolidated statement of comprehensive income. Fill in the appropriate items under each column.

To calculate the non-controlling interest figure, begin with the Gem's profits for the year. Then, consider if any of the adjustments impact on the profits of Gem (the alternatives are that they impact on the profits of Armada or there is no profit implication). Calculate the revised profits of Gem and then calculate 20% to arrive at the profit for the year attributable to the non-controlling interests:

	€000
Profit for the year – Gem	750
Items effecting the profit of Gem	
Adjust X	X
Adjust X	X
Revised profit of Gem	Y
Non-controlling interests @ 20% = 20% of €Y	

3. Consolidated Statement of Changes in Equity This is the final statement that you need to complete. The usual starting point is to begin with a blank template.

SPECIMEN CONSOLIDATED STATEMENT OF CHANGES IN EQUITY

	Ordinary Share Capital	Share Premium	Retained Earnings	Revaluation Surplus	Total Equity	Non-controlling Interests	Total
Opening balance							
Comprehensive income							
Dividend							
Closing balance							

Opening Balance This is the most difficult element of the consolidated statement of changes in equity. Consider each column in turn:

- Ordinary Share Capital: this is the opening balance of the ordinary share capital of the parent company (Armada) only.
- Share Premium: this is the opening balance of the share premium of the parent company (Armada) only.
- Retained Earnings: this is the opening balance of the retained earnings of the parent company (Armada) plus the group share of the opening post-acquisition retained earnings of the subsidiary (Gem).
- Revaluation Surplus: this is the opening balance of the revaluation surplus of the parent company (there is no revaluation surplus in the subsidiary company in this instance).
- Non-controlling Interests: this is 20% of the opening net assets of the subsidiary (no adjustments in this instance).

Of these items, the opening consolidated retained earnings is where most of the marks tend to be allocated:

	€	€
Opening retained earnings of Armada		X
Opening retained earnings of Gem	X	
Less pre-acquisition retained earnings	(Z)	
Opening post-acquisition retained earnings of Gem	Y	
Adjustments to opening post-acquisition retained earnings	0	
Revised opening retained earnings of Gem	Y	
Group share at 80%		V
Consolidated opening retained earnings		V+X

Comprehensive Income The entries into this row are taken from the consolidated statement of comprehensive income.

Dividend Include the dividend paid by the parent to the shareholders (and any dividend paid to the non-controlling interests but not in this case).

Requirement (c) – Guidance

This final part of the case study requires you to comment on the observations made by a shareholder of the Armada Group. This shareholder has observed that there are many different valuation techniques used in the financial statements. He would like to know why this is the case and which valuation method is the correct one to use.

There is no single accounting standard that will address this issue. You will have to use general accounting principles when preparing your answer. *The Conceptual Framework for Financial Reporting* will provide you with some guidance. You should refer specifically to the section on *Measurement of the Elements of Financial Statements.*

Recommended Reading

The accounting standards addressed in this case study may also be referenced in *International Financial Accounting and Reporting*, 3rd Edition, by Ciaran Connolly (Chartered Accountants Ireland, 2011) as follows:

	Chapter	Chapter title	Chapter section	Standard
Requirement (a)				
Outstanding Issue 1	6	Property, Plant and Equipment	6.2	IAS 16
Outstanding Issue 2	6	Property, Plant and Equipment	6.2	IAS 16
Outstanding Issue 3	11	Inventories	11.2	IAS 2
Outstanding Issue 4	15	Events after the Reporting Period	15.2	IAS 10
Requirement (b)				
	27	Consolidated Statement of Financial Position	27.2–27.5, 27.8, 27.11	IFRS 10
	28	Consolidated Statement of Comprehensive Income	28.2	IFRS 10
	26	Business Combinations and Consolidated Financial Statements	26.3, 26.4	IFRS 3
Requirement (c)				
	1	Framework for Financial Reporting	1.3–1.4	

Solution to Armada Group

Requirement (a)

Outstanding Issue 1

IAS 16 *Property, Plant and Equipment* outlines the accounting treatment for tangible non-current assets.

IAS 16, paragraphs 16–22, outlines what costs can be capitalised and what should be expensed. In summary, these paragraphs state that the cost of an item of property, plant and equipment comprises the purchase (or construction) price and any costs directly attributable to bringing the asset to the location and condition necessary for it to be capable of operating in the manner intended by management. Examples of attributable costs and non-attributable costs are outlined in IAS 16, paragraphs 17–22.

In the case study, all costs have been capitalised. In accordance with IAS 16, the following items would not qualify for inclusion. These are:

	€000	
Overtime	180	(abnormal waste IAS 16, paragraph 22)
General Overheads	30	(not allowed IAS 16, paragraph 19(d))
Insurance	90	(operating cost IAS 16, paragraph 19(c))
Site Identification	100	(not a necessary cost IAS 16, paragraph 16(b))
Total	400	

You must next consider the government grant. The company has selected the immediate deduction option for grants relating to assets. The correct entry should be to deduct the grant (€300,000) from the adjusted showroom cost (IAS 16, paragraph 28). The grant is currently included in operating income. An adjustment is required to bring the accounting treatment in line with the company's policy.

Once these adjustments have been put through the asset will be restated as follows:

	€000
Cost per draft financial statements	3,600
Adjustments:	
Overtime, overheads etc.	(400)
Grant	(300)
Revised	2,900

Finally, IAS 16, paragraph 50 states "The depreciable amount of the asset shall be allocated on a systematic basis over its useful life." The depreciable amount of the showroom is €2.3 million. This is the adjusted cost of the showroom less the site cost of €600,000. The site cost has been excluded for the purposes of calculating depreciation in accordance with IAS 16, paragraph 58. This paragraph states "land has an unlimited useful life and therefore is not depreciated."[2]

[2] There are a couple of exceptions to this rule such as quarries and sites used for landfills.

Depreciation will be charged on a monthly basis at a rate of 5% p.a. Depreciation should commence when the asset is available for use (IAS 16, paragraph 55). The showroom was available for use at the end of October 2012.

Two months' depreciation, €19,167, should be charged on the depreciable asset (€2.3m × 5% × 2/12).

The adjustments required to make these changes include:

		€	€
1.	DR Admin expenses	325,000	
	DR Trade and other receivables	75,000*	
	CR PPE		400,000
	(with costs to be excluded from PPE)		
2.	DR Other income	300,000	
	CR PPE		300,000
	(Grant to be credited against PPE cost)		
3.	DR Admin Expenses	19,167	
	CR PPE		19,167
	(with two months' depreciation on €2.3m)		

* The insurance premium is an operating expense and has now been excluded from PPE. Only two months of the premium relates to the current year (November and December). The remaining 10 months' premium is a prepayment and is included in trade and other receivables.

Outstanding Issue 2

PROPERTY Z

The carrying value of property Z, before the 2012 revaluation:

	€
Carrying value of asset	**560,000**
Arrived at as follows:	
Purchased: 1 January 2002	500,000
Depreciation 2002–2007*	(60,000)
	440,000
Revaluation 2007	200,000
Revised value	640,000
Depreciation 2008–2012**	(80,000)
Carrying value 31 Dec 2012	560,000

* Depreciation 2002–2007: €500,000/50 years = €10,000 per year × 6 years = €60,000
** Depreciation 2008–2012: €640,000/40 years = €16,000 per year × 5 years = €80,000

Property Z has now reduced in value to €407,000, a fall of €153,000. This reduction must be reflected in the financial statements in accordance with IAS 16, paragraph 40, which states:

"If an asset's carrying amount is decreased as a result of a revaluation, the decrease shall be recognised in profit or loss. However, the decrease shall be recognised in other comprehensive income to the extent of any credit balance existing in the revaluation surplus in respect of that asset."

As there is an outstanding revaluation surplus of €200,000 relating to this asset, the entire decrease of €153,000 can be set against it.

The journal for this change would be:

	€	€
DR Revaluation surplus	153,000	
CR Property, plant and equipment		153,000

Property X

The carrying value of property X, before the 2012 review was:

	€
Purchased 2006	265,000
Devaluation 2009	50,000
Revised value	215,000

Property X has now increased to €305,000, an increase of €90,000. This increase must be reflected in the financial statements in accordance with IAS 16, paragraph 39, which states:

"If an asset's carrying amount is increased as a result of a revaluation, the increase shall be recognised in other comprehensive income … under the heading of revaluation surplus. However, the increase shall be recognised in profit or loss to the extent that it reverses a revaluation decrease of the same asset previously recognised in profit or loss."

As the increase in value reverses a previous decrease that was included in profit or loss, that part of the increase (€50,000) shall be credited to profit or loss. The excess will be credited to a revaluation surplus.

The journal entry for this change would be:

	€	€
DR Property, plant and equipment	90,000	
CR Profit and loss (Admin expenses)		50,000
CR Revaluation surplus		40,000

The revaluation position as at 31 December 2012 can be summarised as follows:

	Total	**Z**	**X**	**Other**
	€	€	€	€
Opening surplus	200,000	200,000	0	0
2012 revaluation	137,000	(153,000)	40,000	250,000
Closing position	337,000	47,000	40,000	250,000

Outstanding Issue 3

Inventory – first issue "Inventories shall be measured at the lower of cost and net realisable value" (IAS 2, paragraph 9). "The cost of inventories … shall be assigned by using the first-in, first-out (FIFO) or weighted average cost formula" (IAS 2, paragraph 25). Last-in, first-out (LIFO) is not permitted.

The inventory stored in the warehouse in Cork is currently measured on a LIFO basis at €100,000. The correct measurement of cost should be €120,000 on a FIFO basis. A weighted average cost formula would also be acceptable. Weighted average is not relevant in this case study as no information is supplied. The company policy is to use the FIFO basis.

The Net Realisable Value (NRV) of this inventory is €140,000. Inventory should be measured at the lower of cost (€120,000) and NRV (€140,000). Inventory should be measured at €120,000. An adjustment will be required to bring the value of inventory in line with IAS 2.

Inventory adjustments are recorded below.

Inventory – second issue "Inventories shall be measured at the lower of cost and net realisable value" (IAS 2, paragraph 9). This inventory is included at cost €152,000. The net realisable value (NRV) is "the estimated selling price in the ordinary course of business less the estimated costs of completion and the estimated costs necessary to make the sale" (IAS 2, paragraph 6).

The NRV of this inventory is €138,000. This is arrived at as follows:

	€
Selling Price	154,000
Less: Estimated costs necessary to make the sale	16,000
NRV	138,000

The net realisable value of this inventory is lower than cost. Therefore, in accordance with IAS2, this inventory must be written down to NRV. A decrease of €14,000 should be recorded.

Inventory adjustments are recorded below.

Inventory – third issue Some inventory has been pledged as security for liabilities. This should be noted in the financial statements. No adjustments are necessary (IAS 2, paragraph 36(h)).

The inventory adjustment for the first and second issues above is as follows:
(The first issue – an increase of €20,000. The second issue – a decrease of €14,000)

Adjustment	€	€
DR Inventory	6,000	
CR Cost of sales		6,000

Outstanding Issue 4

IAS 10 *Events after the Reporting Period* provides guidance on how to treat information that becomes available after the end of the reporting period but before the financial statements are signed. In the case study you are told that an important customer of the group, Howlett Limited, has ceased trading. There is a balance owing from Howlett Limited of €670,000 included in trade receivables in the draft financial statements. You must decide whether this balance should be adjusted in light of this new information.

IAS 10 classifies events after the reporting period as either "adjusting" events or "non-adjusting" events. Adjusting events are "those that provide evidence of conditions that existed at the end of the reporting period" (IAS 10, para 3(a)), while non-adjusting events are "those that are indicative of conditions that arose after the reporting period" (IAS 10, para 3(b)). At the end of the reporting period, Howlett Limited was a going concern and there was no indication at that time that the business was about to be destroyed. In other words, the event that led to the closure of the company did not exist at the end of the reporting period. This would clearly place this event into the category of a non-adjusting event.

IAS 10, paragraph 10, states how a non-adjusting event should be presented in the financial statements. Paragraph 10 states that an entity shall not adjust for non-adjusting events after the reporting period. However, disclosure of the event, if it is material, is necessary. Paragraph 21 explains why: "… non-disclosure could influence the economic decisions that users make on the basis of the financial statements."

The closure of Howlett Limited is material. Therefore, the event should be fully disclosed in the notes to the financial statements. Disclosure should include "(a) the nature of the event; *and* (b) an estimate of its financial effect, or a statement that such an estimate cannot be made" (IAS 10, para 21).

This presentation will conflict with the CEO's proposal to omit the details from the 2012 financial statements. However disclosure is the correct and ethical way to treat this event.

Note: Occasionally, an event that is non-adjusting will be incorporated into the financial statements. This could occur where the impact of the event is so severe that it would call into question the ability of the entity to continue as a going concern. IAS 10, paragraph 15 states that "if the going concern assumption is no longer appropriate, the effect is so pervasive that this Standard requires a fundamental change in the basis of accounting". (Paragraph 15 is not relevant to this case study. Howlett's closure has a material but not a fundamental effect on Armada's business.)

The adjustments are now completed. They are summarised as follows. (You are not asked to produce these summaries. They are presented for clarity only. The requirement asks you to re-draft the financial statements, this follows over.)

STATEMENT OF COMPREHENSIVE INCOME – adjusted lines only

	Revenue €000	Cost of Sales €000	Other Income €000	Admin Expenses €000	Reval. Surplus €000
Per draft statements	50,000	(32,000)	500	(2,500)	250
Issue (1) PPE				(325)	
Issue (1) Grant income			(300)		
Issue (1) Depreciation				(19)	
Issue (2) Revaluation				50	(113)
Issue (3) Inventory		6			
Revised	50,000	(31,994)	200	(2,794)	137

STATEMENT OF FINANCIAL POSITION – adjusted lines only

	PPE €000	Inventories €000	Other Receivables €000	Retained Earnings €000	Revaluation Surplus €000
Per draft statements	7,500	4,500	2,000	19,500	450
Outstanding issue (1) PPE	(400)		75	(325)	
Outstanding issue (1) Grant income	(300)			(300)	
Outstanding issue (1) Depreciation	(19)			(19)	
Outstanding issue (2) Revaluation	(63)			50	(113)
Outstanding issue (3) Inventory		6		6	
Revised	6,718	4,506	2,075	18,912	337

The revised financial statements are as follows.

Armada Limited
STATEMENT OF COMPREHENSIVE INCOME
for the year ended 31 December 2012

	€000 Draft	€000 Issue 1	€000 Issue 2	€000 Issue 3	€000 Revised
Revenue	50,000				50,000
Cost of sales	(32,000)			6	(31,994)
Gross profit	18,000				18,006
Other Income	500	(300)			200
Selling and distribution costs	(11,000)				(11,000)
Administration costs	(2,500)	(344)	50		(2,794)
Finance costs	(250)				(250)
Profit before tax	4,750				4,162
Taxation	(500)				(500)
Profit for the year	4,250				3,662
Other comprehensive income					
Gain on property revaluation	250		(113)		137
	250				137
Total comprehensive income	4,500				3,799

Armada Ltd
STATEMENT OF CHANGES IN EQUITY
for year ended 31 December 2012

	Ordinary Share Capital €000	Share Premium €000	Retained Earnings €000	Revaluation Surplus €000	Total €000
Opening balance	10,000	3,000	16,250	200	29,450
Comprehensive income			3,662	137	3,799
Dividend			(1,000)		(1,000)
Closing balance	10,000	3,000	18,912	337	32,249

Armada Limited
STATEMENT OF FINANCIAL POSITION
for the year ended 31 Dec 2012

	Draft €000	Outstanding issue 1 €000	Outstanding issue 2 €000	Outstanding issue 3 €000	Revised €000
Non-current Assets					
Property, plant and equipment	7,500	(719)	(63)		6,718
Long-term investments (Gem)	7,500				7,500
Loan to Gem	1,500				1,500
Intangible assets (all development expenditure)	11,000				11,000
	27,500				26,718
Current Assets					
Inventories	4,500			6	4,506
Trade receivables	2,000	75			2,075
Cash and cash equivalents	8,000				8,000
	14,500				14,581
Total Net Assets	**42,000**				**41,299**
Equity					
Ordinary share capital (€1 each)	10,000				10,000
Share premium	3,000				3,000
Retained earnings	19,500	(644)	50	6	18,912
Revaluation surplus	450		(113)		337
	32,950				32,249
Non-current Liabilities					
Bank loans	1,000				1,000
Bonds	2,500				2,500
Provisions	300				300
Retirement benefit obligations	1,200				1,200
Non-current trade payables	200				200
Deferred tax	500				500
	5,700				5,700
Current Liabilities					
Payables	300				300
Intragroup payable	2,500				2,500
Bank loans	300				300
Current tax	250				250
	3,350				3,350
Total Equity and Liabilities	**42,000**				**41,299**

Requirement (b)

Consolidated Statement of Financial Position

In this solution we begin with the consolidated statement of financial position, it does not really matter if you begin with the consolidated income statement; the end point will be the same.

Step 1 – Set out the group structure In this instance, the group structure is straightforward.

This makes Gem a subsidiary of Armada.

Step 2 – The Additional Information

Note 2: Intragroup trading. Under IFRS 10, paragraph B86, all intragroup balances and transactions should be eliminated in full. There are a number of stages to this:

1. Eliminate the intragroup sales and purchases (i.e. Gem has recognised €5,000,000 of sales and Armada has recognised €5,000,000 of purchases which should be reversed).

Adjustment 1 (a):

	€	€
DR (reduce): Revenue	5,000,000	
CR (reduce): Cost of sales		5,000,000
(both are income statement line items)		

2. Remove the profit element of the intragroup goods that are still in inventory. At year end, goods with a sales value of €1,250,000 (one quarter of €5,000,000) were still held by Armada. However, these goods cost the group €1,000,000 (€1,250,000 × 100%/125% = €1,000,000). Therefore the profit element is €250,000.

	€
Total intragroup sales	5,000,000
One quarter still in inventory	1,250,000
Cost of stock in inventory	1,000,000
Profit element	250,000

The intragroup inventory profit needs to be removed. Therefore, closing inventory in the statement of financial position needs to be reduced by €250,000. In addition, closing inventory in the cost of sales calculation also needs to be removed; this has the knock-on effect of reducing profits (i.e. retained earnings). Finally, as Gem, the subsidiary, had originally recognised the profit, the non-controlling interests will need to take their share of the removal of the profit in Gem. The adjustment is as follows:

Adjustment 1 (b):

	€	€
DR Retained earnings	200,000	
DR Non-controlling interests	50,000	
CR Inventory (Statement of Financial Position)		250,000
(Line item on the consolidated statement of comprehensive income is debit/increase cost of sales)		

When an adjustment impacts on a reserve item (e.g. revenue reserves or non-controlling interests) then the likelihood is that there is also an impact on the statement of comprehensive income. In this instance, the impact is via the cost of sales figure.

3. Cash 'in Transit'

At year end Armada had paid €1,500,000 to Gem. Gem had not recorded the receipt of this cash. The general rule with regard to 'in-transit' items is to complete the transit. Therefore, had Gem received the cash it would have recorded the following:

Adjustment 1 (c):

	€	€
DR (increase) Cash	1,500,000	
CR (decrease) Intragroup receivable		1,500,000

4. Eliminate Intragroup Balances

After making adjustment 1(c), the intragroup receivable in Gem decreases to €2,500,000. This matches the intragroup payable in Armada of €2,500,000. These items are not owed or receivable outside the group and should be eliminated.

Adjustment 1 (d):

	€	€
DR (decrease) Intragroup payable in Armada	2,500,000	
CR (decrease) Intragroup receivable in Gem		2,500,000

Item 3: Intragroup financing. This is similar to the previous item. Again IFRS 10, paragraph B86 is invoked and the effect of all intragroup transactions is eliminated. There are two elements to this: the interest on the loan and the loan itself.

1. Interest on the Loan

The total interest on the loan for the period is €60,000. Gem has recorded this as an interest cost while Armada has recorded it as other income. This will have to be fully reversed. Note that the non-controlling interests will get their share of the reduction in finance costs in Gem.

Adjustment 2 (a):

	€	€
DR (reduce) Other income	60,000	
CR (reduce) Finance costs		60,000*
(both line items on consolidated statement of comprehensive income)		

* €48,000 of this will ultimately go to group reserves with €12,000 to non-controlling interests.

2. Intragroup Loan Elimination
Armada is showing an asset of €1,500,000 while Gem is showing a liability of €1,500,000. Outside the group context these items are neither payable nor receivable. Hence, they should be eliminated.

Adjustment 2 (b)		
	€	€
DR (reduce): Loan from Armada	1,500,000	
CR (reduce): Loan to Gem		1,500,000

Step 3 – Prepare the Consolidation Table

There are two sections to this:

1. Taking the information from the statement of financial position
   - Cost of investment in Gem: as per the statement of financial position of Armada, all to the goodwill column
   - Ordinary share capital of Gem: as per the statement of financial position of Gem, split 80% to the goodwill column and 20% to the non-controlling interests column
   - Retained earnings of Gem: as per the statement of financial position of Gem, €3,000,000, split as follows:
     - Pre-acquisition of €2,000,000; split 80% to the goodwill column and 20% to the non-controlling interests column
     - Post-acquisition of €1,000,000 (the balance); split 80% to the retained earnings column (part of the retained profits of the group) and 20% to the non-controlling interests column
   - Retained earnings of Armada: as per the revised statement of financial position of Armada (the answer to requirement (a)), all to group retained earnings.

2. Taking the relevant information from the adjustments made in Step 2.
   - This is a matter of going through the adjustments made and where they impact on goodwill, non-controlling interests or retained earnings, the appropriate amount should be included.
   - For example, adjustment 1(d) affects intragroup payable and intragroup receivable, not goodwill or non-controlling interests or retained earnings, hence it is not included here.

	Goodwill	Non-controlling Interests	Retained Earnings
	€000	€000	€000
Cost of investment in Gem	7,500		
Ordinary share capital: Gem (€1,000,000)	800	200	
Retained earnings – pre-acq (€2,000,000)	1,600	400	
Retained earnings – post-acq (€1,000,000)		200	800
Retained earnings – parent (from the solution to requirement (a)			18,912
Adjustments			
1(a): No net effect on retained earnings			
1(b): Inventory Profit (€250,000 split 20%/80%)		(50)	(200)
1(c): No net effect on retained earnings			
1(d): No net effect on retained earnings			
2(a): Eliminate interest received			(60)
2(a): Eliminate interest paid (€60,000 split 20%/80%)		12	48
2(b): No net effect on retained earnings			
	5,100	762	19,500

Step 4 – Complete the Consolidated Statement of Financial Position

Take the revised statement of financial position for Armada and the statement of financial position for Gem. Combine these with the adjustments highlighted. Include the figures for goodwill, non-controlling interests and retained earnings direct from the consolidation table (Step 3).

Armada Group
CONSOLIDATED STATEMENT OF FINANCIAL POSITION
for the Year Ended 31 December 2012

	€000	€000	€000	€000	€000	€000	€000	€000	€000	€000
			Adj	Adj	Adj	Adj	Adj	Adj	Adj	
Non-current Assets	**Armada**	**Gem**	**1(a)**	**1(b)**	**1(c)**	**1(d)**	**2(a)**	**2(b)**	**X**	**Total**
Property, plant and equipment	6,718	1,000								7,718
Goodwill (from 'consolidation table')	7,500									5,100
Loan to Gem	1,500	0						(1,500)		0
Intangible assets (all development expenditure)	11,000	1,000								12,000
	26,718	2,000								24,818
Current Assets										
Inventories	4,506	500		(250)						4,756
Trade receivables	2,075	750								2,825
Intragroup receivable		4,000			(1,500)	(2,500)				0
Cash and cash equivalents	8,000	2,500			1,500					12,000
	14,581	7,750								19,581
Total Net Assets	41,299	9,750								44,399

Equity	Armada	Gem	Adj 1(a)	Adj 1(b)	Adj 1(c)	Adj 1(d)	Adj 2(a)	Adj 2(b)	Adj X	Total
Ordinary Share Capital (Parent Only)	10,000	1,000								10,000
Share Premium (Parent Only)	3,000									3,000
Retained Earnings (from 'consolidation table')	18,912	3,000								19,500
Revaluation Surplus	337									337
	32,249	4,000								32,837
Non-controlling Interests (from 'table')										762
	32,249	4,000								33,599
Non-current Liabilities										
Bank Loans	1,000	2,000								3,000
Loan from Armada		1,500						(1,500)		0
Bonds	2,500									2,500
Provisions	300	500								800
Retirement Benefit Obligations	1,200	200								1,400
Non-current Trade Payables	200	200								400
Deferred Tax	500	100								600
	5,700	4,500								8,700
Current Liabilities										
Payables	300	800								1,100
Intragroup Payable	2,500					(2,500)				0
Bank Loans	300	250								550
Current Tax	250	200								450
	3,350	1,250								2,100
Total Equity and Liabilities	41,299	9,750								44,399

Requirement (b)

Consolidated Statement of Comprehensive Income

Preparing the consolidated statement of comprehensive income (see **over the page**) is mostly a mechanical exercise. This is because in the previous section (consolidated statement of financial position) the adjustments were considered. It is now just a matter of including the income statement effects of the adjustments, although there will be some analysis required at the end for the non-controlling interests.

Set up the consolidated income statement as indicated in the guidance notes. The column for Armada comes from the solution to requirement (a) (the revised statement of comprehensive income). The column for Gem is provided in the individual financial statements for Gem. The adjustment columns correspond to each of the adjustments arising from the additional information. Note that there is not an entry in every adjustment column. This is because some of the adjustments affect the statement of financial position only.

The final item is to calculate the profits attributable to the non-controlling interests. This is shown in Working 1.

Armada Group
Consolidated Statement of Comprehensive Income
for the Year Ended 31 December 2012

	Armada €000	Gem €000	Adj 1(a) €000	Adj 1(b) €000	Adj 1(c) €000	Adj 1(d) €000	Adj 2(a) €000	Adj 2(b) €000	Adj X €000	Total €000
Revenue	50,000	10,000	(5,000)							55,000
Cost of sales	(31,994)	(5,500)	5,000	(250)						(32,744)
Gross Profit	18,006	4,500								22,256
Other income	200	250					(60)			390
Selling and distribution costs	(11,000)	(2,500)								(13,500)
Administration costs	(2,794)	(1,200)								(3,994)
Finance costs	(250)	(100)					60			(290)
Profit Before Tax	4,162	950								4,862
Taxation	(500)	(200)								(700)
Profit for the Year	3,662	750								4,162
Other Comprehensive Income										
Gain on property revaluation	137	0								137
	137	0								137
Total Comprehensive Income	3,799	750								4,299
Profit for the year Attributable to:										
Equity shareholders										4,050
Non-controlling interests (working 1)										112
										4,162
Total Comprehensive Income Attributable to:										
Equity shareholders										4,187
Non-controlling interests (working 1)										112
										4,299

Working 1: Non-controlling Interests

	€000
Gem: Profit for the year	750
Adjustments affecting Gem's profits	
Adjustment 1(b): intragroup inventory profit	(250)
Adjustment 2(a): intragroup finance cost	60
Gem: revised profit for the year	560
Non-controlling interest's proportion @ 20%	112

Requirement (b)

Consolidated Statement of Changes in Equity

Preparing the consolidated statement of changes in equity (see **over the page**) is a matter of setting out the blank template and filling in the various figures. The most difficult element is determining the opening balances, the remainder is more straightforward.

The ending balances should correspond with the balances on the statement of financial position otherwise an error has occurred.

Armada Group
CONSOLIDATED STATEMENT OF CHANGES IN EQUITY
for Year Ended 31 December 2012

	Ordinary Share Capital	Share Premium	Retained Earnings	Revaluation Surplus	Total Equity	Non-controlling Interests	Total
	€000	€000	€000	€000	€000	€000	€000
Opening balance (working 2)	10,000	3,000	16,450	200	29,650	650	30,300
Comprehensive income			4,050	137	4,199	112	3,299
Dividend (parent only)			(1,000)		(1,000)		(1,000)
Closing balance*	10,000	3,000	19,500	337	32,849	762	33,599

* Take a look at the consolidated statement of financial position. These figures should match the equivalent line items in the consolidated statement of financial position. Any difference indicates that an error has been made. While these errors should be resolved, in an exam situation it is probably better to move onto the next requirement and, if there is time at the end of the exam, any differences can then be investigated further.

Working 2 – Opening Balances The opening balances are the previous year's closing balances. It should be a matter of taking the previous year's closing balances. However, you are not usually provided with the consolidated financial statements of the preceding period. As a consequence the opening balances need to be derived.

In calculating the opening balances try to imagine yourself back at the start of the period. Most of the information for this calculation can be found in the opening balances in the individual statements of changes in equity.

Ordinary Share Capital – Opening Balance Include the ordinary share capital of the parent only. In the revised statement of changes in equity of Armada this was €10,000,000. There was no share capital issued during the period.

Share Premium – Opening Balance Include the share premium of the parent only. In the revised statement of changes in equity of Armada this was €3,000,000. There was no share capital issued during the period which might give rise to an increase in share premium.

Retained Earnings – Opening Balance This is one of the more complex calculations. Include the opening retained earnings of the parent and the group share of opening post-acquisition retained earnings of the subsidiary (a bit of a mouthful). Remember, we are trying to determine what retained profits the group shareholders are entitled to. In the revised statement of changes in equity of Armada the opening retained earnings are €16,250,000 and in the statement of changes in equity of Gem the opening retained earnings were €2,250,000.

	€000	**€000**
Opening retained earnings of Armada (parent)		16,250
Opening retained earnings of Gem (subsidiary)	2,250	
Less: pre-acquisition retained earnings	2,000	
Post-acquisition retained earnings	250	
Any adjustments to opening retained earnings of Gem	0	
Adjusted post-acquisition retained earnings	250	
Group share	80%	200
Group opening retained earnings		16,450

Revaluation Surplus – Opening Balance This is calculated on the same basis as the retained earnings. However, in this instance, the subsidiary does not have a revaluation surplus. The full calculation is shown. This is for illustration purposes only; you are not required to show zeros. In the revised statement of changes in equity of Armada the opening revaluation surplus is €200,000 and in the statement of changes in equity of Gem the opening revaluation surplus is €0.

	€000	€000
Opening revaluation surplus of Armada (parent)		200
Opening revaluation surplus of Gem (subsidiary)	0	
Less: pre-acquisition revaluation surplus	0	
Post-acquisition revaluation surplus	0	
Any adjustments to opening revaluation surplus of Gem	0	
Adjusted post-acquisition revaluation surplus	0	
Group share	80%	0
Group opening revaluation surplus		200

Non-controlling Interests – Opening Balance On 1 January 2012, the non-controlling interests held 20% of the net assets of Gem. From the statement of changes in equity of Gem, it is possible to determine the opening net assets of Gem – it is the opening total equity of Gem (opening ordinary share capital plus opening retained earnings). Remember that since a statement of financial position balances, the opening total equity must equal the opening net assets.

	€000
Gem – opening ordinary share capital	1,000
Gem – opening retained earnings	2,250
Gem – opening net assets/equity	3,250
Any adjustments to opening net assets	0
	3,250
Non-controlling interests @ 20%	650

Statement of Changes in Equity – Other Items

- The comprehensive income line item – these figures are taken from the consolidated statement of comprehensive income which was prepared earlier.
- The dividend line item – this figure is taken from the parent company's statement of changes in equity. In this instance the subsidiary did not pay a dividend.

Requirement (c)

The shareholder has asked you to comment on the valuation techniques used in the preparation of financial statements. He has correctly observed that there are many different techniques used and he would like to know which of the techniques gives the 'true' valuation for the company.

The answer is that there is no one technique that is superior to the others. Different accounting standards assign different valuation techniques to the measurement of assets and liabilities. Financial statements, prepared in accordance with International Accounting Standards, are currently made up of a mix of valuation techniques. This is recognised by the IASB in their document *The Conceptual Framework for Financial Reporting.* A section of this document, dealing with measurement, states that "A number of different measurement bases are employed to different degrees and in varying combinations in financial statements".

The valuation techniques most commonly used include:

- Historical cost
  This is the measurement basis most commonly used today, but it is usually combined with other measurement bases (*Conceptual Framework*, para 4.56). Assets are recorded at the amount of cash or cash equivalents paid or the fair value of the consideration given to acquire them at the time of their acquisition. Liabilities are recorded at the amount of proceeds received in exchange for the obligation or, in some circumstances, at the amounts of cash or cash equivalents expected to be paid to satisfy the liability in the normal course of business.
- Current cost
  Assets are carried at the amount of cash or cash equivalents that would have to be paid if the same or an equivalent asset was acquired currently. Liabilities are carried at the undiscounted amount of cash or cash equivalents that would be required to settle the obligation currently. (This valuation approach would be appropriate in establishing the market value of specialised properties for which market evidence is unavailable.)
- Net realisable (settlement) value
  Assets are carried at the amount of cash or cash equivalents that could currently be obtained by selling the asset in an orderly disposal. Liabilities are carried at their settlement values, i.e. the undiscounted amounts of cash or cash equivalents expected to be paid to satisfy the liabilities in the normal course of business. (This valuation approach would be appropriate when valuing assets on a piecemeal basis in a liquidation scenario.)
- Present Value (discounted)
  Assets are carried at the present discounted value of the future net cash inflows that the item is expected to generate in the normal course of business. Liabilities are carried at the present discounted value of the future net cash outflows that are expected to be required to settle the liabilities in the normal course of business. (This approach is currently applied in certain situations, e.g. long-term provisions are presented in the financial statements at present value equivalents. However, other liabilities such as deferred tax are not discounted.)

Valuation techniques used to measure financial statements have evolved over time. A major feature of IFRS today is the extent to which 'fair value' accounting is used. Many of the accounting standards have introduced fair value measurement as either a mandatory or optional valuation technique for assets and liabilities. Fair value accounting is a type of accounting where assets and liabilities are measured at the price that would be received to sell an asset or paid to transfer a liability on a particular date, e.g. the year end. This type of accounting has many benefits. Assets and liabilities are measured in terms of current valuations giving an up-to-date picture of what a company is actually worth. It has been suggested that financial statements prepared using fair value accounting provide more meaningful and realistic information than traditional forms. IFRS 13 *Fair Value Measurement* provides guidance on fair value accounting. IFRS 13, issued 11 May 2011, establishes a single source of guidance for fair value measurement under IFRS. "IFRS 13 defines fair value, provides guidance on its determination and introduces consistent requirements for disclosure on fair value measurement."[3] However, fair value accounting is not employed across all elements of

[3] "IASB issues new standard on fair value and disclosure" Deloitte,/*iGAAP Alert,* May 2011

financial statements. Fair value accounting, despite its attraction, poses many problems in practice and introduces a lack of verifiability into the financial statements. (Fair values are subjective measures.)

Unfortunately, this mix of valuation techniques will be a feature of financial statements for the foreseeable future.

Case 2

The Knightstown Group

This case study is based on a capital intensive manufacturing group. The accounting standards IAS 1, IAS 2, IAS 10, IAS 11, IAS 16, IFRS 3 and IFRS 10 are addressed in this case.

Background – The Knightstown Group

The Knightstown Group is a capital intensive manufacturing group. The group is made up of Knightstown Holdings Plc and two subsidiaries Sussa Ltd and Finian Ltd. Knightstown acquired both subsidiaries a number of years ago. George O'Shea is the managing director of the group. The financial year end of the Knightstown Group is 31 December. The group is listed on the UK Alternative Investment Market.

It is now almost the end of January 2013, you are part of the audit team that is reviewing the draft financial statements of the group for the year ended 31 December 2012. A number of accounting issues have arisen in respect of the audit. The audit manager has requested that you review these issues and send him a report. Your report should set out the appropriate accounting treatment and disclosures in respect of each accounting issue, together with any necessary associated journal entries.

Once these issues are resolved you hope to move on to preparing the consolidated financial statements. The related companies have submitted their financial statements to you.

The statements of financial position of Knightstown, Sussa and Finian, for the year ended 31 December 2012, are as follows (see **next page**):

The Knightstown Group
STATEMENTS OF FINANCIAL POSITION
for the year ended 31 December 2012

	Knightstown €000	Sussa €000	Finian €000
Non-current Assets			
Property, Plant and Equipment	7,500	7,160	2,540
Investment Properties	5,800		
Long-term Investment – Sussa	9,000		
Long-term Investments – Finian	7,500		
Available for Sale Financial Assets	1,500		
Intangible Asset – Patents	480		
Intangible Asset – Development Expenditure	11,000	1,000	4,850
	42,780	8,160	7,390
Current Assets			
Inventories	4,500	500	600
Intragroup Receivable (from Knightstown)		1,500	
Intragroup Receivable (staff exchange)	200	120	360
Trade Receivables	2,000	750	3,000
Cash and Cash Equivalents	8,000	2,500	900
	14,700	5,370	4,860
Total Net Assets	**57,480**	**13,530**	**12,250**
Equity			
Ordinary Share Capital (€1 each)	10,000	2,000	2,000
Share Premium	9,079		
Retained Earnings	23,021	3,000	4,500
Revaluation Surplus	650		
	42,750	5,000	6,500
Non-current Liabilities			
Bank Loans and Bonds	6,480	2,000	2,000
Provisions	2,800	500	300
Retirement Benefit Obligations	1,200	200	500
Capital Grants	200	200	150
Deferred Tax	500	100	300
	11,180	3,000	3,250
Current Liabilities			
Trade Payables	2,800	4,800	1,800
Intragroup Payable (staff exchange)	200	280	200
Bank Loans	300	250	250
Current Tax	250	200	250
	3,550	5,530	2,500
Total Equity and Liabilities	**57,480**	**13,530**	**12,250**

Outstanding Issues in Respect of the Parent Company Financial Statements

Outstanding Issue 1

Knightstown acquired an item of plant during the financial year. The plant was purchased in February 2012 but was not available for use until the beginning of July 2012. This delay was expected as there were complex shipping arrangements *and* the plant was subject to rigorous testing before it could be used. Details of the plant cost are as follows:

	€000
Invoice price	1,000
Shipping cost	55
Import duties	20
Legal costs	15
Pre-operational testing	25
Administration overheads	25
Lease charges (note)	30
	1,170

Note: In May 2012 Knightstown received a sales order. The new plant was not ready for use at the time and the company had to lease a similar asset for a three-month period to fulfil the order. As a result lease charges incurred for the period were €30,000.

On acquisition of the plant, the entire €1.17 million was capitalised and included in property, plant and equipment. There are, however, two outstanding items that have not yet been considered:

1. For the 10 years of operation, the exterior of the plant will require a layer of protective coating. It is a condition of planning that in 10 years' time this coating should be removed. Removal will involve the application of a chemical solution that will dissolve the original coating. An initial estimate of the cost of this process is €42,000 (at present value rates). As there has been no outlay for this expense to date, no entry has been made in the financial statements.
2. Depreciation has not been charged on this plant. With the exception of the engine, the plant has an estimated life of 10 years with no expected residual value. The engine will need replacing at a present value cost of €400,000 after every 5,000 hours of use. The directors intend to depreciate the full cost of the plant over 10 years *and* make a provision of €80 per hour (€400,000/5,000 hours) of use for the replacement of the engine. It is estimated that 500 hours will be used up to the end of December 2012.

Outstanding Issue 2

Knightstown disposed of a building in December 2012. The company had purchased this building in January 2003 for €900,000 and depreciation is charged over 50 years on a straight line basis. It is the policy of the group to re-value land and buildings and on 31 December 2007 this building was re-valued to €1,270,000. There was no revision to the useful life of the property following the revaluation.

It is also the policy of the company, in accordance with IAS 16, paragraph 41, to transfer the entire revaluation surplus to realised reserves on disposal of assets rather than over the assets' useful lives.

In December 2012 Knightstown sold this property. The company employed the services of a local auctioneer who acted as selling agent for the company. The fee for his service was 2% of the property's selling price. On 20 December an offer of €600,000 was made. This was immediately accepted and the building was taken off the market. On 28 December 2012 the sale was closed and the contracts were signed. A bank draft, equal to the proceeds of the sale less the auctioneer's fee, was transferred to Knightstown on the 31 December 2012.

The only accounting entry that was made for this entire transaction was to debit the bank and credit revenue with the net proceeds of the sale. You can assume that a full year's depreciation has been charged on the building in 2012.

Outstanding Issue 3

Knightstown occasionally carry out construction work on behalf of other entities. On 1 April 2012, the company signed a contract with AVM Ltd to carry out a construction project on their behalf for an agreed price of €5m. The project is due to be completed on 30 September 2013. A condition of the contract is that, if this deadline is not met, Knightstown will be charged a penalty of 2% of the contract price. Equally, if the contract is completed one month early, the company will receive a bonus of the same amount. The directors of Knightstown are confident that they can meet the early target and complete the project by the end of August.

By 31 December 2012 the company had incurred costs on this project of €1.2 million, although only €1 million of these costs related to work that was completed by the year-end. The other €200,000 related to payments that were made in advance of the next stage of construction. The full €1.2 million was debited to cost of sales and credited to the bank account. The construction team now estimates that it will cost another €2.8 million to finish the project but that it can still be completed ahead of schedule. AMV have not yet been invoiced and no stage payments have been made.

It is the policy of the company to recognise profit on construction contracts only when a contract is more than 20% complete.

Outstanding Issue 4

Included in the finished goods inventory is a product called BLT. There are 20,000 units in the inventory figure at the year-end, made up of the following costs:

	BLT €000
Materials	600
Labour/conversion costs	250
Fixed production overhead (note)	400
Patent royalties paid	200
General administration overhead	540
	1,990

Note: The allocation of fixed production overheads to inventory is based on what was actually produced in the year, 200,000 units. Normally production is 20% lower. Production overheads for 2012 amounted to €4 million.

The selling price for this inventory is €2.5 million. Costs to sell are estimated to be €240,000.

Outstanding Issue 5

Finally, Knightstown has a very good relationship with its shareholders and employees. However, it has not paid a dividend for a number of years. On 10 January 2013, the board announced that it would pay a special dividend of €500,000 out of the profits generated in 2012. The shareholders were delighted with this news. It is expected that they are likely to approve this dividend, along with the financial statements, on 10 April 2013. The dividend has been accrued in the 2012 financial statements and is included in provisions as part of non-current liabilities.

Additional Information for the Consolidated Financial Statements

1. Acquisition of Sussa Knightstown acquired 100% of Sussa on 1 January 2004. At that time it gave three shares in Knightstown for every one share in Sussa. Each share in Knightstown was worth €1.50 on 1 January 2004.

On the date of acquisition the ordinary share capital of Sussa was €2,000,000 and the retained earnings were €2,000,000.

The fair values of the assets of Sussa were equal to their carrying values.

2. Acquisition of Finian Knightstown acquired 80% of the share capital of Finian on 1 January 2010. The cost of the investment was €7,500,000 cash.

On the date of acquisition the ordinary share capital of Finian was €2,000,000 and the retained earnings were €3,750,000.

The carrying values of the assets and liabilities were not significantly different from their fair values.

3. Intragroup Trading In the current period Sussa sold €1,500,000 (cost of €1,200,000 plus margin of €300,000) worth of product to Knightstown which is the source of a dispute between the two companies. When the product was received by Knightstown, it was recorded as normal. However, it subsequently transpired that the goods were not of the specification ordered so Knightstown returned the goods to Sussa. In so doing, it booked the goods out of inventory, debited intragroup payable and credited purchases returns (in cost of sales) €1,500,000. Sussa disputes that the goods were not of the appropriate specification. While accepting the goods into the warehouse, it refused to book the goods into inventory and did not record the sales returns. These goods are now sitting in a loading bay in Sussa's warehouse, in the goods-in section. These events all took place before the year end. It is now January 2013 and the goods are still in the 'goods-inwards' section of Sussa's warehouse awaiting a resolution. The goods are not damaged and Sussa will be able to sell the goods at a profit.

4. Intragroup Exchange of Staff In 2012, the group underwent a strategic review. As part of that review it was felt that the organisation would benefit if there was an interchange of staff between the companies within the group. This might help resolve some of the operational issues that are arising (see item 3) as management were of the opinion that communication problems were at the root of many of the issues. Under the arrangements in place, the company that originally employed a transferred staff member would continue to pay the salary of that employee. However, the company that gets the benefit of the employees' work would then reimburse the original employing company for the salary paid.

The following table explains the movement and costs incurred:

	Knightstown	Sussa	Finian	Due to Receive
Knightstown employees sent to:		€80,000 (2 employees)	€120,000 (3 employees)	€200,000
Sussa employees sent to:	€40,000 (1 employee)		€80,000 (2 employees)	€120,000
Finian employees sent to:	€160,000 (4 employees)	€200,000 (5 employees)		€360,000
Due to Pay	€200,000	€280,000	€200,000	

For example, Knightstown sent two employees (at a cost of €80,000) to Sussa. Knightstown paid the salaries of these employees but it will be reimbursed by Sussa for the full cost. Knightstown also received one employee from Sussa (at a cost of €40,000). Sussa paid the salary of this employee and in turn Knightstown will have to reimburse Sussa the full cost.

The amounts payable and receivable have been agreed by the companies in the group but at year end they have yet to be paid, see statements of financial position. The amounts were subsequently paid in early February of 2013.

Requirements

(**Note:** Unless you are specifically required to consider deferred taxation, you can assume that it is not applicable.)

(a) The Parent Company: Knightstown

(i) Prepare a report for the audit manager in respect of outstanding issues 1–5. Your report should set out the appropriate accounting treatment and a summary of the disclosures required in respect of each accounting issue, together with any necessary associated journal entries. (You should support your workings by reference to the relevant accounting rules.)

(40 Marks)

(ii) Prepare the revised statement of financial position of Knightstown Plc, the parent company, as on 31 Dec 2012 incorporating the changes you have recommended in requirement (a)(i) above.

(10 Marks)

(b) Consolidation

(i) Having completed requirement a (ii), prepare the consolidated statement of financial position for the Knightstown Group for the year ended 31 December 2012.

(40 Marks)

(ii) Comment on Knightstown's approach for dealing with intragroup items (in particular the goods in dispute).

(10 Marks)

Guidance Notes – Knightstown Group

Exam Technique

First, read the case carefully, and then read the requirements.

This is the second of three case studies in this book written at an introductory level of financial reporting. The structure of this case study is similar to Armada Plc. This approach is used in many of the case studies in the book.

The requirements for this case study are divided into two:
- Requirement (a) involves the revision of the parent company's financial statements incorporating various adjustments.
- Requirement (b) requires the completion of the group financial statements and, in addition, you are asked to comment on the intragroup procedures within the group.

In this case study you are required to redraft the statements of financial position only. You are not required to prepare the statements of comprehensive income. You should approach this case study by answering requirement (a) *before* you attempt the consolidation. Requirement (a) relates only to the parent company.

The first requirement of the case study is to consider what adjustments are necessary to complete the statement of financial position for Knightstown Plc. There are five separate issues. Some of these issues require computation, others are discursive. You must present answers that are clear *and* are backed up with relevant accounting guidance.

In this part of the case study, you can answer these issues in any order you wish as they are all independent of each other. Begin with an issue that you are reasonably confident with and work on to the most challenging. Please note, however, that this approach will not always be appropriate. In some of the other case studies in this book, the adjustments are interdependent and it will be necessary to complete them in order of presentation.

When you have completed your recommended accounting treatment for the five issues you should then proceed to re-draft the parent's financial statements (requirement (a)(ii)).

Having completed requirement (a), you should then move on to the preparation of the consolidated statement of financial position. You should go directly to your practised technique for statements of financial position:

- Step 1: Set out the group structure
- Step 2: Deal with the 'Additional Information'
- Step 3: Prepare the consolidation table (i.e. calculate the goodwill, non-controlling interests and retained earnings figures)
- Step 4: Bring Step 2 and Step 3 together by preparing the consolidated statement of financial position.

Remember, that most of the marks are awarded for goodwill, non-controlling interests, retained earnings and dealing with the additional information. There may be items in the additional information that you have not come across before, however, try to determine the broader principles in the issue and apply those principles to the information. (In your final exam, it is likely that you will come across circumstances that you have not seen before, therefore, it is important to get some practice applying basic principles and judgment.)

The final requirement relates to the processes that the group has for intragroup items, in particular, the goods that are in dispute between Knightstown and Sussa. This is a discursive requirement and there is no absolutely correct answer. You will score well if you make sensible comments. It can be answered out of sequence to the other requirements.

Answering the Case Study

Requirement (a)(i) – Guidance

Outstanding Issue 1 – Acquisition of New Property This issue tests your knowledge of IAS 16 *Property, Plant and Equipment.* To answer it, you will need to be reasonably familiar with the sections in IAS 16 that deal with the measurement of non-current assets at recognition (IAS 16, paragraphs 16–22) and depreciation (IAS 16, paragraphs 43–64).

When measuring the cost of an asset some items of expenditure may be not be eligible for inclusion in PPE. IAS 16, paragraphs16–18, outlines the costs that **may** be included in property, plant and equipment, while paragraphs 19–22 outlines the costs that **should be excluded**. Excluded costs should be classified as expenses and included in profit or loss. In the case study, all of the costs incurred on the acquisition of the plant are included in property, plant and equipment. You may need to adjust some of these items to bring them in line with the relevant sections of the accounting standard.

There are two items of expenditure that are outstanding and you must decide how to treat them. The first is an estimated charge of €42,000 in five years' time for the removal of an industrial coating from the exterior walls of the plant. You must decide if this future outlay is part of the cost of the plant or if it is a regular operating cost. You should also consider if this expense should be recognized now or in 10 years' time. You will get guidance on this matter in paragraph 16(c) of the standard. (This issue is considered in greater detail in IAS 37 *Provisions, Contingent Liabilities and Contingent Assets*. IAS 37 is not specifically addressed in this case study. Therefore no adjustments have been considered in this solution for the unwinding of the discount rate.)

Finally, you will need to consider depreciation. The plant is made up of two distinct elements, each with a different useful period. The engine needs to be replaced after 5,000 hours of use. The remaining parts of the plant have a useful life of 10 years. You need to decide if it is appropriate to depreciate the entire cost of the plant over 10 years and build up a provision for the future replacement of the engine (as currently proposed). IAS 16, paragraphs 43–49, outlines the appropriate accounting treatment for this issue.

IAS 16 disclosures are outlined in paragraphs 73–79 of the standard.

Outstanding Issue 2 – Disposal of Revalued Property This issue considers the accounting treatment for asset disposals and in particular, the disposal of a revalued asset. The relevant accounting guidance is outlined in IAS 16, paragraphs 67–72.

You must identify how the disposal is to be treated, how the gain or loss on disposal is to be measured and how any outstanding revaluation surplus is treated on disposal. The answer to these questions can be found in the above mentioned paragraphs.

Outstanding Issue 3 – Construction Contracts Knightstown Plc occasionally engages in construction projects, on behalf of other entities. For financial reporting purposes, a distinction is made between construction that is carried out for own company purposes *and* construction work that is carried out on behalf of third parties. An example of construction carried out for own company purposes is the construction of an administrative office building to be used by the company. Construction work carried out for own company purposes is reported in accordance with IAS 16 *Property, Plant and Equipment*. Construction contracts carried out on behalf of third parties are governed by the rules IAS 11 *Construction Contracts*. It is the latter standard that is relevant for this issue.

A feature of many construction contracts is that they take a considerable period of time to complete and their performance is reported over multiple reporting periods. IAS 11 lays down specific guidance as to how on-going contracts are presented in the financial statements.

The contract with AVM Ltd will be carried out over an 18 month period from April 2012 to September 2013. The contract will span two accounting periods.

There are a number of factors you must consider when accounting for construction contracts. When is revenue recognised – at the beginning, the end or during the construction period? How are costs recognised and what is the treatment for on-going payments from the client? In addition, where the contract is incomplete at the end of the reporting period, how is the contract presented in the financial statements? A review of IAS 11 will provide you with the necessary answers.

IAS 11 disclosures are outlined in paragraphs 39–45 of the standard.

Outstanding Issue 4 – Inventory The rules of IAS 2 *Inventories* are tested in this issue. This scenario requires a little bit of thought about how inventory is **measured.** You are given details of an item of inventory and its component parts. You need to identify the costs that should be included in inventory and the costs that should not. Costs that are not included in inventory should be treated as expenses and included in profit or loss. The relevant guidance for this issue is in IAS 2 paragraphs10–18.

Inventory should be measured at the lower of cost and net realisable value (IAS 2 paragraph 9). You should carry out this test to ensure that inventories are not stated above their recoverable value.

IAS 2 disclosures are outlined in IAS 2 paragraphs 36–39.

Outstanding Issue 5 – Dividends There are a number of issues tested in this scenario. First of all, the dividends were declared *after* the year-end. The accounting treatment for events that occur after the year-end and before the accounts are signed is outlined in IAS 10 *Events after the Reporting Period.* IAS 10 classifies events that occur after the reporting period into those that will require adjustment in the current financial statements (i.e. adjusting events) and those that require disclosure only (i.e. non-adjusting events). You must decide into which category this event falls. The appropriate treatment is not immediately obvious but IAS 10 is very specific on the treatment of equity dividends declared after the year end. IAS 10, paragraphs 12–13, will provide you with the answer.

If you consider it appropriate to adjust the 2012 financial statements for the dividend, you must ensure that the correct entry has been made in the financial statements. On the other hand, if you consider it inappropriate you will have to reverse the existing entry.

The disclosures for IAS 10 depend on whether the event is considered to be adjusting or non-adjusting.

Requirement (a)(ii) Guidance

In Requirement (a)(ii) you are instructed to re-draft the statement of financial position for Knightstown Plc incorporating your recommended adjustments from Requirement (a)(i). These revised financial statements will form the basis of Requirement (b) – the consolidated financial statements. The most important aspect of this requirement is that you show a clear trail from the original statement of financial position to the redrafted version.

Requirement (b)(i) Guidance

In this requirement you will have to take the revised financial statements of Knightstown from the previous requirement and consolidate these with the financial statements of Sussa and Finian. You will need to take the four additional information items into account. While it is a time consuming question, if you deal with each item in turn, make your decision and then move on, it becomes an exercise in information management.

It is important to have an approach/technique that you can fall back on to answer these types of question. It is impossible to have a technique that will automatically address all potential scenarios but it will provide you with a starting point and help steady the nerves in an examination situation. The approach set out in this solution is just one approach and you may follow a different system – your system is likely to be equally valid; the end result is what is important.

Approach
- Step 1: Set out the group structure
- Step 2: Deal with the 'Additional Information'
- Step 3: Prepare the consolidation table (i.e. calculate the goodwill, non-controlling interests and retained earnings figures)
- Step 4: Bring Step 2 and Step 3 together by preparing the consolidated statement of financial position

- **Step 1 – Set out the Group Structure** This is not contentious. The information for this is found in additional information item 1 and item 2.
- **Step 2 – Deal with the 'Additional Information'**
  - *Item 1 – Acquisition of Sussa* – There are no fair value issues on acquisition. Just ensure that the ordinary share capital and the retained earnings of Sussa are correctly included in the consolidation table.
  - *Item 2 – Acquisition of Finian* – There are no fair value adjustments on the acquisition of Finian. Just ensure that the ordinary share capital and the retained earnings of Finian are correctly included in the consolidation table.
  - *Item 3 – Intragroup Trading* – IFRS 10, paragraph B86, gives the regulatory guidance here. However, it doesn't provide much detail on how to deal with this particular set of circumstances.

    This issue will need to be resolved but leaving the goods to one side in the warehouse and not recording them into inventory is not appropriate. These should be treated by Sussa as sales returns and recorded accordingly. The goods should become part of Sussa's inventory.
  - *Item 4 – Intragroup Exchange of Staff* – Again IFRS 10, paragraph B86, is the regulation with regard to this – all intercompany transactions should be eliminated at consolidation stage. The payable and receivable do not exist outside the group structure. Check to establish if the intragroup receivable matches the intragroup payable.

- **Step 3 – Prepare the Consolidation Table**

  Using the adjustments from Step 2, you should now be in a position to calculate the goodwill on acquisition of Finian and Sussa, non-controlling interests and retained earnings. A template is presented below:

	100% Goodwill – Sussa	80% Goodwill – Finian	20% Non-controlling Interests	Retained Earnings
Cost of acquisition	XX	XX		
OSC of subsidiary (Sussa)	XX			
OSC of subsidiary (Finian, split 80:20)		XX	XX	
RR of subsidiary (Sussa) – pre-acquisition	XX			
RR of subsidiary (Sussa) – post-acquisition				XX
RR of subsidiary (Finian) – pre-acquisition (split 80:20)		XX	XX	
RR of subsidiary (Finian) – post-acquisition (split 80:20)			XX	XX
RR of parent (Knightstown)				XX
Adjustment 1	?	?		?
Adjustment 2	?	?		?
Adjustment 3	?	?		?
Adjustment X	?	?		?
Adjustment X	?	?		?
	XX		XX	XX

- **Step 4 – Complete the Statement of Financial Position**

  This should be a relatively mechanical exercise as all the thinking has already been done. Take the revised financial statements of Knightstown and those of Sussa and Finian making sure that you correctly include all the adjustments you identified. Be sure to show how each of the figures in the statement of financial position is calculated. If you fail to do this and some of the figures are incorrect, it will not be possible for the examiner to award any marks for the elements of the answer that are correct.

Requirement (b)(ii) Guidance

This requirement asks you to comment on the intragroup processes within the group. Clearly the current situation is not appropriate. What would you propose that the group should do?

Recommended Reading

The above issues are also referenced in *International Financial Accounting and Reporting*, 3rd Edition by Ciaran Connolly (Chartered Accountants Ireland, 2011) as follows:

	Chapter	Chapter title	Standard	Section
Requirement (a)(i)				
Issue 1	6	Property, Plant and Equipment	IAS 16	6.2
Issue 2	6	Property, Plant and Equipment	IAS 16	6.2
Issue 3	12	Construction Contracts	IAS 11	12.2
Issue 4	11	Inventories	IAS 2	11.2
Issue 5	18	Distribution of Profits and Assets		18.2
	15	Events After the Reporting Period	IAS 10	15.2
Requirement (a)(ii)				
Revised SFP	2	Presentation of Financial Statements	IAS 1	2.3
Requirement (b)(i)				
Consolidated SFP	27	Consolidated Statement of Financial Position	IFRS 10, IFRS 3	27.2–27.11
Requirement (b)(ii)				
Intragroup issue	27	Consolidated Statement of Financial Position	IFRS 10	27.8

Solution to Knightstown Group

Requirement (a)(i)

Outstanding Issue 1

Plant cost In the case study, all plant costs are currently included in property, plant and equipment. IAS 16, paragraphs 16–22, outlines what items may be included in plant and what items should be expensed. The following is a list of items that may be included in plant cost:

	Treatment	Guidance	(€000)	Remarks
Invoice Price	allowed	IAS 16.16(a)	1,000	
Shipping	allowed	IAS 16.17(c)	55	
Import Duties	allowed	IAS 16.16(a)	20	
Legal Costs	allowed	IAS 16.17(f)	15	
Pre-operational tests	allowed	IAS 16.17(e)	25	
Admin. overheads	not allowed	IAS 16.19(d)	0	Specifically excluded
Lease charges	not allowed	IAS 17	0	Short-term operating lease
Total			1,115	

The general rule for capitalising costs is to include "any costs directly attributable to bringing the asset to the location and condition necessary for it to be capable of operating in the manner intended by management" (IAS 16, para 16(b)). Administration overheads would not fall into this category. Administration costs are considered to be part of the general operating costs of the business. They are specifically excluded from the asset cost in paragraph 19(d) of IAS 16. An adjustment will be required to reclassify the administration overheads. The adjustment will be to reduce PPE and increase administration expenses by €25,000. The double entry is presented below.

Lease charges have also been excluded from plant cost, but for a different reason. IAS 17 *Leases* classifies leasing contracts into two types – finance leases and operating leases. (A lease is a finance lease if it transfers substantially all of the risks and rewards incidental to ownership. An operating lease is a lease other than a finance lease (IAS 17, para 4).) Only finance leases are included in the cost of PPE. The lease, as described in the case study, would be classified as an operating lease. Operating lease charges should be expensed. The adjustment for leasing charges will be to reduce PPE and increase expenses by €30,000. The double entry for this is presented below.

There are two outstanding items that have not been included above. The first of these relates to the dismantling of the chemical coating on the exterior walls of the plant in 10 years' time. You must consider (a) is this a component part of plant cost and (b) should the cost be accrued now or in 10 years' time? IAS 16, paragraph 16(c), states that the cost of an item of PPE includes "the initial estimate of the costs of dismantling and removing the item". This means that the ***future*** obligation should be included as part of plant cost and the adjustment should be made on acquisition of the asset. (This issue is given greater consideration in IAS 37 *Provisions, Contingent Liabilities and Contingent Assets.*)

The adjustment to incorporate this outlay into PPE will be to increase PPE and increase liabilities by €42,000. The double entry is presented below.

Having considered the above items the adjusted plant cost will now be:

	€000
Plant cost per draft	1,170
Lease charges and admin costs	(55)
Dismantling costs	42
Adjusted Cost	1,157

The double entry required for the above adjustments would be:

	€000	**€000**
DR Expenses	55	
CR PPE		13 (€42,000–€55,000)
CR Liabilities (provisions)		42

Note: As explained in the guidance note on this issue the unwinding of the discount rate has not been considered in this solution.

The second outstanding item is depreciation. You are required to consider the depreciable period of the plant and the consequent depreciation charge for the period. The plant is made up of parts that have different useful lives. (The engine will be depreciated over 5,000 hours, while the body of the plant will last for 10 years.) In accordance with IAS 16, paragraph 43, "each part of an item of property, plant and equipment with a cost that is significant in relation to the total cost of the item shall be depreciated separately".

The separation of parts and the associated depreciation charge for the period would be as follows (€000):

	Plant Cost	**Depreciation Policy**	**Depreciation Rate**	**Period Expired**	**Charge**
Engine	€400,000	5,000 hours	€80 per hour	500 hours	€40,000
Plant	€757,000	10 years	€75,700 per annum	6 months	€38,000
Total	€1,157,000				€78,000

The adjustment to incorporate depreciation will be:

	€000	**€000**
DR Admin Charges	€78	
CR PPE		€78

Note: All figures have been rounded to the nearest thousand.

The relevant disclosures for PPE as specified by IAS 16, paragraphs 73–79, include: measurement basis, depreciation methods, useful lives, a reconciliation between opening and closing PPE for each class of asset, restrictions on title, contractual commitments, construction expenditure on PPE and revaluation details.

Outstanding Issue 2

Knightstown disposed of a building in December 2012. This property had been revalued in a previous accounting period. The only entry that has been made in the financial statements in relation to this sale was to debit the bank and credit revenue with the net proceeds of the sale. This entry is obviously incorrect. The building has not been removed from PPE. Removal should be made by crediting PPE, not revenue. To remove the building from PPE we need to establish both the carrying value of the property and the outstanding balance on the revaluation surplus at the date of sale.

The carrying value of the asset:

	€000	Remarks
Cost 1.1.2003	900	
Depreciation 2003–2007*	90	
NBV	810	
Revaluation 2007	460	(Balance Outstanding)
Revised value	1,270	
Depreciation 2008–2012**	141	
Carrying value at date of sale	1,129	

* Depreciation charge 2003 to 2007: €900,000/50 × 5years = €90,000
** Depreciation charge 2008 to 2012: €1,270,000/45 × 5years = €141,111

The entries for the disposal of an asset would normally include:

1. Remove the asset from PPE at carrying value (in accordance with IAS 16, paragraph 67 (a)).
2. Increase the bank account with the net proceeds of the sale. (This has already been entered). Any difference between (1) and (2) is, in accordance with IAS 16, paragraph 71, the profit or loss on disposal.
3. The revaluation surplus is an unrealised surplus while the building remains unsold. (Unrealised means it cannot be distributed to the shareholders. It is a book gain only.) When the asset to which the revaluation surplus applies is disposed of, the revaluation surplus is transferred from an unrealised surplus to retained earnings (IAS 16, paragraph 41). This surplus can then form part of the entity's distributable reserves.

(There is an alternative approach permitted in IAS 16, paragraph 41. This alternative approach permits the entity to transfer some of a revaluation surplus as the asset is still being used. According to IAS 16, paragraph 41, "the amount of the surplus transferred would be the difference between depreciation based on the revalued carrying amount of the asset and depreciation based on the asset's original cost". This alternative treatment is not relevant to this particular case study but it does arise in another.)

The profit or loss on disposal of the building is calculated as follows:

	€000
Carrying value	1,129
Net proceeds (600,000 – (2% of 600,000))	588
Loss on disposal	541

The adjustments required to bring the disposal of the building in line with IAS 16 would include:

	€000	€000
DR Revenue	588	
DR Loss on disposal (SOCI)	541	
CR PPE (at carrying value)		1,129
DR Revaluation Surplus	460	
CR Retained Earnings		460

The relevant disclosures for disposal of an item of PPE are outlined in IAS 16, paragraphs 73–79, and include the following:

1. The cost and accumulated depreciation on the disposed asset will be included in the reconciliation between opening and closing PPE figures per IAS 16, paragraph 73(e)(ii) and (vii).
2. A single line on the statement of comprehensive income will include the post-tax profit or loss on the disposal of assets (IAS 1, paragraph 82). (**Note:** IAS 1, paragraph 97, states that, when items of income or expense are material, an entity shall disclose their nature and amount separately. This includes the profit or loss on disposal of a non-current asset.)
3. The transfer from unrealised profit revaluation surplus to realised profit reserves will be included as a separate line on the Statement of Changes in Equity.

Outstanding Issue 3

IAS 11 *Construction Contracts* outlines the relevant accounting treatment for the recognition of costs, revenue and profit of construction contracts. This standard is relevant where a contract spans a number of accounting periods. The central issue in IAS 11 is when to recognise revenue and profit on construction contracts. The normal rule for the recognition of revenue[1] is that revenue is recognised when the significant risks and rewards have been transferred to the buyer and the vendor has given up managerial control and interest in the goods (IAS 18, para 14). This means that, normally, revenue is recognised only when a contract is completed. However, IAS 11 acknowledges that, where construction contracts last a significant period of time, it may not be realistic to wait until the contract has been completed to recognise revenue. If this were to happen, the financial statements during the performance period would include only the costs of the contract. Revenue would not be recognised until the contract was completed. This would give a lopsided and unrealistic picture of the contract performance over its life.

IAS 11 *Construction Contracts* permits entities to depart from the normal rules of revenue recognition by allowing revenue to be recognised through-out the contract period rather than at the end. This is done on a stage of completion basis. In the case study the contract between Knightstown and AVM Ltd commenced in April 2012 and is due to be completed in September 2013. The only accounting entry that has been made so far is to debit cost of sales and

[1] The general accounting guidance for the recognition of revenue is IAS 18 *Revenue.* IAS 18 is not addressed in this case study other than to explain how normal principles are waived when reporting for construction contracts.

credit bank with the costs incurred to date, €1.2 million. You will need to review and complete the accounting entries to bring the reporting in line with IAS 11.

To complete the entries you will need to complete the following steps:
Step 1. Identify the total revenue and total cost of the contract
Step 2. Establish if this project is profit-making or loss-making
Step 3. Identify the stage of completion at the reporting date *and*
Step 4. Complete the accounting entries in the Statement of Comprehensive Income and in the Statement of Financial Position (IAS 11, paragraphs 22–35).

- **Step 1 – The Total Revenue and Total Cost of the Contract**

	€000	€000	
Total revenue*		5,100	(5,000+100)
Total costs:			
Costs incurred to date	1,200		
Costs to complete	2,800	4,000	
Total profit		1,100	

* Contract revenue includes the initial revenue agreed (€5 million) and any variations to the price (€5 million × 2% = €100,000) (IAS 11, para 11). Variations are included in revenue when it is probable the customer will approve the variation and the amount can be measured reliably (IAS 11, paragraph 14). The solution assumes these conditions will be satisfied.

- **Step 2 – Profit-making or Loss-making Contract**

The contract is profit-making so revenue and costs can be recognised on a stage of completion basis. (If the project was loss-making the accounting treatment would be different. IAS 11, paragraph 36 states "When it is probable that total contract costs will exceed total contract revenue, the expected loss shall be recognised as an expense immediately.")

- **Step 3 – Identify the Stage of Completion of the Contract**

Assuming the outcome of the contract can be estimated reliably, revenue can now be recognised on a "stage of completion" basis (IAS 11, paragraph 22). IAS 11, paragraph 30, states that the stage of completion can be determined by a variety of methods:
(a) Proportion of costs incurred for work performed to date (i.e. certified costs) bear to the estimated total contract costs;
(b) Surveys of work performed; or
(c) Completion of a physical proportion of the contract work.

The method that best suits the information provided in the case study is method (a). The stage of completion for the AVM contract is calculated as follows:

Costs incurred for work certified	€1,000,000
Total costs	€4,000,000
Completed	25%

- **Step 4 – The entries to the Financial Statement should include:**

The Statement of Comprehensive Income According to company policy, profit may be recognised when the contract is more than 20% complete. As the contract is 25% completed by the end of the reporting period, revenue and profit may be recognised as follows:

		€000	
Revenue	25%	1,275	(€5,100,000 × 25%)
Cost of Sales	25%	1,000	(€4,000,000 × 25%)
Profit :	25%	275	

The Statement of Financial Position IAS 11, paragraph 42, states that an entity "shall present: (a) the gross amount due from customers for contract work as an asset". (Gross amounts due to customers for contract work would be recognised as a liability.)

The gross amount due from customers is the net amount of (IAS 11, para 43):

(a) Costs incurred plus recognised profits, less
(b) The sum of recognised losses and progress billings

The gross amount due from AVM Ltd at 31 December 2012 includes:

	€000
Costs incurred	1,200
Profit recognised	+275
Recognised losses	–0
Progress billings	–0
	1,475

This balance will appear in Trade Receivables in the current assets under the heading **'gross amount due from customers for contract work'.**

The only entry that has been made in the financial statements to take account of outstanding issue 3 was to debit cost of sales and credit the bank €1.2 million. Two adjustments will be required to correct the current entry and complete the accounting presentation:

1. 25% of the contract price should be recognised as revenue.
2. The cost of sales should represent the costs relating to work that was completed in the period (costs certified) and not total costs incurred.

The adjustments required to bring the accounting treatment in line with IAS 11 will be as follows:

	€000	€000
1. DR Gross amount due from customer	1,275	
CR Revenue		1,275
2. DR Gross amount due from customer	200	
CR Cost of sales		200

The relevant disclosures for construction contracts are outlined in IAS 11, paragraphs 39–45, and include:

(a) Contract revenue recognised, methods used to determine revenue and methods used to determine stage of completion.
(b) The aggregate of costs incurred, advances received and retentions withheld at the reporting date.
(c) The gross amount due will be presented as an asset.

Outstanding Issue 4

This issue examines inventory and tests your knowledge of the component parts of inventory cost. IAS 2 paragraph 10 states that "the cost of inventories shall comprise all costs of purchase, costs of conversion and other costs incurred in bringing the inventories to their present location and condition". An explanation of this definition is given in paragraphs 11 to 18 of the standard. In relation to the inventory of product BLT, you must identify what costs should be included in the valuation of inventory and what costs should be excluded.

The inventory of product BLT is currently valued at €1.99 million. In accordance with IAS 2 *Inventories* the cost should be €1.55 million. This is made up as follows:

Item	Treatment	Reference	Amount €000
Material	Allow	IAS 2 paragraph 11	600
Labour conversion costs	Allow	IAS 2 paragraph 12	250
Fixed Production Overheads	Note	IAS 2 paragraph 13	500
Patent Royalties	Allow	IAS 2 paragraph 15	200
General Admin Overhead	No	IAS 2 paragraph 16(c)	0
			1,550

Note: Production overheads should be allocated to inventory on the basis of normal production (IAS 2, paragraph 13). In the case study production overheads have been allocated on the basis of actual production of 200,000 units. Production is normally 20% lower (200,000 units × 80% = 160,000 units).

The existing production overhead figure is made up of the following:

Production overheads	= €4,000,000
Actual production levels	= 200,000 units
Production overhead per unit	= €4,000,000/200,000 units
	= €20 per unit
Closing inventory	= 20,000 units

Production overhead allocated to inventory is €400,000

The correct figure is:

Production overheads	= €4,000,000
Normal production levels	= 160,000 units
Production overhead per unit	= €4,000,000/160,000 units
	= €25 per unit
Closing inventory	= 20,000

Correct production overhead allocated to inventory is €500,000

The allocation of production overheads to closing inventory should be increased by €100,000.

In summary, the adjustments to inventory will be:
- Increase production overhead allocation to inventory by €100,000.
- Reduce inventory by the administration allocation €540,000.
- The net effect is a decrease to inventory of €440,000 to €1.55 million.

The adjustment required to bring inventory in line with IAS 2 is as follows:

	€000	€000
DR Cost of Sales	440	
CR Inventory		440

Inventory should be stated at the lower of cost and Net Realisable Value (NRV). The net realisable value is measured as the estimated selling price less the costs of completion and the estimated costs necessary to make the sale (IAS 2, paragraph 6). The NRV of BLT inventory is:

	€
Selling Price	2,500,000
Costs to sell	240,000
NRV	2,260,000

As the NRV is higher than cost, the inventory will be stated at cost of €1,550,000.

The relevant disclosures for Inventories include (IAS 2, para 36–38):

(a) The accounting policies, the carrying amount of inventories, write-down of inventory, reversal of any write-down and the reasons for the reversal, the carrying amount of inventory pledged as security for liabilities *and*

(b) Classification of inventory (i.e. raw material, WIP, finished goods).

Outstanding Issue 5

Knightstown Plc has declared a special dividend this year. The dividend was proposed after the year-end and has been accrued in the 2012 financial statements.

The treatment of events that occur after the year-end and before the accounts are signed is outlined in IAS 10 *Events after the Reporting Period.* (IAS 10 classifies events that occur after the reporting date into adjusting events and non-adjusting events. Adjusting events are those events that provide evidence of conditions that existed at the end of the reporting period. Non-adjusting events are those events that are indicative of conditions that arose after the reporting period.) IAS 10, paragraph 12, states "If an entity declares dividends to holders of equity instruments … *after* the reporting period, the entity shall not recognise those dividends as a liability at the end of the reporting period" (our italic). (However details should be disclosed in a note to the financial statements in accordance with paragraph 13).

The current treatment is incorrect. The dividend should not be accrued as it was declared after the end of the reporting period. An adjustment will be required to reverse it as follows:

	€000	€000
DR Provisions	500	
CR Retained earnings		500

Note: It is stated in the case study that the dividend will be paid out of the 2012 profits. This is not technically correct. The rules regarding the distribution of company profits are set out in company legislation. The general principle of the law is that dividends can only be paid out of **distributable profits** – distributable profits consist of **accumulated realised** profits less accumulated realised losses.

The term '*accumulated*' means that the dividend can only be paid out of the cumulative balance of retained earnings and not just on the basis of a single year's profit. If the accumulated retained earnings are lower than the current year's profit then the maximum the company can distribute is the retained earnings figure. (Retained earnings of Knightstown per the draft financial statements are €23.021 million.) The term *realised* means the dividend is paid out of profits that have actually been earned. Profits or gains that are *unrealised* may not be distributed. For example, revaluation surplus is considered to be unrealised profit. These profits will normally be realised only when the asset is actually disposed of. Up until that point the revaluation surplus cannot be distributed to shareholders.

Finally, there is an added restriction for companies that have public liability. The total of the net assets of a public company must be equal to or more than the aggregate of the called up share capital plus undistributable reserves at the date of and immediately after the distribution.

Undistributable reserves include the following:

- The share premium account;
- The capital redemption reserve fund (used when buying back shares);
- The excess of accumulated unrealised profits not previously capitalised over accumulated unrealised losses not previously written off by a reduction or reorganisation of capital; and
- Any other reserve which the company is prohibited from distributing by law or the company's own rules.

Summary of Adjustments

The adjustments are now completed. They are summarised as follows. (You are not asked to produce these summaries. They are presented for clarity only. The requirement asks you to re-draft the financial statements – this follows later.)

	PPE	Inventories	Trade Receivables	Provisions	Retained Earnings	Revaluation Surplus
	€000	€000	€000	€000	€000	€000
Per draft statements	7,500	4,500	2,000	2,800	23,021	650
Issue 1 Cost	(13)			42	(55)	
Issue 1 Depreciation	(78)				(78)	
Issue 2 Disposal	(1,129)				(1,129)	
Issue 2 Disposal					460	(460)
Issue 3 Construction			1,275		1,275	
Issue 3 Construction			200		200	
Issue 4 Inventory		(440)			(440)	
Issue 5 Dividends				(500)	500	
Revised balance	6,280	4,060	3,475	2,342	23,754	190
Net Adjustment	(1,220)	(440)	1,475	(458)	733	(460)

Requirement (a)(ii)

The Knightstown Group
Redrafted Statement of Financial Position
as at 31 December 2010

	Original	Issue 1	Issue 2	Issue 3	Issue 4	Issue 5	Revised
	€000	€000	€000	€000	€000	€000	€000
Non-current Assets							
Property, Plant and Equipment	7,500	(91)	(1,129)				6,280
Investment Properties	5,800						5,800
Long-term Investment – Sussa	9,000						9,000
Long-term Investments – Finian	7,500						7,500
Available for Sale Financial Assets	1,500						1,500
Intangible Asset – Patents	480						480
Intangible Asset – Development Expenditure	11,000						11,000
	42,780						41,560
Current Assets							
Inventories	4,500				(440)		4,060
Intragroup Receivable	0						0
Intragroup Receivable (Staff Exchange)	200						200
Trade Receivables	2,000			1,475			3,475
Cash and Cash Equivalents	8,000						8,000
	14,700						15,735
Total Net Assets	**57,480**						**57,295**

Equity							
Ordinary Share Capital (€1 each)	10,000						10,000
Share Premium	9,079						9,079
Retained Earnings	23,021	(133)	(669)	1,475	(440)	500	23,754
Revaluation Surplus	650		(460)				190
	42,750						43,023
Non-current Liabilities							
Bank Loans and Bonds	6,480						6,480
Provisions	2,800	42				(458)	2,342
Retirement Benefit Obligations	1,200						1,200
Capital Grants	200						200
Deferred Tax	500						500
	11,180						10,722
Current Liabilities							
Trade Payables	2,800						2,800
Intragroup Payable (staff exchange)	200						200
Bank Loans	300						300
Current Tax	250						250
	3,550						3,550
Total Equity and Liabilities	**57,480**						**57,295**

Requirement (b)(i)

It is important to have a system for completing the consolidated statement of financial position. This will help speed up the process and help eliminate any mistakes. The system that you employ is your decision (there are a number of different approaches that can be used). In this solution the process followed is as follows:

Step 1: Set out the group structure

Step 2: Deal with the 'Additional Information'

Step 3: Prepare the consolidation table (i.e. calculate the Goodwill, Non-controlling Interests and Retained Earnings figures). These are key figures in a consolidated statement of financial position and attract many marks.

Step 4: Bring Step 2 and Step 3 together by preparing the consolidated statement of financial position.

- **Step 1 – Set out the Group Structure**

  In this instance, the group structure is straightforward.

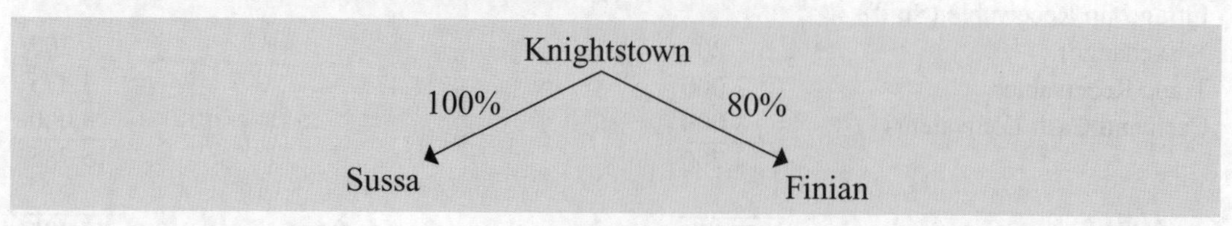

- Sussa and Finian are subsidiaries of Knightstown
- Both subsidiaries were purchased a number of years ago

- **Step 2 – The Additional Information**
  - *Item 1: Acquisition of Sussa* The information provided on the acquisition of Sussa will be considered as part of **Step 3**. There are no fair value issues on acquisition.
  - *Item 2: Acquisition of Finian* The information provided on the acquisition of Finian will be considered as part of **Step 3**. There are no fair value issues on acquisition.
  - *Item 3: Intragroup Trading* Under IFRS 10, paragraph B86, all intragroup balances and transactions should be eliminated in full. The usual approach to this is to eliminate the intragroup sales and purchases, remove the profit element of the intragroup goods that are still in inventory and eliminate any intragroup receivable and payable.

In this instance, the circumstances are slightly different. The dispute means that Knightstown has already removed the effect of the transaction from its records. However, Sussa has not removed the effect of the transaction. This will be discussed further in Requirement (b)(ii) but Sussa would need to book the goods into its inventory and record the sales returns.

	€	€
DR/Increase: Sales returns	1,500,000	
CR/Reduce: Intragroup receivable (from Knightstown)		1,500,000
DR/Increase: Inventory	1,200,000	
CR/Decrease: Cost of sales		1,200,000

The adjustments made to sales returns and cost of sales are both in the statement of comprehensive income, the net effect of which is to reduce profits and subsequently the retained earnings of Sussa by €300,000. The transaction above can be summarised as (all in Sussa):

	€	€
DR/Reduce: Retained earnings	300,000	
DR/Increase: Inventory	1,200,000	
CR/Reduce: Intragroup receivable (from Knightstown)		1,500,000

Once this transaction is made, the intragroup receivable (originally at €1,500,000 in Sussa but now at €0) and the intragroup payable (of €0 in Knightstown) are eliminated so no further adjustment is required.

- *Item 4: Intragroup Exchange of Staff* This is similar to the previous item. Again IFRS 10 paragraph B86 is invoked and the effect of all intragroup transactions is eliminated.

While the circumstances are complex, from a statement of financial position perspective these receivables eliminate against the payables.

	€
Receivables:	
Knightstown	200,000
Sussa	120,000
Finian	360,000
Total receivables	680,000
Payables:	
Knightstown	200,000
Sussa	280,000
Finian	200,000
Total payables	680,000

Therefore the following adjustment is required:

	€	€
DR/Reduce Intragroup payable in Knightstown	200,000	
DR/Reduce Intragroup payable in Sussa	280,000	
DR/Reduce Intragroup payable in Finian	200,000	
CR/Reduce Intragroup receivable in Knightstown		200,000
CR/Reduce Intragroup receivable in Sussa		120,000
CR/Reduce Intragroup receivable in Finain		360,000

To summarise, the additional information gives rise to two adjustments:

	€	€
1. DR/Reduce: Retained Earnings (post-acquisition)	300,000	
DR/Increase: Inventory	1,200,000	
CR/Reduce: Intragroup Receivable (from Knightstown)		1,500,000
2. DR/Reduce Intragroup payable in Knightstown	200,000	
DR/Reduce Intragroup payable in Sussa	280,000	
DR/Reduce Intragroup payable in Finian	200,000	
CR/Reduce Intragroup receivable in Knightstown		200,000
CR/Reduce Intragroup receivable in Sussa		120,000
CR/Reduce Intragroup receivable in Finian		360,000

- **Step 3 – Prepare the Consolidation Table**

There are two sections to this:

1. For each of the acquisitions, take the information from the statement of financial position as presented:
   - Cost of investment in Sussa: as per the statement of financial position of Knightstown.
   - Cost of investment in Finian: as per the statement of financial position of Knightstown.
   - Ordinary share capital: as per the statement of financial position of Sussa, all allocated to the goodwill calculation as this was a 100% acquisition.
   - Ordinary share capital: as per the statement of financial position of Finian, split between goodwill and non-controlling interests.

- Revenue reserves: as per the statement of financial position of Sussa, €3,000,000, split as follows:
  - Pre-acquisition of €2,000,000; all allocated to goodwill as this was a 100% acquisition.
  - Post-acquisition of €1,000,000 (the balance); all allocated to retained earnings as this was a 100% acquisition.
- Retained earnings: as per the statement of financial position of Finian, €4,500,000, split as follows:
  - Pre-acquisition of €3,750,000; split between goodwill (80%) and non-controlling interests (20%).
  - Post-acquisition of €750,000 (the balance); split between revenue reserves (80%) and non-controlling interests (20%).
- Retained earnings of Knightstown: as per the revised statement of financial position of Knightstown (the answer to Requirement (a)(ii)), all to retained earnings.

2. Taking the relevant information from the adjustments made in **Step 2**.
   - This is a matter of going through the adjustments made and where they impact on goodwill, non-controlling interests or retained earnings, the appropriate amount should be included.

	Goodwill Sussa €000	**Goodwill Finian €000**	**Non-controlling Interests €000**	**Retained Earnings €000**
Cost of Investment	9,000	7,500		
Ordinary share capital – Sussa	2,000			
Ordinary share capital – Finian		1,600	400	
Retained earnings – Sussa pre-acq (2,000)	2,000			
Retained earnings – Sussa post-acq (1,000)				1,000
Retained earnings – Finian pre-acq (3,750)		3,000	750	
Retained earnings – Finian post-acq (750)			150	600
Retained earnings – Knightstown (revised SFP)				23,754
Adjustments				
1. Intragroup trading				(300)
	5,000	2,900	1,300	25,054

- **Step 4 – Complete the Consolidated statement of financial position**

Take the revised statement of financial position for Knightstown and the statements of financial position for Sussa and Finian. Combine these with the adjustments highlighted. Include the figures for goodwill, non-controlling interests and retained earnings direct from the consolidation table (**Step 3**).

Knightstown Group
CONSOLIDATED STATEMENT OF FINANCIAL POSITION
for the year ended 31 December 2012

	Knightstown €000	Sussa €000	Finian €000	Adj 1 €000	Adj 2 €000	Total €000
Non-current Assets						
Property, Plant and Equipment	6,280	7,160	2,540			15,980
Investment Properties	5,800					5,800
Goodwill – Sussa	9,000					5,000
Goodwill – Finian	7,500					2,900
Available for Sale Financial Assets	1,500	–	–			1,500
Intangible Asset – Patents	480					480
Intangible Asset – Development Expenditure	11,000	1,000	4,850			16,850
	41,560	8,160	7,390			48,510
Current Assets						
Inventories	4,060	500	600	1,200		6,360
Intragroup Receivable (from Knightstown)	–	1,500	–	(1,500)		0
Intragroup Receivable (Staff Exchange)	200	120	360		(680)	0
Trade Receivables	3,475	750	3,000			7,225
Cash and Cash Equivalents	8,000	2,500	900			11,400
	15,735	5,370	4,860			24,985
Total Net Assets	57,295	13,530	12,250			73,495
Equity						
Ordinary Share Capital (€1 each)	10,000	2,000	2,000			10,000
Share Premium	9,079		–			9,079
Retained earnings	23,754	3,000	4,500			25,054
Revaluation Surplus	190		–			190
	43,023	5,000	6,500			44,323
Non-controlling Interests						1,300
						45,623

Non-current Liabilities					
Bank Loans and Bonds	6,480	2,000	2,000		10,480
Provisions	2,342	500	300		3,142
Retirement Benefit Obligations	1,200	200	500		1,900
Capital Grants	200	200	150		550
Deferred Tax	500	100	300		900
	10,722	3,000	3,250		16,972
Current Liabilities					
Trade Payables	2,800	4,800	1,800		9,400
Intragroup Payable (staff exchange)	200	280	200	(680)	0
Bank Loans	300	250	250		800
Current Tax	250	200	250		700
	3,550	5,530	2,500		10,900
Total Equity and Liabilities	57,295	13,530	12,250		73,495

Requirement (b)(ii)

In the information provided there were two instances of intragroup transactions.
1: The dispute between Sussa and Knightstown over the specification of some goods.
2: The exchange of staff between group companies.

With Regard to Item 1

It is not unusual for companies in the same group to trade with one another. However, the dispute resolution procedures within the group are poor. The two companies are probably wasting a lot of time arguing between themselves and Sussa's refusal to process the goods into inventory is not good practice. Someone within the group needs to adjudicate the dispute and come to a fast and binding decision. This will eliminate the ongoing arguing and stand-off between the companies. The group needs to establish some mechanism for dealing with these disputes quickly rather than letting them fester.

Sussa also needs to consider its own procedures; allowing goods to reside in goods inwards without being processed is bad practice. Sussa effectively has no record of how much of this product is in its inventory. If these goods were booked into inventory they could potentially be sold to a different customer but as long as they are not booked into inventory they are not reflected as available for sale in Sussa's records. Whatever the final resolution is, whether Sussa books the goods in or leaves them in limbo, it should have no bearing on the outcome. Unless the circumstances are extremely unusual, there should be no product on Sussa's premises that is unrecorded on their systems.

From a broader perspective, the group may need to consider their ordering systems. Clearly there was some misunderstanding of the specification of the product (by either Sussa or Knightstown). One wonders if non-group customers are experiencing similar difficulties and these issues are not being conveyed back to the group. The group is potentially running the risk of alienating some of its customers. If these customers find an alternative source of supply, their loyalty may be very limited. This may merit further investigation by management.

The group is already addressing some of the communication problems that this (and possibly other issues) gives rise to. Transferring staff between companies ensures that the barriers that exist within the group are reduced. Also, it may help in resolving the issues somewhat faster as the group companies may understand each other a little better.

With Regard to Item 2

While this is a complicated arrangement, it is being undertaken for a logical reason: the group needs to ensure that there is a greater level of co-ordination and understanding within the group companies. Also, the reimbursement for the salaries of those transferred is logical as companies do not want to pay for staff that do not work for them. The alternative is to transfer the staff between companies, resulting in even more work as existing contracts of employment may need to be terminated and new contracts of employment may need to be drawn up. This is a less desirable way of dealing with temporary, short-term staff transfers.

The mechanism appears to be working quite well as the amounts owed and receivable cancel out and the individual companies in the group have agreed the figures. The only minor issue is that the payment between the group companies takes place quite late. However, this may be done for timing/cash flow purposes, a legitimate rational within a group context.

Case 3

Derrynane Limited

This case study is based on a manufacturing business. The accounting standards, IAS 1, IAS 8, IAS 10, IAS 16, IAS 17, are addressed in this case.

Background – Derrynane Limited

Derrynane Limited is a capital intensive manufacturing business. The company was established in 1979. Paul Sugrue is the Managing Director of Derrynane Limited. The business employs 80 people.

Derrynane is a private company limited by share capital. Although not mandatory, Derrynane has been preparing IFRS compliant financial statements for a number of years. The company made the transition to IFRS in 2004 as a number of its investors are based overseas and are more familiar with IFRS-based statements than with those prepared in compliance with local accounting standards.

It is February 2013 and the 2012 financial statements of Derrynane Limited are being finalised. There are two areas that require attention:

- Property Plant and Equipment, and
- The Statement of Changes in Equity.

During the year the financial accountant, Jenny Brick, had taken an unexpected leave of absence and a temporary bookkeeper was recruited to fill her position. The bookkeeper, although proficient in basic bookkeeping tasks, was unfamiliar with the area of fixed asset accounting. As a result many of the transactions recorded during her tenure were incomplete and incorrect. When Jenny Brick returned to work her schedule was hectic and she did not find time to review the bookkeeper's work before the first set of draft accounts were issued in early January 2013. Towards the end of January, Jenny spent a couple of long lonely nights at her desk poring over the draft accounts. It took some time but, eventually, she managed to identify all of the outstanding accounting issues. These are outlined below. In addition, the disclosure notes for Property, Plant and Equipment and the Statement of Changes in Equity have not yet been completed.

The profit for the period reported in the draft financial statements is €976,000.

The following information is relevant:

Outstanding Issue 1 – Property, Plant and Equipment

The balances on the property, plant and equipment accounts are as follows:

Cost/Valuation as at 1 January 2012: (€000)

Property	Plant	Fixtures	Vehicles	Total
1,600	400	300	280	2,580

Accumulated Depreciation as at 1 January 2012: (€000)

Property	Plant	Fixtures	Vehicles	Total
118	120	90	80	408

As permitted by IAS 16, the company measures its property at revalued amounts. The remaining assets are measured at cost less depreciation and impairment write-downs.

It is the policy of Derrynane Ltd to acquire leasehold interests in plant rather than purchasing outright. At the end of 2012, all of the plant included in Property, Plant and Equipment is leased.

Depreciation is charged using the straight line method at the following rates:

Property	2½% per annum
Plant	10% per annum
Fixtures and fittings	10% per annum
Motor vehicles	20% per annum

A full year's depreciation is charged in the year of acquisition and none in the year of disposal. Depreciation is charged on the closing cost/valuation each year.

The draft financial statements do not include any charge for depreciation for 2012. In addition, they do not take account of the following issues that have now been identified by Jenny Brick:

Transaction (i) Fixtures, which had cost €200,000 in January 2008, were traded-in against new fittings in September 2012. An allowance of €50,000 was received on the old fittings. The new fixtures were delivered and installed in September 2012. The only entry made in the accounts in respect of this transaction was to debit a suspense account and credit the bank account with the net outlay for the replacement fittings of €475,000. The suspense account is included in Trade Receivables.

Transaction (ii) Derrynane Limited owns two buildings – the Highfield property and the Lowlands property. Details of the properties are as follows:

Name of Property	Valuation at 1 January 2012	Accumulated Depreciation 1 January 2012	Remaining Useful Life at 1 January 2012
Highfield	€720,000	€57,000	35 years
Lowlands	€880,000	€61,000	40 years

In 2008 both properties had been revalued. Arising from that revaluation a revaluation surplus of €227,000 was recorded in respect of the Highfield property. None of this revaluation surplus has been written-off. In respect of Lowlands, the 2008 revaluation resulted in a charge to the income statement of €70,400.

The company carried out a further review of its properties in December 2012. In light of depressed market conditions, the value of the Highfield property had fallen significantly since the last valuation. The latest valuation concludes that the Highfield property is now estimated to be worth €395,000. The Lowlands property, which is based overseas, has risen in value. It is now estimated to be worth €986,000.

The bookkeeper ignored any information about revaluations. Therefore no entry has been made in the financial statements in respect of this latest valuation.

Transaction (iii) The company acquired furniture during 2012 in a hire purchase (HP) agreement. The HP contract involves 36 monthly payments of €2,000 each. The cash price for this furniture on the date the contract was signed was €60,000. The HP agreement states that legal title to the furniture will transfer to Derrynane once the final HP instalment has been paid. The HP agreement was signed on the 31 July 2012. Payments are due on the last day of each month, commencing 31 August 2012. The only entry made in relation to this transaction was to debit a rent account and credit the bank each month with the monthly instalment.

Transaction (iv) On the 10 January 2013, the company paid €3,600 to AKH Leasing Ltd. This payment is the first of 12 quarterly instalments of a finance lease. The lease relates to an item of plant that was ordered by Derrynane in October 2012. The plant was delivered to the company's premises on 30 December 2012. The lease agreement was issued on the same day. However, due to the Christmas break, it was not signed until 6 January 2013.

No entries were made in the 2012 financial statements in relation to this lease agreement. The temporary bookkeeper had left the company at that stage but a decision was taken by Jenny Brick and her team that, as there was no actual outlay until 2013, neither the asset nor details of the lease should be included in the 2012 financial statements. The fair value of the plant at the inception of lease was €295,000.

Transaction (v) In the process of her review Jenny Brick discovered that, although the bookkeeper had correctly treated vehicle maintenance costs as an operating expense in 2012, the same charge had been treated as a vehicle acquisition in previous years and included in property, plant and equipment. Jenny was surprised to discover that this treatment had gone unnoticed for a period of three years. On investigation, she identified the relevant maintenance costs but did not make any adjustment to the financial statements. The costs were as follows:

2009: €30,000; 2010: €25,000; 2011: €40,000

In addition, a decision has now been made to change the depreciation policy for the remaining motor vehicles. It is considered to be more appropriate to depreciate motor vehicles over an eight-year period rather than the existing five years. According to Jenny, this will be a better reflection of the consumption of economic benefits embodied in the assets. The change will be effective immediately.

Outstanding Issue 2: Statement of Changes in Equity

The equity position of the company at the beginning of 2012 was as follows:

At 1 January 2012:

	€
Issued Ordinary Share Capital (nominal value €1)	1,000,000 CR
Share Premium	100,000 CR
General Reserve	50,000 CR
Retained Earnings	95,940 CR
Revaluation surplus	227,000 CR
Total Equity 1 January 2012	1,472,940

In addition to any adjustments arising from outstanding issue 1 above, the following changes were made to the equity of Derrynane during 2012:

1. The company issued 120,000 ordinary shares on 25 July. These shares were issued at €1.50 per share. The issue was fully subscribed and all monies due were paid before the end of the financial year. The share issue was correctly treated in the financial statements.
2. The directors propose to transfer €80,000 from retained earnings to general reserves although no action has been taken to effect this transfer. It is the policy of the company not to distribute general reserves.
3. An interim cash dividend of €12,000 was paid on 8 August 2012. This was recorded correctly in the draft financial statements.
4. A final dividend was proposed in December. It was proposed that the shareholders accept a 1 for 10 share bonus issue in lieu of their normal cash distribution. The proposal was made on 10 December and was approved by the majority of shareholders on 15 December. The share transaction was adjusted in the draft statements and the company hopes to issue the share certificates in February 2013.

   One shareholder, who voted against the bonus issue, has written to Jenny Brick. He is disgruntled. This shareholder is of the opinion that the total annual dividend paid to the shareholders of Derrynane is wholly inadequate. Based on his calculations the company is distributing only 5.6% (approx.) of the total equity of the company. He would like to know why the level of distribution is so low.

Requirements

(**Note:** Unless you are specifically required to consider deferred taxation, you can assume that it is not applicable.)

(a) Outline the appropriate accounting adjustments for each of the items (i) to (v) in outstanding issue 1 above. Your answer should include detailed workings for each of the items and you should support your workings by reference to the relevant accounting rules. (50 marks)

(b) Complete the Statement of Comprehensive Income for the year ended 31 December 2012. This should include an *adjusted profit figure* (incorporating the adjustments in **requirement (a)** above) *and* a statement of Other Comprehensive Income for the period.
(5 marks)

(c) Complete the disclosure notes for Property, Plant and Equipment in accordance with IAS 16 *Property, Plant and Equipment*. Your notes should incorporate the transactions in **requirement (a)** above.
Note: You may assume there were no movements in Property Plant and Equipment other than those that are outlined in the case.
(20 marks)

(d) Prepare the Statement of Changes in Equity for Derrynane for the year ended 31 December 2012 in accordance with IAS 1 *Presentation of Financial Statements.*
(15 marks)

(e) Prepare the outline of a brief letter to the shareholder setting out the principal limitations on the distribution of profits in Irish companies.
(10 marks)

Ignore Taxation.

Guidance Notes – Derrynane Ltd

Exam Technique

Read the case carefully, then read the requirements.

This is the third of the introductory case study trilogy. The structure of this case study is different to **Armada** and **Knightstown**, the other case studies written at this level. This case study concentrates on disclosure notes rather than the redrafting of financial statements. The case focuses on two of the most significant disclosure notes on a set of financial statements namely: Property, Plant and Equipment and the Statement of Changes in Equity. The case study is divided into a number of sections:

1. In this first section you are required to complete the Property, Plant and Equipment note in accordance with IAS 16. In order to complete this note you must make a number of adjustments to the asset schedule. These adjustments incorporate IAS 16 *Property, Plant and Equipment,* IAS 17 *Leases,* IAS 10 *Events after the Reporting Period* and IAS 8 *Accounting Policies, Changes in Accounting Estimates and Errors.* There are *five* separate transactions to consider in this section. (This incorporates **requirements (a)–(c)** of the case study.)
2. In the second section of the case study, **requirement (d)**, you are asked to complete the Statement of Changes in Equity for inclusion in the financial statements. This note should be prepared in accordance with paragraphs 106 to 110 of IAS 1 *Presentation of Financial Statements.* As well as an increase in profits for the period, there will be other equity movements to consider when completing this section.
3. The final section of the case study, **requirement (e)**, is a discursive section. In this section, you are asked to outline the limitations on distributable profits. Your answer to this section should be reasonably short.

This case study should be approached in the order in which it is presented. This is particularly important. Each requirement builds on the previous one. **Requirements (a)** to **(c)** must be completed before attempting **requirement (d)**.

The discursive element to the case study is best answered at the end.

Manage your time. You should establish at the outset how much time should be allocated to each section. This should be done based on the marks awarded to each requirement. Remember to allow some time at the beginning for reading the case study.

Answering the Case Study

Requirement (a) – Guidance

Requirement (a) requires you to complete the accounting adjustments for five separate transactions. Each of these transactions relate to the property, plant and equipment of Derrynane Limited. You are presented with the opening balances as at 1 January 2012 for each class of asset held by the company. You are also provided with the depreciation policy for the various assets held by the company. You are also given details on the outstanding issues in relation to PPE. This information is presented to you in five separate transactions (i) – (v). You should consider each of these transactions separately.

Your adjustments should be presented clearly and professionally, identifying the debits and credits to each transaction. You will need to compile a summary of adjustments as you work through the case study. This will make it easier to answer each of the requirements of the case study.

Transaction (i) The company replaced some fixtures during the year. An allowance was given for the old fixtures. The net outlay was €475,000. The only entry made was to debit a suspense account and credit the bank account with the net payment. IAS 16 requires that assets disposed of are treated separately to acquisitions. The disposal of assets should be treated in accordance with IAS 16, paragraph 67–72. Paragraphs 15–28 outline the treatment of asset acquisitions. You should refer to these sections when completing the accounting transactions for the replacement of fixtures.

Transaction (ii) This transaction addresses the revaluation of property. Derrynane Limited owns two properties – Highfield and Lowlands. Both properties, revalued previously in 2008, are now subject to a second review. The results of the current review indicate that the Highfield property has fallen in value while Lowlands has increased. Paragraphs 31–42 of IAS 16 outline the accounting treatment for the revaluation of assets. Paragraph 39 describes the appropriate accounting treatment where a revalued asset has increased in value while paragraph 40 outlines the treatment when there has been a decrease. You should refer to these sections. No entries have been made in relation to the current revaluation.

Transaction (iii) This transaction outlines details of a Hire Purchase (HP) agreement. The temporary book-keeper entered some basic details about the contract but the accounting entries were not complete. You will need to consider the appropriate accounting treatment for HP agreements. You should refer to IAS 17 *Leases.* Although, in law, a HP agreement is distinctly different to a lease, the accounting treatment for hire purchase arrangements is the same as for finance leases. You should refer to the accounting guidance for finance leases in the financial statements of lessees (IAS 17, para 20–32).

Transaction (iv) Derrynane Ltd acquired plant in a lease agreement at the end of 2012. The plant was installed and operational before the end of the accounting period but the leasing agreement was not signed until the beginning of 2013. A decision was made by the finance team to omit the asset and the lease from the 2012 financial statements as the documentation was not signed until January 2013 and no payments were made until then.

You must decide if this is the most appropriate approach to take. Does the current treatment comply with international accounting guidance? To answer, you should review IAS 10 *Events after the Reporting Period.* You could consider, when making your recommendation, why the finance team may wish to defer recognition until 2013. Would a proposed application for external funding have any bearing on the decision?

Transaction (v) As part of the financial statements review an error was discovered. Maintenance costs have been included in the cost of vehicles. This error has been on-going for a number of accounting periods (from 2009–2011). Jenny Brick has identified the amounts but has not adjusted the financial statements. You should consider how to do this. You should also consider how to present this information in the financial statements. Bear in mind that as the maintenance costs were capitalised they would have been included as part of the depreciable asset each year.

IAS 8 *Accounting Policies, Changes in Accounting Estimates and Errors* will provide the appropriate guidance for the correction of this error.

Finally, a decision has been made to amend the depreciation policy for motor vehicles. You must consider how this change should be reflected in the financial statements. Is this a change in accounting policy or a change in accounting estimate? IAS 8 will give appropriate guidance.

Requirement (b) – Guidance

This is a short requirement. You simply need to adjust the draft profit figure given in the introduction to the case study for each of the items (i) to (v) in requirement (a). You should then combine the adjusted profit with any Other Comprehensive Income arising in the period. These are easier marks to earn but be careful with your presentation.

Requirement (c) – Guidance

The next stage is to complete the property, plant and equipment note. The purpose of the PPE note is to show the movement in the company's assets over the financial period. There are a number of disclosure requirements outlined in IAS 16, paragraphs 73–79. You should review these guidelines before completing this note.

In the case study, you are presented with the opening balances for each class of asset held by the company (for the cost/valuation of each asset class *and* for depreciation). These opening balances, combined with the PPE effects of transactions (i) to (v) in **requirement (a)** above will form the basis for the PPE note (remember you are told there is no other movement in Property, Plant and Equipment other than what is presented in the case).

A template for the presentation of the movement in PPE over the financial period is presented as follows:

	Property	**Plant**	**Fixtures**	**Total**
Cost/Valuation				
At 1 January 2012	xxx	xxx	xxx	xxx
Additions	xxx	xxx	xxx	xxx
Revaluations	xxx	xxx	xxx	xxx
Disposals	xxx	xxx	xxx	xxx
At 31 Dec 2012	xxx	xxx	xxx	xxx
Accumulated Depreciation				
At 1 January 2012	xxx	xxx	xxx	xxx
Charge for the period	xxx	xxx	xxx	xxx
On Disposal	xxx	xxx	xxx	xxx
On Revaluation	xxx	xxx	xxx	xxx
At 31 December 2012	xxx	xxx	xxx	xxx
Net Book Value 31/12/2012	xxx	xxx	xxx	xxx
Net Book Value 1/1/2012	xxx	xxx	xxx	xxx

In addition to the table note (above), IAS 16 requires further disclosures about property, plant and equipment. The purpose of these additional disclosures is to give further information to the user of the financial statements about the assets held by the company. This additional information relates to, among other things, the revaluation of tangible assets, assets held on leasehold interests and assets pledged as security on financial liabilities.

Requirement (d) – Guidance

In **requirement (d)** you are asked to complete the Statement of Changes in Equity of Derrynane Limited for the financial period.

The Statement of Changes in Equity is a statement outlining the movement of each class of equity over the accounting period. IAS 1 requires an entity to present this information as a separate component of the financial statements. The requirements are laid down in paragraphs 106 to 110 of the standard. Have a look at this section and review the necessary information.

The information relating to the Statement of Changes in Equity is given in outstanding issue 2. In this section you are given the opening position for each category of equity as well as information on the movement over the financial period. In addition, the 'Total Comprehensive Income' for the period, as calculated in **requirement (b)** of the case, will form part of this note.

There are no difficult calculations in this section. You need only concern yourself with the presentation of the information. A template for the presentation of the Statement of Changes in Equity is presented as follows:

STATEMENT OF CHANGES IN EQUITY
for year ended 31 December 2012

	Share Capital	**Share Premium**	**General Reserves**	**Retained Earnings**	**Revaluation Surplus**	**Total Equity**
Balance at 1 January 2012	xxx	xxx	xxx	xxx	xxx	xxx
Prior Period effects				xxx		xxx
Restated balance	xxx	xxx	xxx	xxx	xxx	xxx
Changes in equity for 2012						
Issue of Shares	xxx	xxx				xxx
Total Comprehensive Income for the year				xxx	xxx	xxx
Dividends				(xxx)		(xxx)
Transfers			(xxx)	xxx		
Total changes in equity	xxx	xxx	xxx	xxx	xxx	xxx
Balance at 31 December 2012	**xxx**	**xxx**	**xxx**	**xxx**	**xxx**	**xxx**

Requirement (e) – Guidance

This final section requires you to prepare the outline of a brief letter for the shareholder. The letter should give a brief summary of the principal restrictions under Irish Company Law on the distribution of profits and assets. In practice, the law on the distribution of profits is quite detailed. However, as the recipient is not a financial expert, you are required to provide only a brief overview of the principal restrictions laid down in company law. The relevant guidance can be found in the Companies Acts.

Recommended Reading

The above issues may also be referenced in *International Financial Accounting and Reporting,* 3rd Edition, by Ciaran Connolly (Chartered Accountants Ireland, 2011) and the relevant accounting standards as follows:

Case	Chapter	Chapter Title	Chapter Section	Standard
Requirement (a)				
Transaction (i)	6	Property, Plant and Equipment	6.2	IAS 16
Transaction (ii)	6	Property, Plant and Equipment	6.2	IAS 16
Transaction (iii)	8	Leases	8.3	IAS 17
Transaction (iv)	15, 8	Events After the Reporting Period, Leases	15.2, 8.3	IAS 10, IAS 17
Transaction (v)	21	Accounting Policies, Changes in Accounting Estimates and Errors	21.2, 21.3	IAS 8
Requirement (b)				
Revised IS	2	Presentation of Financial Statements	2.3	IAS 1
Requirement (c)				
PPE Note	6	Property, Plant and Equipment	6.3	IAS 16
Requirement (d)				
Statement of Changes in Equity	2	Presentation of Financial Statements	2.3	IAS 1
Requirement (e)				
Letter to shareholder	18	Distribution of Profits and Assets	18.2	

Solution to Derrynane Limited

Requirement (a)

Transaction (i)

Fixtures and Fittings traded in during the financial year have not been recorded correctly in the financial statements. The only entry made by the bookkeeper was to debit a suspense account and credit the bank with the net payment to acquire the new fixtures. No adjustments were made to the fixed assets schedule.

This transaction comprises both an acquisition of an asset and the disposal of an asset. In accordance with IAS 16 *Property Plant and Equipment* acquisitions and disposals should be treated separately.

Acquisitions:

IAS 16, paragraph 15, states "An item of property, plant and equipment that qualifies for recognition as an asset shall be measured at its cost."

The *cost* of the fixtures acquired in 2012 was €525,000. The amount actually paid out was €475,000. The difference is the trade-in allowance on the old fixtures. The trade-in allowance forms part of the disposal entries in the financial statements. It is not part of the acquisition cost.

Therefore the journal entry to incorporate the new fixtures (and correct the original entry) is:

	€	€
DR Fixtures (PPE)	525,000	
CR Suspense Account		475,000
CR Disposal Account		50,000

Disposals:

The following is relevant on the disposal of an asset:

1. "The carrying amount of an item of property, plant and equipment shall be derecognised ... on disposal" (IAS 16, para 67).
2. "The gain or loss arising from the derecognition of an item of property, plant and equipment shall be included in profit or loss when the item is derecognised" (IAS 16, para 68).

The gain or loss arising from the derecognition is the difference between the net disposal proceeds and the carrying amount of the item (IAS 16, para 71).

The loss on the disposal of the fixtures is:

	€	
Carrying value	120,000	(Cost €200,000 less depreciation of €20,000 per annum for four years)
Proceeds	50,000	
Loss	70,000	

The journal entries required for the disposal of the fixtures will include:

	€	€
DR Disposal	120,000	
DR Accumulated Depreciation	80,000	
CR PPE (cost)		200,000
(Derecognition IAS 16, paragraph 67)		
DR Operating Expenses	70,000	
CR Disposal Account		70,000
(Loss on Disposal IAS 16, paragraph 68)		

Transaction (ii)

Derrynane Ltd measures its property at revalued amounts. The company has two properties; the Highfield property and the Lowlands property. Both properties are currently stated at 1 January 2012 values. You are presented information on the latest revaluation in December 2012. The bookkeeper has ignored the new valuations and hence you must process the information.

IAS 16, paragraphs 31–42, outlines the guidance for assets held at re-valued amounts. The standard states that where assets have increased in value "the increase shall be recognised in other comprehensive income and accumulated in equity under the heading of revaluation surplus. However, the increase shall be recognised in profit or loss to the extent that it reverses a revaluation decrease of the same asset previously recognised in profit or loss" (IAS 16, para 39).

Where assets have decreased in value the decrease shall be recognised in profit or loss unless it reflects the reversal of a previous increase for same asset, in which case the revaluation surplus is reversed (IAS 16, para 40).

Finally, on revaluation, we restate the gross value of the asset as the revalued amount. When an item of PPE is revalued, any accumulated depreciation at the date of revaluation is eliminated (IAS 16, para 35(b)).

The Highfield property has fallen in value from its current carrying value of €663,000 (valuation of €720,000 less accumulated depreciation €57,000) to €395,000. Lowlands has increased from a carrying value of €819,000 (valuation of €880,000 less accumulated depreciation €61,000) to €986,000. This will be presented in the financial statements as follows:

	€	€	
Highfield Property:			
DR Operating expenses	41,000		(devaluation IAS 16, para 40)
DR Revaluation surplus	227,000		(devaluation IAS 16, para 40)
DR Accumulated depreciation	57,000		(depreciation IAS 16, para 35(b))
CR PPE (to new valuation)		325,000	

	€	€	
Lowlands Property			
DR PPE (to new valuation)	106,000		
DR Accumulated depreciation	61,000		(depreciation IAS 16, para 35(b))
CR Operating expenses		70,400	(devaluation IAS 16, para 39)
CR Revaluation surplus		96,600	(revaluation IAS 16, para 39)

Transaction (iii)

Derrynane acquired furniture during the year. The furniture was acquired under a hire purchase (HP) agreement. A HP agreement is a method of buying goods by making instalments over time. Ownership of the goods does not transfer to the buyer until the final instalment has been made. The accounting guidance for hire purchase agreements is outlined in IAS 17 *Leases*.

Hire purchase agreements are similar to lease agreements in many ways. Both involve the use of an asset without having legal ownership. The principal difference lies in the eventual ownership of the asset. In a HP arrangement legal ownership transfers to the buyer once the final instalment has been made. In a finance lease legal ownership may never transfer.

Hire purchase agreements are expressly included in IAS 17. Paragraph 6 of IAS 17 states that "The definition of a lease includes contracts for the hire of an asset that contain a provision giving the hirer an option to acquire title to the asset upon fulfilment of agreed conditions. These contracts are sometimes known as hire purchase contracts."

HP agreements are presented in the financial statements as finance leases. IAS 17, paragraph 10(a), states that a lease is a finance lease if "it transfers ownership of the asset to the lessee by the end of the lease term." (IAS 17, paragraphs 10 and 11, also outlines examples of other situations where a lease would be classified as a finance lease.)

Finance leases are accounted for as follows:

1. "At the commencement of the lease term lessees shall recognise finance leases as assets and liabilities in their financial statements at amounts equal to the fair value of the leased property or, if lower, the present value of the minimum lease payments" (IAS 17, para 20).
2. The subsequent "minimum lease payments shall be apportioned between the finance charge and the reduction of the outstanding liability. The finance charge shall be allocated to each period to produce a constant periodic rate of interest on the remaining balance of the liability" (IAS 17, para 25). An approximation to simplify calculations is permitted (IAS 17, para 26).

The HP contract is as follows:

	€	
Minimum Lease Payments	72,000	(36 instalments of €2,000)
Fair value	60,000	
Finance Charge	12,000	

These figures must be incorporated into the financial statements in accordance with IAS 17 *Leases.*

The journal entries necessary to incorporate the HP details include:

At the inception of the lease on 31 July 2012:

	€	€
DR Furniture (PPE)	60,000	
CR Lease Liability		60,000

With instalments made August to December 2012 (5 months)

	€	€
DR Finance Charges (W1)	3,063	
DR Lease Liability	6,937	
CR Rent		10,000

Working 1: Finance Charge – sum of digits method

Digits: $\frac{N(N+1)}{2}$ (where N = number of instalments)

$$\frac{36(36+1)}{2} = 666$$

From August 2012 to December 2012 there are five instalments. Finance will be charged to these periods as follows:

$$\frac{\text{(sum of first five instalments in descending order)}}{\text{(sum of total instalments)}} \times \text{Total Finance Charges}$$

$$= \frac{36+35+34+33+32}{666} \times €12{,}000$$

$$= \frac{170}{666} \times €12{,}000$$

$$= €3{,}063$$

Transaction (iv)

Derrynane Limited acquired plant at the end of 2012. The plant was acquired under a leasing contract. The plant was delivered and installed on 30 December 2012. As the leasing contract was not signed until 2013 and no payments were made before signing, no entries have been made in the financial statements. The bookkeeper ignored the contract altogether and Jenny Brick and the finance team agreed that the lease should remain off the Statement of Financial Position until 2013. The appropriate guidance for this can be found in IAS 10 *Events after the Reporting Period.*

IAS 10 categorises events that occur after the end of the financial period into adjusting and non-adjusting events. Adjusting events are defined as those events that occur after the end of the reporting period that "provide evidence of conditions that existed at the end of the reporting period" (IAS 10, para 3(a)). These events should be recognised in the current financial statements. Non-adjusting events are those events that occur **after the end** of the reporting period that "are indicative of conditions that arose after the reporting period" (IAS 10, para 3(b)). These events should be not be recognised in the current financial statements.

The plant was acquired before the end of the reporting period. It was delivered, installed and available for use by 31 December 2012. The contract was also issued before the 31 December 2010. The evidence would suggest that the leasing contract was in place at the end of the reporting period and that this event is, therefore, an adjusting one. The lease is a finance lease (we are given this information in the case) and should be presented in accordance with IAS 17 *Leases*. IAS 17, paragraphs 20–35, outlines the recognition rules for finance leases in the financial statements of the lessee. These rules have already been summarised in the answer to **transaction (iii)** above.

In accordance with IAS 17, paragraph 20, the contract would be brought on to the financial statements as follows:

	€	€
DR Plant (PPE)	295,000	
CR Lease Liability		295,000

There is no need to accrue for the first instalment or the allocation of interest. Finance charges will not accrue until 2013.

Transaction (v)

A material error has been discovered in the financial statements. Maintenance costs relating to the upkeep of the fleet of commercial vehicles were included in property plant and equipment for a period of three years from 2009 to 2011.

The schedule of maintenance payments included in property plant and equipment is as follows:

	2009	2010	2011	Total
	€	€	€	€
Included in motor vehicles (PPE)	30,000	25,000	40,000	95,000
Depreciated @ 20% pa	6,000	5,000	8,000	
Number of years of depreciation	3	2	1	
Total depreciation charged	18,000	10,000	8,000	36,000
Remaining in PPE as at 31 December 2012	12,000	15,000	32,000	59,000

Paragraphs 41–53 of IAS 8 *Accounting Policies, Changes in Accounting Estimates and Errors* give the appropriate guidance for the correction of errors. Guidance is given for errors relating to the current period and errors relating to prior periods. The error in the case study relates to prior periods.

Paragraph 42 of IAS 8 states that errors relating to prior periods should be corrected retrospectively in the first set of financial statements authorised for issue after their discovery by "restating the comparative amounts for the prior period(s) presented in which the error occurred; or … if the error occurred before the earliest prior period presented, restating the opening balances of assets, liabilities and equity for the earliest prior period presented."

As the case study does not include comparative amounts, the prior period error will be corrected by restating the opening balances of assets, liabilities and equity for "the earliest prior period presented".

This will be as follows:

	€	€
DR (opening) Retained Earnings	59,000	
DR (opening) Accumulated Depreciation	36,000	
CR (opening) Vehicles (PPE)		95,000

You should note that the *opening* retained earnings adjustment will be presented as a separate figure on the Statement of Changes in Equity. The opening balances for vehicles and related accumulated depreciation will incorporate the adjustment above. (Refer to the solution to requirements (c) and (d) for an illustration.)

Finally, the company has decided to alter its depreciation policy on motor vehicles. Up until 2012, the company charged depreciation at a rate of 20% per annum straight line. It is now proposed to change the rate to 12.5% (the effective rate for straight-line depreciation over eight years), effective immediately. According to IAS 8, paragraphs 32–40, this proposal is a change in accounting estimate (as opposed to a change in accounting policy). A change in accounting estimate occurs where a business revises its financial estimates. Paragraph 32 of IAS 8 gives examples of what might be constituted as an accounting estimate. Included in this list is "the useful lives of, or expected pattern of consumption of the future economic benefits embodied in, depreciable assets".

Changes in accounting estimates are applied prospectively, i.e. going forward to future periods. "The change shall be included in profit or loss in the period of the change and future periods" (IAS 8, para 36). No adjustment need be made to the opening reserves.

You have now completed the adjustments for transactions (i) to (v) of outstanding issue 1, thus meeting requirement (a) of the case study.

Before moving on to requirement (b), the adjustments made to Property Plant and Equipment will be summarised below. This will form the basis of the depreciation charge for the period.

These include:

COST/VALUATION

	Property	**Plant**	**Furniture and Fittings**	**Vehicles**
	€	**€**	**€**	**€**
Cost/valuation (per case study)	1,600,000	400,000	300,000	280,000
Transaction (i)			525,000	
Transaction (i)			(200,000)	
Transaction (ii)	(325,000)			
Transaction (ii)	106,000			
Transaction (iii)			60,000	
Transaction (iv)		295,000		
Transaction (v)				(95,000)
	1,381,000	695,000	685,000	185,000

Depreciation is charged on the closing cost/valuation of the assets each year. This is to keep the calculations relatively simple. The depreciation charge for 2012 for each class of asset, based on the company's depreciation policy is as follows:

	Property	**Plant**	**F&F**	**Vehicles**	**Total**
Depreciation Charge	€36,900*	€69,500	€68,500	€23,125**	€195,650

* (395,000/34) + (986,000/39)
** This is based on the revised useful life of the vehicles per transaction (v).

The journal entry to incorporate depreciation for the period is:

	€	€
DR Operating expenses	198,025	
CR Accumulated Depreciation (PPE)		198,025

Requirement (b)

In requirement (b) you are asked to prepare a revised profit figure and, along with any other relevant information, to complete the statement of comprehensive income for the period. The analysis has already been undertaken to complete this section. It is a matter of summarising the effects of transactions (i) to (v) above on the statement of comprehensive income.

The adjusted profit for the period is as follows:

		€
Profit per case study		976,000
Transaction (i)	Loss on sale of fixtures	(70,000)
Transaction (ii)	Valuation decrease	(41,000)
Transaction (ii)	Valuation increase	70,400
Transaction (iii)	HP – finance charge	(3,063)
Transaction (iii)	HP – rent error	10,000
Transaction (iv)	Lease contract	0
Transaction (v)	Error adjustment	0
	Depreciation charge	(198,025)
Revised Profit figure		744,312

The Statement of Comprehensive Income is presented as follows:

Derrynane Limited

STATEMENT OF COMPREHENSIVE INCOME

for the Year Ended 31 December 2012

	€
Profit for the period	744,312
Other Comprehensive Income	
Revaluation gains or losses	(130,400)
Total other comprehensive income	(130,400)
Total Comprehensive Income for the period	613,912

Requirement (c)

You are asked to prepare the property, plant and equipment note. This note should be presented in accordance with IAS 16, paragraphs 73–79. A suggested template was included in the guidance notes above. The completed note would appear as follows:

Property Plant and Equipment Note

	Property	Plant	Furniture and Fittings	Vehicles	Total
	€	€	€	€	€
Cost/Valuation:					
At 1 January 2012	1,600,000	400,000	300,000	185,000*	2,485,000
Additions		295,000	585,000		880,000
Revaluations	(219,000)				(219,000)
Disposals			(200,000)		(200,000)
At 31 December 2012	1,381,000	695,000	685,000	185,000	2,946,000
Accumulated Depreciation					
At 1 January 2012	118,000	120,000	90,000	44,000**	372,000
Charge	36,900	69,500	68,500	23,125	198,025
On Disposal			(80,000)		(80,000)
On Revaluation	(118,000)				(118,000)
	36,900	189,500	78,500	67,125	372,025
NBV 31/12/2012	1,344,100	505,500	606,500	117,875	2,573,975
NBV 1/1/2012	1,482,000	280,000	210,000	141,000	2,113,000

* The opening balance per the case study of €280,000 is reduced by the motor expenses that were incorrectly capitalised per transaction (v) €95,000.
** The opening accumulated depreciation per the case study of €80,000 is reduced by the accumulated depreciation on the motor expenses that were incorrectly capitalized in transaction (v) above €36,000.

Other disclosures that would be relevant include:

- the depreciation policy (IAS 16, para 73(a)–(d));
- the restriction on asset titles (e.g. plant is leasehold) (IAS 16, para 74(a));
- the nature and effect of a change in accounting estimate (IAS 16, para 76);
- revaluation details (IAS 16, para 77), including:
  - the effective date of revaluation;
  - whether an independent valuer was involved;
  - the methods and significant assumptions applied in estimating fair value;
  - the extent to which the fair values were determined by reference to active market prices;

- for each revalued class of asset, the carrying amount that would have been recognised had the assets been carried under the cost model;
- the revaluation surplus, indicating the change for the period and any restrictions on the distribution of the balance to shareholders.

Requirement (d)

The final schedule you must present is the statement of changes in equity. As explained in the guidance notes above, the statement of changes in equity should be presented in accordance with IAS 1 *Presentation of Financial Statements.* Paragraphs 106–110 outline what should be included.

The statement must show (IAS 1, para 106) (the elements in bold are relevant to this case study):

- **total comprehensive income for the period**, showing separately amounts attributable to the owners of the parent and to non-controlling interests;
- **the effects of retrospective application,** when applicable, for each component;
- **reconciliations between the carrying amounts** at the beginning and the end of the period for each component of equity, separately disclosing:
  - **profit or loss;**
  - **each item of other comprehensive income;**
  - **transactions with owners, showing separately contributions by and distributions to owners;** and
  - changes in ownership interests in subsidiaries that do not result in a loss of control.

The following amounts may also be presented on the face of the Statement of Changes in Equity, or they may be presented in the notes (IAS 1, para 107):

- **amount of dividends recognised as distributions;** and
- the related amount per share.

A template was presented in the guidance notes above. The completed note would appear as follows:

Derrynane Limited
STATEMENT OF CHANGES IN EQUITY
for the year ended 31 Dec 2012

	Share Capital	Share Premium	General Reserves	Retained Earnings	Revaluation Surplus	Total
	€	€	€	€	€	€
Balance at 1 January	1,000,000	100,000	50,000	95,940	227,000	1,472,940
Prior period effects				(59,000)		(59,000)
Restated balance	1,000,000	100,000	50,000	36,940	227,000	1,413,940

Changes in equity during 2012:						
Issue of share capital*	232,000	60,000				292,000
TCI for the period				744,312	(130,400)	613,912
Dividends**				(124,000)		(124,000)
Transfers			80,000	(80,000)		0
Total changes in equity	232,000	60,000	80,000	540,312.2	(130,400)	781,912
Balance at 31 December 2012	1,232,000	160,000	130,000	577,252.2	96,600	2,195,852

* Issued share capital during 2012 is made up of a new share issue of €120,000 and a bonus issue of €112,000 (1,120,000/10).
** Interim dividend €12,000. Final dividend €112,000 (1 for 10 bonus issue).

Requirement (e)

In this final section you are asked to prepare the outline of a brief letter addressing the disgruntled shareholder's concerns. The letter should contain the principal legal limitations on the distribution of profits and assets in an Irish company. A suggested reply would be as follows:

Re: Dividend levels 2012

Dear Mr/Ms X

First of all I am sorry you are dissatisfied with the level of dividend declared for 2012. It is true that 2012 was a profitable year for the company and a more generous dividend may have been warranted in such circumstances. However, although the financials of the business are good, it is always necessary to control the level of distribution. Retained earnings are continually re-invested to ensure long-term growth and profitability for the shareholders. You state that the company is distributing only about 5.6% of equity. Your figure appears to be based on the total equity of the company at the end of December (€124,000/€2,195,892). However, you must remember that not all equity may be distributed. Under Company Law certain elements of equity are prohibited from distribution. It might help to summarise what the legal restrictions are.

A company is prohibited by law from distributing the following reserves:

- The share premium account.
- Unrealised profits, e.g. revaluation surplus. (See below).

- The capital redemption reserve fund (used when buying back shares).
- Any other reserve which the company is prohibited from distributing by law or the company's own rules.

In relation to revaluation reserves, the Companies Act makes exceptions to the distribution restriction. One of these exceptions (Section 45(d) 1983 Companies Act) occurs where a revaluation surplus is recorded on an item of property, plant and equipment that gives rise to a higher depreciation charge than would have been charged if the asset were carried at historical cost. In this situation the difference between the revalued depreciation and the historical cost depreciation is distributable. (We are not given the historical cost depreciation in the case study but we can find this figure by dividing the balance in the revaluation reserve over the remaining useful life of the asset concerned.)

What a company *may* distribute, therefore, are accumulated realised profits less its accumulated realised losses (as determined by Irish Generally Accepted Accounting Principles (GAAP) and the Companies (Amendment) Act 1983. Rules are unchanged for International GAAP).

Using the legal framework, it is clear that the only profits that are available for distribution by Derrynane Ltd are the accumulated retained profits. It is the policy of the company *not* to distribute general reserves. The remaining reserves are non-distributable by law.

There are further restrictions for a company that is publicly quoted but, as Derrynane is a private company, these additional restrictions are probably not of any interest to you. However, if you do want to discuss this matter further, it can be arranged.

Finally, given that the total reserves available for distribution is €703,729 (opening retained earnings €36,940 + profits €744,312 + section 45(b) 2477 – transfers €80,000) and the actual distribution is €124,000, the dividend payout is actually 17.6% of profits available for distribution. While not all of the dividend is in the form of cash, this is in excess of the original 5% that was quoted and we believe is a generous level of dividend bearing in mind the company policy on re-investment for growth and profitability.

Finally, the directors are concerned by the need to conserve cash given the current restrictions on the availability of credit, hence the stock dividend. The payment of a large cash dividend could be counterproductive and harm the long-term sustainability of the financing model of the business. Paying out large amounts of cash will result in a business that is less flexible to deal with any future shocks (albeit none are anticipated) that may occur.

I hope this answers your query.

Yours sincerely,
Jenny Brick

Case 4

Stay Inn Limited

This case study is based on a group of hotel companies. The accountancy standards addressed in this case study include IAS 1, IAS 8, IAS 10, IAS 16, IAS 18, IAS 19, IAS 20, IAS 21, IAS 36, IAS 37, IAS 38, IAS 40, IFRS 3, IFRS 5 and IFRS 10.

Background – Stay Inn Limited

Stay Inn is an international group of hotels. The parent company is Stay Inn Ltd. Stay Inn Ltd operates the Irish and UK Hotels in the group and also holds the investments in the other companies in the group.

The group has expanded in recent years and there are a number of people working in the financial reporting and control function at head office. Your job is to manage the statement of comprehensive income reporting function for the group. The company uses a sophisticated reporting package which has drawn up a draft statement of comprehensive income for the company. However, there are a number of items that have not been fully reflected in the draft. These issues are outlined below. Your first task will be to ensure that these items are all reflected in the financial statements of Stay Inn (the parent). You will then move on to completing the consolidated financial statements of the group. There are also discursive issues to deal with.

Parent Company – Stay Inn Limited
DRAFT STATEMENT OF COMPREHENSIVE INCOME
for the Year Ended 31 December 2012

	€000
Revenue	55,000
Cost of sales	(22,000)
Gross Profit	33,000
Administration expenses	(6,050)
Distribution expenses	(1,100)
Income from group companies	400
Gain on disposal of Rest	18,000
Other expenses	(2,750)
Profit from operations	41,500

Finance costs	(1,545)
Profit before Tax	39,955
Taxation	(1,200)
Profit for the Year	38,755
Other comprehensive income	0
Total Comprehensive Income	38,755

Stay Inn Limited
DRAFT STATEMENT OF CHANGES IN EQUITY
for the Year Ended 31 December 2012

	Ordinary Share Capital €000	Share Premium €000	Retained Earnings €000	Revaluation Surplus €000	Total €000
Opening balance	8,500	18,720	78,565	12,095	117,880
Share issue	500	19,500			20,000
Total comprehensive income			38,755		38,755
Dividends			(5,500)		(5,500)
Closing balance	9,000	38,220	111,820	12,095	171,135

Outstanding Issues in Respect of Stay Inn Ltd (the Parent Company) Financial Statements

Outstanding Issue 1

1. Discounted booking scheme Revenue from the company's hotels represents income earned from room rentals and food and beverage sales. During the year, Stay Inn Ltd introduced a discounted booking scheme whereby customers who book rooms on-line are offered an 8% discount on the reservation rate if they accept a non-cancellation clause. Customers booking under this scheme pay in full, by credit card, when the reservation is made. The policy of Stay Inn Limited is to recognise a sale when a non-cancellation reservation is made. The justification for this policy is that the income is guaranteed as the customer does not have the right to rescind the booking.

Included in revenue is €4 million of discounted bookings relating to reservations for 2013.

2. Management fees In 2012, Stay Inn Ltd extended its revenue generating base by securing a number of long-term management contracts with other hotel owners. Stay Inn manages hotels on behalf of these other owners and earns management fees for the services it provides. The fees are based on a percentage of annual hotel revenue and are recognised when they are earned. €3 million in management fees has been correctly included in revenue in the draft financial statements.

Four contracts in total were secured during 2012. Two of the contracts are for a period of 10 years each while the remaining two are secured for five years. In order to secure these contracts, the company incurred procurement costs in January 2012 of €1 million. These costs have been written off in full in 2012 and are included in administration costs in the draft financial statements. It is estimated that an equal amount was spent securing each contract.

3. Value added tax (VAT) In 2012, the Government announced a cut in the rate of VAT charged on hotel accommodation. The rate was cut from 15% to 12%. The new VAT rate was applicable from 1 November 2012. Due to a systems error at head office the new rate was not applied to any sales made by Stay Inn Limited in November and December 2012. It was only when a customer queried his bill in early January 2013 that the error came to light. Accommodation invoices (including VAT at 15%) for the final two months of the year amounted to €8.6 million and these were all settled before the year end. The VAT return for this period was paid on 15 January 2013. The management of Stay Inn Limited intend to refund customers with the excess charge but no entries have been made in the financial statements to reflect this.

Outstanding Issue 2

Details of two of the Stay Inn hotels are as follows:

Hotel	Carrying value at 1 January 2012	Valuation at 31 December 2012	Revaluation surplus at 1 January 2012	Remaining useful life at 31 December 2012
	€m	€m	€m	
Snug	4	2.2	0.8	40 years
Pamper	6.5	6.8	1.5	40 years

Note 1: Both hotels are currently stated at their carrying value at 1 January 2012.
Note 2: A full year's depreciation is charged in the year of acquisition and none in the year of disposal. Depreciation on hotels is charged to cost of sales.

Hotel Snug The Stay Inn group has a policy of revaluing its properties. One of its hotels, Hotel Snug, is located in an area of active regeneration. The National Tourist Board awards government grants to businesses in the area who incur significant costs upgrading their facilities. In 2011, Stay Inn Limited spent €1.1 million upgrading Hotel Snug. In October of that year, a government grant of €500,000 was received. On receipt of the grant, the accountant credited it, in full, to revenue. The normal accounting policy for government grants related to property is to treat them as deferred income and recognise them in profit or loss over the useful life of the assets – you can assume this is 40 years. This error only came to light at the beginning of 2013 and no corrections have yet been made.

Hotel Pamper Hotel Pamper is a five-star luxurious hotel located in the UK. The hotel has won many top awards and has been regularly voted as one of the Top 10 Resort Properties in Europe. Because of its prestigious position, Stay Inn Limited incurs considerable expenditure each year maintaining the hotel to the highest possible standards. A maintenance charge for Hotel Pamper of €300,000 is included in administration expenses in 2012.

A review of the depreciation policies of the group was undertaken in 2012. A decision was made to stop charging depreciation on the Pamper hotel. The CEO of Stay Inn has argued that the level of maintenance expended on this hotel compensates for any wear and tear charge. "And isn't this what depreciation is all about?" he adds. The financial director has proposed that the change in depreciation policy for Hotel Pamper be treated as a change in accounting estimate in accordance with IAS 8 *Accounting Policies, Changes in Accounting Estimates and Errors*.

Outstanding Issue 3

Stay Inn Ltd operates a variety of post-employment benefit arrangements including both defined contribution and defined benefit schemes. The most significant of these schemes are the defined benefit pension schemes for employees in the UK and the Republic of Ireland. At 1 January 2012, the net obligation for defined benefit schemes was €6 million. This was made up of the present value of obligations of €66 million less the market value of plan assets of €60 million.

The re-assessment of the defined benefits obligations and scheme assets for the current year has not yet been reflected in the financial statements. (The defined contribution plan has already been adjusted.) The following information has now been gathered:

The cost of providing service benefits	€5m
Contributions made (but not yet paid) to the retirement fund	€7m
Benefits paid to retired employees	€8m
Interest cost on 1 January 2012	5%
Expected return on plan assets on 1 January 2012	3%

There were no actuarial gains or losses in the current year.

Outstanding Issue 4

One of the shareholders of Stay Inn Limited has written to the company seeking clarification on how the hotels are classified in the group's Statement of Financial Position.

The hotels are currently classified as owner-occupied properties and presented in property, plant and equipment in the Statement of Financial Position. This shareholder is concerned that the properties have been misclassified. He believes that the hotels should be presented as investment properties in accordance with IAS 40 *Investment Property*. He quotes the definition of an investment property (IAS 40, para 5), "Investment property is held to earn rentals or for capital appreciation or both." His specific argument is that, as the principal form of revenue for the hotel group is the income derived from *renting out* the rooms, it would be more appropriate to present them as investment properties.

The Consolidated Financial Statements

When the parent company's financial statements are complete your next task is to prepare the consolidated financial statements. All of the companies in the group have now reported their figures, details shown below:

Rest, Relax and Cool

DRAFT STATEMENTS OF COMPREHENSIVE INCOME

for the Year Ended 31 December 2012

	Rest	Relax	Cool
	€000	€000	$000
Revenue	25,000	10,000	18,000
Cost of sales	(11,750)	(8,000)	(7,560)
Gross Profit	13,250	2,000	10,440
Administration expenses	(3,000)	(1,000)	(2,340)
Distribution expenses	(750)	(300)	(180)
Other expenses	(1,250)	(800)	(1,080)
Finance costs	(2,000)	(1,400)	(950)
Operating Profit	6,250	(1,500)	5,890
Taxation	(550)	(20)	(2,500)
Profit for the Year	5,700	(1,520)	3,390
Other comprehensive income	0	0	0
Total Comprehensive Income	5,700	1,520	3,390

You have been provided with the following additional information regarding the entities in the Stay Inn group. This information will be of assistance in the preparation of the consolidated financial statements:

Acquisition Details

Company	Date of Acquisition	% Owned	Ord Share Capital on Acquisition 000	Retained Earnings on Acquisition 000	Consideration 000
Rest	1/1/11	80%	€1,000	€37,000	€42,000 (note 1)
Relax	30/9/12	75%	€1,000	€2,500	€7,000
Cool	30/6/12	90%	$2,000	$14,000	$20,000

Additional Information

Note 1 – Further Details on Acquisition

Stay Inn has elected to value the non-controlling interest at its proportionate share of the fair value of the subsidiary's identifiable net assets, i.e. the traditional method.

Rest When Rest was acquired €42,000,000 was paid to the former shareholders. In addition, if profits exceed €4,500,000 per annum an additional €5,788,000 would become payable on the third anniversary of the acquisition, i.e. on 1 January 2014. The current level of profits of Rest is similar to those in previous years. This potential payment has not been recognised in the financial statements of the parent company. The group can borrow at a rate of 5% per annum.

Relax Relax operates a number of hotels in France. They have a policy of not revaluing their property. This is in opposition to Stay Inn's policy. You have been provided with the following information.

As per Relax's financial statements:

Cost of hotels	€5,000,000 (on acquisition date)
Accumulated depreciation	€2,000,000 (on acquisition date)
Net Book Value	€3,000,000 (on acquisition date)
Estimated useful life when purchased	20 years
Remaining estimated useful life on acquisition date	12 years
Annual depreciation charge	€250,000

If the hotels had been re-valued on the acquisition date (based on a 12-year remaining useful life), they would have been worth €6,000,000.

Relax's financial statements have been prepared on the basis of their original policy. No buildings have been acquired or disposed of since acquisition. No valuation of Relax's hotels has taken place for the purposes of the year-end financial statements. The depreciation expense is included as part of cost of sales.

Since acquisition, Relax's business has suffered greatly and is now loss-making. The directors believe that the company will only be able to continue if it receives additional funding from its shareholders. All of the shareholders (including the minorities) have agreed to invest a further €10 million in Rest through a rights issue in early 2013; however, by year end, no announcement had been made to the workforce. Some corporate finance advisors have been approached but none have yet been appointed. This €10 million will be used to fund losses up to the end of 2013. After 2014 it is envisaged that the company will be in a position to trade profitably again. In addition, the directors believe that the goodwill of Relax is now impossible to substantiate and have agreed to write off 100% of the goodwill arising on acquisition.

Cool Cool is a US-based company. It operates the Cool brand of Hotels and Spas. The management of Cool is allowed to run the business as it sees fit, most of its non-equity finance (i.e. debt finance) is sourced in the US (in dollars). You have been provided with the following exchange rates (€1 = $X.XX)

On 1/1/12:	€1 = $1.35
On 30/6/12:	€1 = $1.40
On 31/12/12:	€1 = $1.45
Average January–June:	€1 = $1.37
Average July–December:	€1 = $1.43
Average January–December:	€1 = $1.41

Cool's financial statements have been prepared using US GAAP. You have reviewed the accounting policies adopted by Cool and the only difference between Cool's policies and Stay Inn's policies is on their approach to provisions. The management of Cool have set aside some large provisions for redundancies which they had begun to consider well before the acquisition date. In November 2012, management decided to set aside $3 million being the expected cost of the redundancies (included in cost of sales). In January 2013 the management of Cool announced the redundancies to its workforce who agreed to the proposals. The affected employees will leave in March 2013.

Note 2 – Disposal of Rest

On 31 March 2012 Stay Inn disposed of all of its shareholding in Rest for €60,000,000. The retained earnings of Rest on disposal were €50,500,000 (there was no change to share capital since acquisition, i.e. €1,000,000).

When carrying out the due diligence on the acquisition the new owners noted the original contingent payment (see note 1). It was agreed that Stay Inn would continue to take responsibility for this item.

Note 3 – Dividends Paid/Income from Group Companies in Stay Inn

At year end Cool paid a dividend on profits earned in the second half of the year. The €400,000 of 'income from group companies' in the income statement of Stay Inn is the parent company's share of the dividend converted into euro.

Note 4 – Intragroup Management Fee

On 31 December 2012 Stay Inn levied a management fee on all of its subsidiaries. This was recorded as revenue by Stay Inn but at year end none of the subsidiaries had recorded their portion of the fee. The subsidiaries are not disputing the amount of the fee.

Company	Fee
Rest	€0 (no longer in group)
Relax	€1,000,000
Cool	€1,000,000 = $1,450,000

Consolidation Issue

The Managing Director has come to you with a technical issue which has concerned him:

The investment in Cool was made on the understanding that it would be possible to transfer some of the profits of Cool to Stay Inn. This would result in those profits being taxed in the ROI at lower rates than in the US. One of the approaches was for Stay Inn to charge a management fee to all of the subsidiaries in the group. He then notes that on consolidation the effect of intragroup transactions are eliminated and is concerned that the group will not get the benefit of the reduced tax rates in the ROI.

Requirements

(**Note:** Unless you are specifically required to consider deferred taxation, you can assume that it is not applicable.)

(a) You are required to redraft the statement of comprehensive income and the statement of changes in equity of Stay Inn Ltd for the year ended 31 December 2012. (This incorporates outstanding issues 1–3.) Your answer should include detailed workings for each of the issues.

(22 marks)

(b) Prepare a brief report addressing the concerns of the shareholder as outlined in outstanding issue 4.

(5 marks)

(c) Prepare the consolidated statement of comprehensive income of the Stay Inn Group for the year ended 31 December 2012. (You are **not** required to prepare a consolidated statement of changes in equity.)

(28 marks)

(d) Write a memo to the MD outlining why it is necessary to eliminate intragroup transactions on consolidation and how the tax position will still be effective.

(5 marks)

(60 marks)

Guidance Notes – Stay Inn Limited

Exam Technique

Read the case carefully and then read the requirements.

The structure of this case study is similar to many others in this book. It involves, first, a review of the parent company's financial statements, then the consolidation of the parent's financial statements with the subsidiary's results. There are also discursive elements to this case study that will require a little reflection.

This case concentrates on the statement of comprehensive income. You are required to prepare the statement of comprehensive income and the statement of changes in equity for the parent company. This case study does not consider the statement of financial position (although you are asked to refer to it in outstanding issue 4).

Having completed the redrafting of the parent company's financial statements, you are asked to prepare a consolidated statement of comprehensive income. It is important that you have a well-practised approach for answering these types of questions. Use your basic approach but be flexible; amend it for any unique elements of this case study. The statement-of-financial-position implications of any adjustment can be ignored. **Note**: you are not required to prepare a consolidated statement of changes in equity.

This case study is based on a hotel group. Bear this in mind: you should consider the industry as you are working through the case study. Think clearly and logically. You will score highly in the case if you apply your answers to the industry rather than giving generalised blanket responses.

As has been noted in other case studies, allocate your time according to the marks awarded for each section. You will score better marks if you *attempt* all parts of the case rather than completing some sections and not answering others at all.

Finally, you must attempt requirement (a) before the consolidation exercise in requirement (c). Other than that, the remaining elements of the case study require narrative answers (requirements (b) and (d)) and can be answered in any order, although you may find it more structured to answer the requirements in the order that they appear in the case.

Answering the Case Study

Requirement (a) – Guidance

Outstanding Issue 1

1. Discounted booking scheme The issue here is the timing of revenue. IAS 18 *Revenue* is the international accounting standard governing revenue recognition. Paragraphs 14–19 of the standard outline the conditions that must be satisfied before revenue can be recognised in the financial statements. You should review these paragraphs before writing your answer. You need to consider if the current treatment for discounted bookings is appropriate or not. Look carefully at the terms of the reservations. Have the conditions of sale been fulfilled by the end of 2012 on bookings made in 2013?

2. Management fees Stay Inn Ltd earned management fees in 2012 as part of long-term service contracts secured with other hotel owners. €3 million in management fees has been included in revenue. There is no issue here; you are told that this revenue has been correctly treated in the draft financial statements.

The issue therefore, is with the *costs* of securing these contracts. A total of €1 million was spent in 2012 in securing these contracts. These costs have been written off in full to profit or loss in 2012. You must consider if this treatment is correct. You could use basic financial accounting concepts to figure out the answer or you could refer to the specific guidance given on this matter (IAS 18, illustrative examples, para 14(b)). Have a look at this paragraph to determine what to do.

3. Value added tax (VAT) A reduced rate of VAT on hotel accommodation, applicable from 1 November 2012, was not applied to sales of hotel nights in November and December 2012. Customers were overcharged during this period. This was an error. You must consider how to correct it. IAS 18, paragraph 8 will give you some basic guidance. You may also need to refer to IAS 8 *Accounting Policies, Changes in Accounting Estimates and Errors*.

Outstanding Issue 2 This issue concerns the accounting policy applied to hotels held by the company. Stay Inn Ltd has a policy of revaluing its hotels. You are given details of the opening and closing valuations of two of the hotels in the company's portfolio – Hotel Snug and Hotel Pamper. Before you deal with the valuations however, you must address some other matters that have arisen in relation to these properties. These matters must be resolved before the closing valuations are applied.

There are a number of accounting standards that are relevant when answering this issue.

IAS 16 *Property, Plant and Equipment* Hotels are carried at revalued amounts. The guidance for revaluation is outlined in IAS 16, paragraphs 31–40. Hotel Snug has fallen in value while Hotel Pamper has risen.
Note: Depreciation on hotel buildings is included in cost of sales.

IAS 20 *Accounting for Government Grants and Disclosure of Government Assistance* Hotel Snug received a government grant during 2011. Guidance on accounting for government grants is given in IAS 20. You will need to consider what type of grant Stay Inn Ltd has received. Is it a grant related to assets *or* to income*?* You will find the answer in IAS 20, paragraph 3.

You are told that the grant was credited to profit or loss. The presentation of grants related to assets is outlined in paragraphs 24–28 of the standard while grants related to income are covered in paragraphs 29–31.

IAS 8 *Accounting Policies, Changes in Accounting Estimates and Errors* You will need to refer to this standard to complete your answer. IAS 8, paragraphs 7–31, deals with accounting policies, paragraphs 32–40 deal with changes in accounting estimates and errors are considered in paragraphs 41–49.

Outstanding Issue 3 There is nothing hidden within this issue. You must simply apply double-entry principles to the retirement obligation and scheme assets.

IAS 19 *Employee Benefits* outlines the accounting treatment for employee benefits. Paragraphs 55–152 give guidance on the accounting treatment for post-employment defined benefit plans. It is this section of the standard to which you need refer. Paragraphs 63–65 outline the presentation of defined benefit plans in the statement of financial position while profit or loss entries are outlined in paragraphs 120–122 of the standard. This case study concentrates on the income statement entries.

You should work through each of the retirement changes as outlined in the case and consider if they affect the statement of comprehensive income and, if they do, make an adjustment.

The net changes to retirement benefits and scheme assets will be included in staff costs in administration expenses in the statement of comprehensive income. Additional information about employee benefits expense must be disclosed in the notes to the financial statements in accordance with IAS 1 and IAS 24.

The final element of requirement (a) is to re-draft the statement of comprehensive income and the statement of changes in equity of Stay Inn Ltd for the year ended 31 December 2012, incorporating any changes you propose to make.

The revised financial statements will form the basis for requirement (c) – the consolidated financial statements.

Requirement (b) – Guidance

Outstanding Issue 4 This requires a discursive answer. You could answer this section either at the start of the case or wait until the end. Answering simple narratives at the beginning can sometimes calm the nerves and boost confidence.

Your narrative should explain to the shareholder why hotel properties would be presented as owner occupied rather than investments. This particular issue is outlined in IAS 40 *Investment Property* (IAS 40, para 11–12). Classification depends on the level of service provided while the property is let.

You would start your answer by defining what an investment property is. You would then explain how investment properties differ from owner-occupied properties. Finally, you would refer to the provisions of paragraphs 11–12 explaining why the letting of hotel rooms would be considered an owner-occupied service rather than an investment property.

Do not spend very long on this section as there are only five marks available.

Requirement (c) – The Consolidated Statement of Comprehensive Income

This is the consolidation element of the case study, so you will need to manage your time carefully. You will be using Stay Inn's redrafted statement of comprehensive income from requirement (a) along with the financial statements provided for Rest, Relax and Cool.

While it is a time-consuming question, if you deal with each item in turn, make your decision, and then move on, it then becomes an exercise in information management.

To assist in the preparation of the consolidated statement of comprehensive income it is often beneficial to have a process to follow. This will allow you to spend some time addressing the more complex issues. A four-step process is employed in this case study. (This was detailed in the Armada case study.) There are other approaches but it is important that you have your own, reliable system.

- **Step 1 – Set out the group structure.**
- **Step 2 – Prepare a template for the statement of comprehensive income.** There should be a column for each of the entities involved (four in total) and additional columns for each of the subsequent adjustments.
- **Step 3 – Consider each adjustment in turn and evaluate the impact it has on items in the consolidated statement of comprehensive income.** Fill in the appropriate items in each column.
- **Step 4 – Complete the consolidated statement of comprehensive income and calculate the non-controlling interest figure.**

Step 1 – The Group Structure Setting out the group structure is not a difficulty in this instance, as the percentages are provided. However, note that some of the subsidiaries were acquired part way through the current period. This will have an impact on the amounts included in the statement of comprehensive income – see IFRS 10, paragraph 20. It should also be noted that Rest was disposed of three months into the current period.

Step 2 – The Consolidated Statement of Comprehensive Income Template This is where a broad outline of the consolidated statement of comprehensive income is set out in a spreadsheet type format. There should be columns for each of the companies in the group and columns for each of the adjustments. The rows should represent the individual income and expense headings. See the guidance to the Armada case study for more detail.

Step 3 – Resolve the Additional Information Items

1. *There is contingent consideration on the acquisition of Rest (note 1)* You will need to decide if this should have been part of the consideration at the time of acquisition – see IFRS 3, paragraph 39.

   Depending on the decision you make, you may have to consider how to value this consideration: should the consideration be included at the full amount due (€5,788,000) or at some other amount? As a general rule, IFRS 3 uses fair value for most aspects of an acquisition but what is fair value in the case of contingent consideration?

   Next, decide on the statement of comprehensive income implication of the contingent consideration. If contingent consideration does exist then it will usually result in increasing the goodwill on acquisition. This will affect the statement of financial position but not the statement of comprehensive income. Can you think of any potential statement of comprehensive income consequences? Hint: unwind the discount, see IAS 37 *Provisions, Contingent Liabilities and Contingent Assets*, paragraph 60, for guidance on the effect of discounting over time.

2. *The revaluation of Relax's hotels* Should the hotels be revalued on the date of acquisition and, if so, is market value appropriate? See IFRS 3 paragraphs 18 and 20.

   If the decision is to revalue the hotels what, if any, is the impact on the statement of comprehensive income?

   Should all companies in a group have similar accounting policies? – see IFRS 10, paragraph 19. If the answer to this question is "Yes", then should a valuation of the property be obtained at year end or is the valuation on acquisition date sufficient? See IAS 16, paragraph 34.

3. *The rights issue in Relax* The rights issue is due to take place after the year end. Is this an event after the reporting period as defined by IAS 10, paragraphs 10, 11 and 22? Consider the implication on the income statement, if any.
4. *Write off of goodwill in Relax* The goodwill on the acquisition of Relax is clearly impaired (see IAS 36 *Impairment of Assets*). Calculate the goodwill on acquisition. Remember to include the fair value adjustment in respect of the hotel properties in Relax. How should the goodwill impairment loss be recognised? See IAS 36, paragraphs 59 and 60.
5. *Cool – the redundancies* Has Cool been correct in recognising the redundancies in the statement of comprehensive income for the current period? See IAS 37 *Provisions, Contingent Liabilities and Contingent Assets*, in particular, consider if there has been an obligating event (IAS 37, para 14 and 17). Specific guidance in relation to restructuring is given in IAS 37, paragraphs 72–75. If there is no obligating event, what changes are required to the financial statements of Cool?

   If the decision is taken to remove the provision, is this an adjusting event after the reporting period? See IAS 10 *Events after the Reporting Period*, paragraphs 10, 11 and 22.
6. *Cool – the foreign exchange issue* IAS 21 *The Effects of Changes in Foreign Exchange Rates* sets out the procedures on the translation of the statement of comprehensive income of the US subsidiary into a different presentational currency (i.e. from US Dollars to Euro). See IAS 21, paragraphs 39 and 40. Pick an appropriate exchange rate, remember that the subsidiary joined the group on 30 June 2012.
7. *Disposal of Rest* There are two issues here: the calculation of the gain or loss on disposal and the disclosure of the profits (or losses) from discontinued operations.

   The calculation of the gain/loss on disposal is outlined in IFRS 10, paragraphs 25 and B98. To calculate the gain/loss, compare the sales proceeds (€60,000,000) with both the percentage share of net assets of the subsidiary and the carrying value of goodwill remaining since acquisition.

   The gain on disposal currently included in the statement of comprehensive income of Rest is not correct from a group perspective. It is just the sales proceeds (€60 million) minus the cost of purchase (€42 million).

   The profits (or losses) of the discontinued operations will be disclosed separately as per IFRS 5 *Non-current Assets Held for Sale and Discontinued Operations*, paragraphs 30 and 33. See also illustrative example 11 in IFRS 5 Implementation Guidance (IG).
8. *Intragroup dividend from Cool in the statement of comprehensive income of Stay Inn* See IFRS 10 *Consolidated Financial Statements,* paragraph B86(c), on how to deal with intragroup items.
9. *Intragroup management fee* See IFRS 10 *Consolidated Financial Statements,* paragraph B86(c), on how to deal with intragroup items.

Step 4: Prepare the Consolidated Statement of Comprehensive Income and Calculate the Non-controlling Interests While dealing with each of the adjustments, the relevant figures should be included in the template for the statement of comprehensive income. Thus, the preparation of the statement of comprehensive income should be an arithmetic exercise. One element that will still be awaiting completion will be the calculation of the profit attributable to the non-controlling interests.

The full income and expenses of the subsidiaries have been included in the consolidated statement of comprehensive income. The non-controlling interests will need to be removed; remember to include the effect of any adjustment that also impacts upon the non-controlling interests. See IAS 1 *Presentation of Financial Statements*, Implementation Guidance (IG) for illustrative financial statements.

Requirement (d) – The Consolidation Issue

This requirement is written in the context of the current case. However, the managing director's confusion is a general question on the nature of group accounts versus individual company accounts. The solution to this issue will need to be explained in a manner that the MD will understand. You can refer to technical documents (e.g. the standards) but you cannot expect that he/she will have read these or even know of their existence.

Without undertaking any analysis it should be clear that the MD is correct in saying that intragroup items are eliminated upon consolidation. The MD is also correct in saying that the reason companies use the ROI as a base is to get the benefit of reduced tax rates. There is no contradiction here but you will need to explain how both situations can persist – perhaps the MD is at cross-purposes. You do not need to go into a detailed discussion on tax regimes and double taxation treaties to answer this.

Recommended Reading

The accounting standards addressed in this case study may also be referenced in *International Financial Accounting and Reporting,* 3rd Edition, by Ciaran Connolly (Chartered Accountants Ireland, 2011) as follows:

	Chapter	Chapter title	Chapter section	Standard
Requirement (a)				
Outstanding Issue 1	4	Revenue	4.2	IAS 18
	9	Intangible Assets	9.2	IAS 38
Outstanding Issue 2	6	Property plant and equipment	6.2	IAS 16
	21	Accounting policies, changes in accounting estimates and errors		IAS 8
	16	Accounting for government grants and the disclosure of government assistance		IAS 20
Outstanding Issue 3	17	Employee benefits	17.2	IAS 19

Requirement (b)

Outstanding Issue 4	5	Investment property	5.3	IAS 40

Requirement (c)

	28	Consolidated Statement of Comprehensive Income	28.2, 28.3	IFRS 10
	26	Business Combinations and Consolidated Financial Statements	26.4	IFRS 3
	31	Foreign Currency Transactions and Translation of Foreign Operations	31.3	IAS 21
	32	Disposal of Subsidiaries	32.3	IFRS 10, IFRS 5

Note: to answer requirement (c) other chapters will also be relevant (but to a lesser extent), they include: Chapter 6, Property, Plant and Equipment; Chapter 2, Presentation of Financial Statements; Chapter 10, Impairments; Chapter 14, Provisions, Contingent Liabilities and Contingent Assets; Chapter 15, Events After the Reporting Period

Requirement (d)

	26	Business Combinations and Consolidated Financial Statements	26.3	IFRS 10, IAS 27

Solution to Stay Inn Limited

Requirement (a)

Outstanding Issue 1

1. IAS 18 *Revenue* provides the standard guidance on revenue recognition. IAS 18, paragraphs 14–19, gives guidance on the recognition of revenue from the sale of *goods*. Paragraphs 20–28 deal with revenue earned from the rendering of *services*. The question is whether the provision of hotel accommodation represents the sale of goods or of services. It is a service sale. In accordance with paragraph 20 of the standard, revenue from the provision of services should be recognised by reference to the stage of completion of the transaction at the end of the reporting period. At the end of 2012, none of the services relating to the 2013 advance bookings have been rendered. In other words 0% of the service transaction has been completed.

The advance bookings should be presented as deferred income rather than as revenue in the 2012 financial statements.

An adjustment is required to reverse the recognition of advance bookings as follows:

	€000	**€000**
DR Revenue	4,000	
CR Accruals – deferred income		4,000
(Being deferral of 2013 revenue)		

2. *Management fees* The entire cost incurred in securing the four management contracts was charged to profit or loss in 2012. In accordance with IAS 18 only €150,000 should be charged in the current year. IAS 18 Appendix, paragraph 14 (b) explains this concept. This paragraph states that "Incremental costs that are directly attributable to securing an investment management contract are recognised as an asset if they can be identified separately and measured reliably and if it is probable that they will be recovered". "The asset represents the entity's contractual right to benefit from investment management services and is amortised as the revenue is recognised." In the case study revenue will be recognised over either 10 years or five years.

(IAS 18 Appendix, paragraph 14(b) refers to investment management fees in relation to the financial services industry. However the same principles apply to other industries. IFRS 3 *Business Combinations*, IE 34 also recognises the principle of capitalising costs incurred in securing contracts under the heading of 'contract-based intangible assets'). In the case study the costs of the contracts will be amortised as follows:

	Contract (1)	**Contract (2)**	**Contract (3)**	**Contract (4)**	**Total**
Costs	€250,000	€250,000	€250,000	€250,000	€1,000,000
Period of contract in years	10	10	5	5	
Charge to profit or loss p.a.	€25,000	€25,000	€50,000	€50,000	€150,000

As the €1 million was charged to profit or loss in 2012, an adjustment is required to bring it in line with recommended practice as follows:

	€000	€000
DR Intangible assets	850	
CR Admin expenses		850
(Being deferral of procurement costs)		

3. *Value added tax (VAT)* The incorrect rate of VAT was charged on sales of bed nights in November and December 2012. This error affects the amounts charged to the customers' accounts but not the revenue figure in the financial statements. In accordance with IAS 18, paragraph 8, "Amounts collected on behalf of third parties such as sales taxes.... are excluded from revenue."

The amount of VAT overcharged in 2012 is:

	€000
Invoices including VAT at 15% (November and December)	8,600
Invoices including VAT at 12% (November and December)	8,376
Overcharge	224

This excess VAT will be refunded to the guests in 2013. At 2012 year end this will be presented in the financial statements as a liability.

To correct the error

	€000	€000
DR Tax liabilities	224	
CR Refunds owing to guests (liabilities)		224

Outstanding Issue 2

Hotel Snug There are *three* items in relation to Hotel Snug that require your attention.

First of all an error has been identified. The error relates to the treatment of the government grant when it was received in 2011. The grant was credited directly to operating income. This treatment is not in accordance with IAS 20 *Accounting for Government Grants and Disclosure of Government Assistance*. IAS 20 states "Government grants related to assets … shall be presented in the statement of financial position either by setting up the grant as deferred income or by deducting the grant in arriving at the carrying amount of the asset"[1] (IAS 20, para 24). The accounting policy of the Stay Inn Group is to set up a deferred income account. In relation to this policy IAS 20, paragraph 26 states, "One method[2] recognises the grant as deferred income that is recognised in profit or loss on a systematic basis over the useful life of the asset."

[1] The immediate deduction method is prohibited under Irish law.

[2] The deferred income approach.

Although the error originated in 2011 it will be necessary to make the correction in the 2012 financial statements. The correction will be treated in accordance with IAS 8 *Accounting Policies, Changes in Accounting Estimates and Errors* paragraphs 42–49. IAS 8, paragraph 41, states "... material errors are sometimes not discovered until a subsequent period, and these prior period errors are corrected in the comparative information presented in the financial statements for that subsequent period" or, as per IAS 8, paragraph 42(b), by " … restating the opening balances of assets, liabilities and equity for the earliest prior period presented."

Note: In this case study you are not presented with 2011 comparative information. Therefore the correction of the error will be made by adjusting the opening figures in 2012 as follows:

	€000	**€000**
DR Opening retained earnings	488	
CR Cost of sales		13
CR Deferred income (liabilities)		475

The adjustment to opening retained earnings is the original grant less one year's amortisation €12,500 (40 years).

A further year's amortisation is credited against profit or loss for 2012. The remaining element (38/40yrs) is deferred to future periods.

The figures are rounded up and down on alternate years.

Once the grant issue has been resolved, depreciation should be charged for the year. You are told in the case study that Hotel Snug has 40 years' remaining useful life. Depreciation for 2012 will be charged as follows:

	€000	**€000**
DR Cost of sales	100	
CR Accumulated depreciation		100
(€4,000,000/40 years)		

Finally, Hotel Snug must be revalued. At 31 December 2012 the hotel has an adjusted carrying value of €3.9 million (i.e. €4 million opening valuation less €0.1 million depreciation = €3.9 million) and a valuation of €2.2 million. There is a net fall of €1.7 million and this should be incorporated into the financial statements as follows:

	€000	**€000**
DR OCI (note)	800	
DR Cost of Sales (note)	900	
CR Property, plant and equipment		1,700

Note: IAS 16 *Property, Plant and Equipment*, paragraph 40 states "If an asset's carrying amount is decreased as a result of a revaluation, the decrease shall be recognised in profit or loss. However, the decrease shall be recognised in other comprehensive income to the extent of any credit balance existing in the revaluation surplus in respect of that asset. The decrease recognised in other comprehensive income reduces the amount accumulated in equity under the heading of revaluation surplus."

Hotel Pamper There are *two* items that require your attention. The first is depreciation and the second is revaluation.

The CEO of Stay Inn has made a decision to stop depreciating Hotel Pamper. This decision was made on the grounds that the high level of maintenance on the hotel negates the need for depreciation. IAS 16 specifically prohibits this practice. IAS 16, paragraph 52, states "Depreciation is recognised even if the fair value of the asset exceeds its carrying amount, as long as the asset's residual value does not exceed its carrying amount. Repair and maintenance of an asset do not negate the need to depreciate it."

Depreciation should be charged on the hotel as follows:

	€000	€000
DR Cost of sales	163	
CR Accumulated depreciation		163
(€6,500,000 carrying value over 40 years (rounded))		

Next, the revaluation: Hotel Pamper now has an adjusted carrying value of €6.34 million at 31 December 2012 (€6.5m – €0.163m depreciation = €6.34m) and a valuation of €6.8 million. There is a net increase in the value of the hotel of €463,000 and this should be incorporated into the financial statements as follows:

The revaluation adjustment:		
	€000	€000
DR Property, plant and equipment	463	
CR Revaluation surplus *		463

* **Note:** IAS 16 *Property, Plant and Equipment*, paragraph 39, states "If an asset's carrying amount is increased as a result of a revaluation, the increase shall be recognised in other comprehensive income … under the heading of revaluation surplus."

Outstanding Issue 3

The accounting treatment for pension obligations is outlined in IAS 19 *Employee Benefits.*

In accordance with IAS 19, paragraph 120, an entity shall recognise the components of defined benefit cost, except to the extent that another IFRS requires or permits their inclusion in the cost of an asset, as follows:

(a) service cost (IAS 19, para. 66–112) in profit or loss;
(b) net interest on the net defined benefit liability (asset) (IAS 19, paras. 123–126) in profit or loss; and

(c) Re-measurements of the net defined benefit liability (asset) (IAS 19, para 127–130) in other comprehensive income. (There is none in the case study.)

The adjustments required for the Stay Inn defined benefit plan are as follows:

	Statement of Comprehensive Income (SOCI)	Obligation	Asset	
	€000	€000	€000	
Opening balance		66,000	60,000	
Service cost	5,000	5,000		(DR SOCI, CR Obligations €5m)
Contributions			7,000	(DR Assets, CR Accruals €7m)
Benefits paid		(8,000)	(8,000)	(DR Obligations, CR Assets €8m)
Interest cost	3,300	3,300		(DR SOCI, CR Obligations €65m × 5%)
Return on investment	(1,800)		1,800	(DR assets, CR SOCI 3% × €60m)
	6,500	66,300	60,800	

(Interest cost and return on investment are netted and recognised as net interest on the defined liability.)

The net adjustment to the *Defined* Benefit Pension scheme is as follows:

	€000	€000
DR Administration expenses	6,500	
DR Net Obligation	500	
CR Accruals		7,000

The adjustments for outstanding issues 1–3 have now been completed.

Finally, the above adjustments can be summarised, as follows:

	Statement of Comprehensive Income Effects				Other Comprehensive Income	
Issue	Revenue	Cost of Sales	Distribution	Admin	Other Comprehensive Income	Opening Retained Earnings
(1) Discounted bookings	(4,000)					
(1) Management fees				(850)		
(1) VAT (no effect SOCI)						
(2) Snug grant		(13)				(488)
(2) Snug depreciation		100				
(2) Snug revaluation		900			(800)	
(2) Pamper depreciation		163				
(2) Pamper revaluation (no effect SOCI)					463	
(3) Pension charges			–	6,500		
	(4,000)	1,150	0	5,650	(338)	(488)

Stay Inn Limited
REVISED STATEMENT OF COMPREHENSIVE INCOME
For the Year Ended 31 December 2012

	Original	Adjustments	Revised
	€000	**€000**	**€000**
Revenue	55,000	(4,000)	51,000
Cost of sales	(22,000)	(1,150)	(23,150)
Gross Profit	33,000		27,850
Administration expenses	(6,050)	(5,650)	(11,700)
Distribution expenses	(1,100)		(1,100)
Income from group companies	400		400
Gain on disposal of Rest	18,000		18,000
Other expense	(2,750)		(2,750)
Profit from Operations	41,500		30,700
Finance costs	(1,545)		(1,545)
Profit before Tax	39,955		29,155
Taxation	(1,200)		(1,200)
Profit for the Year	38,755		27,955
Other comprehensive income		(338)	(338)
Total Comprehensive Income	38,755		27,618

Stay Inn Limited
STATEMENT OF CHANGES IN EQUITY
for the Year Ended 31 December 2012

	Ordinary Share Capital	Share Premium	Retained Earnings	Revaluation Surplus	Total
	€000)	**€000**	**€000**	**€000**	**€000**
Opening Balance	8,500	18,720	78,565	12,095	117,880
P/Y adjustment			(488)		(488)
Revised Opening	8,500	18,720	78,078	12,095	117,393
Share issue	500	19,500			20,000
Total Comprehensive Income			27,955	(338)	27,618
Dividends			(5,500)		
	9,000	38,220	100,533	11,758	165,010

Requirement (b)

Outstanding Issue 4

The answer to the shareholder's query is given in IAS 40 *Investment Property.*

IAS 40, paragraph 11, states "In some cases, an entity provides ancillary services to the occupants of a property it holds. An entity treats such a property as investment property if the services are insignificant to the arrangement as a whole. An example is when the owner of an office building provides security and maintenance services to the lessees who occupy the building."

Paragraph 12 carries on "In other cases, the services provided are significant. For example; if an entity owns and manages a hotel, services provided to the guests are significant to the arrangement as a whole. Therefore, an owner-managed hotel is owner-occupied property, rather than investment property."

This is self-explanatory and requires no further explanation.

Requirement (c)

Consolidation

Step 1 – Set out the group structure The starting point for any consolidation question is to set out the group structure. At this stage, any relevant items of information should be noted, for example, when the company joined or left the group.

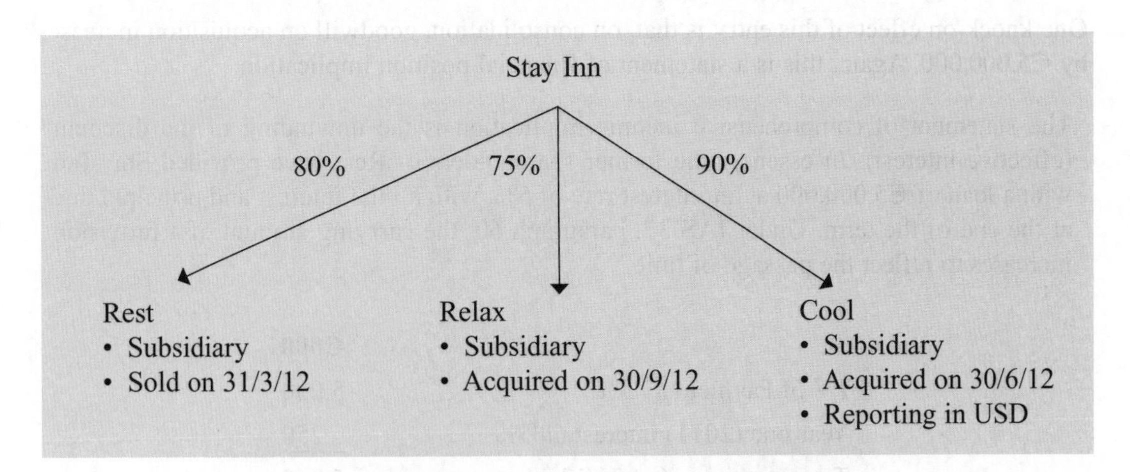

Step 2 – The Consolidated Statement of Comprehensive Income Template This step involves setting out the broad format of the statement of comprehensive income. The method described in this solution follows a spreadsheet style approach. One column is allocated to each company in the group and a column for each adjustment. This should make it easier to keep control over all of the adjustments that you propose as part of your solution. Rather than present a blank version of the solution here, the completed version is set out at the end.

However, you should follow the process: enter in the figures for each of the subsidiaries and the information for each of the adjustments as you proceed with your solution.

Step 3 – Resolve the Additional Information Items Consider each of the adjustments (as provided in the 'additional information') in turn. Try to break the information into manageable sections, make your mind up and move on to the next item. Do not dwell for too long on any one item as it will probably not attract any additional marks. You may notice, in some of the instances, no adjustment is required.

1. Deferred Payment on Rest There are a number of issues here but there are only limited statement of comprehensive income implications. Under IFRS 3, paragraph 39, the fair value on the acquisition date of the contingent consideration should be recognised. The payment is conditional on Rest's profits exceeding €4,500,000. The current year's profits are €5,700,000. This is similar to previous years. Consequently, it appears from the information that, on the acquisition date, the likelihood of the payment of this amount was all but guaranteed. Thus, this amount should be included as part of the overall consideration for Rest.

The next stage is to calculate the fair value of the consideration on the acquisition date. The cash payment is going to be €5,788,000. However, the fair value on acquisition date of this amount is €5,000,000 (i.e. €5,788,000/$(1.05)^3$). This would need to be recorded in the records of Stay Inn Limited (debit investment in Rest of €5,000,000 and credit provision for deferred consideration €5,000,000) but this entry only impacts upon the statement of financial position.

One knock-on effect of this entry is that, on consolidation, goodwill on acquisition increases by €5,000,000. Again, this is a statement of financial position implication.

The statement of comprehensive income implication is the unwinding of the discount (effective interest). In essence, the former shareholders of Rest have provided Stay Inn with a loan of €5,000,000 at an interest rate of 5%, with all the interest and principal due at the end of the term. Under IAS 37, paragraph 60, the carrying amount of a provision increases to reflect the passage of time.

	€000
PV of Payment @ 5%	5,000
Year one (2011) interest @ 5%	250
Total provision (on 31/12/11)	5,250
Year two (2012) interest @ 5%	263
Total provision (on 31/12/12)	5,513

This solution assumes that this issue was correctly identified at consolidation stage in previous years. Thus, only the current-year effects need be considered.

Thus the entry required

	€	€
Debit/Increase: Finance charges	263,000	
Credit/Increase: Provision for deferred consideration (statement of financial position item)		263,000

2. Revaluation of Relax's Hotels Under IFRS 3, paragraphs 18 and 20, the hotels should be valued at fair value (market value in this instance is acceptable, see IFRS 13 *Fair Value Measurement* for the detailed guidance on measuring at fair value).

In addition, all companies in the group should have similar accounting policies (IFRS 10, para 19) and Stay Inn does revalue its hotels. At year end no revaluation had taken place. However, the acquisition was just three months earlier (30 September) and unless there was a reason to indicate a large increase or decrease in value over the intervening three months (October to December) then the valuation on acquisition would still be regarded as current (IAS 16, para 34).

The revaluation of hotels will have a statement of financial position impact. However, the knock on effect of the additional depreciation needs to be considered.

	€
Original depreciation (€5,000,000/20 years)	250,000
Revised depreciation (€6,000,000/12 years)	500,000
Additional depreciation (annual)	250,000

The subsidiary was in the group for only three months, thus the additional depreciation charge will just be applied over three months, €250,000 × 3 months/12 months, €62,500 (i.e. €63,000, when rounded up to the next €000)

	€	€
Debit/Increase Depreciation (in cost of sales)	63,000	
Credit/Increase Accumulated depreciation (SOFP item)		63,000

3. Relax Rights Issue The rights issue takes place after the year end. Thus, the question is whether or not this is an adjusting event after the reporting period (31 December 2012). IAS 10, paragraph 22(f), would indicate that major ordinary share transactions are generally not adjusting events. In addition, it appears that, by year end, the company had not progressed the transaction to a stage where it was effectively committed to it.

There would appear to be no implications for the current financial statements. However, the Stay Inn Group would need to disclose the event in the notes to the financial statements.

4. Write Off of Goodwill in Relax Under IAS 36, paragraph 10, goodwill should be tested annually for impairment. Consequently, the full amount of the goodwill should be written off (as instructed in the information). However, the amount of the goodwill needs to be calculated. This will need to take into account the revaluation of hotels from item 2 above.

The first stage is to calculate the goodwill on acquisition.

	€000	€000	
Fair value of consideration		7,000	
Fair value of net assets acquired:			
Ordinary share capital	1,000		
Retained earnings	2,500		
Fair value adjustment	3,000		(increase in value of hotels)
Total	6,500		
Group – 75%		4,875	
Goodwill		2,125	

On acquisition date the fair values of the hotels were €6 million but the carrying value was just €3 million, hence the fair value adjustment of €3 million.

The entire amount of this goodwill will need to be written off:

	€000	€000
Debit/Increase: Impairment expense	2,125	
Credit/Decrease: Goodwill (SOFP item)		2,125

5. *Cool* Under IAS 37, paragraph 72, there does not appear to be a constructive obligation on the part of Cool at period end.

The constructive obligation appears to be entered into after the reporting period. Thus, the question is whether or not this is an adjusting event after the end of the reporting period (31 December 2012). IAS 10, paragraph 22(b), would indicate that announcing a plan to discontinue an operation is not an adjusting event. It appears that, by year end, the company had not progressed the transaction to a stage where it was effectively committed to it.

Therefore by recording the transaction the management of Cool were in error. This will need to be reversed.

	$	$
Credit/Decrease: Cost of sales	3,000,000	
Debit/Decrease: Provisions (SOFP item)		3,000,000

The next step is to convert the statement of comprehensive income of Cool into Euro. At issue here is the exchange rate to use. IAS 21, paragraph 39 and 40, would indicate that the transactions in the statement of comprehensive income should be translated using an actual rate at the date of the transactions. However, realising that this may be impractical, the standard does permit an average rate to be used. For the period in question (July to December 2012) the average rate was €1 = $1.43. Only six months of income and expenses are included for Cool.

	USD		EUR
	$000	**Rate**	**€000**
Revenue	9,000	1.43	6,294
Cost of sales*	(2,280)	1.43	(1,594)
Gross Profit	6,720	1.43	4,699
Administration expenses	(1,170)	1.43	(818)
Distribution expenses	(90)	1.43	(63)
Other expenses	(540)	1.43	(378)
Finance costs	(475)	1.43	(332)
Operating Profit	4,445	1.43	3,108
Taxation	(1,250)	1.43	(874)
Profit for the Year	3,195	1.43	2,234

* Cost of sales = $7,560,000 – $3,000,000
= $4,560,000

Cost of sales for 6 months = $2,280,000

6: Disposal of Rest This is probably the most complex technical issue in this requirement. The income and expenses of Rest up until it left the group (the three months from January to March) will have to be included. In addition, the gain or loss on disposal of Rest will need to be calculated. This will replace the current amount included in the statement of comprehensive income of Stay Inn. These two items will combine to be reported as 'Profit (/Loss) from Discontinued Activities'.

The income and expenses of Rest for the first three months of the period are calculated on a time-apportioned basis (3 months/12 months) for each line item.

	€000
Revenue	6,250
Cost of sales	(2,938)
Gross Profit	3,312
Administration expenses	(750)
Distribution expenses	(188)
Other expenses	(313)
Finance costs	(500)
Operating Profit	1,561
Taxation	(138)
Profit for the Year	1,423

The procedure for calculating the gain/loss on disposal is outlined in IFRS 10, paragraph B98. The amount currently included in the financial statements of Rest is inaccurate from a consolidation perspective. This €18 million is the proceeds of the disposal (€60 million) less the original cost of purchase (€42 million). It does not include the goodwill that is also being derecognised from the group financial statements. In addition, the effective carrying amount of the subsidiary increased (or decreased) each year as the subsidiary earned profits (or losses). Thus, when Rest was sold, it was not being carried in the group financial statements at cost but at cost plus any goodwill on acquisition plus the group's share of profits (or losses) since acquisition.

The foregoing explanation appears convoluted. However, on the date of disposal, the gain or loss on disposal is calculated by comparing the disposal proceeds with the net assets disposed of (including goodwill disposed of). The disposal proceeds are given in the information – €60,000,000. The net assets at the date disposed of are not directly provided, however, the ordinary share capital and retained earnings are disclosed. On the date Rest was sold, the net assets of the business were €51,500,000 (ordinary shares of €1,000,000 and retained earnings of €50,500,000). The group share of this total was 80%.

The goodwill on acquisition was also disposed of. This will need to be calculated (going back to the acquisition date). When Stay Inn purchased Rest, it paid €42,000,000 cash and €5,000,000 of deferred consideration (see item 1 above), giving a total of €47,000,000. At the time of acquisition, the net assets of Rest were €38,000,000: this comprises €1,000,000 of ordinary share capital and €37,000,000 of retained earnings. The group acquired 80% of this €38,000,000 paying €47,000,000. This gives rise to goodwill on acquisition of €16,600,000.

Combining these, on the date of disposal, Stay Inn received €60,000,000 for 80% of net assets worth €51,500,000 and goodwill with a carrying value of €16,600,000. This gives a gain on disposal of €2,200,000. The calculations are set out below:

Calculation of Gain on Disposal of Rest

	€000	€000
Proceeds		60,000
Net assets disposed:		
Ordinary share capital	1,000	
Retained earnings	50,500	
	51,500	
Group (80%)	41,200	
Goodwill (W1)	16,600	
Total disposed of		57,800
Gain on disposal		2,200

W1: Goodwill on Acquisition

	€000
Fair Value of Net Assets on Acquisition	
Ordinary share capital	1,000
Retained earnings	37,000
	38,000
Group (80%)	30,400
Fair Value of Purchase Consideration	
Consideration	42,000
Deferred consideration	5,000
	47,000
Goodwill	16,600

To summarise:

For the three months that Rest was part of the group it contributed €1,423,000 in profits. In addition, there was a gain on the disposal of €2,200,000. This gives a total of 'Profits from discontinued operations' of €3,623,000.

7. Intragroup Dividend Under IFRS 10, paragraph B86(c), intragroup transactions should be eliminated in full. Thus, the dividend income in Stay Inn will need to be removed. The other side of the transaction is against 'Dividends' in Cool – this appears in the statement of changes in equity which is not required as part of the solution to this question.

Elimination of intragroup dividend:

	€	€
Debit/Decrease: Income from group companies	400,000	
Credit/Decrease: Dividend (Cool) (SOCE item)		400,000

8. Intragroup Management Fee This is similar to item 7 above. Under IFRS 10, paragraph B86(c), this type of intragroup transaction should be eliminated in full. None of the subsidiaries has recorded the item in expenses thus no adjustment needs to be made to expenses. The required adjustment is:

	€	€
Debit/Decrease: Revenue	2,000,000	
Credit/Decrease: Intragroup Receivable (statement of financial position item)		2,000,000

Summary of Adjustments from Step 3

		€
1:	Debit/Increase: Finance charges	263,000
2:	Debit/Increase: Cost of sales	63,000
3:	No implications	
4:	Debit/Increase: Impairment expense	2,125,000
5:	Cool – include the EUR equivalent figures as calculated	
6(a):	Profits from discontinued operations	3,623,000
6(b):	Debit/decrease gain on disposal of Rest	18,000,000
7:	Debit/Decrease: Income from group companies	400,000
8:	Debit/Decrease: Revenue	2,000,000

Step 4 – Preparing the Consolidated Statement of Comprehensive Income

The final stage of this process is to complete the consolidated statement of comprehensive income. You should now revert to your standard process for completion of consolidated statements of comprehensive income. This should involve a spreadsheet style system. There should be a column for each subsidiary in the group and a column for each of the adjustments. The final calculation will involve the allocation of profits between the non-controlling interests and the equity holders.

The first four columns in the consolidated statement of comprehensive income comprise the information from each of the members of the group:

- Remember, the column for the parent company, Stay Inn, should include the figures as calculated in your solution to requirement (a).
- The column allocated to Rest will not include any figures as the business is no longer in the group.
- The column for Relax should only include three months of figures as the subsidiary was only acquired with three months remaining in the current period.
- Finally, the column for Cool should include just 6 months of figures converted into EUR (see adjustment item 5).

Stay Inn Group

CONSOLIDATED STATEMENT OF COMPREHENSIVE INCOME
for the Year Ended 31 December 2012

	Stay Inn: Revised	Rest: Discount	Relax: 3 months	Cool: 6 months	Adj. 1	Adj. 2	Adj. 3	Adj. 4	Adj. 5	Adj. 6	Adj. 7	Adj. 8	Total
	€000	€000	€000	€000	€000	€000	€000	€000	€000	€000	€000	€000	€000
Continuing Operations													
Revenue	51,000		2,500	6,294								(2,000)	57,794
Cost of Sales	(23,150)		(2,000)	(1,594)		(63)							(26,807)
Gross Profit	27,850		500	4,699									30,986
Administration Expenses	(11,700)		(250)	(818)									(12,768)
Distribution Expenses	(1,100)		(75)	(63)									(1,238)
Income from Group Companies	400										(400)		
Gain on disposal of Rest	18,000									(18,000)			0
Goodwill Impairment								(2,125)					(2,125)
Other Expenses	(2,750)		(200)	(378)									(3,328)
Finance Costs	(1,545)		(350)	(332)	(263)								(2,490)
Operating Profit	29,155		(375)	3,108									9,037
Taxation	(1,200)		(5)	(874)									(2,079)
Profit for the Year Continuing Ops	27,955		(380)	2,234									6,958

	Stay Inn: Revised	Rest: Discount	Relax: 3 months	Cool: 6 months	Adj. 1	Adj. 2	Adj. 3	Adj. 4	Adj. 5	Adj. 6	Adj. 7	Adj. 8	Total
	€000	€000	€000	€000	€000	€000	€000	€000	€000	€000	€000	€000	€000
Discontinued Operations													
Profit for the year discontinued operations (note 1)													3,623
Profit for the Year													10,581
Other Comprehensive Income													
Gain/(Loss) on Revaluation	(338)												(338)
Total Comprehensive Income	27,618		(380)	2,234									10,244
Total Comprehensive Income attributable to:													
Equity Holders													10,184
Non-controlling interests (W2)													397
													10,581
Total Comprehensive Income attributable to:													
Equity Holders													9,846
Non-controlling interests (W2)													397
													10,244

Stay Inn Group
NOTES TO THE CONSOLIDATED STATEMENT OF COMPREHENSIVE INCOME
for the Year Ended 31 December 2012

Note 1: Discontinued Activities (From adjustment 6)

On 31 March 2012 the group disposed of its entire shareholding in Rest Limited. Rest Limited operated and owned hotels.

	€000
Consideration Received	60,000
Net Assets Disposed	57,800
Gain on Disposal	2,200

	€000
Revenue	6,250
Cost of sales	(2,938)
Gross Profit	3,312
Administration expenses	(750)
Distribution expenses	(188)
Other expenses	(313)
Finance costs	(500)
Operating Profit	1,561
Taxation	(138)
Profit for the Year	1,423
Gain on Disposal	2,200
Total	3,623

Working 2 – Calculation of Non-controlling Interests In the consolidated statement of comprehensive income all of the income and expenses of the subsidiaries are included. It is at this stage that the amounts attributable to non-group shareholders is analysed. IAS 1 requires the analysis to be carried out on both 'Profit for the Year' and 'Total Comprehensive Income'.

The process involves taking the profit for the year of the subsidiaries as included and allowing for any consolidation adjustments that directly affect the income or expenses of the subsidiaries.

The only adjustment that directly impacts on the profit of a subsidiary is adjustment 2. The additional depreciation on Relax's hotels will reduce its profits by €63,000. All of the other adjustments impact on the parent company only.

	Rest	Relax	Cool	Total
	€000	€000	€000	€000
Profit for the Year	1,423	(380)	2,234	
Adj 2: Additional depreciation on hotels		(63)		
Profit after consolidation adjustments	1,423	(443)	2,234	
Non-controlling interests	20%	25%	10%	
Profit attributable to non-controlling interests	285	(111)	223	397

	Rest	Relax	Cool	Total
	€000	€000	€000	€000
Total Comprehensive Income	1,423	(380)	2,234	
Adj 2: Additional depreciation on hotels		(63)		
Profit after consolidation adjustments	1,423	(443)	2,234	
Non-controlling interests	20%	25%	10%	
Comprehensive income attributable to non-controlling interests	285	(111)	223	397

Requirement (d)

Consolidation Issue

The key issue here is that a group is not a legal entity. The individual companies in the group (Stay Inn Limited, Rest Limited, Relax Limited and Cool Inc.) are the legal entities.

The notion of a group was devised for financial reporting purposes so that stakeholders could better understand the overall performance of those entities under common control. A group is an artificial construct that is used to present information as if all the individual entities in the group were a single entity.

A group in itself does not pay tax (or dividends). Thus any consolidation adjustment has no impact on the tax liability of the entities that make up the group. Under IFRS 10, paragraph B86(c), the effect of all intragroup transactions (e.g. the management fees) should be eliminated on consolidation.

It is the individual entities (Stay Inn Limited, Rest Limited, Relax Limited and Cool Inc.) that pay tax on their reported profits. When intragroup items are eliminated, this only takes place at the 'group' level; each individual entity's financial statements are left unchanged thus the tax situation is unaffected.

There are however complicated taxation regulations on transfer pricing that impact on the extent to which groups can 'transfer' profits from one company to another. However, in this case, it is assumed that the amount charged for the central management services is reasonable in comparison to the value of the management services actually provided.

Case 5

Pickle Products Plc

This case study is based on a food ingredients business. The accountancy standards addressed in this case study include IAS 1, IAS 8, IAS 16, IAS 19, IAS 23, IAS 37, IAS 39, IFRS 3, IFRS 9, IFRS 10 and IFRS 13.

Background – Pickle Products Plc

You are the financial accountant of Pickle Products Plc, a food ingredients business located in Co. Kildare. The group manufactures and supplies a range of food ingredients to internationally renowned food companies.

Pickle Products was set up by Rory Keogh in 1995. Rory had identified an opening in the Irish market for a range of imported food ingredients. He established the business, initially, as a sole trader. However, the business grew rapidly and it was converted to a limited company in 1997.

Pickle Products made a number of successful acquisitions over the following five years. The company was launched on the Irish stock exchange in 2003. It currently has a listing on both the Irish and the London stock exchanges. The group is headquartered in Co. Kildare but employs staff across the world. The group is currently made up of Pickle Products and its two subsidiaries DSM and Akzo.

It is 13 January 2013 and you are preparing the financial statements for the year ended 31 December 2012. This is a pressurised time of the year and you need to have final figures for publication in two days' time. You are based in head office and have just finished the first draft of the financial statements of the parent company. There are a number of outstanding issues that you need to discuss with the finance director. Once these are resolved you hope to move on to preparing the consolidated financial statements.

Parent Company (Pickle Products Plc)
DRAFT STATEMENTS OF FINANCIAL POSITION
as at 31 December 2012

	€000	€000
Non-current Assets		
Property, plant and equipment		13,600
Investments in:		
DSM	2,000	
Akzo	1,500	3,500
Financial assets – equity instruments		4,400
Intangible assets		1,500
		23,000
Current Assets		
Inventories		9,000
Trade receivables		4,000
Cash and cash equivalents		2,000
		15,000
Total Net Assets		**38,000**
Equity		
Ordinary share capital (€1 each)		2,000
Share premium		6,900
Reserves		11,000
		19,900
Non-current Liabilities		
Bank loans		2,000
Bonds		5,000
Provisions		1,000
Retirement benefit obligations		1,200
Deferred income		600
Deferred tax		2000
		11,800
Current Liabilities		
Payables		5,200
Bank loans		600
Current tax		500
		6,300
Total Equity and Liabilities		**38,000**

Outstanding Issues in Respect of the Parent Company's Financial Statements

Outstanding Issue 1

As part of the production process, Pickle Products blends and packages a range of food formulations. This process is carried out in clean-room facilities. The formulations are either in liquid form or powder form, depending on client requirements.

During 2012 one of these clean rooms was upgraded. Building work commenced on the facility in February 2012 and was completed in August 2012. The facility was not available for use until 1 October 2012.

Pickle incurred construction costs at various intervals throughout this period all of which are included in property, plant and equipment. Material costs were incurred on the following dates: 1 February €300,000, 1 May €150,000 and 1 August €100,000. Labour costs of €180,000, €240,000 and €300,000 were paid on 1 February, 1 May and 1 August respectively. Fees of €100,000, incurred on professional services, were paid on 1 May 2012.

To ensure that the clean room and its equipment installation was safely built and met the required regulatory standards, Pickles was obliged to have a cleanroom inspection carried out on the facility. This inspection took place in September 2012 (and all inspection costs were paid for at the end of that month). The total cost of this inspection was €200,000. Included in these inspection costs was €28,000 incurred on staff training. Four members of staff were sent on a seven-day course to be trained in clean-room operations.

In addition, during the inspection process, a sample of food products was manufactured. These samples were sold to customers at reduced prices. Net proceeds of €70,000 was generated from this process and this income is included in group revenue in the statement of comprehensive income.

Pickle Products financed the project with a €2 million, 4% fixed interest rate loan that was made available to the company from 1 January 2012. The company had hoped to secure variable rate funding but the bank would only agree to lend at fixed rates. Indeed, they could only secure this rate for the first six months. In July 2012, the rate was increased by 1.5% to reflect a general upward trend in commercial rates interest rates. Interest is charged and paid monthly. However, capital repayments will not commence until January 2013.

Borrowing costs have been charged in full to profit or loss.

Finally, work on the clean room was disrupted in March 2012 due to an unofficial dispute by construction workers. Although the dispute lasted for four weeks, construction of the clean room was still completed on time and within budget.

(You can ignore depreciation for this issue.)

Outstanding Issue 2

Up until 2012, Pickles ran a chain of health food stores. During 2012, as part of an overall review of the business, Pickles decided to close the health food stores and concentrate solely on the wholesale supply of food ingredients. A re-organisation plan was finalised in November 2012 and, on 20 December 2012, a public announcement of the closure was made. A letter was sent to each member of staff notifying them of the imminent closure. The directors expect that the re-organisation will commence in the spring of 2013 and be completed by 31 August 2013.

The costs of the plan are estimated to be €980,000, made up of the following:

	€
Redundancy costs	600,000
Operating losses from 1 January 2013 to 31 August 2013	250,000
Anticipated loss on the disposal of property	100,000
Professional Fees	30,000
	980,000

The directors intend noting the details of the plan in the 2012 financial statements but do not intend accruing the costs this year. The opinion of the board is that as restructuring did not begin in 2012, there is no need to provide for the cost this year. The company are under no obligation, legal or otherwise, to carry out the plan in 2012. They have simply announced their intention to do so. No obligation will arise until the restructuring process commences in 2013.

Outstanding Issue 3

During the audit, it was discovered that goods, sold in December 2011, were not removed from inventory and were included in the closing inventory figure for that year. The cost price of these goods was €480,000 and they were sold at a mark-up of 20%. At the time of sale the customer had requested that the goods be delivered *after* 12 January 2012 as they were not in a position to accept them before that date.

Pickle Products had invoiced the customer in December 2011 and the sale was properly recorded at that time. However, due to an oversight, the goods were not removed from inventory until the date of delivery.

In addition, Pickle Products depreciate computer equipment over 12 years. On 1 January 2012 the group's computer equipment had a carrying value of €700,000 with 10 years' remaining useful life. On the same date, management reviewed the useful lives of all assets and decided that computer equipment had a remaining useful life of 5 years. No depreciation has been charged on computer equipment for 2012.

Outstanding Issue 4

Pickle Products operates a defined benefit retirement plan for its senior executives. At 1 January 2012, the market value of the assets in the scheme was €2.38 million and the present value of retirement obligations €3.5 million. During 2012, the following entries were correctly made to the financial statements in relation to the retirement scheme:

1. Additional service costs of €150,000
2. Contributions to the fund of €70,000
3. Benefits paid to retired employees of €50,000.

The following additional information has become available since the year-end but has not yet been accrued in the financial statements. It has been established that the discount rate applied to the retirement obligation at 1 January 2012 was 5% and at 31 December 2012 was 6% while the expected return on plan assets was 3% on 1 January 2012 and 2% on 31 December 2012.

The actuarial valuation at 31 December 2012 now suggests that the market value of the plan assets is €2.2 million and the present value of the defined obligations is €190,000 more than it was at the start of the year.

The Consolidated Financial Statements

Consolidation Issue

Having resolved outstanding issues 1–4 your next task is to prepare the consolidated financial statements. There are two subsidiaries in the group. The draft statements of financial position are presented although there is an issue with obtaining the financial statements of one of the subsidiaries (see below).

Before Christmas you contacted both of the subsidiaries in the group. You decided on a timetable with the accountants in each unit and everyone agreed to submit their financial statements to you on 7 January 2013 so that you would be able to prepare the group financial statements.

It is now the 13 January 2013 and one of the subsidiary operating-units, Akzo, has not yet submitted its results. You have attempted to contact the accountant but to no avail. The situation is now critical as the consolidated results are to be announced to the market tomorrow. The finance director is livid and is blaming you for the mess. The subsidiary did submit results as normal for November. He has declared to the finance team that the consolidation will continue without Akzo, the missing subsidiary.

He justifies this on the basis of the results for November, which showed that the company had only just broken even for the first 11 months. In addition he knows, from discussions with the managing director (MD) of Akzo, that there was no material change in December. He maintains that Pickle Products' shareholding in Akzo could hardly constitute control if they cannot get a set of financial statements from the company. He wants the investment to be carried at cost on the consolidated statement of financial position (IFRS 9, para B5.4.14). (There is no quoted market price for the shares in Akzo.)

The Draft Statements of Financial Position as at 31 December 2012 for the subsidiaries are shown below:

	DSM €000	Akzo €000
Non-current Assets		
Property, plant and equipment	3,600	
Current Assets		
Inventories	600	
Trade receivables	300	
Cash and cash equivalents	100	
	1,000	
Total Net Assets	4,600	
Equity		
Ordinary share capital (€1 each)	200	
Reserves	2,100	
	2,300	
Non-current Liabilities		
Bank loans	400	
Bonds	830	
Provisions	100	
Retirement benefit obligations	300	
	1,630	
Current Liabilities		
Payables	450	
Provisions (dividend)	150	
Bank loans	50	
Current tax	20	
	670	
Total Equity and Liabilities	4,600	

Additional Information

You have been provided with the following information regarding the subsidiaries. This will be of assistance in the preparation of the consolidated financial statements.

Note 1 – Purchase of Investment in DSM

On 29 May 2002 Pickle Products purchased 80% of DSM for €2,000,000 when its retained earnings were €500,000.

Pickle Products agreed to pay a further €300,000 if certain profit targets were met. Those targets were met in 2012 and on 30 June 2012 the €300,000 was paid to the original shareholders of DSM. The finance director handled this transaction but was unsure of how to account for it. He credited cash and debited an expense account calling the item an exceptional expense in the records of Pickle Products. Originally at the time of the acquisition, it appeared very unlikely that this amount would be payable. In order to fund the amount paid to the old shareholders of DSM, Pickle Products forced DSM to pay it a special dividend of €375,000. This special dividend was paid on 30 June 2012. Both companies have recorded the dividend.

At the time of the acquisition a fair value review was carried out into the assets and liabilities of DSM. The following items were noted:

- Machine: €300,000 carrying value on acquisition date.
  There has been very little activity in the second hand market for this type of machine in 2002. The amount above relates to a 20-year-old machine (original cost €1,500,000). Machines of this nature have a life of 25 years. A new machine of similar size would have cost €3,000,000 to purchase in 2002.
- Intangible Assets: €0 carrying value on acquisition date.
  At the time of the acquisition Pickle Products put a value of €200,000 on the brand name of DSM. This value had not previously been recognised by DSM as it was internally generated. There has been no event since to indicate that this valuation has been impaired.
- Financial Assets: €700,000 carrying value on acquisition date.
  These represent a small equity stake (6%) in a private company, Galactic Ltd. The company is involved in the manufacture and sale of heating equipment. There is no market value for the shares as the company's shares are not traded. However, the shares of similar companies tend to trade at 10 times the earnings or twice their net asset value. At the time of the acquisition a recent set of financial statements of Galactic revealed the following:

	€
Operating profit	2,000,000
Interest	200,000
Profit before tax	1,800,000
Tax	200,000
Profit after tax	1,600,000
Net assets	9,000,000

The shares were sold for a profit in 2008.

- Provisions: €100,000 carrying value on acquisition date.
  At the time of the acquisition DSM had a provision in its financial statements for €100,000. This was a provision for the expected reorganisation costs of the acquisition. The directors of DSM included the provision as a pre-emptive strike by the directors to negotiate large redundancy payments for themselves. Their estimate was not incorrect as, in 2003, the cost of the re-organisation was almost €100,000.
- Sales Contract: €0 carrying value on acquisition date.

At the time of the acquisition DSM had negotiated a long-term sales agreement with a customer for 2003. The agreement was that DSM would supply 10,000 units of product to the customer for a guaranteed price of €10 per unit. However, due to increases in the cost of raw material, each of these products will cost €12 to make. The contract was not cancellable; in 2003 DSM did uphold its side of the agreement.

None of these adjustments was made in the individual accounts of DSM but all of the items (except the Brand Name) have subsequently resolved themselves.

Note 2 – Purchase of Investment in Akzo

The investment in Akzo was purchased on 23 May 2003 for €1,500,000 cash. Pickle Products bought 75% of the business, which makes chemicals to order. The company is located in France and is managed locally. Akzo had share capital of €400,000 and retained earnings of €800,000 on the date of the acquisition transaction and the fair value of assets acquired was approximately equal to their carrying values.

Note 3 – Dividend from DSM

On 10 December 2012 the directors of DSM proposed a dividend for the year ended 31 December 2012 of €150,000 (this is in addition to the special dividend in the additional information note 1). The dividend has been voted on by the shareholders and is properly authorised. The dividend has been provided for in the financial statements of DSM (included in provisions under current liabilities and against retained earnings).

Pickle Products has not accounted for its portion of the dividend.

Note 4 – Review of DSM

In light of the dividend payments that Pickle Products are insisting on from DSM, there is some concern that the directors of Pickle Products are running down the operation and squeezing as much cash from the business as they possibly can. This lack of investment into the business will have some impact on the goodwill that arose on acquisition. It is considered that the goodwill on acquisition is impaired and 30% of this goodwill should be written off.

Shareholder Concern

The finance director has also asked you to draft a reply to some correspondence which he has received from a shareholder.

The shareholder has written to the financial director seeking information about the value of their shares. This shareholder owns 3,000 shares in Pickle Products. The group's shares are trading on the Irish Stock Exchange at €20 per share and this price has remained steady for the past 12 months. This puts a value on the shareholder's holding of €60,000 and a market capitalisation of the group, based on two million issued shares, at €40 million.

"However," the shareholder has written, "when I review the group's statement of financial position, I note that the valuation of equity is only €20 million*. I don't understand why this is so. Why is there a difference between the quoted value of the business and the financial statements? Can you explain? Can you also advise me which valuation is a better indicator of what my holding is worth today?"

* This is a rounded figure. It is based on the completed consolidated statements (requirement 3). You may have arrived at a different figure when working through the question. The exact figure is irrelevant when you are answering this section. This section requires only general discussion.

Requirements

(**Note:** Unless you are specifically required to consider deferred taxation, you can assume that it is not applicable.)

(a) You are required to redraft the statement of financial position of Pickle Products Plc for the year ended 31 December 2012. (This incorporates outstanding issues 1–4.) Your answer should include detailed workings for each of the issues. You should justify your answers. (Ignore taxation.)

(40 marks)

(b) With regard to the situation in Akzo (the 'consolidation issue'), outline the current regulatory position. Evaluate the response of the finance director. How would you propose to remedy the situation?

(10 marks)

(c) Prepare the consolidated statement of financial position for the Pickle Products Group as at 31 December 2012. Although you may not agree, follow the wishes of the finance director in respect of Akzo. (Use the redrafted statement of financial position from requirement (a) for Pickle Products Plc.)

(40 marks)

(d) Prepare a brief report addressing the concerns of the shareholder as outlined in the final section of the case study above.

(10 marks)

Guidance Notes – Pickle Products Plc

Exam Technique

Read the case carefully.

There are four requirements to this case study. The first requirement involves a review of the parent company's financial statements. There are some problems with the Pickle Products financial statements and you are required to address them. Once these issues have been resolved, a revised statement of financial position must be prepared for the parent company. Requirements (b) and (c) of the case study involve consolidation. In the case study it is important to be aware of the scheduling of the requirements. Only after the parent company's financial statements are revised can the consolidated financial statements be completed.

Requirement (b) requires a discursive answer while requirement (c) involves the preparation of the consolidated statement of financial position of the Pickle Products Group. When you are preparing the consolidated financial statements, you should work methodically through the consolidation process. You should not worry too much about the consequences of the occasional error – it may not have a material impact on the final mark that you achieve. For example, if you make an error on one of the issues in requirement (a) which results in an incorrect statement of financial position for Pickle Products, this will almost certainly result in an incorrect statement of financial position for the group under requirement (c). However, you will not be overly penalised for each individual mistake – therefore, if one error has a number of knock-on effects, you will not be penalised for the resultant errors arising from the original error.

You will score more marks if you *attempt* all parts of the case rather than completing some sections and not answering others at all.

Requirements (b) and (d) do not require much technical analysis; they require discursive style answers. These can be answered out of sequence. This is worth considering as they may require less time to complete.

Answering the Case Study

Requirement (a) – Guidance

Outstanding Issue 1 This issue tests your knowledge of IAS 16 *Property, Plant and Equipment* (IAS 16) and IAS 23 *Borrowing Costs* (IAS 23).

IAS 16 outlines the accounting treatment for property, plant and equipment (PPE). The principal issues in IAS 16 are the recognition of the assets, the determination of their carrying amounts, the depreciation charges and impairment losses to be recognised in relation to them (IAS 16, paragraph 1). IAS 16 applies to those costs incurred *initially* to construct or acquire an item of property, plant and equipment *and* those that are incurred *subsequently* to add to or replace part of the asset (IAS 16, paragraph 10). In this case study, it is the latter situation that is presented to you. The clean room, constructed in a previous reporting period, has undergone an upgrade in the current year. You must establish how this upgrade should be recognised in the financial statements.

To answer this section, you will need to be reasonably familiar with the sections of IAS 16 dealing with the measurement of non-current assets at recognition (upgrade in this instance). (IAS 16, para 16–22). These paragraphs outline the costs that *may* be included in PPE (IAS 16, para 16–18) and those costs that should be expensed (IAS 16, para 19–22). Currently in the case study, all costs incurred in the upgrade of the clean-room facility are included in PPE. You may need to reconsider some of these.

When you have established the final cost of the upgrade to be included in PPE, you can move on to the borrowing costs. You will need to decide whether the borrowing costs should be included as part of the cost of the upgrade (and therefore included in property, plant and equipment) *or* if they should be included as finance charges in the statement of comprehensive income. IAS 23 *Borrowing Costs* gives the appropriate guidance.

Outstanding Issue 2 This issue deals with restructuring costs. In the case study, a restructuring programme was *planned* in 2012 but will not be implemented until spring 2013. You must decide when to include the effects of the restructuring programme in the financial statements. Without appropriate guidance you could, potentially, treat this matter in a number of different ways:

1. make a full provision for all of the restructuring costs in the 2012 financial statements as the company has announced the plan;
2. include a disclosure note only in the 2012 financial statements as the company has only announced their intention to restructure; or
3. ignore the restructuring altogether this year as it has not been implemented.

In the case study Pickles has made a decision to include a disclosure note only in the 2012 financial statements. You must decide if this is an appropriate treatment.

IAS 37 *Provisions, Contingent Liabilities and Contingent Assets* will provide the appropriate guidance. The guidance for restructuring costs is given in IAS 37, paragraphs 70–83. IAS 37, paragraphs 71–79 outlines *when* re-structuring costs should be accrued and IAS 37, paragraphs 80–83, outlines *what costs* should be accrued. The guidance is very clear so it should not be too difficult to arrive at an appropriate answer.

Outstanding Issue 3 IAS 8 *Accounting Policies, Changes in Accounting Estimates and Errors* gives guidance on how to treat changes in accounting policies, changes in accounting estimates and the correction of errors in the financial statements. There are two separate transactions to this issue:

Inventory Goods sold in 2011 were correctly reported in revenue in 2011 but the goods were not removed from inventory. The customer had requested a delay on delivery until January 2012. The goods were not removed until they were delivered to the customer. This was clearly an error. You must figure out how to correct this error. You should bear in mind that the error affects both closing inventory of 2011 and the opening inventory in 2012. How will you deal with this?

IAS 8, paragraphs 41–49, outlines how to treat errors in the financial statements. These sections offer guidance where the errors relate to the current period and where the errors relate to previous periods. You will find the appropriate accounting guidance in these sections.

Depreciation on Computer Equipment Pickle Products has decided to revise the remaining useful life of the company's computer equipment. You must decide if this change is a change in accounting policy, a change in accounting estimate or requires the correction of an error. The definitions of each of the terms outlined in IAS 8, paragraph 5 will provide you with the appropriate answer. You should review this section of the standard. Once you have established how to classify this item you should then establish the appropriate accounting treatment. This can be found in the following paragraphs: changes in accounting policy – IAS 8, paragraphs 14–31, changes in accounting estimates – IAS 8, paragraphs 32–40, and errors – IAS 8, paragraphs 41–49.

Outstanding Issue 4 You will need to review the provisions of IAS 19 *Employee Benefits* to answer this section. IAS 19 covers the accounting treatment for all employee benefits (except share options which are covered in IFRS 2 *Share-based Payment*) including those relating to current and former employees. IAS 19, paragraphs 26–152, outlines the appropriate treatment for post-employment benefits or, in other words, occupational pension schemes. There are two types of occupational pension scheme outlined in the accounting standard – defined contribution plans and defined benefit plans. You must identify the type of pension scheme that is being offered to Pickle Products' employees. The details of each scheme are briefly explained and the distinction between them outlined in IAS 19, paragraphs 26–30.

When you have identified the *type* of scheme, you will then need to follow the appropriate accounting guidelines for presentation in the financial statements. The accounting treatment for defined contribution plans is outlined in IAS 19, paragraphs 50–54. The accounting treatment for defined contribution plans is quite straightforward and requires only a few disclosures. The accounting treatment for defined benefit plans is outlined in paragraphs 55–152 of the standard. The accounting treatment is detailed and extensive disclosures are required.

The paragraphs of the standard that will be most relevant for this scenario are paragraphs 54 and 61.

When you have completed the adjustments for the four outstanding issues you can then proceed to the next step which is to redraft the parent's financial statements.

Requirement (b) – Guidance

This is an unusual situation. IFRS 10 gives some guidance on when a company can be excluded from consolidation, if at all (IFRS 10, para 4). Does this include situations where it appears that it is not possible to obtain a set of financial statements from a subsidiary?

You will need to consider if this is a failure of management and organisation rather than a legitimate reporting issue.

Finally, do not forget to consider some remedies – what should the company do now? Is the finance director's suggestion appropriate?

Requirement (c) – Guidance

This is the long consolidation element of the case study, so you will need to manage your time carefully. You will be using Pickle Product's redrafted statement of financial position from requirement (a) along with the financial statements provided for DSM and Azko (not actually available).

While it is a time-consuming question, if you deal with each item in turn, make your decision, and then move on, it becomes an exercise in information management.

To assist in the preparation of the consolidated statement of financial position it is often beneficial to have a process to follow. This will allow you to spend more time addressing the more complex issues. In addition, it may also prevent some basic errors that may arise from failing to identify the effect of the standard items of information. A four-step process is employed in this case study. This process was elaborated upon in more detail in the Armada case study. There are other approaches but it is important that you have your own system that you can rely on.

- **Step 1 – Set out the group structure**
- **Step 2 – Deal with the 'additional information'**
- **Step 3 – Prepare the consolidation table** (i.e. calculate the figures for goodwill, non-controlling interests and retained earnings). These are key figures in a consolidated statement of financial position and attract many marks.
- **Step 4 – Bring step 2 and step 3 together** by preparing the consolidated statement of financial position.

Step 1 – Set out the group structure This is not usually a difficult task as often the percentages are provided. You will need to decide whether the companies in the group are subsidiaries, associates or financial investments.

Step 2 – Deal with the 'additional information' This is a key element of the question, most of the available marks will be awarded for this step and step 3. You should consider each item in turn; decide on the journal entry to make (if any) and then move on to the next item.

We will now consider each item in turn:

1. The Purchase of DSM The adjustments made at this stage will impact on the calculation of the goodwill on acquisition and on the subsequent profits of DSM that the group will be able to recognise.

Cost of Consideration: The first item to deal with is the contingent consideration of €300,000 which became payable in 2012. Originally, it was felt that the probability of making the payments was unlikely. However, during 2012, the amount was paid. The issue here is to decide if, 10 years after the acquisition, the cost of the acquisition should be adjusted and, as a result, goodwill increased, or should the amount be written off? IFRS 3, paragraph 58, may be of some help. Alternatively, perhaps this item could be considered to be a change to an accounting estimate. IAS 8, paragraph 36, provides the guidance if that is your decision.

A second issue surrounds the dividend paid by DSM to Pickle Products. This dividend was made to fund the additional payment of €300,000 to the original shareholders of DSM. You will need to decide if this dividend is legitimate and, if so, has it been correctly recorded?

Fair Value of Assets Acquired: At the time of the acquisition, you will need to consider the basis for valuing the assets acquired and the liabilities assumed. Is the carrying value appropriate or should fair value be used? IFRS 3, paragraph 18, gives clear guidance here.

Then, for each of the items listed, you will need to decide how the fair value should be arrived at. This will depend on the asset involved:

- Machine: there is no market-based evidence of fair value so what would an appropriate alternative be, if any?
- Intangible assets: should they now be included separately? – see IFRS 3, paragraph 13.
- Financial assets: how should these be valued? – see IFRS 9, paragraph 5.2.1.
- Integration provision: can these provisions be recognised as part of the acquisition? – see IFRS 3, paragraph 11; is there a constructive obligation? – see IAS 37, paragraph 14.
- Sales Contract: this appears to be onerous on DSM – see IAS 37, paragraph 66.

Once the adjustment to fair value is determined, you will need to decide how to record the adjustment – is the other side of the adjustment to pre-acquisition retained earnings (and consequently to goodwill) or to post-acquisition retained earnings (and consequently to group retained earnings)?

Reversal of Fair Value Adjustments: Any adjustment made as part of the fair value process can have a knock on effect on the post-acquisition profits of the combined entity. For instance, increases to the value of plant can result in subsequent depreciation charges being higher. For each of the adjustments to fair value above, consider the impact on the asset/liability and post-acquisition retained earnings. Set out each adjustment to reflect this.

2. Purchase of Investment in Akzo Given the difficulties in getting the financial statements of Akzo, this company will not be consolidated. You have been requested to include the investment as a financial asset at cost (€1,500,000). This matter has already been discussed in requirement (b).

3. Dividend from DSM The dividends have been recorded by DSM but not by Pickle Products. Try to decide which company was correct – does this item come within IAS 10 *Events after the Reporting Period* (IAS 10, para 13) or did DSM have a constructive obligation to make the payment at year end (IAS 37, para 14).

- If DSM was correct in recording the dividend then Pickle Products should record the dividend income. Consider any intragroup effects which may need to be eliminated.
- If DSM was incorrect in recording the dividend then the entry will have to be reversed.

4. Impairment review of DSM There is little debate here – the amount has already been decided upon. IAS 36, paragraph 60, describes what to do with the impairment loss.

Step 3 – Prepare the consolidation table Using the adjustments from step 2, you should now be in a position to calculate the goodwill on acquisition of DSM, non-controlling interests and retained earnings. A template is presented below:

	Goodwill 80%	Non-controlling Interests 20%	Retained Earnings
	€	€	€
Cost of acquisition	XX		
Adjustment to cost	XX		
	XX		
Ordinary share capital of subsidiary (split 80:20)	XX	XX	
Retained earnings of subsidiary – pre-acquisition (split 80:20)	XX	XX	
Retained earnings of subsidiary – post-acquisition (split 20:80)		XX	XX
Retained earnings of parent – all group			XX

Adjustment 1	?	?	?
Adjustment 2	?	?	?
Adjustment 3	?	?	?
Adjustment X	?	?	?
Adjustment X	?	?	?
	XX	XX	XX

Step 4 – Complete the Statement of Financial Position This should be a relatively mechanical exercise as all the thinking has already been done. Just make sure that you correctly include all the adjustments that you have identified. Be sure that you show how each of the figures in the statement of financial position is calculated. If you fail to do this and some of the figures are incorrect, it will not be possible for the examiner to award any marks for the elements of the answer that are correct.

Requirement (d) – Guidance

This question requires a discursive answer. You are presented with two valuations for the Pickle Group. One valuation is based on the quoted share price of the group – the other is on the financial statements, or in other words, the book value. The quoted value of Pickles is higher than the book value and you are asked to comment on which is the 'true' value.

This issue is slightly different to a 'normal' financial reporting question, but it is an important issue. It requires you to step back from the detail of the accounting standards and look at the bigger picture, i.e. what is the true value of a company and do the financial statements reflect this true value? There is a link here with corporate finance studies on the topic of share valuations.

This case study does not require you to produce a comprehensive report on share valuation methods. (However, for tutorial purposes they could be summarised.) The issue is about the relevance of financial statements and whether or not they are a good indicator of an entity's true worth. You should reflect on the statement of financial position, in particular. Is this a statement of the true value of an entity at the end of its reporting period (as its title would suggest) or is it simply an addition of the net assets of the business based on what they had cost in the past?

You could answer this question by discussing the merits and demerits of historical cost accounting as the traditional basis for preparing financial statements. You could also mention the fair value developments that are on-going with the International Accounting Standards Board (IASB) (in conjunction with the Financial Accounting Standards Board in the US (FASB) in an effort to make financial statements more relevant. Finally, you could give a brief summary of how the quoted price is arrived at. This will require you to draw from your knowledge of corporate finance.

Recommended Reading

The accounting standards addressed in this case study may also be referenced in *International Financial Accounting and Reporting,* 3rd edition, by Ciaran Connolly (Chartered Accountants Ireland, 2011) as follows:

Case	Chapter	Chapter Title	Chapter Section	Standard
Requirement (a)				
Outstanding Issue 1	6	Property, Plant and Equipment	6.2	IAS 16
	7	Borrowing Costs	7.2	IAS 23
Outstanding Issue 2	14	Provisions, Contingent Liabilities and Contingent Assets	14.2	IAS 37
Outstanding Issue 3	21	Accounting Policies, Changes in Accounting Estimates and Errors	21.2	IAS 8
Outstanding Issue 4	17	Employee Benefits	17.2	IAS 19
Requirement (b)				
	26	Business Combinations and Consolidated Financial Statements	26.2, 26.4	IFRS 10
Requirement (c)				
	27	Consolidated Statement of Financial Position	27.2–27.6, 27.8, 27.11	IFRS 10
	26	Business Combinations and Consolidated Financial Statements	26.3, 26.4	IFRS 3
	25	Financial Instruments	25.3, 25.5	IFRS 9
Requirement (d)				
	1	Framework for Financial Reporting	1.3–1.4	

Solution to Pickle Products Group

Requirement (a)

Outstanding Issue 1

Currently, costs totalling €1.57 million, relating to the upgrade of the company's clean-room facilities, are included in property, plant and equipment. A review of IAS 16, paragraphs 16–22, will indicate that the following adjustments should be made to this figure. These adjustments include:

Staff training costs are not included in PPE cost Staff training is a cost arising from the operation of the clean-room facility, not the construction. Staff training costs should be expensed in full and *not* included in property, plant and equipment (IAS 16, para 19(c)).

	€	€
DR Retained earnings	28,000	
CR PPE		28,000

Revenue from Sample products included in Sales The net proceeds from the sale of samples when testing equipment are deemed to be a deduction from attributable costs (IAS 16, para 17 (e)). In the case study, the net proceeds from the sale of the sample products has been included in revenue. This is not correct. The net income from the sale of samples should be deducted from the cost of the asset and not included in revenue.

	€	€
DR Retained earnings	70,000	
CR PPE		70,000

Borrowing costs to be Capitalised The borrowing costs incurred on the upgrade of the clean-room facility have been charged in full to profit or loss, €95,000, i.e. (€2m × 4% × 6/12) + (€2m × 5.5% × 6/12). This treatment does not comply with the rules of IAS 23 *Borrowing Costs*. IAS 23 gives guidance on *what* borrowing costs should be capitalised and the *period* for which they should be capitalised. The principle of IAS 23 is that "borrowing costs that are directly attributable to the acquisition, construction or production of a qualifying asset[1] form part of the cost of that asset. Other borrowing costs are recognized as an expense" (IAS 23, paragraph 1).

[1] A qualifying asset is an asset that necessarily takes a substantial period of time to get ready for its intended use or sale (IAS 23, para 5).

In the case study the qualifying asset (incorporating the adjustments for staff training costs and testing) is now:

	€
Per the case study	1,570,000
Staff training	(28,000)
Samples	(70,000)
Restated qualifying asset	€1,472,000

Pickle Products has borrowed €2 million to fund the cost of this construction work. IAS 23, paragraph 8 states "an entity shall capitalise borrowing costs that are directly attributable to the acquisition, construction or production of a qualifying asset." Or, in other words, "the borrowing costs that would have been avoided if the expenditure on the qualifying asset had not been made" (IAS 23, para 9). Further detail is given in the following paragraphs of IAS 23:

- Paragraph 17: "the commencement of capitalisation is the date when the entity first meets all of the following conditions (i) it incurs expenditure on the asset (ii) it incurs borrowing costs and (iii) it undertakes activities that are necessary to prepare the asset for its intended use or sale.
- Paragraph 20: "An entity shall suspend capitalisation of borrowing costs during extended periods in which it suspends active development of a qualifying asset". (There are exceptions to this rule. These are outlined in IAS 23, paragraph 21.)
- Paragraph 22: "An entity shall cease capitalising borrowing costs when substantially all of the activities necessary to prepare the qualifying asset for its intended use or sale are complete."

Various dates are given in the case study:

Loan facility drawn down	January 2012
Construction commenced	February 2012
Construction – in stages	Over seven months
Construction suspended	March 2012
Construction completed	August 2012
Available for use	October 2012
Loan repayments	Commencing 2013

When the rules of IAS 23 and the relevant dates are applied to the case study, the borrowing costs that will be capitalised for the period will be for 4 months at 4% (Feb, April, May, June) and for 3 months at 5.5% (July, Aug, Sept). (Although the construction work is completed in August 2012 the asset is not available until 1 October 2012.)

The borrowing costs to be capitalised can be presented in a table as follows:

Date	Costs	4%	5.50%	Total	
	€	€	€	€	
1 February 2012	480,000	6,400	6,600	13,000	(4 months 4%, 3 months 5.5%)
1 March 2012					(construction suspended)
1 May 2012	490,000	3,267	6,738	10,004	(2 months 4%, 3months 5.5%)
1 August 2012	400,000		3,667	3,667	(2 months 5.5%)
1 September* 2012 (adjusted)	102,000		468	468	(1 month 5.5%)
Total	1,472,000	9,667	17,472	27,139	

* (September €200,000 per case study less samples €70,000 and staff training €28,000)

The adjustment required to capitalise borrowing costs in accordance with IAS 23 is:

	€	€
DR PPE	27,139	
CR Retained earnings		27,139

Outstanding Issue 2

IAS 37, paragraph 71 states "a provision for restructuring costs is recognised only when the general recognition criteria are met." The general recognition criteria as outlined in paragraph 14 of the standard are:

(i) An entity has a present obligation as a result of a past event and
(ii) It is probable that an outflow of funds will be required to settle the obligation and
(iii) A reliable estimate can be made of the amount of the obligation.

An obligation, as explained in paragraph 17, can be one that is enforced by law or is constructive in nature. A constructive obligation exists where an action by the entity "creates valid expectation in other parties that the entity will discharge the obligation".

When an entity announces a restructuring plan, it is creating a constructive obligation. Paragraph 72 of the standard expands on this point:

"A constructive obligation exists when an entity:

(i) Has a detailed formal plan for the restructuring identifying at least (i) the business or part of the business concerned (ii) the principal locations affected (iii) the location, function, and approximate number of employees who will be compensated for terminating their services (iv) the expenditures that will be undertaken and (v) when the plan will be implemented and
(ii) Has raised valid expectations in those affected that it will carry out the restructuring by starting to implement that plan or announcing its main features to those who are affected by it."

Pickle Products made a formal announcement of the reorganisation before the end of the current financial period. A constructive obligation has, therefore, been made and, in accordance with IAS 37, paragraph 71, a restructuring provision should be made in the 2012 financial statements.

IAS 37, paragraph 80, outlines what costs should be included in a restructuring provision: "direct expenditure arising from the restructuring, which are those that are both (i) necessarily entailed by the restructuring and (ii) are not associated with the on-going activities of the entity".

Paragraphs 81–83 include further details on what costs should be included and excluded from the provision.

Pickles has not made any provision in the financial statements so far, although it has identified the total costs of the restructuring. In accordance with IAS 37 the costs will be accrued as follows:

Item	Provision	No Provision	
	€	€	
Redundancy	600,000		(IAS 37, para 80)
Operating losses		250,000	(IAS 37, para 82)
Loss on disposal		100,000	*(IAS 37, para 51)
Professional fees	30,000		(IAS 37, para 80)
	630,000	350,000	

* The loss on disposal will be recognised when the property is sold.

An adjustment is necessary to incorporate this provision:

	€	€
DR Retained earnings	630,000	
CR Provisions		630,000

Outstanding Issue 3

Inventory There is an error in the 2011 financial statements. Goods that were sold in 2011 were not withdrawn from inventory. The effect of this error is that closing inventory and profits of 2011 were overstated (cost of sales was understated therefore the reported profit was overstated). This error has carried forward into 2012. The opening inventory for 2012 is overstated as are the retained profits brought forward.

To correct this error we will need to refer to IAS 8 *Accounting Policies, Changes in Accounting Estimates and Errors* which states that an entity must correct all material prior period errors retrospectively in the first set of financial statements authorised for issue after their discovery by

- restating the comparative amounts for the prior period(s) presented in which the error occurred; or
- if the error occurred before the earliest prior period presented, restating the opening balances of assets, liabilities and equity for the earliest prior period presented (IAS 8, para 42 (a)).

As there are no comparative amounts presented in the case study, the correction of the error will be made to the opening figures.

To correct this error:

	€	€
DR Opening reserves	480,000	
CR Opening inventory		480,000

(This adjustment will have no effect on the closing SOFP as the goods were removed from inventory in January 2012. The transaction was completed at that date.)

Depreciation The original estimate for depreciation on computer equipment was too low. The remaining useful life has been revised to five years. In accordance with IAS 8, paragraph 32 this change will be classified as a change in accounting estimate rather than a change in accounting policy. Paragraph 32 states "As a result of the uncertainties inherent in business activities, many items in financial statements cannot be measured with precision but can only be estimated. Estimation involves judgments based on the latest available, reliable information. For example . . . (d) the useful lives of, or expected pattern of consumption of the future economic benefits embodied in, depreciable assets".

A change in accounting estimate is recognised prospectively, i.e. from now on. Paragraph 36 states "the effect of a change in accounting estimate . . . shall be recognised prospectively by including it in the profit or loss in . . . the period of the change and future periods, if the change affects both".

Applying these rules to the case study, the depreciation charge for computer equipment in 2012 should be based on a five-year remaining useful life as follows:

	€	€
DR Retained earnings	140,000	
CR PPE		140,000
700,000/5 years = €140,000		

Outstanding Issue 4

The basic principle of IAS 19 *Employee Benefits* is that an entity should recognise employment costs when service has been provided and *not* when payment is made.

Pension contributions made by an entity on behalf of employees, are considered to be a form of remuneration and should be treated in accordance with this accounting standard.

The retirement plan offered to the employees of Pickle Products Plc is a defined benefit plan. A defined benefit pension plan is one where an entity has promised (and therefore incurred an obligation) to pay benefits to employees when they retire based on pre-agreed terms (e.g. a pension may be based on the final year's salary of an employee's working life). The provisions of IAS 19 require entities to present (the present value of) all future post-retirement obligations as a liability at the end of each reporting period. The accounting treatment for the presentation of defined benefit pension plans is outlined in paragraphs 55–152 of the accounting standard.

In accordance with IAS 19, paragraph 57, accounting by an entity for defined benefit plans involves the following:

(a) Determining the deficit or surplus on the pension scheme. This involves:
   (i) Using an actuarial technique, the projected unit credit method, to make a reliable estimate of the ultimate cost to the entity of the benefit that employees have earned in return for the service in the current and prior periods (IAS 19, para 67–69)
   (ii) Discounting that benefit in order to determine the present value of the defined benefit obligation and the current service cost (IAS 19, para 67–69 and 83–86)
   (iii) Deducting the fair value of any plan assets (IAS 19, para 113–115) from the present value of the defined benefit obligation.

(b) Determining the amount of the net benefit liability (asset) as the amount of the deficit or surplus determined in (a) above adjusted for the effect of an asset ceiling (IAS 19, para 64).

(c) Determining the amount to be recognised in profit or loss:
   (i) Current service cost (IAS 19, para 70–74)
   (ii) Any past service costs and gain or loss on settlement (IAS 19, para 99–112)
   (iii) Net interest on the net defined liability (paragraphs 123–126). *(This figure is made up of the net interest on the defined liability, interest income on plan assets and interest on the effects of asset ceiling.*

(d) Determining the re-measurements of the net defined benefit liability (asset) to be recognised in other comprehensive income:
   (i) Actuarial gains and losses (IAS 19, para 128–129)
   (ii) Return on plan assets excluding amounts included in (c)(iii) above
   (iii) Any change in the effect in the asset ceiling.

In the case study the entries to profit or loss have been partly completed (for service cost, contributions and benefits paid). The remaining entries: the interest rate charge, the return on plan assets and the actuarial gains and losses, must be accrued. The table below summarises the movement in the liability over the period.

	Pension Asset	Pension Obligation	SOCI/Other Comprehensive Income	Summary Statement of Financial Position	
	€	€	€	€	
Balance 01/01/12	2,380,000	3,500,000		(1,120,000)	
Service cost		150,000	150,000	(150,000)	*already*
Contributions	70,000			70,000	*entered*
Benefits paid	(50,000)	(50,000)		0	*in f/s*
Sub Total	2,400,000	3,600,000		(1,200,000)	
Discount rate 5%		175,000	175,000	(175,000)	*To be*
Return on plan 3%	71,400		(71,400)	71,400	*entered*
Subtotal	2,471,400	3,775,000		(1,303,600)	*in f/s*
Actuarial valuation 31/12/12	2,200,000	3,690,000			
Actuarial (loss) or gain	(271,400)	85,000	(186,400)	(186,400)	*(balancing)*
Closing balance 31/12/12				(1,490,000)	

An adjustment is required to incorporate the outstanding entries:

	€	€
DR SOCI (€175,000 – €71,400)	103,600	
DR Other comprehensive income	186,400	
CR Retirement benefit obligation		290,000

The adjustments for outstanding issues 1–4 have now been completed. We can now summarise the adjustments (see **opposite**):

SUMMARY OF ADJUSTMENTS

		Retained Earnings for the Period	PPE	Provisions	Retirement Obligation
		€	€	€	€
Per draft statement		11,000,000	13,600,000	1,000,000	1,200,000
Outstanding Issue 1	Training	(28,000)	(28,000)		
	Samples	(70,000)	(70,000)		
	Borrowing costs	27,138	27,138		
Outstanding Issue 2	Provisions	(630,000)		630,000	
Outstanding Issue 3	Inventory	0			
	Depreciation	(140,000)	(140,000)		
Outstanding Issue 4	Retirement benefit	(290,000)			290,000
		9,869,138	13,389,138	1,630,000	1,490,000

Note: This is not required as part of the solution but is presented to show how the figures have changed in the statement of financial position of Pickle Products Plc which follows (see **over the page**).

Pickle Products Plc
REVISED STATEMENT OF FINANCIAL POSITION
as at 31 December 2012

	Original	Outstanding Issue 1	Outstanding Issue 2	Outstanding Issue 3	Outstanding Issue 4	Adjusted
	€000	**€000**	**€000**	**€000**	**€000**	**€000**
Non-current Assets						
PPE	13,600	(71)		(140)		13,389
Investment in DSM	2,000					2,000
Investment in Akzo	1,500					1,500
Financial assets – equity instruments	4,400					4,400
Intangible assets	1,500					1,500
	23,000					22,789
Current Assets						
Inventories	9,000					9,000
Trade receivables	4,000					4,000
Cash and cash equivalents	2,000					2,000
	15,000					15,000
Total Net Assets	**38,000**					**37,789**
Equity						
Ordinary share capital	2,000					2,000
Share premium	6,900					6,900
Reserves	11,000	(71)	(630)	(140)	(290)	9,869
	19,900					18,769

Non-current Liabilities				
Bank loans	2,000			2,000
Bonds	5,000			5,000
Provisions	1,000	630		1,630
Retirement benefit obligations	1,200		290	1,490
Deferred income	600			600
Deferred taxation	2,000			2,000
	11,800			12,720
Current Liabilities				
Payables	5,200			5,200
Bank loan	600			600
Current tax	500			500
	6,300			6,300
Total Equity and Liabilities	**38,000**			**37,789**

Requirement (b)

Under IFRS 10, paragraph 4, a parent "shall present consolidated financial statements" for all entities that it controls.

IFRS 10 details a situation where a parent does not have to present consolidated financial statements (IFRS 10, para 4(a)). This is where the parent itself is a subsidiary of another entity and as long as the highest entity in the structure presents consolidated financial statements then this will suffice. The scenario just described is not similar to that of Akzo, indeed, it describes a completely different set of circumstances.

The only legitimate reason for excluding a subsidiary is where control does not exist i.e. where the subsidiary is not really a subsidiary. This is alluded to by the finance director. However, unless there are very unusual extenuating circumstances it is difficult to classify an investment as a financial asset (or associate) where the parent owns 80% of the company. It is clear that there are no such extenuating circumstances in this instance. Pickle Products does have control of the subsidiary, failure to get a set of financial statements is not necessarily due to a lack of control.

This appears to be a case of poor management. No one at group level was keeping in contact with the subsidiary to see if they had any difficulties in preparing their financial statements. Perhaps the financial accountant in Akzo was sick over the period and nobody took over his/her role. (Alternatively, perhaps the financial accountant does not want to submit the financial statements as he/she cannot stand over them. This could be a signal of deeper problems in the subsidiary.)

The remedy put forward by the finance director is flawed and is contrary to the pronouncements of IFRS 10. At a practical level, some members of the accounting team (including the finance director) should visit the subsidiary with a view to helping them produce a set of financial statements. In addition, some consideration should be given to delaying the release of the figures but this would need to be handled with care as the market will suspect the worst. It may be possible to give an indication of profit but an exact number may be difficult to ascertain. There are no easy solutions to this as the impact on the financial reputation of the group will be a negative one.

Requirement (c)

Consolidated Statement of Financial Position

Step 1 – Set out the Group Structure

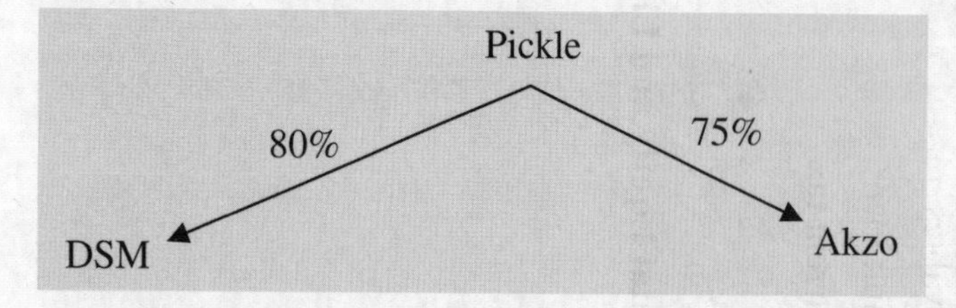

As illustrated above, both DSM and Akzo are subsidiaries of Pickle Products.

Step 2 – Deal with the 'additional information'

1. The Purchase of DSM There are two elements to the purchase of DSM

- the cost of the consideration; and
- the fair value of the net assets acquired.

The cost of the consideration is the original €2 million (as per the statement of financial position of Pickle Products). However, should the €300,000, which was paid in 2012 (10 years after the acquisition), be included as part of the consideration? The requirement to pay the €300,000 was unexpected and only became apparent in 2012. It could be that in previous years it was felt that the conditions under which the €300,000 would become due were unlikely to arise. Then (for whatever reason – a substantial increase in profitability, perhaps), in 2012 the conditions were unexpectedly satisfied and the amount was paid. The issue is: did the finance director correctly expense the amount or should the amount be added to the original fair value of the consideration (thereby increasing the value of goodwill by €300,000)?

IFRS 3, paragraph 45 would appear to indicate that any adjustments to fair values that arise more than 12 months after the acquisition date cannot be retrospectively incorporated. IFRS 3, paragraph 58 deals with this issue of contingent consideration and its subsequent measurement. Given the inherent uncertainty surrounding contingent consideration, it is possible that the fair value of the contingent consideration could change outside of the 12-month measurement period. In these instances any gain or loss should be recognised in the statement of comprehensive income (i.e. no change to the fair value of the consideration at acquisition and the resultant goodwill on acquisition, IFRS 3, paragraph 58b(i)). Thus, the original treatment by the finance director was correct so no further adjustment is required.

The payment of the dividend has been properly authorised and has been recorded. There is no adjustment required here. While the subsidiary may have been 'forced' to pay a dividend, this is the precise reason why these types of investments are undertaken. Pickle Products bought DSM to earn a return, most likely through the payment of dividends. There is a potential knock-on effect; if a subsidiary is constantly paying back cash to the parent then there may be little left for reinvestment hence the value of goodwill may be damaged. This matter is addressed later.

On acquisition, the assets acquired should be remeasured to fair value (IFRS 3, para 18). However, the standard only provides limited guidance on the practical issue of determining fair values. Instead, this is provided in some detail in IFRS 13 *Fair Value Measurement*. This standard is intended to present a comprehensive framework for the measurement of fair value across all the IFRSs and IASs. IFRS 13, paragraph 9, defines fair value as the "price that would be received to sell an asset or paid to transfer a liability in an orderly transaction between market participants on the measurement date".

The fair value of the machine: Where there is no active market, IFRS 13, paragraph B8 permits the use of depreciated replacement cost. Therefore a 20-year-old 'new' machine should be worth €600,000 (€3,000,000 – (€3,000,000 × 20 years/25 years)). The carrying value of the machine needs to be increased by €300,000.

Fair value of intangible assets: IFRS 3, paragraph 13, permits the recognition of previously unrecognised assets such as brands. Once the asset is identifiable and can be sold separately (even if there is no intention to sell separately) then it should be valued at fair value. The value of brands needs to be increased by €200,000 (the previous value was zero).

Fair value of financial assets: Where no quoted price on an active market exists, IFRS 13, paragraph 61 states that a valuation technique can be used to arrive at an estimate for fair value. An assessment will need to be made as to the reliability of the valuation. However, for the purposes of this case study, such an assessment is not possible and the inputs into the valuation techniques can be taken to be reliable.

Fair Value using PER	
Profits of Galactic	€1,600,000
PER of peers	10 times
Value of Galactic	€16,000,000
6% shareholding	960,000
Fair Value using Times Book Value	
Net assets of Galactic	€9,000,000
Times Net Assets of peers	2 times
Value of Galactic	€18,000,000
6% shareholding	€1,080,000
Average of fair values	€1,020,000*
Carrying value at acquisition	€700,000
Increase required to fair value	€320,000

* The use of an average of the fair values calculated is an assumption. Any reasonable calculation would be acceptable but would need to be justified.

Reorganisation provision: A provision of €100,000 has already been included. Under IAS 37, paragraph 14, there does not appear to be a present obligation at the date of acquisition to pay the €100,000. The cost (if any) of a reorganisation will depend on future decisions regarding the integration of DSM. In addition, IFRS 3, paragraph 11, specifically states "costs the acquirer expects but is not obliged to incur in the future….. are not liabilities at the acquisition date". Therefore, reduce the carrying value of the provision (a liability) by €100,000.

Onerous sales contracts: It appears that DSM has locked itself into losing €20,000. All else being equal, the existence of this contract should result in Pickle Products paying less to acquire DSM. At the moment DSM has not recognised the loss-making contract. Under IAS 37, paragraphs 66–68, this loss is unavoidable and a provision should be established for the full amount of the expected loss. Therefore, increase the carrying value of provisions (a liability) by €20,000.

Summary of Fair Value Adjustment (Adjustment 1a)

	€	€
DR (Increase) PPE	300,000	
DR (Increase) Intangible assets	200,000	
DR (Increase) Financial assets	320,000	

DR (Decrease) Provisions	100,000	
CR (Increase) Provisions		20,000
CR (Increase) Pre-acquisition retained earnings		900,000

Reversal of Fair Value Adjustments: Any fair value adjustment has a knock on effect on subsequent year's results. For example, if the value of machinery is increased then this will result in a higher depreciation charge in subsequent years. Each fair value adjustment needs to be reconsidered to determine if it has reversed. Keep in mind that the acquisition took place over 10 years ago.

When reversing a fair value adjustment, the correct treatment is to reverse the original entry, except, instead of entering the reversed amount into pre-acquisition retained earnings, it goes to post-acquisition retained earnings. For example, the increase in the value of machinery will increase the value of the company at acquisition (pre-acquisition retained earnings) but the additional depreciation will reduce profits after the acquisition (post-acquisition retained earnings).

Reversal of PPE adjustment (machinery): The increase in the value of machinery would have been expensed (as depreciation) over the five years immediately following the acquisition as the machine was 20 years into an expected 25-year useful life. Therefore, the full amount is reversed as the acquisition was 10 years ago. Therefore, reduce the value of PPE by €300,000.

Reversal of Brand Valuation: The information clearly states that the brand still exists and we assume (as we are not told otherwise) that there has been no diminution in value. Therefore, the value of the brand at acquisition is still valid. Consequently, there is no reversal necessary of the brand value.

Reversal of Financial Asset Valuation: The shares in Galactic were sold in 2008, thus any increase in value has reversed itself as the shares no longer belong to DSM. Therefore the value of financial assets needs to be reduced by €320,000.

Reversal of Provision: The provision was not recognised in the group financial statements but was included in the accounts of DSM. When the obligation was subsequently incurred, the impact would be to reduce the profits of the group (as the group had not provided for the amount on acquisition). Therefore, increase the value of provisions back to original amount by €100,000.

Reversal of Onerous Contract: The onerous contract was not recognised in the financial statements of DSM but was included in the group financial statements. In the year after acquisition, DSM fulfilled its side of the contract; therefore this provision is no longer needed in the group financial statements (it was never provided for in the individual financial statements of DSM). Therefore, provisions need to be reduced by €20,000.

SUMMARY of REVERSAL OF FAIR VALUE ADJUSTMENT (ADJUSTMENT 1B)

	€	€
DR (Decrease) Provisions	20,000	
DR (Decrease) Post-acquisition retained earnings	700,000	

CR (Decrease) PPE	300,000
CR (Decrease) Financial Assets	320,000
CR (Increase) Provisions	100,000

2. Purchase of Investment in Akzo The instructions in the case study indicate that the investment is to be recorded at cost, i.e. €1,500,000. This is not the correct treatment but the requirement clearly states to follow the wishes of the finance director – see the solution to requirement (b). The investment is currently recorded in the financial statements of Pickle Products at €1,500,000; therefore no adjustment is required.

3. Dividend from DSM The dividends have been recorded by DSM but not by Pickle Products. It is clear that the dividend was authorised pre year-end thus this transaction is not governed by IAS 10 *Events after the Reporting Period*. As the dividend has been voted on, there is now a constructive obligation on DSM to pay the dividend. Consequently, it is not unreasonable for Pickle Products to account for the dividend (there is no reason to suggest that DSM will not be in a position to pay the dividend).

As DSM was correct to account for the dividend, Pickle Products should record its portion of the dividend. The appropriate adjustment (in Pickle Products) is for €120,000, i.e. 80% of €150,000 (adjustment 3a):

	€	€
DR (Increase): Dividends receivable	120,000	
CR (Increase) Retained earnings (Pickle)		120,000
('Other income' in the statement of comprehensive income)		

However, in the statement of financial position, there is an asset in Pickle Products (€120,000) and a liability in DSM (80% of €150,000) that is an intragroup transaction; no liability and associated asset exists outside the group. To eliminate the intragroup element of the dividends (adjustment 3b):

	€	€
DR (Decrease): Dividends payable	120,000	
CR (Decrease): Dividends receivable		120,000

4. Review of DSM: Goodwill Impairment Under IAS 36, paragraph 10, an annual impairment review of goodwill should be carried out. This has been done in the case of DSM and the result was to write 30% off the value of goodwill. Any reduction in the value of goodwill should be recognised immediately in the consolidated statement of comprehensive income (IAS 36, para 60). However, the amount of goodwill has not yet been ascertained (see following section). Once known, the appropriate adjustment is (adjustment 4):

DR (Decrease) Post-acquisition retained earnings	30% of value of Goodwill
CR (Decrease) Goodwill	30% of value of Goodwill

Step 3 – Prepare the Consolidation Table At this stage, the adjustments from the previous step are accumulated together and the goodwill, non-controlling interests and retained earnings figures are calculated. These figures attract most of the marks in an examination scenario. At this point, the hard work has already been done in step 2 and it is only a matter of following a process; this is why an approach similar to that set out in the following consolidation table is beneficial.

CONSOLIDATION TABLE

	Goodwill €000	Non-controlling Interests €000	Retained earnings €000
Investment in DSM (from statement of financial position)	2,000		
Ordinary share capital – DSM (€200,000)	160	40	
Pre-acquisition retained earnings DSM (€500,000)	400	100	
Post-acquisition retained earnings DSM (€1,600,000)*		320	1,280
Retained earnings – Pickle Products			9,869
Fair Value adjustment (adjustment 1a, €900,000 split 80:20)	720	180	
Fair Value adjustment reversal (Adj 1b, €700,000 split 80:20)		(140)	(560)
Dividends 'in transit' (Adjustment 3a)			120
Total	720	500	10,709
Goodwill write off (Adj 4, 30% of goodwill)	(216)		(216)
Final Total	504	500	10,493

* Total retained earnings of DSM per the statement of financial position are €2,100,000. We know that €500,000 of these profits existed on the date of acquisition (pre-acquisition) thus, by deduction, €1,600,000 of profits have been generated while DSM has been part of the group (post-acquisition).

Step 4 – Complete the Statement of Financial Position This is an information management exercise. It is a matter of taking the revised statement of financial position of Pickle Products (answer to requirement (a)), the statement of financial position of DSM along with the adjustments set out in step 2 and the final figures from the 'Consolidation Table' and stitching them together into a consolidated statement of financial position.

Pickle Products Group
CONSOLIDATED STATEMENT OF FINANCIAL POSITION
as at 31/12/12

	Pickle	DSM	Adj 1a	Adj 1b	Adj 3a	Adj 3b	Adj 4	Total
	€000	**€000**	**€000**	**€000**	**€000**	**€000**	**€000**	**€000**
Non-current Assets								
PPE	13,389	3,600	300	(300)				16,989
Goodwill (from consolidation table)	2,000							504
Investment in Akzo at cost	1,500							1,500
Financial assets – equity instruments	4,400		320	(320)				4,400
Intangible assets	1,500		200					1,700
	22,789	3,600						25,093
Current Assets								
Inventories	9,000	600						9,600
Dividend Receivable					120	(120)		0
Trade receivables	4,000	300						4,300
Cash and Cash equivalents	2,000	100						2,100
	15,000	1,000						16,000
Total Net Assets	**37,789**	**4,600**						**41,093**
Equity								
Ordinary share capital	2,000	200						2,000
Share premium	6,900							6,900
Retained earnings (from consolidation table)	9,869	2,100						10,493
	18,769	2,300						19,393
Non-controlling interests (from consolidation table)								500
								19,893

Non-current Liabilities						
Bank loans	2,000	400				2,400
Bonds	5,000	830				5,830
Provisions	1,630	100				1,730
Retirement benefit obligations	1,490	300				1,790
Deferred income	600					600
Deferred taxation	2,000					2,000
	12,720	1,630				14,350
Current Liabilities						
Payables	5,200	450				5,650
Onerous contract provision			20	(20)		0
Acquisition provision			(100)	100		0
Dividend payable		150			(120)	30
Bank loan	600	50				650
Current tax	500	20				520
	6,300	670				6,850
Total Equity and Liabilities	37,789	4,600				41,093

Notes on the Consolidated Statement of Financial Position

1. A number of items are shown separately that could be combined under a single line item; i.e. goodwill and intangible assets; investments in Akzo and financial assets.
2. Onerous contract provision and restructuring provision have zero balances and do not need to be identified separately – this was done to show how the transactions were recorded.
3. The investment in DSM (€2,000,000) was replaced with goodwill as calculated.

Tutorial Note on Reversal of Fair Value Adjustments (Not part of the solution – for explanatory purposes only) This often presents a difficulty for students. However, all that is happening is that profits are being moved around (legitimately) from post- to pre-acquisition and, sometimes, vice-versa. The logic of the adjustment will be explained in the case of the machinery adjustment and the Galactic share valuation adjustment.

1. Machinery Adjustment: Consider the fair value adjustment on machinery. At the date of acquisition it was determined that the machine was worth €300,000 more than its carrying value. The knock-on effect of this adjustment is the increased depreciation charge on

post-acquisition profits. Every year, for the following five years (the remaining life of the machine), the profits of the subsidiary will be €60,000 p.a. less than reported in its individual financial statements.

At the end of five years, post-acquisition profits will have been reduced by a cumulative €300,000. In addition, while the value of the machine was originally increased by €300,000, the effect of the increased depreciation charge post-acquisition will be to reduce the carrying value by €300,000 (or €60,000 p.a. for 5 years). As the acquisition was 10 years ago, to give effect to the reversal of the fair value adjustment, the following should be done:

	€	€
DR (Reduce) Post-acquisition retained earnings	300,000	
CR (Reduce) PPE		300,000

2. Galactic Share Valuation Adjustment: The shares in Galactic had a carrying value of €700,000 and were revalued to €1,020,000 on acquisition. The valuation on acquisition more accurately reflects the shares' fair value. Also note that DSM did not reflect this increase in valuation in its own financial statements.

Then in 2008 the shares were sold (let's assume two scenarios: the shares were sold for €900,000 and the shares were sold for €1,200,000).

This is how DSM would have reported the sale of the shares:

	Scenario 1	Scenario 2
	€	€
Proceeds	900,000	1,200,000
Carrying value	700,000	700,000
Gain/(loss)	200,000	500,000

However, from a group perspective the calculation of the gain/loss is based on the fair value of the Galactic shares at the date of acquisition (this more accurately measures the increase/decrease in the value of the shares while they were in the possession of the group). The gain/loss on the shares should have been reported from a group perspective as follows:

	Scenario 1	Scenario 2
	€	€
Proceeds	900,000	1,200,000
Carrying value	1,020,000	1,020,000
Gain/(loss)	(120,000)	180,000

The difference between how DSM accounts for the transaction and how the transaction should be accounted for within the group is as follows:

	Scenario 1	Scenario 2
	€	€
Gain/(loss) per DSM	200,000	500,000
Gain/(loss) for group	(120,000)	180,000
Difference	(320,000)	(320,000)

In both cases, because DSM never recorded the fair value of the shares in Galactic, the profits since acquisition of DSM are overstated by €320,000, i.e. the amount of the original fair value adjustment.

Thus, to reverse the fair value adjustment:

	€	€
DR (reduce) Post-acquisition retained earnings	320,000	
CR (reduce) Financial assets		320,000

Requirement (d)

Discussion

The statement of financial position, is a statement prepared as part of the financial statements of a business. It is prepared at least once a year. The objective of the statement of financial position (balance sheet) is to show the net worth of a business.

There are many definitions of what a balance sheet is. Explanations vary greatly depending on your reading material.[2] The common theme that runs through all of these definitions is that the purpose of a statement of financial position is to exhibit the *overall value of a business*. However, this is not always the case (and in the case study this is what the shareholder is querying).

The principal difference between the quoted price of a business and the value of the financial statements is all about perspective. The price of a quoted share is a 'forward-looking' measure. In financial literature the value of a share is based on the present value of all future income streams that may be earned from the share. In other words, the current value is based on future expectations.

On the other hand, the value of a business based on a set of financial statements, is backward looking. Traditionally, financial statements were prepared on a historical cost basis. The statement of financial position was simply a sum of the net assets of a business, based on what was *paid for them*, rather than what they were worth at any point in time or the income they might generate in the future. As an accounting concept, historical cost has many benefits. Records are based on objectively verifiable amounts (actual cost of assets etc.), it is simple and cheap to prepare historical financial statements and the concept of profit is well understood. However, historical cost accounting does not show the value of the enterprise and, as a result, it provides a poor basis for assessing future performance.

The IASB has recognised, for some time, that there are serious issues with historical cost accounting. In recent years, the IASB have been actively involved in the '*Fair Value*

[2] These definitions range from '*A balance sheet is a statement that shows the value of a company's assets and its debts*' (Definition of balance sheet noun from the Cambridge Advanced Learner's Dictionary) TO 'A condensed statement that shows the financial position of an entity on a specified date' (businessdictionary.com).

Measurement' project. (This project is a joint effort by the IASB and the USA's Financial Accounting Standards Board (FASB)). This project aims to move financial statements from a 'historical cost' basis towards a 'fair value' basis. Their work is evident in many of the accounting standards that have been revised over the past five years.[3]

However, although good progress has been made, there is a lot more work to do. International Financial Statements are currently in a state of flux. They are not fully cost based nor are they completely based on fair values. They are a *mixture* of both. This mixture can be confusing and misleading and, as a platform for analytical comparison, they are of limited use.

A further problem with the relevance of financial statements is the issue of internally generated intangibles. Internally generated intangible assets include own brands, logos, trademarks etc. The standard that governs this area is IAS 38 *Intangible Assets*. This standard states that internally generated intangible assets cannot be recognised as assets. The justification for this is that the measurement of own intangibles is subjective and open to abuse and, inclusion as an asset would do little to help comparative analysis. In reality, an entity's brand, logo or trademark is an asset that is vital to the earning power of the business. In market terms, the quoted price of shares will incorporate a value for these assets, even though the statement of financial position does not.

Conclusion

A statement of financial position does not necessarily 'value' a company, where assets and liabilities are measured at 'historical cost' and some intangible assets (e.g. brands, quality of management, market leadership) are not included. The quoted share price may give a better indication of the shareholders' true value. However, there are many other valuation techniques available to value shares. These are not mentioned in the case but do give an equally valid measure of what the company is worth.

[3] Many of the accounting standards now require the inclusion in the balance sheet of a fair value measurement (IFRS 3, IFRS 9, IFRS 13, IAS 19, IAS 40, IAS 39, etc.).

Case 6

Howard Retail Group

This case study is based on a retail business, called the Howard Retail Group. The accounting standards IAS 1, IAS 12, IAS 16, IAS 17, IAS 18, IAS 23, IAS 28, IAS 32, IAS 37, IAS 38, IAS 40, IFRS 7, IFRS 9 and IFRS 13 are addressed in this case.

Background – The Howard Retail Group

The Howard Retail Group is a long-established retail business. The business dates back to 1960, when two business men, Arthur McSwinney and James Delaney, opened a department store on the main shopping area of Dublin city. The company grew steadily over the intervening years and is now one of the main players in the Irish retail industry. The Group has its head office and flagship store in Dublin city centre and also owns a number of department stores around the country. The group has recently expanded into the UK, opening its first store in Hammersmith, London in 2012.

The stores offer a selection of merchandise from fashion to furniture, footwear, sportswear, kitchenware, electrical goods, children's wear and corporate clothing.

In addition to its trading stores, the group also owns a substantial property portfolio. The company is headquartered in Dublin, and employs 5,014 people. It is privately owned. Its financial year-end is 31 December.

The Group is structured as follows (all 100% owned apart from Cara Fashions):

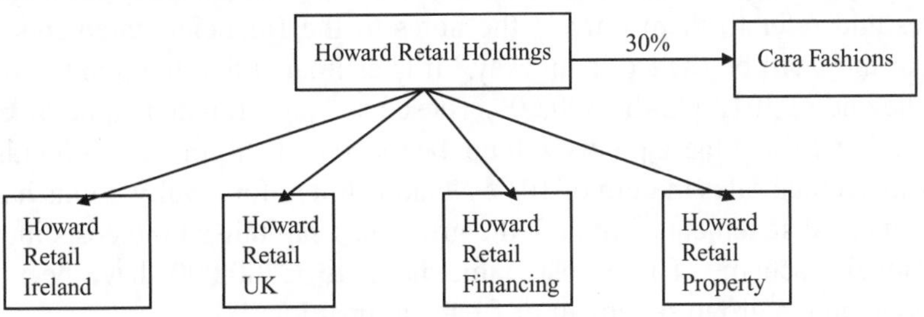

Howard Retail Ireland Ltd runs the Irish operations of the group. Howard Retail UK Ltd operates the UK business. Howard Retail Financing Ltd arranges the financing for the other units in the group. Howard Retail Property Ltd holds the properties of the group. Howard Retail Holdings Ltd is parent of the group and holds the investments in the subsidiaries and associate along with some smaller trade investments.

It is now the middle of Janaury 2013. You are an auditor with Pipe, Pope & Co, Auditors and you have been assigned to the audit team of the Howard Group. You have just come from a planning meeting with the audit manager. Howard Retail is a new client of Pipe, Pope & Co. You have been given a copy of the 2012 draft consolidated financial statements. In addition, you have been given a list of outstanding issues that need your consideration before the financial statements can be finalised. Howard Retail prepares IFRS compliant financial statements each year.

Outstanding Issues

Outstanding Issue 1 – Revenue

The note to the group's financial statements regarding the accounting policy for the recognition of revenue states "Revenue comprises sales of goods to customers outside the Group less an appropriate deduction for actual and expected returns and discounts and is stated net of value added tax and other sales taxes. Revenue is recognised when the significant risks and rewards of ownership have been transferred to the buyer. Sales of furniture and online sales are recorded on delivery to the customer."

Loyalty Schemes In an effort to boost market share, Howard Retail introduced its own loyalty card in 2012. Customers who sign for a loyalty card receive points every time they shop in a Howard store. The more a customer buys the quicker the points add up. Once a customer has earned a certain level of points the points are converted into Reward Vouchers which can be spent on anything in Howard's stores. Reward Vouchers are valid for 15 months from date of issue.

Your audit manager has asked you to pay particular attention to this issue for two reasons: First, it is a new scheme *and* secondly, the senior directors of Howard Retail have had a series of heated discussions about the accounting treatment of these schemes. The finance director has proposed that a liability be made for the full value of the outstanding points. The sales director, however, would like to ignore any such adjustment. His response to the liability proposal is always "We do not owe cash to anybody. We should treat the loyalty points as contingencies and refer to them only in the notes to the financial statements. There is no guarantee that they will be cashed in anyway." It is estimated that the number of points outstanding at the end of 2012 will be 800,000. These have an estimated value of €6.4 million. It is estimated that 20% of these points will not be redeemed within the 15-month period. The group earns an average sales margin of 10%. No adjustment for loyalty points has been made in the draft financial statements although the group has capitalised the costs incurred in setting up the loyalty scheme. These costs, amounting to €700,000, have been included as intangible assets in the group statement of financial position.

Sales Promotions In order to boost sales, Howard ran a number of special offers in 2012. One such offer was on a particular line of furniture. The offer ran for the entire 12 month period. The details of the scheme were that, for every item purchased in excess of €2,000, customers would receive 20% off the recommended retail price. Sales from this line of furniture had a gross retail value of €6 million (and each sale was in excess of €2,000). The accountant included these sales in revenue at their original selling price and the discount has been included as a promotional cost under administration expenses.

Concession Agreements ('store-in-store' arrangements) The Howard Group operates a number of concession agreements with independent retailers (licensees). These agreements offer floor space to retailers within the Howard stores. These concession agreements generally follow a standard format. Howard allocates a section of a store to the retailer, Howard fits out the floor space according to the retailer's specifications and Howard's design standards. Each licensee is required to pay a lump sum upon signing (to cover set-up costs), followed by a monthly commission of 25% of sales. When the concession period ends, the licensee has the right to take possession of the fixtures and fittings in their section of the store.

In 2012 Howard signed a concessionary agreement with *Soiree Perfumes*. Soiree Perfumes paid a total of €900,000 to Howard, all of which has been credited to group revenue. €520,000 of this payment was to cover set-up costs. Howard has spent an equal amount fitting out the stores and has debited the cost to Property, Plant and Equipment. The remaining receipts were monthly commissions. No depreciation has been charged on store renovations.

In a separate agreement, a customer has taken legal action against the licensee *and* the Howard group for damages caused when a shelving unit collapsed. Faulty workmanship was deemed to be the cause of the accident. Howard has accepted full responsibility for the damage. Legal costs have been estimated at €620,000.

One of the conditions of Howard's concession agreements is that each licensee is required to give an indemnity to Howard against all actions, costs, proceedings, losses, damage or injury arising from their products. Licensees are required to indemnify 70% of all costs. On this basis Howard has made a provision in the financial statements for legal costs as follows:

	€
Legal costs – claim	620,000
Reimbursed from licensee	434,000
	186,000

In the audit file there is a copy of an email sent by the licensee to Howard. The email states that they (the licensee) are 'vehemently opposed' to contributing anything to the cost of this dispute. They claim that, as Howard was responsible for the store fit out, the faulty workmanship is their responsibility alone and the licensee should not have to pay for the damage.

Maintenance Contracts The Howard Group sells electronic equipment in all of its stores. When a customer purchases equipment they are offered a maintenance service as part of the sale. The maintenance service is optional. If purchased, the maintenance agreement will last for two years only. The average price of an item of equipment with a maintenance package is €2,000.

Howard also provides maintenance services and equipment separately. If sold separately, the average price of a maintenance contract is €175 per annum and the cost of the equipment is €1,750; 2,400 sale/maintenance packages were sold across the stores in 2012 and the total value of the contracts is included in revenue.

Outstanding Issue 2 – Taxation

The current taxation charge for the period, included in the draft financial statements, is €145 million.

The deferred taxation liability included in the draft financial statements represents the deferred tax position at the beginning of 2012 (***due entirely to an excess of capital allowances over book depreciation***). No adjustments have been made for the current period.

Additional differences between the tax base and the accounting base have now been identified as follows:

	€000
Permanent differences	3,000
Temporary differences including:	
Taxable timing differences	25,000
Deductible timing differences	(10,000)
Taxable other differences (equity)	5,000

The rate of corporation tax for 2012 is 12.5%. The rate in 2011 was 11%. All of differences in existence at the beginning of 2012 still exist at the end of 2012.

Outstanding Issue 3 – Property Portfolio

The Howard Group holds an extensive property portfolio as follows:

Properties	Number	Standard	Measurement
Owner occupied	18	IAS 16	Cost (50 years)
Held under lease arrangements and occupied by the lessee	16	IAS 17	Cost (50 years)
Investment properties	8	IAS 40	Fair value

Owner occupied During 2012 Howard completed six store extensions, 12 refurbishments and acquired three new trading stores. (This excludes any effects from Soiree Perfumes in outstanding issue 1.) The total capital expenditure for the year, excluding borrowing costs, was €15.6 million. This was incurred as follows: €5 million on 1 January 2012, €8.4 million on 1 July 2012 and the balance on 1 November 2012.

All of this expenditure is included in Property, Plant and Equipment in the draft financial statements. The expenditure was financed partly from specific borrowings of €5 million drawn down on 1 January 2012 and partly from a pool of general construction finance available to the group.

Borrowing costs are currently expensed in the statement of comprehensive income.

Details of Howard's funding arrangements are as follows:

Loan	Cost	Period	Repayments Commence
Specific:			
€5m	10%	1 year	2014
General pool of finance:			
€60m	9%	10 years	2016
€40m	7.5%	20 years	2017

Investment Properties The group manages a very active investment property portfolio. One of these properties, Property Acorn, was acquired in January 2004 and had been leased to a third party for number of years.

On 1 March 2012, a decision was made to change the use of this property. In order to accommodate the group's growing workforce, additional office space was required. The Acorn property would provide this additional space.

The existing tenants were given one month's notice at the beginning of March 2012. They vacated the premises on 1 April 2012. The property was then renovated and Howard staff eventually moved in on 1 July 2012.

The re-classification of this property in the financial statements from investment to owner occupied was not made during the financial year. The property is currently included in the draft financial statements, as an investment property, at its fair value, on 1 January 2012, of €3 million. You have now established that the property was worth €2.9 million on 1 March 2012, €2.82 million on 1 April 2012 and €2.4 million on 1 July 2012.

The Acorn property has 40 years' remaining useful life.

Held under lease arrangements and occupied by the lessee Howard trades in a number of stores that are leased rather than owned. Some of these leases are classified as finance leases while others are operating leases. Finance Leases are capitalised and operating leases are expensed in accordance with IAS 17 *Leases*. The total operating lease charges included in the Statement of Comprehensive Income in 2012 is €8 million.

One of the properties held under a non-cancellable operating lease is a property in Cork City, Property ASH. The total lease period for Property ASH is 25 years of which five have already expired. In January 2012, a decision was made to vacate the Ash premises and relocate to larger premises. On that same date, a new tenant for the Ash property was secured who has agreed to rent the Ash premises for the remaining lease term.

As a result of this arrangement Howard is now paying rent of €800,000 per annum to the owner of Ash property and receiving €805,000 per annum for the sublet. Both payments are made in advance each year and the 2012 charges are included in the operating profit for the period.

James Delaney has inquired if the Ash property, although not legally owned by the Howard Group, could now be presented in the financial statements as an investment property as it is being leased out by the Group. This would bring the accounting treatment of Ash in line with the group's other investment properties.

The implicit rate of interest in the lease agreement is 10%.

Investment Property valuations at 31 December 2012 Investment properties outstanding at 31 December 2012 (excluding Acorn and Ash) are currently stated at their 2011 valuations. You have now established that the fair value of these properties at 31 December 2012 is €98 million and Ash is valued at €5.5 million. The year-end valuations have not yet been incorporated into the financial statements. In addition, a review of the Property Times suggests that, by the time the financial statements are ready to be signed, property prices will have fallen in value by a further 10%.

Outstanding Issue 4 – Financing

On 30 September 2012, €100 million of Howard Retail's borrowings came due. Given the stressed nature of the Irish capital markets, the group found it difficult to obtain financing at a competitive rate. However, a French bank was prepared to lend €100 million with no interest payment attached (i.e. 0%) but Howard Retail would have to repay €133.1 million on 30 September 2015.

In the draft financial statements, the receipt of this loan has been recorded as follows:

	€000	€000
DR Bank	100,000	
CR Borrowings (non-current liabilities)		100,000

No further entries in respect of this loan have been made.

Outstanding Issue 5 – Trade Investments

Apart from the investments in its subsidiaries, Howard Retail Holdings has a number of smaller investments. In each case the holding represents less than 1% of the issued share capital of the companies. The group classifies these investments as 'measured at fair value' and has elected to present changes in fair value through other comprehensive income.

The investments are as follows:

Name	Public/Private	Number of Shares	Price on 31/12/11 €	Value on 31/12/11 €
Carrefour SA	Public	10,000	100	1,000,000
Inditex SA	Public	1,000,000	12	12,000,000
Wed Ltd	Private	500,000		1,000,000
Total Value on 31/12/11				14,000,000

On 31 December 2012 the shares in Carrefour were quoted at €95 and the shares in Inditex were quoted at €11.50.

The issued share capital of Wed Ltd is 50,000,000 shares. There is no market value for the shares as the company's shares are not traded. However, similar companies tend to trade at 11 times earnings or three times their net asset value. A recent set of financial statements of Wed revealed the following (Wed Ltd's year end is 30 November 2012):

	€000
Operating profit	20,000
Interest	2,000
Profit before tax	18,000
Tax	2,000
Profit after tax	16,000
Net Assets	55,000

No entries have been made in the draft consolidated financial statements to reflect the change in value of these investments.

Outstanding Issue 6 – Investments in Associates

The group has a 30% shareholding in Cara Fashions, a clothing distribution company. This was purchased many years ago. The amount included in the draft financial statements was €187 million which was the carrying value on 31 December 2011 (i.e. no transaction has been recorded for year end 31 December 2012). At the time the draft accounts were prepared the financial statements of Cara Fashions were unavailable. These have since become available – there is an extract below.

Cara Fashions has a 31 October 2012 year end. However, the finance director of Cara Fashions prepared a set of financial statements for the year to 31 December 2012 to ensure that Howard Retail comply with IAS 28 *Investments in Associates and Joint Ventures*. However, these financial statements will not be audited as it is not Cara Fashions' year end. Cara Fashions has not paid a dividend in the past two years.

You have been provided with the following information:

	€m
Original cost of investment (30% shareholding)	100
Ordinary share capital of Cara Fashions on acquisition date	40
Retained earnings of Cara Fashions on acquisition date	200

Extracts from Financial Statements

	31 Oct 2011 audited	31 Dec 2011 unaudited	31 Oct 2012 audited	31 Dec 2012 unaudited
	€m	€m	€m	€m
Ordinary share capital	40	40	40	40
Retained earnings	450	490	580	550

The directors of Howard Retail are concerned at the use of unaudited financial information in their financial statements and would like your view on using the Cara Fashions year end information (i.e. 31 October 2012) as the basis for their consolidated financial statements.

In addition, Pipe, Pope & Co also acts as auditor to Cara Fashions. In fact, the audit manager is located just down the corridor.

Outstanding Issue 7 – Cash and Cash Equivalents

The group has considerable cash (and cash equivalent) balances. It has become apparent that €1 billion of this cash arrived into one of the group's bank accounts on 27 December 2012 and left the same bank account on 4 January 2013.

It has transpired that the amount relates to a transaction with South Quarter Development Co Limited. South Quarter Development Company Ltd is involved in developing a new shopping centre in Dublin. Howard Retail has agreed to be the anchor tenant of the shopping centre. James Delany (a director and major shareholder of Howard Retail) is a director of South Quarter Development Co Ltd but only holds a minor number of shares in the company (less than 0.1%).

On the 31 March 2012, Howard Retail gave a loan of €1,000 million to South Quarter Development Co Limited with a repayment date of 27 December 2012. There was an interest rate of 10% attached to the loan and it was secured on the partially finished property. The loan and interest were paid on time. This was recorded in the financial statements.

A new loan arrangement was entered into on 4 January 2013 and on similar terms.

You are concerned that any new shopping centre developments will find it difficult to obtain tenants. You have read in the media that work on the site has slowed considerably.

Requirements

(**Note:** Unless you are specifically required to consider deferred taxation, you can assume that it is not applicable.)

(a) Summarise the adjustments that are required to be made to the group financial statements of Howard Retail Group Ltd for the year ended 31 December 2012.
This incorporates outstanding issues 1–6 (not issue 7).
(Your answer should include detailed workings and a justification for each adjustment.)
(60 marks)

(b) Summarise the impact the adjustments will have on the group total comprehensive income for the year ended 31 December 2012.
(10 marks)

(c) Prepare a brief memo dealing with the following issues:
(i) The use of audited and unaudited financial statement data for associates in the financial statements of Howard Retail **(issue 6)**
(ii) The ethical implications for Pipe, Pope & Co of using the knowledge gained on the audit of Cara Fashions in their valuation of investments in associates in Howard Retail **(issue 6)**
(iii) How the cash/loan transaction with South Quarter Development Company should be recorded **(issue 7)**.
(30 marks)

Howard Retail Group
DRAFT CONSOLIDATED STATEMENT OF COMPREHENSIVE INCOME
for the Year Ended 31 December 2012

	€m
Revenue	8,040
Cost of sales	(5,870)

Gross profit	2,170
Administration	(987)
Other operating income	27
Profit from operations	1,210
Finance income	250
Finance costs	(148)
Share of post-tax profit/loss from associate	0
Profit before tax	1,312
Taxation charge (current tax)	(145)
Profit for the financial year	1,167
Other comprehensive income	
Actuarial losses on defined benefit pension schemes	(145)
Foreign exchange translation gains	122
Cashflow hedges: Fair value movement (increase)	4
Total other comprehensive income/expense for the period (net of tax)	(19)
Total Comprehensive Income for the Period	**1,148**

Howard Retail Group

DRAFT CONSOLIDATED STATEMENT OF CHANGES IN EQUITY

for the Year Ended 31 December 2012

	Called Up Share Capital €m	**Share Premium €m**	**Retained Earnings €m**	**Other Reserves €m**	**Total €m**
At 1 January 2012	80	310	1,173	889	2,452
Issue of shares	20	60			80
Profit for the period			1,167		1,167
Other comprehensive income:					
Actuarial losses on defined benefit pension schemes				(145)	(145)
Foreign exchange translation gains				122	122
Cash flow hedges: Fair value movement				4	4
At 31 December 2012	**100**	**370**	**2,340**	**870**	**3,680**

Howard Retail Group
DRAFT CONSOLIDATED STATEMENT OF FINANCIAL POSITION
As at 31 December 2012

	€m
Non-current Assets	
Goodwill	344
Property, plant and equipment	1,431
Intangible assets	101
Investments in associates	187
Investment properties	112
Financial assets	14
	2,189
Current Assets	
Inventories	375
Trade and other receivables	213
Derivative financial instruments	200
Cash and cash equivalents	1,340
	2,028
Total Assets	**4,317**
Current Liabilities	
Trade and other payables	153
Taxes payable	20
Provisions	18
Obligations under finance leases	125
Other liabilities	0
Borrowings	8
	323.5
Non-current Liabilities	
Borrowings	258
Retirement Benefit Obligations	45
Deferred tax liability	11
	314
Equity	
Share capital	100
Share premium	370
Other reserves	870
Retained earnings	2,340
	3,680
Total Equity and Liabilities	**4,317**

Guidance Notes – Howard Retail Group

Exam Technique

Read the case carefully then read the requirements.

This case study is based on the financial statements of a retail business. The approach to this case study is different to other case studies in the book as there is no significant consolidation element to it. Instead, the case study consists of a series of separate issues. You should consider each issue in turn. For each issue, you should explain the accounting implications using the appropriate IAS/IFRS references to back up your statements. You should then set out any adjustments that are required.

When you have dealt with the first six issues you are then required to set out the impact on the Statement of Comprehensive Income for the year. You are not required to re-draft the financial statements.

The final requirement of the case study is discursive. This section incorporates some of the wider elements of financial reporting. Each section requires only a brief answer. This requirement can be completed in a short time particularly if you can get to the core issues quickly.

The normal time management guidance continues to apply.

Answering the Case Study

Requirement (a) – Guidance

Issue 1 examines IAS 18 *Revenue* and to a lesser degree IAS 37 *Provisions, Contingent Liabilities and Contingent Assets* and IAS 38 *Intangible Assets.*

There are two overriding principles in IAS 18 – *when* to recognise revenue and *how* to measure revenue. This issue examines both principles.

Issue 1 is made up of four separate transactions.

Transaction (1) The Howard group introduced a loyalty scheme in 2012. At 31 December 2012 loyalty points to the value of €6.4 million were outstanding. These loyalty points represent advances on future revenue, i.e. customers have made a contribution in 2012 towards future purchases. What you must decide is: first, should these points be included in current revenue or should they be deferred to a future period; secondly, if you decide to defer this revenue, where will you present it in the financial statements; and, finally, should you defer the full value of the points or only the 80% that are likely to be redeemed?

To answer this section you should consider the following:

- IAS 18, paragraph14, outlines the conditions that need to be satisfied before revenue can be recognised, i.e. if certain conditions are not satisfied, we cannot recognise revenue.
- IFRIC 13 *Customer Loyalty Programmes* outlines the appropriate accounting treatment for loyalty schemes.

Included in 'intangible assets' are the costs of setting up the loyalty scheme, €700,000. You must decide if it is acceptable to capitalise these costs. IAS 38 *Intangible Assets* outlines the appropriate treatment for intangible assets that are externally acquired and those that are internally generated. You must decide which the expenditure is. You must also decide the most appropriate accounting treatment for this intangible. Accounting guidance for externally acquired intangibles is outlined in IAS 38, paragraphs 24–47 and internally generated intangibles at IAS 38, paragraphs 51–67.

Transaction (2) Howard ran a special offer on the sale of furniture during the year. Items of furniture sold above a certain price attracted a generous discount. The sales have been recorded at gross value and the discount included as a promotional expense. You need to decide if this is an acceptable treatment or is Howard overstating revenue? IAS 18, paragraphs 9–12 covers the measurement of revenue. You should find your answer here.

Transaction (3) deals with 'store-in-store' (concession) arrangements which are a common feature in the retail industry. There are no specific accounting rules in force for these types of arrangement. General accounting principles apply.

The first part of the transaction deals with a concession arrangement with a business called *Soiree Perfumes*. Howard has received a total of €900,000 from Soiree Perfumes all of which is included in revenue. €520,000 of this total amount is to reimburse Howard's 'fit-out' costs and the remainder is commission. You must decide how to present this information. Is it appropriate to include all €900,000 in revenue? The €520,000 is a reimbursement of capital costs. The commission fees should be accounted for in accordance with IAS 18, Illustrative Examples, paragraphs 10–19.

The second part of this transaction requirs you to consider whether a provision, already included in the financial statements, is appropriate. The provision is made up of impending legal costs and is reduced by a (possible) re-imbursement from the licensee. Is this correct? IAS 37 will give sufficient guidance on this matter. IAS 37, paragraph 14, defines a provision (and this definition is explained in paragraphs 15–26). Guidance for re-imbursements is given in IAS 37, paragraphs 53–58.

Transaction (4) The sale of electronic equipment along with a two-year maintenance package is a 'bundled transaction'. IAS 18, paragraph 13, refers to this issue. This paragraph requires that bundled transactions are separated into 'identifiable components' that can be separately assessed. In addition, IAS 18, Illustrative Example 11, gives guidance on how these separate parts should be measured. You should review these paragraphs.

A further complication arises in the case study as the value of the bundled transaction is lower than the sum of the parts. In other words, the bundled transactions have been sold at a discount. You must decide how this discount should be allocated.

Issue 2 You need to update the provision for deferred tax. Guidance on deferred taxation is outlined in IAS 12 *Income Taxes*. In the case study you are given certain details about the deferred tax provision including the tax rates for the current and previous years, opening details (1 January 2012) and additional differences between the tax base and the accounting base that have been identified in the 2012 accounting period.

To deal with this issue you must be familiar with the following definitions (IAS 12, para 5 and 17):

- Taxable temporary timing differences;
- Deductible temporary timing differences; and
- Permanent differences.

When you have reviewed these terms, you must next decide *which* differences (temporary, permanent, deductible) should be recognised. IAS 12, paragraphs 15–18, gives guidance on temporary taxable differences. IAS 12, paragraphs 24–30, gives guidance on deductible temporary differences. How should permanent differences be treated?

Once you have identified the appropriate differences you must charge tax on these differences. The tax rate for the current year is 12.5%. In 2011 it was 11%. Which rate should you use? Does the 2011 tax rate affect your calculations for the current year? IAS 12, paragraph 47, will give you the answer.

Finally, you must decide where the deferred tax charge (or credit) is to be expensed (or credited). Should it be to the income statement or to another account? IAS 12, paragraphs 58–68 will give you the appropriate guidance.

Issue 3 deals with the group's property portfolio. Accounting guidance for property is covered in a number of accounting standards including IAS 16 *Property, Plant and Equipment,* IAS 23 *Borrowing Costs,* IAS 40 *Investment Property* and IAS 17 *Leases*. This issue covers all of the above standards. (It is longer than a normal exam question but is designed to incorporate as many property issues as possible.)

Issue (3) is made up of *four* separate transactions.

Transaction (1) Owner-occupied properties This transaction tests your understanding of IAS 23 *Borrowing Costs* and, in particular, the capitalisation rate to be applied to borrowings for qualifying projects. In this transaction a total of €15.6 million was spent on capital projects in 2012. This expenditure was funded by a combination of a €5 million loan (raised specifically for these projects) and a pool of construction finance available to the group. You need to figure out what rate to apply to the capital expenditure. Should you use the cost of the loan specifically raised for the projects or should you take into account the cost of all funding sources? IAS 23, paragraphs12 and14, gives the appropriate guidance.

Transaction (2) Investment property – Acorn This transaction examines how properties, whose use has changed during the financial period, should be treated in the financial statements. Property Acorn, originally leased to a third party, is now occupied by the Group. How should this change in use be presented in the financial statements? IAS 40 *Investment Property,* paragraphs 57 to 65, outlines the appropriate treatment when transfers are made to or from investment property during the financial year.

You will need to identify whether a change in use has taken place. Look at IAS 40, paragraph 57, which outlines examples of *when* a change of use has taken place.

You must also establish the date that the change in use took place. A number of different dates are given in this scenario – 1 March, 1 April and 1 July 2012. Which is the appropriate one?

Finally, the transfer value must be determined. IAS 40, paragraphs 60–65, outlines how the transfer value should be determined and how it should be treated in the financial statements.

Once the Acorn property has been transferred to property, plant and equipment, it will be presented in accordance with IAS16 *Property, Plant and Equipment*. You will need to include a depreciation adjustment for 2012.

Transaction (3) Investment property – Ash This transaction also addresses the change in use of property. The Ash property, leased by the Howard Retail group, was vacated during the year and is now being sublet to a third party. (The property has changed from being occupied to becoming an investment property.) There is an additional consideration here; the Ash property is not legally owned by the Howard Group but is held under a non-cancellable operating lease. The current accounting treatment is to treat the rental charges and the sublet rental income as profit or loss entries in accordance with IAS17 *Leases*. The CEO has proposed an alternative treatment. You should consider if this alternative presentation would be permissible. You will find some guidance on this matter in IAS 40 *Investment property*, paragraph 6 and IAS17 *Leases* paragraph 19.

Transaction (4) Year-end valuations Investment properties held in the Howard Retail Group are measured at *fair value*. IAS 40, paragraphs 33–55, outlines how fair value should be determined and measured.

The case study identifies what the fair value of the group's investment properties are at 31 December 2012. We are also told that the valuation will have fallen by a further 10% before the accounts are signed. You have to decide which valuation is most appropriate for the financial statements. IAS 10, paragraph 11, will give you the appropriate answer.

Issue 4 Obtaining a loan at anything other than a market rate should raise some concerns – perhaps the interest is being obtained using other means. In this instance, it is possible that the final payment includes an interest element and a capital element.

You will need to calculate the effective interest rate on the loan (IAS 39, para 9 and IFRS 9, para 4.2.1). This can be done by considering the cash flows of the loan and using the IRR methodology, i.e. interpolation or extrapolation (same approach as for your finance studies) to calculate the interest rate inherent in the loan.

Then calculate the interest that should have been applied in the current year – remember that the company has only had the loan for three months. Finally once the amount is calculated, record the amount. The interest has not been paid, hence it will have to be accrued.

Issue 5 There are a number of items to note here:

- The investments represent less than 1% of the outstanding share capital of the companies concerned. Therefore, the standards on subsidiaries and associates (IFRS 10, IAS 28, IFRS 3…) do not apply. Howard does not have any control over the companies and as a result these investments will be classified as financial assets. Therefore, the appropriate standard is IFRS 9 *Financial Instruments*.

- Next you will need to determine the implications of the designation of 'measured at fair value'.
  - This means that the investments are valued at fair value. As a general guide, the IASB has embraced the fair value approach to valuation. Thus, as a very general rule of thumb,

if you do not have a good reason to do otherwise, fair value should be used. Have a look at IFRS 9, paragraphs 4.1.2 and 4.1.4.
  - Secondly, if the answer to the previous question gives rise to a change in value then where does this increase/decrease go? The answer to this will be either direct to the 'income statement' or to 'other comprehensive income'. As indicated in the information provided Howard had elected to present changes to fair value through 'other comprehensive income'. This is an option that is available in respect of investments in equity instruments in IFRS 9, paragraph 5.7.5.

- Wed Ltd does not have a quoted market price. However, can an alternative be used and, if so, under what circumstances? Take a look at IFRS 13 *Fair Value Measurement*, paragraphs 61 and B5–B7.

Issue 6 Cara Fashions has a different year end to that of the Howard Retail Group. The issue here is to decide whether the financial statements can be prepared using the audited information for the year ended 31 October or the unaudited information for the year ended 31 December. IAS 28, paragraphs 33–34, gives some guidance here.

Once the decision is made, calculate the carrying value of the investment in associates. The final element is to decide whether any increase or decrease in value (the previous carrying value was €187 million) should be reported in the current period's financial statements.

Requirement (b) – Guidance

In this requirement you are not asked to redraft the financial statements. Instead, you are asked to summarise the impact of the adjustments from **requirement (a)** on the group income statement. You should note that there are just four marks allocated to this requirement so it should not take very long. You are not required to do any new thinking, just bring together your answer from the previous requirement.

An important element of this requirement is to ensure that your workings are easy to follow: you will need to highlight clearly where the adjustments are coming from; your answer should not be a series of random numbers thrown on a page.

There should be two sections to your answer:
1. Take the 'profit for the financial year' (currently €1,167 million) and restate this for the adjustments made in the previous requirement.
2. Take the 'total other comprehensive income/expense for the period' (currently an expense of €19 million) and restate for the adjustments that impact on 'other comprehensive income'.

The resultant figure (item 1 and item 2) will give the restated 'Total Comprehensive Income for the Period'.

Requirement (c) – Guidance

The first item you should note here is that the requirement is asking for a memo to be prepared. There are usually one to two 'soft' marks in any question for presentation. Should you omit to present your answer as a memo then these marks may be needlessly lost.

This requirement does not require any technical accounting to be performed – it is a more discursive style question. In order to score well in this section you will need to get to the point quickly and relate your answer to the information in the case. Students often score well on these types of questions but tend to write too much information in the hope that some of it will be correct. The implication of this is that there is less time for answering other sections of the paper.

Use of audited and unaudited financial statements for the associate You will have already considered this as part of your answer to **requirement (a)**, now you are being asked to explain your thinking in more detail. Perhaps consider the relevance of information versus reliability of information debate and whether there is any regulatory guidance.

Use of knowledge and information gained from another audit carried out by the firm While there are financial reporting implications, this is more of an ethical issue. There are benefits and risks to discussing the audit of Cara Fashions with the in-charge audit manager. You should outline both sides to the argument.

You could also consider using one of the ethical frameworks to analyse this decision – is a utility type framework appropriate here (i.e. take the solution that results in the greatest net benefit) or would a rights-based approach be more appropriate (i.e. take the solution that considers all the rights of everyone involved)?

It might also be valuable to take into account the *Standards of Professional Conduct* and the *Code of Ethics* of Chartered Accountants Ireland (or the relevant professional body). Does the notion of 'confidentiality' apply here?

Finally, can you propose a simple solution to this dilemma?

The South Quarter Development Company transaction There are two issues here: the reporting of the transaction at the year end and the potential impairment of the 'post-year-end loan' to the South Quarter Development Company.

The reporting of the transaction at year end This transaction certainly appears unusual. However, currently the transaction 'appears' correctly accounted for. Ask yourself – how would this appear to the man on the street?[1] Incidentally, this scenario is not too dissimilar to the 'liquidity support' provided by Irish Life and Permanent to Anglo Irish Bank around its 30 September 2008 year end.[2]

How else could this transaction be reported? Are there any regulations that would support an alternative approach? Finally, what clarification and additional information surrounding this transaction would you seek to obtain?

---

[1] This is a version of the test famously referred to as the 'man on the Clapham omnibus' i.e. how would it appear to a reasonably educated person but without any particular specialist knowledge of the area. For some time this became a standard against which conduct in negligence cases was judged. It was first used in a legal sense in *McQuire vs Western Morning News*, 1903.

[2] See http://www.rte.ie/news/2009/0210/angloirish.html for further details (accessed 21 June 2012) and Anglo Irish Bank, 2008, Annual Report and Accounts 2008, accessed on www.angloirishbank.ie (30 June 2011).

The potential impairment of the 'post-year-end loan' The treatment of this may be dependent on your answer to the item immediately above. The work on the shopping centre has stalled. This is certainly an indication that the loan to the South Quarter Development Company could be impaired. The exact amount is unknown but it could be material. Should the amount of the impairment be provided for in the current year financial statements or should it just be disclosed by way of a note (i.e. any impairment charge reported as part of next year's profits/losses)?

Recommended Reading

The above may also be referenced in *International Financial Accounting and Reporting,* 3rd edition, by Ciaran Connolly (Chartered Accountants Ireland, 2011) and the relevant accounting standards as follows:

	Chapter	Chapter title	Chapter section	Standard
Requirement (a)				
Issue 1	4	Revenue Recognition	4.2	IAS 18
			4.4	IFRIC 13
	9	Intangible Assets	9.2	IAS 38
	37	Provisions, Contingent Liabilities and Contingent Assets	14.2 & 14.3	IAS 37
Issue 2	13	Income Taxes	13.3	IAS 12
Issue 3	7	Borrowing Costs	7.2	IAS 23
	5	Investment Property	5.2	IAS 40
	6	Property, Plant and Equipment	16.2	IAS 16
	8	Leases	8.2 & 8.3	IAS 17
	15	Events after the Reporting Period	15.2	IAS 10
Issue 4	25	Financial Instruments	25.3	IAS 39
				IFRS 9
Issue 5	25	Financial Instruments	25.3	IFRS 9
				IFRS 13
Issue 6	29	Associates	29.2	IAS 28
Requirement (b)				
Summary of adjustments	2	Presentation of Financial Statements	2.3	IAS 1
Requirement (c)				
Issue 6	29	Associates	29.2	IAS 28
Issue 7	25	Financial Instruments	25.3	IAS 39

Solution to Howard Retail Group

Requirement (a)

Outstanding Issue 1 – Revenue

Loyalty Schemes A sale should be recognised only when the conditions outlined in IAS18, paragraph 14, are satisfied. This will happen when:

- the seller has transferred to the buyer the significant risks and rewards of ownership;
- the seller retains neither continuing managerial involvement to the degree usually associated with ownership nor effective control over the goods sold;
- the amount of revenue can be measured reliably;
- it is probable that the economic benefits associated with the transaction will flow to the seller, and
- the costs incurred or to be incurred in respect of the transaction can be measured reliably.

Loyalty points represent an advance on future sales. At the end of the year, points to the value of €6.4 million remain outstanding. Conditions relating to a sale have not been satisfied for these advances. The seller has not transferred any of the risks and rewards of ownership to the customer as no actual sale has taken place. Therefore these advances should be presented as deferred income and included in Current Liabilities in the Statement of Financial Position.

Although only 80% of the loyalty points are expected to be redeemed in the exercise period, IFRIC 13 *Customer Loyalty Programmes* requires companies to estimate the value of points ***to the customer*** and defer this amount of revenue as a liability until they have fulfilled their obligations to supply awards. Therefore 100% of the loyalty points should be deferred.

The following journal entry is required:

DR Revenue	€6.4 million	
CR Provisions (Liabilities)		€6.4 million

Loyalty schemes generate economic benefits for the company. However, the expenditure on a loyalty card scheme cannot be distinguished from the cost of developing the business as a whole. Therefore such an item should not be treated as a separate intangible asset. The cost of developing a loyalty scheme is considered to be an internally generated intangible and cannot be recognised as an asset (IAS 38, para 64). It should be expensed.

The following journal entry is required:

DR Administration expenses	€0.7 million	
CR Intangibles Assets		€0.7 million

Sales Promotion Revenue should be measured at the fair value of the consideration received or receivable. Discounts should be considered (IAS 18, para 10). Revenue should be stated net of discounts. Discounts should not be included as promotional expenses:

	€m	€m
DR Revenue	1.2	
CR Admin expenses		1.2

Concession Agreements (It is assumed that the leasing of the retail area does not quality as an IAS 40 investment property.)

Agreement one Retailers, and in particular department stores, frequently operate an element of their business on a 'store-in-store' or concession basis whereby independent retailers are offered floor space within the store. These agreements can come in many forms. The recognition of revenue generated from a concession agreement depends on how the arrangement is structured. If the independent retailer is responsible for the generation, collection etc., of their own sales, the department store is simply providing the space and location and the revenue should be any commissions received or receivable in the period (€900,000 - €520,000 = €380,000). This has been correctly treated in the financial statements.

With regard to the set-up costs, the treatment depends upon the terms of the agreement. Some agreements require the independent retailer to contribute to the costs of redesigning the stores. These are the terms of the Soiree Perfume agreement. Howard has incurred capital costs of €520,000 and these have been incorrectly debited to Property, Plant and Equipment.

The fittings are not part of the asset base of the Howard Group. They belong to Soiree Perfumes. (Soiree Perfumes are entitled to remove these fittings when the licence ends.) Howard is simply carrying out the construction work on behalf of Soiree and this expenditure will (and has been) reimbursed by the end of the year. The correct accounting treatment for these costs should have been to debit trade and other receivables as the costs were incurred and then credit this account with the capital costs reimbursed by Soiree Perfumes. The existing entries need to be corrected. As the costs were reimbursed before the year-end there is no need to adjust the trade receivable account. We can correct the error with the following single journal entry:

DR Revenue	€0.52 million	
CR PPE		€0.52 million

Agreement two The provision should be for the full cost of €620,000. The re-imbursement cannot be considered for adjustment until it is virtually certain that it will be received. As the licensee is disputing the claim the reimbursement is anything but certain (IAS 37, para 53).

DR Administration expenses	€0.434 million	
CR Provisions		€0.434 million

A contingency could be considered for the reimbursement. A contingent asset is 'a possible asset that arises from past events and whose existence will be confirmed by the occurrence or non-occurrence of one or more uncertain future events not wholly within the control of the entity' (IAS 37, para 10).

However, 'a contingent asset is disclosed only where an inflow of benefits is *probable* (IAS 37, para 34).

At the end of the reporting period, the re-imbursement remains uncertain and there does not appear to be any indication that Howard will receive this income. The inflow is neither certain or probable. In conclusion, this is not an asset, nor is it a contingency. It would be recommended that it be excluded from the financial statements altogether.

Maintenance Contracts The sale of electronic equipment is a bundled sale. In accordance with IAS 18, paragraph 13, and ED *Revenue from Contracts with Customers*, paragraph 23, the sale should be split into its component parts. The bundled sale is priced at €2,000 per item. If sold separately, the price of the equipment would be €1,750 and the two year maintenance package €350 (€175 pa for two years). The sum of the two separate components is €2,100. Therefore, if the bundled package is bought, the customer will receive a discount of €100 on the entire transaction. In this situation the exposure draft requires an entity to 'allocate the transaction price to the performance obligations in proportion to their stand-alone selling prices (i.e. on a relative stand-alone selling price basis). Any discount within the contract is allocated proportionally to all of the separate performance obligations in the contract.' This would be calculated as follows:

Sale of goods	€1,750 × €2,000/€2,100 =	€1,667	(i.e.5/6 of €2,000)
Maintenance service	€350 × €2,000/€2,100 =	€333	(i.e.1/6 of €2,000)
		€2,000	

In 2012, a total of 2,400 sales-maintenance packages were sold. This generated income of €4.8 million (2,400 × €2,000).
In accordance with the exposure draft this income will be allocated as follows:

Sale of goods	(€4.8m × 1,667/2,000)	= €4.0m	(i.e. 5/6 of €4.8m)
Maintenance services	(€4.8m × 333/2,000)	= €0.8m	(i.e. 1/6 of €4.8m)
Total		= €4.8m	

The revenue appropriate for 2012 is €4 million for the sale of goods plus one year's maintenance. The maintenance income for the second year should be deferred and included as a current liability. (For simplicity purposes, it is assumed that all bundled contracts were sold at the beginning of year one and that one year's maintenance has been provided by the end of the reporting period.) As the full €4.8 million is currently included in revenue, an adjustment should be made equal to the amount that is to be deferred.

	€m	€m
DR Revenue	0.4	
CR Deferred income (liability) (€0.8m × ½)		0.4

Outstanding Issue 2 – Taxation

Background Deferred taxation tends to cause students difficulties but the principle behind it is rather straightforward. The purpose of financial statements is to present the *accounting* consequences of all transactions carried out in a financial period. However the tax charge does not follow this rule. The current[3] tax charge in a financial period is charged, not on the basis of accounting profits but on *taxable* profits. Thus there is no direct link between the reported accounting profit and its tax charge as they are based on two different figures. The objective of deferred taxation is to bridge this gap or, in other words, to bring the tax charge back in line with accounting profits so that the basic accounting principles are followed through-out the financial statements.

Take the following example of ABN Plc (not part of the case study):

	€m
Accounting base	100
Taxable base	90
Tax rate	10%
Current tax charge (90 × 10%)	9
Tax charge based on accounting profits (100 × 10%)	10

Deferred taxation for ABN Plc works as follows:

	€m
Current tax	9
Adjustment to bring back in line with accounting profits (i.e. deferred)	1
Total tax expense	10

[3] Current tax is the tax payable in respect of the taxable profit for the period (i.e. it excludes the effects of deferred tax).

In practice, the process can be a little more complex and the terminology is difficult but the basic principle remains the same.

The guidelines in the standard (IAS 12) include:

Deferred taxation is provided where, at the end of the reporting period, there is a difference between the carrying value of an asset (or liability) and its tax base. Deferred tax should be provided on the difference, in accordance with IAS 12 *Income Taxes*.

The principal rules of deferred tax include:

1. Deferred taxation should be provided on *temporary* differences between the carrying value of an asset (or liability) and its tax base (IAS 12, para 15).
2. Temporary differences may either be *taxable* differences or *deductible* differences (IAS 12, para 5).
3. Taxable temporary differences are those differences that will result in taxable amounts in determining taxable profit (or loss) of future periods. Deductible temporary differences are those differences that will result in amounts that are deductible in determining future taxable profit (or loss) (IAS 12, para 5).
4. Deferred tax is not provided on PERMANENT differences.
5. Some temporary differences originate in the income statement. These differences are known as 'timing differences'. The deferred tax charge/credit for timing differences is included in the tax expense in the income statement (IAS 12, para 17).
6. Some differences do not originate in the income statement. For example, a gain recorded on the revaluation of an asset. The deferred tax charge/credit for these other differences should be charged/credited directly against equity (IAS 12, para 18–61).
7. Deferred tax should be measured at rates that are expected to apply when the liability/asset is realised (IAS 12, para 47).

Howard's situation is as follows:

There is an opening deferred tax liability of €11 million (€100m × 11%) in the draft financial statements. This, we are told in **issue 2**, is based on the difference between book depreciation and capital allowances.[4]

A number of additional differences have been identified during the period:

	€m
Permanent differences	3
Temporary differences including:	
Taxable timing differences	25
Taxable 'other' differences (equity)	5
Deductible timing differences	(10)

The permanent differences of €3 million should be excluded from any deferred tax charge in accordance with IAS 12, paragraph 15.

[4] An opening deferred tax *liability* means that the opening tax base of assets is lower than the carrying value. This implies that the cumulative amount of capital allowances deducted from PPE is greater than cumulative book depreciation at the beginning of the current period. A deferred tax charge would have been made in a previous period to bring the tax expense in line with book profits.

The temporary differences, €20 million, are subject to deferred tax (€25m + €5m – €10m). Deferred tax is charged at the current rate of tax 12.5% giving rise to a charge of €2.5 million (IAS 12, para 47).

€5 million of these differences are equity related. The deferred tax on this €5 million will be debited against 'other comprehensive income' while the balance will form part of the tax expense for the period.

	€m	€m	
DR Taxation expense	1.875		(€15m × 12.5%) (IAS 12, para 15)
DR Other comprehensive income	0.625		(€5m × 12.5%) (IAS 12, para 61)
CR Deferred taxation provision		2.5	

The additional differences that were identified in the period have now been measured at current rates but the opening provision has been measured at rates that applied to 2011, 11%. The opening provision must be adjusted to bring it in line with 2012 tax rates (€100m at 11% – €100m at 12.5%).

	€m	€m
DR Taxation expense	1.5[5]	
CR Deferred taxation provision		1.5

Outstanding Issue 3 – Property Portfolio

Owner Occupied This issue examines the capitalisation rate of funds borrowed for the purposes of constructing assets. IAS 23 *Borrowing Costs* (IAS 23), outlines the rules for capitalising borrowing costs on qualifying assets. A qualifying asset is an asset that necessarily takes a substantial period of time to get ready for its intended use or sale (IAS 23, para 5).

In the case study a total of €15.6 million has been spent on the construction and acquisition of qualifying assets. Howard has funded this capital programme with a mixture of loans. €5 million has been borrowed specifically for the programme and the remainder, €10.6 million, has come from a general construction fund.

The interest rates of the various loans are as follows:

Specific Finance	€5 million	interest rate of 10%
General Funds :	€60 million	interest rate of 9%
	€40 million	interest rate of 7.5%

The total finance charge on these loans, included in profit or loss for 2012, is:

	€m
Specific Finance of €5 million at 10% for 12 months	= 0.50
General Finance of €60 million at 9% for 12 months	= 5.40
General Finance of €40 million at 7.5% for 12 months	= 3.00
Total interest (all expensed)	= 8.90

[5] The adjustment to bring the opening provision in line with 2012 tax rates is charged in full to the income statement (and not equity) as the opening provision relates purely to timing differences.

In accordance with IAS 23, a portion of this charge should be capitalised and included in the capital cost. IAS 23, paragraph 14, states that "the entity shall determine the amount of borrowing costs eligible for capitalisation by applying a capitalisation rate to the expenditures on that asset. The capitalisation rate shall be the weighted average of the borrowing costs applicable to the borrowings of the entity that are outstanding during the period, other than borrowings made specifically for the purpose of obtaining a qualifying asset."

The weighted average cost of capital will be based on the €60 million and the €40 million loans and will be calculated as follows:

(9% × €60/€100) + (7.5% × €40/€100) = 8.4%

The capitalised borrowing cost will be calculated as follows:

	€m	
Loan on 1 Jan: €5 million at 10% for 12 months	= 0.500	(Specific Finance)
Loan on 1 July: €8.4 million at 8.40% for 6 months	= 0.350	(General Finance)
Loan on 1 Nov: €2.2 million at 8.40% for 2 months	= 0.030	(General Finance)
Total interest to be capitalised	= 0.884	

An adjustment will be required to capitalise this borrowing cost:

	€m	€m
DR PPE	0.884	
CR Finance Charges		0.884

Investment properties

Acorn The use of this property has changed from an investment property to an owner-occupied property. This re-classification must be reflected in the financial statements. IAS 40 *Investment Property*, paragraph 57, states that 'transfers to or from investment property shall be made when, and only when, there is a change in use.' It is evident from the information given in the case study that a change in use has taken place. However, the actual date of change in use requires some thought. Should it be the date that notice is given to the tenant (1 March) *or* the date the property is actually vacated (1 April) *or* should it be the date that Howard's staff occupy the premises (1 July). On the balance of the information given, the change of use will have taken place on the 1 April, the date that the existing tenants moved out. Up until that date the property was leased out and would have been correctly presented as an investment property. After 1 April the property, although not actually occupied by Howard staff, was in the process of being developed for owner occupation and should therefore have been classified as owner-occupied from that date. This point is made, in IAS 40, paragraph 9, which, in giving examples of items that are ***not*** investment property, includes the following: property held for future development and subsequent use as owner occupied' (IAS 40, para 9(c)).

IAS 40, paragraph 60, states that 'for a transfer from investment property carried at fair value to owner occupied property or inventories, the property's deemed cost for subsequent accounting in accordance with IAS 16 or IAS 2 shall be its fair value at the date of change of use.' The fair value is then deemed to be the cost base under IAS 16. The fair value of Acorn on 1 April 2012 was €2.82 million.

To make this transfer from investment property to owner occupied property, the following adjustment is required:

DR PPE	€2.82 million	
DR Admin Expenses	€0.18 million	
CR Investment Properties		€3 million (valuation at 1 January 2012)

In addition, once the asset is transferred to PPE, it must be depreciated. The depreciation charge would be calculated as €2.82m/40years for nine months, as follows:

DR Admin Expenses/Depreciation	€0.053 million	
CR PPE		€0.053 million

Ash This is a transfer of property from one that was occupied by the group to one that is now held as an investment property. The snag here is that the property was not owned by Howard but held under a 25-year operating lease. Up until now, the lease payments have been correctly included as expenses in profit or loss. From 1 January 2012, the property has been sublet. IAS 40, paragraph 6, states that "a property interest that is held by a lessee under an operating lease may be classified and accounted for as investment property if, and only if, the property would otherwise meet the definition of an investment property and the lessee uses the fair value model … for the asset recognised."[6] This is the policy that the Howard team would like to pursue. To reclassify an operating lease into an Investment Property you are, in effect, turning an operating lease into a finance lease (IAS 40, para 25). To do this you will need to capitalise the remaining payments on the lease. This is carried out as follows:

Minimum lease payments = (€.8m × 20)
= €16m (*This is the sum of the remaining lease charges)*

PV of minimum lease payments = (€0.8m × 8.514*)
= €6.81m (*This is the present value of the minimum lease payments)*

* (10% for 20 years is a cumulative factor of 8.514)

Finance charge = minimum lease payments minus PV of minimum lease payments
= €16m – €6.81m
= €9.19m

The present value of the minimum lease payments is capitalised as follows:

	€m	€m
DR Investment Property	6.81	
CR Lease Creditor		6.81

[6] The other option in IAS 40, paragraph 6, is to continue to treat the property as an operating lease in accordance with IAS 17.

The subsequent lease payments are split between a reduction of the liability and a finance charge. The finance charge is calculated at a constant periodic rate on the outstanding liability. For 2012 this would be calculated as follows:

	€m
Opening liability	6.81
Lease payment (1/1/2012)	0.80
Outstanding for period	6.01
Charge at 10%	0.60

The lease charge for 2012 is currently included in operating profit for the period. This needs to be reclassified in accordance with the elected change in presentation:

	€m	€m
DR Finance charge	0.60	
DR Lease creditor	0.20	
CR Rent expense		0.80

The treatment of rental income will remain unchanged. It will continue to be credited to SOCI.

Investment Property valuations

	€m
Carrying value at 31 December 2011	112.00 (per draft statements)
Acorn (now transferred to PPE)	(3.00)
Ash (now reclassified as an investment)	6.81
Carrying value at 31 December 2012	115.81
Fair value at 31 December 2012	
Investment properties	98.0
Ash	5.5
Fair value at 31 December 2012	103.5

Adjustment to fair value = €115.81m – €103.5m = €12.31m

The adjustment is as follows:

	€m	€m
DR Expenses (Income Statement)	12.31	
CR Investment Properties		12.31

Note: The fall in value post-year-end is not relevant. IAS 10, paragraph 11, states that an example of a non-adjusting event after the reporting period is a decline in the market value of investments between the end of the reporting period and the date when the financial statements are authorised for issue. This information should be disclosed in a note.

Outstanding Issue 4 – Financing

Obtaining a loan at anything other than a market rate should raise some concerns. In this instance, the final repayment of the loan of €133.1 million includes both interest and capital.

The notion that the loan has a 0% interest payment is incorrect – the payment of the interest has been deferred until the end of the term of the loan. This is not an unusual arrangement and it may have been done for legitimate cash flow reasons.

Under IAS 39, paragraph 9, and IFRS 9, paragraph 4.2.1, the effective (i.e. real) interest rate on the loan will have to be calculated. This involves setting out the cash flows attached to the loan and calculating the effective interest rate by using the internal rate of return methodology (from your finance studies). From the information provided there is a cash inflow on 30 September 2012 of €100 million followed by just one cash outflow of €133.1 million on 30 September 2015. This can be modelled as follows:

	30/09/2012	30/09/2013	30/09/2014	30/09/2015
	Now	**Year 1**	**Year 2**	**Year 3**
	€m			**€m**
Cash Flows	100			(133.10)

To determine the effective interest rate, first discount cash flows to their present value at, say, 8% (selecting 8% a good starting point because it is likely that the interest rate is somewhere between 5% and 12%). Using a discount rate of 8%, the cash flow in year 3 is –€133.10/ $(1 + 0.08)^3$ or –€105.66.

	Now	Year 1	Year 2	Year 3	Total
	€m			**€m**	**€m**
PV @ 8%	100.00			(105.66)	(5.66)

At a discount rate of 8%, the PV of the cash flows is –€5.66, thus the effective interest rate must be higher than 8%.

The next step is to repeat the previous process using a higher interest rate, say, 12%. 12% is a rate that is higher than 8% (11% or 13% or 10% could also have been used). Using a discount rate of 12% the cash flow in year 3 is –€133.10/$(1 + 0.12)^3$ or –€94.74.

	Now	Year 1	Year 2	Year 3	Total
	€m			**€m**	**€m**
PV @ 12%	100.00			(94.74)	5.26

At a discount rate of 12%, the PV of the cash flows is €5.26, thus the effective interest rate must be lower than 12%.

At this stage we know that at an interest rate of 8% the cash flows have a present value of negative €5.66 million, while at 12% there is a positive present value of €5.26 million. We need to determine the interest rate that will result in the present value of the cash flows being zero. If you can recall from your previous studies, there are two approaches: the graphical method and interpolation. This solution uses the graphical method.

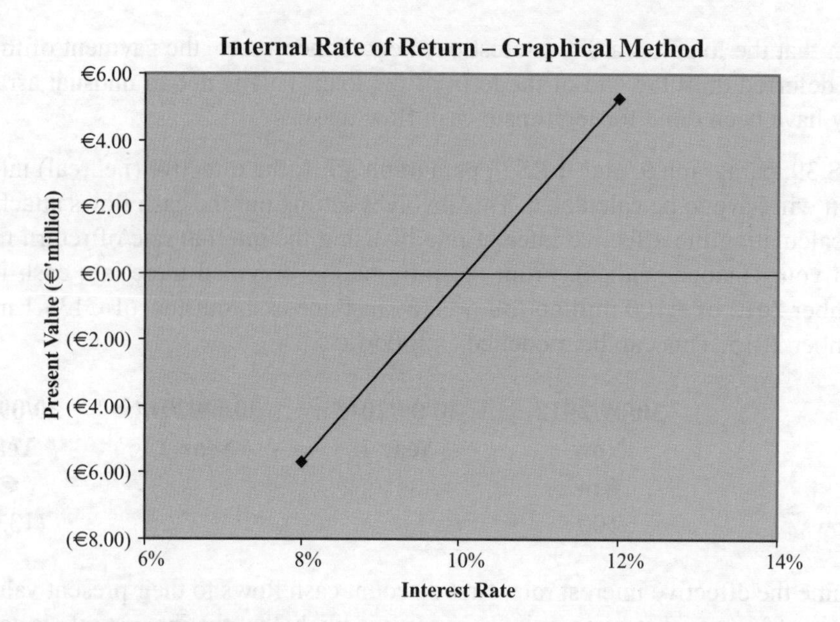

The point at which the line crosses the x-axis gives an approximate internal rate of return. From the graph above it appears that 10% is the rate at which the present value of the cash flows are exactly zero.[7]

The effective interest rate on the loan is 10% i.e. borrowing €100 million on 30 September 2012 and repaying €133.1 million on 30 September 2015 with no periodic interest payment is the equivalent to borrowing at a rate of 10%. This was a long-winded calculation but once the method is performed a number of times it does get quicker.

Alternatively, a mathematical calculation can be performed as follows:

$$\text{Effective Interest rate} = 8\% + ((5.66/(5.66 + 5.26) \times (12\% - 8\%)) = 10\% \text{ (approx)}$$

The formula is as follows:

$$\text{Effective interest rate } = IRR_{(\text{rate }1)} + ((IRR\ 1/(IRR\ 1 + IRR2) \times (IRR_{(\text{rate }2)} - IRR_{(\text{rate }1)})$$

The next stage is to calculate the interest on the loan that should be applied to the current period. Given an interest rate of 10%, the interest on a loan of €100 million in the first year of the loan is €10 million. However, the loan was taken out on 30 September 2012 therefore the amount will be time-apportioned to €2.5 million[8].

Finally, the amount will need to be recorded. The interest of €2.5 million has not been paid and payment will not occur until 30 September 2015. Instead, the interest is added to the

[7] If you had been lucky enough to select 10% as one of the trial percentages then you would have had to go no further.

[8] This is not an exact answer – the solution assumes that the interest is added to the loan on an annual basis, however, most lenders apply daily compounding. The difference is unlikely to be significant. Applying a methodology that uses daily compounding is beyond the scope of this book.

outstanding principal and the total amount is paid at the end of the term of the loan. Therefore to record the interest:

	€m	€m
DR (increase) Finance Costs	2.5	
CR (increase) Borrowings – non-current		2.5

Outstanding Issue 5 – Trade Investments

With a shareholding of less than 1% of the outstanding share capital, Howard Retail Holdings has no control or influence over the operations of the companies involved. As a result these investments will be classified as financial assets. Therefore, the appropriate standard is IFRS 9 *Financial Instruments.*

Under this standard there are two categories of financial assets: financial assets measured at fair value and financial assets measured at amortised cost (IFRS 9, para 4.1.2–4.1.4). The information in the case study clearly states that the company has opted to classify the investments as 'measured at fair value'.

The next stage is to determine the implications of classifying an asset as 'measured at fair value'. Under IFRS 9 the measurement of these investments is at fair value. IFRS 13 *Fair Value Measurement* provides guidance in how to determine fair value. IFRS 13, paragraph 13, states that "if there is a quoted price in an active market … an entity should use that price". Therefore valuing the instruments in Carrefour and Inditex is straightforward. In the case of Wed Ltd, IFRS 13, paragraph 61, permits the use of valuation techniques. The use of market multiples is suggested in IFRS 13, paragraph 136.

It is now possible to determine the value of the investments:

	€
Carrefour: 10,000 shares @ €95	950,000
Inditex: 1,000,000 shares @ €11.50	11,500,000
Wed: no quoted price (note 1)	1,705,000
Total	14,155,000
Previous valuation (31/12/11)	14,000,000
Increase in fair value	155,000

The final stage is to record this increase in valuation – under IFRS 9, paragraph 5.7.5, Howard has elected to show that the increase in value in 'other comprehensive income':

	€	€
DR (Increase) Financial assets	155,000	
CR (Increase) Other comprehensive income/Gain on revaluation of financial assets		155,000

Note 1: Wed Fair Value: From the information provided there is no quoted market price for the shares in Wed Ltd. In such situations the next best approach is to use a valuation technique. This will involve a significant amount of judgement but if the resultant valuation is sufficiently reliable then it is acceptable to use a valuation technique.

In this instance there is the possibility of estimating the fair value of the investment based on some simple valuation techniques.

- Using PE Ratios

Profit after Tax of Wed	€16m
PE ratio of similar companies	11 times
Estimated Fair Value	€176m
1% shareholding (50,000 shares)	€1.76m

- Using Market to Book Ratios

Net Assets of Wed	€55m
Market to Book Ratio	3 times
Estimated Fair Value	€165m
1% shareholding (50,000 shares)	€1.65m
Average of Values	€1.705m

Although we are not really in a position to judge, the next stage will be to determine how reliable these values are. There does not appear to be a significant variation in the range of the values calculated (€1.65 million versus €1.76 million) therefore, on that basis, the average value (€1.705 million) can be used (IFRS 12, para 63).

Outstanding Issue 6 – Investments in Associates

There are various extracts of financial statement information provided for Cara Fashions. First, decide which is the appropriate one to use. The choice is between:

- 31 October 2012 – the most recent audited financial statements; **or**
- 31 December 2012 – unaudited financial statements prepared by Cara Fashions but with the same year end as Howard Retail Holdings.

IAS 28, paragraph 33, states that financial statements of the associate should be for the same period as that of the parent. If they are not, then the associate should prepare, for the use of the parent, financial statements as of the same date. This is what Cara Fashions has done. Therefore it is appropriate to use the 31 December 2012 financial information. The reliability of this information is an audit issue but there are approaches that can be used to provide some assurance to the auditor.

From this point then it is a matter of applying the equity method (IAS 28, para 10). The investment is recognised at cost plus (or minus) share of profits (or losses) since acquisition.

	€m	€m
Cost of investment		100
Retained earnings (31 December 2012)	550	
Retained earnings (on acquisition)	200	
Increase since acquisition	350	
Group Share (30%)		105
Value of investment in associate		205
Previous valuation (no transaction recorded for current year)		187
Increase required		18

To record this amount, the following transaction is appropriate:

	€m	€m
DR (Increase) Investment in associate	18	
CR (Increase) Share of profits of associate		18

Requirement (b)

Bringing all the adjustments from the previous requirement together:

	€m
Profit for the financial year as originally stated	1,167.00
Issue 1: Loyalty points – deferred revenue	(6.40)
Issue 1: Loyalty points – cost of scheme	(0.70)
Issue 1: Sales promotion – discounts (net effect)	0.00
Issue 1: Concession 1 – deferred income	(0.52)
Issue 1: Concession 2 – dispute over reimbursement	(0.43)
Issue 1: Maintenance contracts – deferred income	(0.40)
Issue 2: Deferred tax – timing differences	(1.88)
Issue 2: Deferred tax – rate change	(1.50)
Issue 3: Capitalisation of borrowing costs	0.88
Issue 3: Acorn, transfer at fair value	(0.18)
Issue 3: Acorn, subsequent depreciation	(0.05)
Issue 3: Ash, reclassification of rent as finance charges	(0.60)
Issue 3: Ash, reclassification of rent	0.80
Issue 3: Investment property, fair value adjustment	(12.31)

Issue 4: Finance costs – effective interest on loan	(2.50)
Issue 6: Share of profit of associate	18.00
Profit for the financial year, restated	1,159.21
Other Comprehensive Income/(Expense) as originally stated	(19.00)
Issue 2: Deferred tax – equity related timing differences	(0.63)
Issue 5: Gain on revaluation of financial assets	0.16
Other Comprehensive Income/(Expense) – restated	(19.47)
Total Comprehensive Income for the Period – restated	1,139.74

Alternatively, this requirement could be answered by representing the income statement as shown opposite:

Alternative Presentation of Summary of Changes to Income Statement

		Issue 1	Issue 2	Issue 3	Issue 4	Issue 5	Issue 6	Adjusted
	€m	€m	€m	€m	€m	€m	€m	€m
Revenue	8,040.00	(8.52)						8,031.48
Cost of Sales	(5,870.00)							(5,870.00)
Gross Profit	2,170.00							2,161.48
Administration	(987.00)	0.07		(11.74)				(998.68)
Other operating income	27.00							27.00
Profit from operations	1,210.00							1,189.80
Finance Income	250.00							250.00
Finance costs	(148.00)			0.28	(2.50)			(150.22)
Share of post tax profit/loss from associates	0.00						18.00	18.00
Profit before tax	1,312.00							1,307.58
Taxation charge (current tax)	(145.00)		(3.13)					(148.38)
Profit for the financial year	1,167.00							1,159.21
Other Comprehensive Income								
Actuarial losses on defined benefit pension schemes	(145.00)							(145.00)
Foreign currency translation gains	122.00							122.00
Cash flow hedges: Fair value movement (+)	4.00							4.00
Gain on revaluation of financial assets						0.16		0.16
Deferred tax on equity items			(0.63)					(0.63)
Total Other Comprehensive Income/expense for the period (net of tax)	(19.00)							(19.47)
Total Comprehensive Income for the Period	1,148.00							1,139.74

Requirement (c)

Memo

To: File

From: An Auditor

Re: Issues raised at audit planning meeting

1. Audited versus unaudited financial statements for associates From the point of view of reporting financial information, this is a classic example of the trade-off between relevant and reliable information. The 31 December 2012 information is more relevant but the 31 October 2012 information is more reliable. The framework for the preparation and presentation of financial information raises this trade-off but it does not provide any direction when faced with a practical application.

IAS 28, paragraph 33 states that financial statements of the associate should be for the same period as that of the parent. If they are not, then the associate should prepare, for the use of the parent, financial statements as of the same date. This is what Cara Fashions has done. Therefore it is appropriate to use the 31 December 2012 financial information.

This may give rise to some audit issues (note: not financial reporting issues) as the auditor will need to get some assurance that the change in position of Cara Fashions between 31 October and 31 December is real.

2. Using knowledge gained on other audits If you approach the other audit manager to discuss the results of Cara Fashions you may be in breach of the fundamental principle of client confidentiality. Confidentiality is defined in terms of disclosure of information to third parties therefore, it could be argued that your colleague, in the same firm, is not a third party.

However, using semantic loopholes to avoid rules of professional conduct is ill-advised for a professional accountant.

It could also be argued that the benefit to be gained from the more reliable information from your audit manager colleague outweighs the loss (if any) incurred by Cara Fashions of disclosing the information without their knowledge. In addition, there are reputational risks to be considered for Pipe, Pope and Co if their attitude to client's confidential information was made public. Balancing the benefits against the risks and associated probabilities, it could be argued that the audit manager of Cara Fashions should be approached. The preceding argument uses a utility-based approach to analyse an ethical situation – it is not an appropriate methodology in this case. There are weaknesses to using this type of approach: you do not know for certain the attitude of Cara Fashions or the implications of disclosure on their business.

A rights-based approach recognises the rights of all those affected by the decision. Does the right of Cara Fashions to confidentiality supersede the right of the auditor of Howard Retail Holdings to seek greater assurance on information obtained? There is no straightforward answer here. However, Cara Fashions have probably assumed that their information would be treated confidentially in their dealings with Pope, Pipe and Co.

Perhaps a solution would be to approach Cara Fashions with a view to seeking permission to speak to the audit manager. You could ask Howard Retail Holdings to use their influence (remember they should have significant influence) to ensure that the information can be divulged.

3. The cash/loan transaction with South Quarter Development Company This is a very unusual transaction. It appears to have taken place merely to improve the cash position of the group at year end. The motivation behind the transaction will need to be ascertained (if possible).

There is a general characteristic of financial information of substance over form (as per the conceptual framework for financial reporting). This states that information should report faithfully what it purports to represent. This general guideline would indicate that the transaction should continue to be recorded as a loan. However, the framework is not a standard but it can be used by preparers of financial statements to deal with topics where a standard does not exist.

There is no standard that specifically deals with this issue. The IASB has used substance over form in other unrelated areas (e.g. in distinguishing between equity and debt in IAS 32).

If the facts of this transaction were disclosed to users, it is likely that their reaction would be to reinstate the loan. While user reaction should not dictate financial reporting, it is important the financial statement information continues to be credible in the eyes of users. It is a factor to consider.

Before a final decision is made, it may be beneficial to find out how South Quarter Development was able to find the finance to repay the loan. For example, did a bank forward the money on the understanding that the funds were only required for a couple of days?

The facts of the case do indicate that this was a sham transaction and the loan should be reinstated.

This then gives rise to the possibility that the loan may be impaired. The work on the shopping centre has stopped. Thus, the collectability of the loan will need to be determined. There are many factors that will impact on this – it is not possible to establish the extent of impairment (if any) based on the information provided.

Case 7

Doherty Holdings Plc

This case study is based on a construction business. The accounting standards IAS 1, IAS 2, IAS 10, IAS 11, IAS 12, IAS 18, IAS 33, IAS 36, IAS 37, IAS 38, IAS 40 and IFRS 5 are addressed in this case.

Company Profile – Doherty Holdings Plc

Doherty Holdings Plc is a large Irish construction company. The business was founded in the 1960s by two brothers, Alan and Mark Doherty. The company enjoyed steady growth in its early years and expanded rapidly in the 1990s. This growth was due to an unprecedented building boom *and* a strategic move by the brothers into property development. This strategy proved so successful that, in 1997, the brothers decided to float the company. The shares are traded on both the Irish and London Stock exchanges. At their peak, in early 2008, the shares traded at a price of €10.56. Now, in 2013, the shares are currently worth just €0.34.

It is now March 2013 and the company has just completed its draft consolidated financial statements for the year ended 31 December 2012. There are, however, a number of outstanding issues that need to be resolved before the accounts can be finalised. The financial director has sought your advice on these matters.

The draft financial statements and the list of unresolved issues are presented as follows:

Doherty Holdings Plc
CONSOLIDATED STATEMENT OF COMPREHENSIVE INCOME
for the year ended 31 December 2012

	€000
Revenue	150,400
Cost of sales	(134,000)
Gross Profit	16,400
Administrative expenses	(21,300)
Share of results from joint ventures	6,800
Profit from operating activities	1,900
Investment Income	780
Finance Costs	(10,220)
Loss before tax	(7,540)
Taxation	(800)
Group loss for the financial period	**(8,340)**
Other Comprehensive Income/(Expense)	
Currency translation effects	(6,000)
Actuarial (loss)/gain on group defined benefit pension obligations	(258)
Total Other Comprehensive Expense	**(6,258)**
Total Comprehensive Loss for the year	(14,598)

Loss for the year and total comprehensive loss for the year are fully attributable to the equity shareholders.

Doherty Holdings Plc
CONSOLIDATED STATEMENT OF FINANCIAL POSITION
as at 31 December 2012

	€000
Non-current Assets	
Goodwill	19,489
Property, plant and equipment	10,469
Intangible assets	2,100
Interests in joint ventures	3,160
Investment property	3,690
Deferred tax assets	1,100
	40,008
Current Assets	
Inventories	156,000
Trade and other receivables	46,000
Cash and cash equivalents	14,190
	216,190
Total Assets	**256,198**

Equity	
Share capital	2,885
Share premium	31,001
Other reserves	870
Hedging and translation reserves	5,674
Retained earnings	8,460
Total Equity	**48,890**
Current Liabilities	
Trade and other payables	68,222
Tax liabilities	4,400
Provisions	7,901
Obligations under finance leases	125
Bank loans and overdrafts	76,000
	156,648
Non-current Liabilities	
Bank loans	48,000
Retirement benefit obligations	1,006
Provisions	1,654
	50,660
Total Equity and Liabilities	**256,198**

Doherty Holdings Plc

CONSOLIDATED STATEMENT OF CHANGES IN EQUITY
for the year ended 31 December 2012

	Ordinary Share Capital €000	**Share Premium €000**	**Hedging Translation €000**	**Other Reserves[1] €000**	**Retained Earnings €000**	**Total €000**
Balance at 1 January 2012	2,000	30,886	11,674	1,128	16,600	62,288
Prior year adjustment	-	-	-	-	-	-
Comprehensive Income/(Loss)	-	-	(6,000)	(258)	(8,340)	(14,598)
New share issue	1,200					1,200
Share buyback	(315)	115	-	-	200	-
Balance at 31 December 2011	2,885	31,001	5,674	870	8,460	48,890

[1] 'Other Reserves' comprise Share Option Reserve, Retirement Benefits Reserve and other items that are recognised direct in equity (of which there were none in the current period).

Outstanding Issues in Respect of the Group Financial Statements

Note: Ignore the tax effects of all adjustments other than Issue (6)

Outstanding Issue 1

The inventory figure in the draft financial statements is made up of the following

	€000
Development land at cost	94,000
Work-in-progress:	
Irish housing	24,000
UK housing	19,000
Leisure and commercial developments	9,000
Other	10,000
	156,000

In 2010 Doherty Holdings acquired a 50-acre plot of development land in Roscommon. The land was in an area known as 'Marsh Meadows'. The land cost €125,000 per acre including all ancillary acquisition costs and it is included in the financial statements as part of 'development land at cost' at that figure.

It has now transpired that the land is unfit for development. The area is a floodplain and, given recent meteorological changes, building on the land is considered too risky. The company has abandoned its development plans. A recent valuation suggests the land is now worth €90,000 per acre. The company now wishes to sell the land. However in order to sell, remedial drainage work is required. This is estimated to cost about €1.3 million.

Doherty Holdings is seeking reimbursement of the drainage costs from the original vendors. They claim that this drainage work should have been carried out by the vendor when the original sale took place in 2010. The vendor's reply to this claim was *caveat emptor*, i.e. buyer beware. They have dismissed the claim completely.

Outstanding Issue 2

The trade and other receivables include construction contract balances totalling €23 million.

One of these contracts is for the construction of an apartment complex in the Temple Bar area of Dublin. The contract is with Boyd McNamara Ltd. The contract was signed in January 2011 but, due to planning difficulties, construction did not commence until November 2011. The original fixed contract price was €15 million, with estimated total costs of €10 million over the duration of the project period. Doherty successfully sought an additional fee of €1 million to compensate for loss of earnings during the period of delay, as the group could not tender for other contracts during this time. By 31 December 2012, 60% of the total costs had been incurred and the project was deemed to be 60% complete. No profit had been recognised in 2011 as the project was only in its initial stages. Boyd McNamara paid 10% of the original contract price in August 2012. All of this information has already been incorporated into the draft financial statements in accordance with IAS11 *Construction Contracts.*

On 6 January 2013, Boyd McNamara was declared bankrupt. Business operations ceased on that date. Doherty Holdings were not officially notified until February 2013. No adjustments have been made to the financial statements to reflect this bad debt. Initial indications are that unsecured creditors will not receive anything.

Doherty Holdings has committed itself to further costs in 2013 of €800,000 in relation to this project. These commitments cannot be cancelled.

Outstanding Issue 3

In an effort to boost housing sales the group launched a Rent to Buy Property Purchase Scheme in 2012.

The scheme operates as follows:

1. A customer selects a property they would like to own.
2. A price is fixed for the property. This price will be fixed for three years.
3. The customer signs a Rent to Buy letting agreement and moves into the property.
4. The customer has up to three years to make a decision to purchase the property.
5. If a decision is made to purchase the property, all rental payments already made will be deducted from the purchase price. If the customer chooses not to buy they simply vacate the premises.

This scheme has proved very successful. During 2012, 500 properties were occupied under this scheme. Rental income of €4.5 million was generated in the period, all of which has been credited to cost of sales. The rental charged on the properties represents a market rent, there is no additional charge for the inherent option to buy the property at a fixed price in the future, this option has zero value.

On 31 December 2012, formal agreements were signed relating to the unconditional purchase of 100 of these properties. The agreed price for each of these properties was €290,000 and the total rental income received on these properties up to 31 December 2012, was €900,000. No adjustment has been made to the financial statements to reflect these sales. The cost of constructing each property was €210,000.

Outstanding Issue 4

The accounting policy for investment properties held by the group is to measure them at cost less depreciation and impairment write downs.

Included in the investment property portfolio is a complex of 10 apartments in Portugal that have a carrying value of €2 million. In October 2012 Doherty Holdings made a decision to sell the entire complex. Initial interest has been very positive and Doherty Holdings believe they will have no trouble securing a sale in 2013. The fair value less costs to sell of the complex in October 2012 was estimated to be €2.8 million but had fallen to €1.8 million by the end of December 2012. Given the likelihood of a sale, the company did not depreciate the apartments in the final quarter of the year.

The remaining investment properties in the group had a recoverable value of €1.45 million at the year end.

Outstanding Issue 5

Paul Hogarty, the financial director of Mallon Ltd, a UK construction company, contacted Alan Doherty in 2012 with an unusual request. His company wished to acquire land in the South East of Ireland. Although there was plenty of land available, the company was not in a position to raise finance to settle a deal in cash. Instead, what was proposed, in a letter dated 12 November 2012, was that Mallon Ltd and Doherty Holdings exchange land holdings. Mallon Ltd would give Doherty 150 acres of development land in the UK that has a current value of €9,733 per acre in exchange for 120 acres of agricultural land in the South East of Ireland and a draft of €500,000 payable to Mallon Ltd. A holding of this size in the South East is currently trading at €8,000 per acre and you can assume that it is also included in the group's inventory at this value.

Doherty and Mallon signed contracts for the exchange of land on 4 December 2012 but no adjustments have been made to reflect this transaction.

Outstanding Issue 6

The deferred tax balance in the draft Statement of Financial Position relates to 2011. The adjustments for 2012 have not yet been considered. All temporary differences were taxed at a rate of 12.5% in 2011. This tax rate is not expected to change in 2012.

At 31 December 2012 the following were relevant:

1. The tax written down value of the group's non-current assets exceeded its book value by €2.8 million. This difference is due entirely to the different rates of depreciation and capital allowances on the company's tangible assets.
2. At 31 December 2012 the defined benefit pension obligation was €1.006 million. The equivalent tax base was €300,000. You may assume that, for tax purposes, the pension expense is allowed only when it is paid.
3. Included in 'trade and other payables' is an accrual for interest charges. The accrual relates to interest on a €10 million 5% bank loan that was issued on 1 January 2012. Interest is charged semi-annually on the loan and is paid, in arrears, in August and February of each year. A payment for the first six months of the year was duly made on 1 August 2012. The capital sum is due to be repaid in one lump-sum in 2019.
4. One of the group's 100% subsidiaries, OMIY Ltd, made a tax adjusted loss of €2.54 million during the year. The only relief for this tax loss is to carry it forward for offset against future taxable profits of the company. OMIY Ltd is expected to be profitable in future years.
5. The remaining temporary *taxable* timing differences affecting the statement of comprehensive income in 2012 amount to €2,970,000.

Note: You may assume that deferred tax assets and liabilities may be offset against each other for the purposes of presentation in the statement of financial position.

Outstanding Issue 7

In 2012, Doherty Holdings incurred €2 million researching new building technologies. These costs have been capitalised but not yet amortised. Currently, the costs are included as part of Intangible Assets. 2012 was the first time the group ventured into research activities and the company justified the accounting treatment on the basis that new building technologies should eventually improve the construction process and ultimately reduce the overheads of the business. Doherty Holdings intends to amortise these development costs over a five-year period commencing in 2013.

Outstanding Issue 8

The group is made up of a number of subsidiaries, all wholly owned by the group. Many of these subsidiaries were either acquired on incorporation (hence there is no goodwill) or any goodwill arising has already been written off. The goodwill figure in the consolidated statement of financial position (€19,489,000) relates, in its entirety, to the acquisition of 100% of Green Energy Construction Ltd.

An impairment review of the goodwill figure needs to be undertaken and the following information has been provided.

Green Energy Construction comprises two cash generating units (CGUs): the Green Construction Division and the Insulation Division. On acquisition €14,000,000 of the goodwill was attributable to the Green Construction CGU and €5,489,000 to the Insulation Division CGU.

It was not possible to arrive at a fair value less cost to sell for the subsidiary or its CGUs – due to the depressed state of the property market there are not many similar transactions to benchmark the company against.

Instead, the directors provided an estimate of the future cash flows for each of the CGUs. These estimates are based on board-approved forecasts.

Green Construction Division

	2013	2014	2015	2016	2017
	€000	€000	€000	€000	€000
Operating Cash	1,500	1,500	1,500	2,500	2,500
Interest	(200)	(200)	(200)	(200)	(200)
Tax	(300)	(300)	(300)	(300)	(300)
Net Cash	1,000	1,000	1,000	2,000	2,000

The appropriate pre-tax cost of capital for the Green Construction Division is 9%.

Insulation Division

	2013	2014	2015	2016	2017
	€000	€000	€000	€000	€000
Operating Cash	1,000	1,000	1,000	1,500	1,500

Interest	(200)	(200)	(200)	(200)	(200)
Tax	(200)	(200)	(200)	(200)	(200)
Net Cash	600	600	600	1,100	1,100

The appropriate pre-tax cost of capital for the Insulation Division is 6%.

Note 1: The interest cost was split 50:50 between the divisions as the management have argued that it is not possible to identify what division the bank finance was applicable to.
Note 2: The management do not intend to sell either division. After 2017 each CGU will generate the 2017 cash flows in perpetuity less €500,000 on annual expenditure to maintain the productive capacity.

The current carrying values of the assets and liabilities of the CGUs are as follows:

	Green Construction Division	Insulation Division
	€000	€000
PPE	3,000	1,500
Inventory	6,500	250
Receivables	11,000	5,000
Cash	850	900
Payables	(5,500)	(2,500)
	15,850	5,150

Outstanding Issue 9

Doherty Holdings had two million €1 shares in issue at the beginning of the financial year. In February 2012 the company issued 1.2 million additional €1 ordinary shares at €1 per share. The proceeds of the shares was received in two stages: €0.2 per share on application on 1 February 2012 and the balance on the allotment date of 1 August 2012. In addition, on 30 November 2012, as part of a proposed financial restructuring plan, Doherty Plc bought back 315,000 shares at full market price.

There are also 1.5 million outstanding share options in the group. The options were issued in 2010 and are exercisable in 2015 at €6.50 per share. The average market price of the company's shares in 2012 was €0.50. There was no change in the fair value of these options over the period.

Outstanding Issue 10

A news report has come to the attention of Mark Doherty, now CEO of Doherty Holdings. The report includes the following comment:

'Live Register analysis by IRB Consulting estimated that, in April 2012, employment in construction was down 40% from its peak in 2007 or 110,000 job losses in construction alone. The ESRI are predicting a decline of 37% commercial and retail construction in 2013.'

Mark Doherty is concerned about the long-term viability of the group. 2012 was a bad year for the company. In addition to the collapse of Boyd McNamara's business, there are rumblings in the industry about a number of other property developers sinking into deep financial crisis.

Mark believes that Doherty Holdings may have a going-concern issue in the near future if the economy does not improve. He is also aware that under stock exchange listing rules of both the Irish and London Stock Exchanges, listed entities are required to include a statement by the directors that the business is a going concern, together with supporting assumptions or qualifications as necessary.

Requirements

(**Note:** Unless you are specifically required to consider deferred taxation, you can assume that it is not applicable.)

(a) Advise the financial Director of **Doherty Holdings Plc** on the appropriate accounting treatment for outstanding matters (1) to (8) above.
Your answer should give a reasoned rationale for the appropriate treatment in each case.
(**Note:** you are not asked to redraft the financial statements)

(40 marks)

(b) Summarise the impact the adjustments will have on the Group Total Comprehensive Income for the year ended 31 December 2012.

(4 marks)

(c) Using the adjusted profit figure from requirement (b), above, and the information outlined in **Outstanding Issue 9,** calculate the basic and diluted Earnings/(Loss) per Share to be included in the Group Financial Statements for the accounting period.

(10 marks)

(d) In relation to **Outstanding Issue 10,** prepare a brief analysis of performance over the period and then comment briefly on how an analysis of the 2012 financial statements may provide meaningful information on the going-concern capability of the group.

(6 marks)

(Total: 60 marks)

Guidance Notes – Doherty Holdings Plc

Exam Technique

Read the case carefully and then read the requirements.

Requirement (a) of this case study is similar to the requirements of 'The Howard Retail Group'. In both cases consolidation forms only a minor part of the case study. Instead, the case is made up of a series of issues that you must address. In **requirement (a)** there are eight separate issues. The issues address a wide range of accounting standards. You are asked to produce a comprehensive answer to each of these issues. Your answer should include a reasoned rationale along with journal entries, where appropriate. Although it is possible to approach these adjustments in any order, it is advisable that you answer them in the order in which they appear. This may avoid unnecessary confusion.

You are not required to redraft the financial statements. Instead, you are asked, in **requirement (b)**, to summarise the impact the adjustments will have on the Group Total Comprehensive Income for the year.

Requirement (c) requires the calculation of the Earnings per Share ratios for the period. You should not attempt this section until you have finalised **requirement (b)** as you will need the adjusted profit for the period to correctly calculate the EPS for the period.

Finally, **requirement (d)** is discursive. You are asked to address how an analysis of the 2012 financial statements may provide meaningful information about the long-term viability of the group. This section is very general and should not take too long to complete. No calculations are required.

As mentioned in all of the case studies, *manage your time*. You should establish, at the outset, how much time you have and you should allocate the time accordingly. You will score better marks if you *attempt* all parts of the case, rather than completing some sections and not answering others at all.

Answering the Case Study

Requirement (a) – Guidance

Outstanding Issue 1 This issue addresses the valuation of inventory. A common feature for many construction companies in the post-Celtic Tiger era is the significant loss in value of their inventory. This issue highlights how these losses should be presented in the financial statements.

To answer this issue you must be familiar with the provisions of IAS 2 *Inventories*. In particular, you need to know how inventory is measured. The measurement of inventory is outlined in IAS 2, paragraphs 9–33. You will need to complete a calculation to establish the net realisable value (NRV) of development land. This will be used in arriving at the final valuation of inventory. The guidance on NRV is outlined in IAS 2, paragraphs 28–33.

Finally, you must consider the claim for drainage costs. Doherty Holdings is seeking reimbursement of these costs from the original vendor of the property. How should this claim be presented in the financial statements? IAS 37 *Provisions, Contingent Liabilities and Contingent Assets* will provide you with the appropriate guidance.

Outstanding Issue 2 One of Doherty's customers had been experiencing trading difficulties and in early January 2013 was declared bankrupt. Doherty Holdings was under contract with this customer to construct an apartment complex in the Temple Bar area of Dublin. Construction was partially complete at the end of 2012. The news of the customer's difficulties became public knowledge in February 2013 but no entries have been made in the financial statements to reflect this changed status.

In order to resolve this issue, you will need to:

1. Establish the outstanding balance on the Boyd McNamara receivable at the end of 2012. It is stated that the contract has been accounted for in accordance with IAS 11 *Construction Contracts.* (This standard outlines how partly completed construction contracts should be presented in the financial statements.) To establish the year-end balance you will need to understand the principles of IAS 11.
2. Next you will need to determine what to do with the outstanding balance on the Boyd McNamara receivable account. Although the company ceased trading on 6 January 2013, it was experiencing difficulties throughout 2012. You must decide whether this bad debt should be written off in the 2012 or 2013 accounts and what the correct disclosures are. IAS 10 *Events after the Reporting Period* will provide you with the appropriate guidance.
3. Finally, although the contract will not now be completed, Doherty Holdings are committed to €1.3 million of further costs. These commitments cannot be cancelled or modified. You must consider how to include this information in the financial statements. IAS 37 *Provisions, Contingent Liabilities and Contingent Assets* will provide the appropriate guidance, in particular, paragraphs 66-69 of the standard on onerous contracts.

Outstanding Issue 3 Doherty launched a 'rent to buy' property purchase scheme in 2012. This is a concept employed by construction entities to generate some income from their large stock of unsold housing. The option allows the (potential) buyer to rent a property for a period of time while deciding whether or not to buy.

There are no specific accounting guidelines for 'rent to buy' purchase schemes but IAS 18 *Revenue* will help. You need to consider the classification of the rent generated from the scheme during the 2012 accounting period *and,* in addition, the appropriate presentation for the 100 properties sold at the end of 2012. IAS 18, paragraphs 14–18, outlines *when* revenue should be recognised. Paragraphs 9–12 provide guidance on *how* revenue should be measured. You should find the appropriate answers here.

Outstanding Issue 4 Many companies hold properties for investment purposes rather than for occupation or stock-in-trade. In financial reporting, properties held for investment purposes are presented in accordance with IAS 40 *Investment Property.* In this accounting standard, properties can be measured at either cost or fair value. Doherty Holdings chose to measure investment properties at cost. The appropriate accounting guidance is outlined in IAS 40, paragraph 56.

Doherty Holdings made a decision in 2012 to sell a section of their investment property portfolio, although no buyer had been secured by the end of the reporting period. You must decide how to present these properties in the financial statements. Should they continue to be presented in accordance with IAS 40 *or* should they be presented in accordance with IFRS 5 *Non-current Assets Held for Sale and Discontinued Operations* as a sale is imminent? The conditions to be satisfied before the properties can be classified as 'held for sale' will help you decide on the most appropriate presentation. These are outlined in IFRS 5, paragraphs 7–12.

Outstanding Issue 5 A barter transaction has taken place between Doherty Holdings and a UK-based construction company, Mallon Ltd. The companies have swapped holdings of land. The legal exchange was completed before the year-end but no accounting entries have been made to reflect this transaction. The exchange involves both a purchase and sale of property. IAS 18 *Revenue* includes a section on the appropriate accounting treatment for barter transactions (IAS 18, para 12). You will need to review these provisions to establish how this transaction should be presented in the financial statements.

Outstanding Issue 6 In this section you need to update the provision for deferred tax. Guidance on deferred taxation is outlined in IAS 12 *Income Taxes.* In the case study, you are given certain details about deferred taxation including the opening position on 1 January 2012 and a list of differences between the financial statements and the tax base at the end of the reporting period. You must decide what to do with this information.

The guidance in IAS 12 is reasonably detailed. The deferred tax implications of the transactions arising in this issue are outlined as follows:
1. The net book value and the tax written down value of assets (IAS 12, para 17(b)).
2. Retirement obligations paid and accrued (IAS 12, para 26(a)).
3. Accruals (IAS 12, para 17(a)).
4. Losses recorded in accounting profit and losses recorded for tax purposes (IAS 12, para 34–36).
5. Other temporary differences (IAS 12, para 17–18).

You will need to review these sections before attempting the deferred taxation adjustment for 2012.

Outstanding Issue 7 This issue addresses the accounting treatment for research and development costs. The accounting guidelines are outlined in paragraphs 51–67 of IAS 38 *Intangible assets.* This part of the standard recommends that research expenditure be treated as an operating expense of the business and included in accounting profit (or loss), and development expenditure be capitalised and included as an intangible asset in the statement of financial position. In the case study you are told that the costs of researching new building techniques have been capitalised. You must decide if this is the appropriate treatment of these costs. You should consult IAS 38, paragraph 57. This paragraph sets out the conditions that must be satisfied before expenditure can be classified as development expenditure. If the conditions of paragraph 57 are satisfied, the expenditure has been correctly classified, and no adjustment is required. If the conditions of paragraph 57 are not satisfied, an adjustment will be necessary to write off the expenditure to the income statement.

Outstanding Issue 8 IAS 36 addresses impairment of assets including goodwill.

The first task is to determine the carrying value of each of the cash generating units (CGUs) – remember, the carrying value of the CGUs includes both the goodwill allocated and the individual assets less liabilities. This is not an onerous task as the figures are presented.

The next step will be to calculate the recoverable amount of the CGU (see IAS 36, paragraph 74 and paragraphs 18–57, in particular paragraphs 30–39). As no figure is provided for 'fair value less costs to sell', then the recoverable amount is determined by the 'value in use' of each CGU.

Your decision on how to deal with the cash flows beyond year 5 will have a big bearing on the outcome. Take a look at IAS 36, paragraphs 35–38, however, bear in mind that these paragraphs discuss growth rates not absolute amounts.

Finally, if a CGU is impaired then you will need to allocate the impairment to the assets of the CGU – this process is described in IAS 36, paragraphs 104–105.

Requirement (b) – Guidance

In this requirement you are **not** asked to redraft the financial statements. Instead, you are asked to summarise the impact on the adjustments from **requirement (a)** on the group statement of comprehensive income. You should note that there are just four marks allocated to this requirement so it should not take very long. You are not required to do any new thinking; you are just required to bring together your answer from the previous requirement.

An important element of this requirement is to ensure that your workings are easy to follow, so you will need to highlight clearly where the adjustments are coming from.

There should be two sections to your answer:

1. Take the loss for the financial year (currently €8.34 million) and restate this for the adjustments made in the previous requirement.
2. Take the total other comprehensive expense for the year (currently an expense of €6.258 million) and restate for the adjustments that impact on other comprehensive expense.

The resultant figure (item 1 and item 2) will give the restated total comprehensive income/loss for the period.

Requirement (c) – Guidance

Paragraph 66 of IAS 33 *Earnings per Share* states that an entity whose securities are publicly traded (or in process of public issuance) "shall present in the statement of comprehensive income basic and diluted EPS for profit or loss from continuing operations attributable to the ordinary equity holders of the parent entity and for profit or loss attributable to the ordinary equity holders of the parent entity for the period, for each class of ordinary shares that has a different right to share in profit for the period … "

In this section you are required to calculate the Earnings/Loss per Share of Doherty Holdings for the reporting period. You are required to calculate both the *basic* earnings per share and the *diluted* earnings per share. To complete these calculations you will need to determine the following:

1. *The adjusted profit/loss of the group.*
   This will be determined on completion of **requirement (b)** of the case study, *and*
2. *The average number of shares in issue for the reporting period.*
   Outstanding issue 9 provides details about the movement in share capital during the reporting period.
3. *Outstanding convertible instruments, options and warrants, contingent shares.*
   Outstanding issue 9 provides the necessary details.

IAS 33 *Earnings per Share* provides detailed guidance for EPS calculations. IAS 33 is divided into two sections. Paragraphs 9–29 outline the rules for calculating the basic earnings per share while paragraphs 30–65 deal with diluted earnings per share.

It should be noted that you will need to complete the basic EPS before you can complete the diluted EPS.

Requirement (d) – Guidance

The purpose of this section is to introduce an element of analysis to the case study.

You are required to comment on how the 2012 financial statements can provide meaningful information about the future viability of an organisation. Your answer to this part of the case study should be in a discursive format. You are asked to *comment* on the financial statements in the context of a possible going-concern problem; you are not required to produce any calculations. Bear in mind that going concern is a matter of judgement and it will be possible to draw both favourable and unfavourable indications from the financial statements and other information provided.

Recommended Reading

The above issues are also referenced in *International Financial Accounting and Reporting*, 3rd Edition, by Ciaran Connolly (Chartered Accountants Ireland, 2011) as follows:

Requirement (a)

Case	Chapter	Chapter title	Standard	Chapter section
Issue 1	11	Inventories	IAS 2	11.2
	14	Provisions, Contingent Liabilities and Contingent Assets	IAS 37	14.2
Issue 2	12	Construction Contracts	IAS 11	12.2
	15	Events after the Reporting Period	IAS 10	15.2
Issue 3	4	Revenue Recognition	IAS 18	4.2
Issue 4	20	Non-current Assets Held for Sale and Discontinued Operations	IFRS 5	20.3
	5	Investment Property	IAS 40	5.2
Issue 5	4	Revenue Recognition	IAS 18	4.2
Issue 6	13	Income Taxes	IAS 12	13.3
Issue 7	9	Intangible Assets	IAS 38	9.2
Issue 8	10	Impairment	IAS 36	10.1

Requirement (c)

Case	Chapter	Chapter title	Standard	Chapter section
Issue 9	23	Earnings per Share	IAS 33	23.6, 23.7

Requirement (d)

Case	Chapter	Chapter title	Standard	Chapter section
Issue 10	35	Analysis and Interpretation of Financial Information		

Solution to Doherty Holdings Plc

Requirement (a)

Outstanding Issue 1

Development land is included in inventories. As a construction business, development land is part of the inventory of the business and is governed by the rules of IAS 2 *Inventories*. This land should be valued at the lower of cost and net realisable value (NRV) in accordance with IAS 2, paragraph 9. It is currently included in inventory at cost of €6.25 million.

The case study states that, at the end of the 2012, the value of this inventory has fallen below cost. An adjustment will be required to write this land down from cost to net realisable value.

NRV is measured in accordance with IAS 2, paragraph 6, as "the estimated selling price in the ordinary course of business less the estimated costs of completion and the estimated costs necessary to make the sale". For this tranche of development land the NRV is as follows:

	€000
Estimated selling Price (50 × €90,000)	4,500
Costs necessary to make sale	(1,300)
NRV	3,200

An adjustment of €3.05 million is required to write the inventory down from its cost of €6.25 million to its NRV of €3.2 million as follows:

	€000	**€000**
DR Cost of Sales	3,050	
CR Inventory		3,050

In addition, Doherty Holdings are seeking reimbursement for the drainage costs that are likely to be incurred by the group. IAS 37, paragraphs 53–58, gives clear guidance on how reimbursements should be presented in financial statements. In accordance with paragraph 53, a reimbursement is recognised "when, and only when, it is virtually certain that reimbursement will be received". As initial indications of recovery appear remote, this transaction should *not* be recognised as an asset.

If it is probable (but not virtually certain) that the funds will be recovered, disclosure as a contingent asset would be appropriate. IAS 37, paragraph 89, outlines the treatment of contingent assets as follows:

> "Where an inflow of economic benefits is probable, an entity shall disclose a brief description of the nature of the contingent assets at the end of the reporting period, and, where practicable, an estimate of their financial effect ..."

The case study indicates that that there is little hope of recovering the costs. Therefore, the claim cannot be classified as 'probable'. Disclosure would not be appropriate as it could be misleading. The most appropriate treatment for this claim is to omit it from the financial statements altogether.

Outstanding Issue 2

Boyd McNamara, a customer of Doherty Holdings, has run into financial difficulty. The company was declared bankrupt on 6 January 2013. Unsecured creditors will not receive anything. This receivable has become a bad debt.

The first step is to establish the outstanding balance on the McNamara receivable at the end of the reporting period. The case study states that the contract has been accounted for in accordance with IAS 11 *Construction Contracts*. You need to apply the rules of the standard in order to establish the current balance on the contract. Under paragraph 42 of the standard "An entity shall present … the gross amount due from customers for contract work as an asset".

Paragraph 43 explains what this means. The gross amount due from customers is "the net amount of: (a) costs incurred plus recognised profits; less (b) the sum of recognised losses and progress billings".

The gross amount due from McNamara and included in the 2012 statement of financial position would be:

	€000	
Costs incurred	6,000	(60% of total costs)
Profit recognised	3,600	(60% of total profit of €6,000,000*)
Progress billings	(1,500)	
Balance	8,100	

* Total Profit on the contract, €6 million, is made up of revenue €16 million (€15 million plus €1 million alteration) less costs €10 million. An alternative calculation may also be acceptable if the view is taken that the additional €1 million was earned in full before the contract commenced. The €1 million was claimed for loss of profits suffered prior to the commencement of the contract. If this view is taken the €1 million can be credited to profit or loss in full immediately and the contract profit of €5 million would be spread over the contract period.

You must now decide whether this balance should remain in the accounts or whether it should be written-off as a bad debt. Although the announcement of the bad debt was made in early 2013, the bad debt should be written off in the 2012 financial statements. The reason for this is outlined in paragraph 9(b)(i) of IAS10 *Events after the Reporting Period.* This paragraph states that "the bankruptcy of a customer that occurs after the reporting period usually confirms that a loss existed at the end of the reporting period on a trade receivable and that the entity needs to adjust the carrying amount of the trade receivable".

A journal entry to reflect the bad debt would be required as follows:

	€000	€000
DR Expenses (Exceptional)	8,100	
CR Trade Receivables		8,100

Finally, Doherty Holdings is committed to further costs of €800,000 on this project. These costs cannot be cancelled and, as the contract will now be discontinued, it is assumed that no economic benefits will be derived from them. This situation is known as an onerous contract. Paragraph 66 of IAS 37 *Provisions, Contingent Liabilities and Contingent Assets* states that if an entity has an obligation that is onerous, "the present obligation under the contract shall be recognised and measured as a provision".

An adjustment will be required to reflect this onerous contract as follows:

	€000	€000
DR Expenses	800	
CR Provisions		800

Outstanding Issue 3

There are two issues to consider here. First, the classification of the rental income and, secondly, presentation of the sale of properties at the period end.

The most appropriate classification for rental income is to include it in 'Other Operating Income' in the statement of comprehensive income. The current classification, a deduction from cost of sales, is clearly incorrect. The cost of constructing these properties has not been reduced by these rental contributions. These contributions are providing a return on unsold properties.

The second issue is the sale of 100 'rent and buy' properties at the end of the financial period. No adjustment has yet been made in the financial statements to reflect these sales. These properties have been sold unconditionally. It is, therefore, appropriate to treat them as revenue in the 2012 financial statements. IAS 18, paragraph 14, states that revenue shall be recognised when "the entity has transferred to the buyer the significant risks and rewards of ownership of the goods" and "the entity retains neither continuing managerial involvement ... nor effective control over the goods sold". When recording the sale, the rental income already received should be deducted from the selling price of each property in accordance with the terms of the contract.

The adjustments necessary to reflect the above transactions include:

1. To adjust the classification of rental income from 'Cost of Sales' to 'Other Operating Income':

	€000	€000
DR Cost of Sales	4,500	
CR Other Operating Income		4,500

2. To record the sale of properties:

	€000	€000
DR Receivables	28,100	
CR Revenue		28,100

(100 properties at €290,000 each, giving €29 million less €900,000 of rent recognised.)

3. To remove these properties from Inventory:

	€000	€000
DR Cost of Sales	21,000	
CR Inventory		21,000
(100 properties at cost price of €210,000)		

Outstanding Issue 4

IAS 40 Investment Property permits entities to measure investment properties at either cost or fair value. The information provided states that the policy of the Doherty Holdings is to measure these properties at cost. Investment properties are included in the draft statement of financial position at €3.69 million.

A decision was made in October 2012 to dispose of part of this portfolio, an apartment complex in Portugal. The complex is included in the financial statements at €2m (cost). No adjustment has been made for the impending sale.

In accordance with IFRS 5 *Non-current Assets Held for Sale and Discontinued Operations*, non-current assets that are held for sale at the year-end should be presented separately to other non-current assets in the statement of financial position. However, in order for IFRS 5 to apply, there are certain conditions that must be fulfilled:

1. IFRS 5 only applies to investment properties that are accounted for using the cost model in IAS 40. As the policy of the group is to measure investment property at cost, this condition has been satisfied.
2. IFRS 5, paragraph 8, states that, in order to be classified separately, the sale must be "highly probable, the appropriate level of management must be committed to a plan to sell the asset … , and an active programme to locate a buyer and complete the plan must have been initiated". We are told that initial interest has been very positive. This would indicate that the property has been well advertised or, in other words, that an active programme to locate a buyer had been initiated by the period end. As a result the property should be classified in accordance with IFRS 5.

IFRS 5, paragraph 15, states "An entity shall measure a non-current asset … classified as held for sale at the lower of its carrying value and fair value less costs to sell." In October 2012 the carrying value of the complex was €2 million and the fair value less costs to sell was €2.8 million. The transfer from non-current assets should have been made as follows:

	€000	€000
DR Non-current assets held for sale	2,000	
CR Investment properties		2,000

Depreciation should not be charged on an asset while it is classified as held for sale (IFRS 5, paragraph 25).

At 31 December 2012, the fair value of the complex has fallen below its carrying value. IFRS 5, paragraph 20, states that "An entity shall recognise an impairment loss for any initial or subsequent write-down of the asset … to fair value less costs to sell." The property should be written down to €1.8 million as follows:

	€000	€000
DR Expenses	200	
CR Non-current assets held for sale		200

Finally, the remaining investment property portfolio of €1.69 million is also impaired. The recoverable value of these properties is €1.45 million at the end of the reporting period. These also need to be written down to recoverable value as follows:

	€000	€000
DR Expenses	240	
CR Investment Properties		240

Outstanding Issue 5

The Doherty Holdings and a UK construction company, Mallon Ltd, have entered into a barter arrangement by swapping land holdings. Paragraph 12 of IAS 18 *Revenue* outlines the accounting treatment for barter transactions. The accounting treatment depends on whether or not goods or services are swapped for goods and services of a similar nature and value.

The standard states that, where the swap is of goods and services of a similar nature and value, "the exchange is not regarded as a transaction which generates revenue" (IAS 18, para 12). Alternatively, if the swap is of goods and services of a dissimilar nature and value "the exchange is regarded as a transaction which generates revenue". In the case of Doherty and Mallon the land holdings are of a dissimilar nature and value and therefore the transaction would give rise to revenue.

In these situations, revenue is measured at "the fair value of the goods and services received, adjusted by the amount of any cash or cash equivalents transferred. When the fair value of goods or services received cannot be measured reliably, revenue is measured at the fair value of goods or services given up, adjusted by the amount of any cash or cash equivalents transferred" (IAS 18, para 12).

In this swap arrangement the fair value of land received is €9,733 per acre. Revenue will be measured at the fair value of land received, adjusted by any cash that has been exchanged as part of the contract as follows:

Value of the transaction:	
	€000
Value of land received (€9,733 × 150 acres)	1,460
Cash transaction	(500)
Barter element of transaction (Revenue)	960

The journal entry to incorporate the barter transaction:

	€000	€000
DR Purchases (land received)	1,460	
CR Trade Payables		500
CR Revenue (land transferred)		960

In addition, inventory at 31 December 2012 will require adjustment to reflect the change in land holding:

	€000	€000
DR Closing inventory (SOFP)	500*	
CR Cost of Sales (SOCI)		500

* Addition of €1,460,000 and transfer of €960,000. Net Inventory change €500,000

Outstanding Issue 6

The deferred tax balance requires updating. The opening position, a deferred tax asset of €1.1 million, is included in non-current assets. The opening position represents cumulative net temporary deductible differences at 1 January 2012 of €8.8 million taxed at 12.5%. The opening position and the updated information are made up of temporary taxable differences and temporary deductible differences. We are told that Doherty Plc has the right to offset deferred tax assets and liabilities. This right is laid down in IAS 12, paragraph 74, which states that the offset is permitted where "the deferred tax assets and … liabilities relate to income taxes levied by the same taxation authority".

The updated information relating to deferred taxation is made up of five separate points. Guidance on each point is dealt with separately in IAS 12. A revised 'deferred tax table' and the relevant guidance is as follows:

	Accounts Base	Tax Base	Temporary Difference	Deferred Asset (A)/ Liability (L)	Taxed at 12.50%	IAS12 para.
	€000	€000	€000		€000	
31 December 2012						
Non-current assets			2,800	A	350	17(b)
Retirement obligation	1,006	300	706	A	88	26(a)
Interest accrual	250	0	250	A	31	17(a)
Taxable Losses	2,540	0	2,540	A	318	34–36

Other *taxable* temporary differences	(2,970)	L	(371)	17–18
Cumulative differences	3,326		416	
less Opening differences (1,100/0.125)	8,800		1,100	
Change (reduction in the asset)	(5,474)		(684)	

The net cumulative temporary difference at the end of the reporting period was €3.326 million. Taxed at a rate of 12.5%, this represents a deferred tax asset of €0.416 million. This is a reduction in the opening deferred tax asset of €1.1 million. The difference of €0.684 million will be charged as a deferred tax expense in the 2012 financial statements and will be included in the tax expense for the period as follows:

	€000	**€000**
DR Taxation expense	684	
CR Deferred Tax Asset		684

The 2012 closing deferred tax balance of €0.416 million will be included in the non-current assets section of the statement of financial position.

Outstanding Issue 7

IAS 38, paragraph 55, states that "In the research phase of an internal project, an entity cannot demonstrate that an intangible asset exists that will generate probable economic benefits. Therefore, this expenditure is recognised as an expense when it is incurred."

The expenditure incurred by the Doherty Holdings falls into this category and therefore it should be included in profit or loss and not as an intangible asset in the financial statements.

An adjustment is required to correct the accounting treatment for this expenditure as follows:

	€000	**€000**
DR Expenses	2,000	
CR Intangible assets		2,000

Outstanding Issue 8

Under IAS 36 there is a requirement to test goodwill for impairment on an annual basis (IAS 36, paragraph 10). As goodwill does not exist on its own, it is necessary to allocate goodwill to its associated CGU. The detail of the case study has already done this. The carrying value of each CGU is as follows:

	Green Construction Division	Insulation Division
	€000	**€000**
Net assets carrying value	15,850	5,150
Goodwill carrying value	14,000	5,489
Total carrying value	29,850	10,639

The future cash flows (or fair value less costs to sell) is what underpins the above valuations. In this instance, there is no fair value less costs to sell hence the recoverable amount is determined solely based on the present value of the future cash flows of each CGU.

The next issue is to determine which cash flows should be included and the appropriate discount rate that should be applied. The discount rate used is the pre-tax discount rate (IAS 36, para 55). Consistent with this discount rate is the notion that interest costs and taxation are not included as part of the cash flows (IAS 36, para 50). Based on the information provided, the operating cash flows form the basis for the calculation.

The cash flows beyond year five should also be included in the analysis; IAS 36 permits this as long as the growth rate is steady or declining. In the information provided, the growth rate is zero (IAS 36, para 35–37). The costs of maintaining the CGU should also be deducted as long as there is no 'enhancement or improvement' in the CGU (IAS 36, para 44). Therefore, in the case of the Green Construction Division, the years six to perpetuity cash flows (2018 and forward) are €2,000,000 (€2,500,000 of operating cash flows less €500,000 of annual expenditure to maintain the CGU). Similarly the years six to perpetuity cash flows (2018 and forward) of the Insulation Division are €1,000,000 p.a. (€1,500,000 of operating cash flows less €500,000 of annual expenditure to maintain the CGU).

Value in Use – Green Construction CGU

	2013	2014	2015	2016	2017	2018+
	€000	**€000**	**€000**	**€000**	**€000**	**€000**
Cash Flows	1,500	1,500	1,500	2,500	2,500	2,000

To calculate the value of the annuity, the present value of the annuity from 2018 forward will be its value in 2017 and is calculated using the formula:

$$PV_{2017} = \frac{Cash\ Flow_{2017}}{r}$$

$$PV_{2017} = \frac{2{,}000{,}000}{9\%}$$

$$PV_{2017} = €22{,}222{,}000$$

Therefore the cash flows can be restated as follows:

	2013	2014	2015	2016	2017	2018+
	€000	€000	€000	€000	€000	€000
Cash Flows	1,500	1,500	1,500	2,500	2,500 + 22,222	

The present value of the cash flows above using a discount rate of 9% is €21,636 (this is the Value in Use of the Green Construction Division).

Value in Use – Insulation Division CGU

	2013	2014	2015	2016	2017	2018+
	€000	€000	€000	€000	€000	€000
Cash Flows	1,000	1,000	1,000	1,500	1,500	1,000

Using the same methodology as for the Green Construction Division, the Value in Use for the Insulation Division is €17,436,000.

The next stage in the process is to determine whether either of the CGUs is impaired. This is done by comparing the carrying value (calculated earlier) with the recoverable amount for each division.

	Green Construction Division €000	Insulation Division €000
Fair Value less costs to sell	n/a	n/a
Value in Use	21,636	17,436
Recoverable Amount (higher of Value in Use and Fair Value))	21,636	17,436
Carrying Value (from earlier)	29,850	10,639
Impairment	Yes	No
Impairment amount	8,214	0

The final stage in the process is to allocate the impairment loss against the assets of the Green Construction Division. The order of allocation is first against any assets that are obviously impaired (none in this case, but an example would be an asset that was damaged), then against goodwill and any remaining balance on a pro-rata basis across the other assets of the CGU (IAS 36, paras. 104–105).

In this instance the goodwill of the Green Construction Division is €14 million. This is enough to absorb all of the impairment. Therefore the journal entry required is:

	€000	€000
DR Expenses*	8,214	
CR Goodwill		8,214

* This expense may be material enough to appear as a separate line item on the face of the statement of comprehensive income in accordance with IAS 1, paragraph 97.

Requirement (b)

This requirement brings together all of the adjustments from **Requirement (a).** Note that you are not asked to redraft the income statement, you are only required to summarise the adjustments made.

Impact of Changes on the Statement of Comprehensive Income

		€000
Group loss for the period as originally stated		**(8,340)**
Adjustments:		
Issue 1	Write-down of inventory	(3,050)
Issue 2	Bad debts written off	(8,100)
	Onerous contract	(800)
Issue 3	Rental income reclassification	0
	Revenue from sale of houses	28,100
	Cost of sale of houses	(21,000)
Issue 4	Re-statement of non-current assets held for sale	(200)
	Re-statement of investment property	(240)
Issue 5	Barter transaction – (purchases €1,460,000 and sale €960,000)	(500)
	Barter transaction – increase in closing inventory	500
Issue 6	Deferred taxation	(684)
Issue 7	Research expenditure reclassified	(2,000)
Issue 8	Impairment loss	(8,214)
Revised Group Loss for the Period		**(24,528)**
Other Comprehensive Expense as originally stated		**(6,258)**
Adjustments:		
None		0
Revised Comprehensive Loss		**(6,258)**
Revised Total Comprehensive Loss		**(30,786)**

Overall reduction in Total Comprehensive Income is €16,188,000.

Requirement (c)

Earnings Per Share

Basic earnings/(loss) per share Basic earnings/(loss) per share is calculated by "dividing profit or loss attributable to ordinary equity holders of the parent entity (the numerator) by the weighted average number of ordinary shares outstanding (the denominator) during the period" (IAS 33, para 10).

Earnings IAS 33, paragraph 12, states that, for the purpose of calculating basic earnings per share, the amounts attributable to ordinary equity shareholders shall be profits, adjusted for the after-tax amounts of preference dividends, differences arising on the settlement of preference shares and other similar effects of preference shares classified as equity.

Doherty Plc has no preference shares in issue. The earnings for the EPS calculation will be the adjusted after-tax loss for the period, i.e. €24,528,000.

Shares IAS 33, paragraph 19, states that "For the purpose of calculating basic earnings per share, the number of ordinary shares shall be the weighted average number of ordinary shares outstanding during the period."

Paragraph 20 explains that the weighted average shares outstanding during the period is "the number of ordinary shares outstanding at the beginning of the period, adjusted by the number of ordinary shares bought back or issued during the period multiplied by a time-weighting factor".

The only exception to the weighting process is if shares are issued (or reduced, e.g. in a reverse share split) without a corresponding change in resources (e.g. a bonus issue or a bonus element of a rights issue). In these situations the shares are adjusted "as if the event had occurred at the beginning of the earliest period presented" (IAS 33, para. 28).

In the case of Doherty Holdings the changes in capital structure in 2012 included:

1. An issue at full market price in February (payable in two stages). Appendix A15 (application guide) states that "Where ordinary shares are issued but not fully paid, they are treated in the calculation of basic earnings per share as a fraction of an ordinary share to the extent that they were entitled to participate in dividends during the period relative to a fully paid ordinary share."
2. A repurchase, at full market price, on 30 November 2012.

The weighted average share capital for the purposes of calculating the basic EPS for the year ended 31 December 2012 is calculated as follows:

Dates		Number of Shares 000s	Fraction Paid	Number of Equivalent Shares 000s	Weighting Period	Weighted Shares 000s
1 Jan to 31 Jan	Opening share capital	2,000	100%	2,000	1 month	166.7
1 Feb	Partly paid shares	1,200	20%	240		
1 Feb to 31 Jul	New shares outstanding			2,240	6 months	1,120.0
1 Aug	Partly paid shares	1,200	80%	960		

1 Aug to 30 Nov	New shares outstanding			3,200	4 months	1,066.7
30 Nov	Buyback of shares	(315)	100%	(315)		
30 Nov to 31 Dec	New shares outstanding			2,885	1 month	240.4
	Total Weighted Shares in Issue					**2,593.8**

The basic earnings per share is as follows:

$$\frac{\text{Earnings (loss)}}{\text{Weighted Average Shares}} = \frac{(\text{€}24{,}528{,}000)}{2{,}593{,}800}$$

This gives a loss per share of (€9.46).

Diluted Earnings Per Share A dilution in basic earnings per share occurs when there is a "reduction in earnings per share or an increase in loss per share resulting from the assumption that convertible instruments are converted, that options or warrants are exercised, or that ordinary shares are issued upon the satisfaction of specified conditions" (IAS 33, para. 5).

In the case study there is only one convertible instrument in force, an issue of share options. These options are exercisable from 2015 onwards at a price of €6.50 per share. The average market price of the company's shares during 2012 was €0.50 per share.

If shareholders can purchase shares at €0.50 per share on the stock exchange secondary market it is unlikely they will pay €6.50 to acquire a share by exercising their options. The share option in this situation does not hold any value for the shareholder. The technical description for this is that the options are 'out of the money'. If a shareholder is unlikely to exercise their options then there will be no additional shares issued and consequently no dilution of the basic EPS.

Paragraph 47 of IAS 33 makes reference to this point. This paragraph states that "Options and warrants have a dilutive effect only when the average market price of ordinary shares during the period exceeds the exercise price of the options or warrants."

As there is no dilutive effect there is no need to calculate the diluted earnings per share.

Requirement (d)

Analysis of Financial Statements

An analysis of the financial statements may give information about the going concern assumption of a business in the following ways:

- The Statement of Financial Position indicates negative net worth.
  - Even after the adjustments the group has positive net worth, although the retained earnings have been absorbed by losses made in the current period.

- Financial gearing levels are very high.
  - The total of Bank Loans and Overdraft is €124 million. This combined with trade payables does indicate quite high gearing.
- Fixed term borrowings may be approaching maturity with no realistic plans for renewal of repayment.
  - Short-term loans and overdrafts are significant; progress on their renegotiation is not presented in the financial statements.
- Reliance on short-term borrowing to fund long-term assets.
  - This appears to be the case for the Doherty Holdings as their land holdings seem to be for the longer term due to the depressed nature of the property market.
- New shares issued to obtain financing in an attempt to restructure the business.
- Substantial sale of assets (not intended to be replaced).
  - No evidence provided.
- Negative operating cash flows indicated by historical financial statements.
  - No evidence provided.
- Adverse key financial ratios (including sales growth, profit growth, return on capital employed, total shareholder return, EPS, dividend per share, capital expenditure).
  - No specific evidence provided although the company is finding it difficult to sell property, i.e. sales are probably declining.
- Substantial operating losses.
  - This is certainly true (loss for the period is €24,528,000).
- Arrears or discontinuance of dividends.
  - No dividends paid for the current period.
- Reduction in the terms of credit from suppliers.
  - No evidence provided.
- Significant contingent liabilities and guarantees including legal or regulatory claims against the entity.
  - No significant evidence provided.
- Major losses or cash flow problems that have been noted in accordance with IAS 10 *Events after the Reporting Period*.
  - Major customer has gone bankrupt after year end (although this is provided for in the revised figures) and rumours of other potential bankruptcies are rife.
- Excessive dependence on a few product lines.
  - Overly dependent on residential property which is in significant decline.
- The market value of the company's shares are trading below nominal value.

Clearly the group does have a potential going-concern problem and, as outlined above, the financial statements provide valuable information in this review. Further analysis would need to be undertaken to fully assess the applicability of the going concern principle to Doherty Holdings.

Case 8

Dove Air Group

This case study is based on an airline company, Dove Air. The international accounting standards addressed in this case include IAS 7, IAS 17 and the *Standards of Professional Conduct, Code of Ethics* (Chartered Accountants Ireland).

Background Information

You are the financial accountant of Dove Air Group, an airline company with operations in many different markets.

The Consolidated Statement of Financial Position, the Consolidated Statement of Comprehensive Income and the Consolidated Statement of Changes in Equity have already been prepared for the year ended 31 December 2012. You are satisfied that all items have been correctly recorded in these statements. You have been asked to prepare the Consolidated Statement of Cash Flows.

The finance director has been reviewing the financial statements of other airline operators with a view to analysing their financing strategies. He is looking for your input into his suggestion to make greater use of operating leases similar to the approach of Iberia (the Spanish airline, now merged with British Airways).

Also, unknown to your superiors you have been approached by a competitor airline. You are considering the implications of the approach made.

Dove Air Group
CONSOLIDATED STATEMENT OF COMPREHENSIVE INCOME
for the Year Ended 31 December 2012

	€000
Revenue	65,920
Cost of sales	(39,600)
Gross Profit	26,320
Other income	480
Operating expenses	(12,000)
Share of profit of associate	840
Finance costs	(860)
Goodwill impairment	(360)
Profit on disposal of intangible assets	110
Loss on disposal of PPE	(1,680)
Profit before Tax	12,850
Tax	(2,820)
Profit for the Year	10,030
Other Comprehensive Income	
Gain on investments in equity instruments	180
Revaluation gain	120
Total Comprehensive Income	10,150
Profit for the year attributable to:	
Equity shareholders	9,130
Non-controlling interests	900
	10,030
Total Comprehensive Income attributable to:	
Equity shareholders	9,250
Non-controlling interests	900
	10,150

Dove Air Group
CONSOLIDATED STATEMENT OF CHANGES IN EQUITY
for the Year Ended 31 December 2012

	Ordinary Share Capital €000	Share Premium €000	Retained Earnings €000	Revaluation Surplus €000	Surplus on Investments in Equity Instruments €000	Total Equity €000	Non-controlling Interests €000	Total €000
Opening Balance	33,600	840	23,410	240	150	58,240	3,480	61,720
Share issue	1,800	540				2,340		2,340
Total Comprehensive Income			9,130	120	180	9,430	900	10,330
Acquisitions						0	240	240
Dividends			(3,600)			(3,600)	(120)	(3,720)
Closing Balance	35,400	1,380	28,940	360	330	66,410	4,500	70,910

Dove Air Group
CONSOLIDATED STATEMENT OF FINANCIAL POSITION
as at 31 December 2012

	2012	2011
	€000	€000
Non-current Assets		
Property, plant and equipment	51,680	46,400
Investments in associates	8,400	7,800
Intangible assets – goodwill	4,500	4,500
Non-current assets held for sale	1,100	0
Intangible assets – landing rights	1,660	1,500
Financial assets – equity instruments	6,180	6,000
	73,520	66,200
Current Assets		
Inventory	7,200	2,400
Trade receivables	12,000	7,200
Cash	1,620	3,840
	20,820	13,440
Total Assets	94,340	79,640
Equity		
Ordinary share capital	35,400	33,600
Share premium	1,380	840
Retained earnings	28,940	23,410
Surplus on investments in equity instruments	330	150
Revaluation surplus	360	240
	66,410	58,240
Non-controlling interests	4,500	3,480
Total equity	70,910	61,720
Non-current Liabilities		
Borrowings	9,600	8,640
Obligations under finance leases	5,850	4,250
Deferred tax	96	84
	15,546	12,974
Current Liabilities		
Trade payables	4,500	2,160
Obligations under finance leases	800	750
Tax	2,304	1,836
Deferred income	280	200
	7,884	4,946
	94,340	79,640

Additional Notes

Additional Note 1 – Details of Property, Plant and Equipment

Included in operating expenses is €1,500,000 of depreciation. The items of PPE disposed of had a carrying value of €4,680,000. During the year a revaluation of PPE was undertaken. The result of this was a revaluation gain of €120,000. See note 2 for transfers to 'non-current assets held for sale'.

Additional Note 2 – Non-current Assets Held for Sale

In addition to the aircraft actually disposed of during the year, as at 31 December 2012, the group identified three aircraft that it intends to sell. The aircraft (all Boeing 747-400s) were transferred from Property, Plant and Equipment at a NBV of €1,100,000. It is group policy to value non-current assets held for sale at the lower of carrying value and fair value less costs to sell. As the fair value is considerably higher than €1,100,000, the aircraft are valued at their carrying amount (net book value). On 31 December 2011 there were no non-current assets held for sale.

These three aircraft will be replaced in 2013 with three new aircraft for which the group has already entered into a purchase agreement at a total cost of €2,100,000. €1,000,000 of this amount has already been paid to the vendor (Boeing). This payment has been recognised in PPE as part of acquisitions.

Additional Note 3 – Capitalised Interest

Included in the cost of PPE is €100,000 of capitalised interest. This was interest incurred on borrowings to finance the purchase of aircraft prior to the introduction of the aircraft into service. This capitalisation has been correctly carried out under IAS 23 *Borrowing Costs*.

Additional Note 4 – Leases

Dove Air has entered into a number of leases in respect of a number of aircraft. These leases are classified as finance leases.

During 2012 the group acquired an additional €2,500,000 worth of aircraft under finance leases.

Additional Note 5 – Details of Subsidiary Acquired

During the period Dove Airlines purchased a 90% interest in Ground Handling Limited. Details are as follows.

FV of Consideration:

	€
600,000 €1 ordinary shares in Dove	780,000
Cash paid	1,740,000
Total cost	2,520,000

FV of Assets Acquired:

	€
PPE	1,560,000
Inventory	600,000
Receivables	1,200,000
Cash	120,000
Payables	(960,000)
Tax	(120,000)
Net Assets Acquired	2,400,000

Subsequent to the acquisition, Ground Handling Limited lost a major contract and all of the goodwill arising on acquisition was written off (see the Consolidated Statement of Comprehensive Income). Dove Airlines values non-controlling interests based on the proportionate share of net assets (the traditional method).

Additional Note 6 – Sales of Tickets in Advance

Revenue is recognised when the transportation service is provided. Many customers pay for their tickets in advance. These amounts are recognised in 'deferred income' until the service is provided at which time the revenue is recognised. This practice is in accordance with IAS 18 *Revenue*. On 31 December 2012 there was €280,000 of ticket sales in advance compared to €200,000 on 31 December 2010.

Additional Note 7 – Landing Rights

Dove Air has recognised the value of landing rights[1] that it has purchased at cost from other airlines. These landing rights are tested every year for impairment but they are not amortised as they are deemed to have an indefinite life; this is common industry practice.

As at 31 December 2011, Dove Air had recognised landing rights purchased at €1,500,000 (this includes the landings rights swapped at a cost of €40,000, see below).

During 2012, Dove Air entered into a transaction with Avion Direct, a French airline company. Dove Air had 10 daily landing rights at Charles de Gaulle Airport which it was not using. Avion Direct had 8 daily landing rights at Heathrow which it was not using. Therefore Dove Air swapped its 10 landing rights at Charles de Gaulle for 8 landing rights at Heathrow. As landing rights at Heathrow are more valuable than Charles de Gaulle, Dove Air also had to pay €50,000 to Avion Direct.

[1] A landing right is the right to land a plane at a particular airport. In some airports there is a scarcity of available time to land a plane. For instance, in Heathrow there are more airlines who want to land their planes than there are available landing slots. Thus, not every airline that wishes to operate a service to Heathrow can do so. As a consequence, the right to land a plane at Heathrow has a value.

One daily landing right at Charles de Gaulle was recently valued at €15,000 and one daily landing right at Heathrow was valued at €25,000. These are arm's-length valuations based on recent sales of landing rights at the two airports. Dove Air was carrying the Charles de Gaulle landing rights at a value of €4,000 per right, the amount it had originally purchased the landing rights for (many years ago).

The transaction was accounted for as follows:

Purchase of 8 Heathrow Landing Rights

	€
Value of 10 Charles De Gaulle Landing Rights (10 × €15,000)	150,000
Additional cash payment	50,000
Total cost	200,000

Disposal of 10 Charles de Gaulle Landing Rights

	€
Deemed sales proceeds (10 × €15,000)	150,000
Carrying value (10 × €4,000)	40,000
Profit on disposal	110,000

(You can assume that the transaction was correctly accounted for.)

Additional Note 8 – Financial Assets – Equity Instruments

Dove Air has a number of investments (all less than 5% shareholding) in other airlines. These investments are all quoted on a recognised stock exchange and are valued at closing market price on 31 December.

The investments are classified as 'financial assets – equity instruments', with any gains or losses recognised as part of 'other comprehensive income'. Any dividend income is recognised in income as 'other income' when received. During the year, Dove Air received €480,000 of dividend income from its investments. The investments increased in value by €180,000 during the period.

No investments were purchased or sold during the period.

Additional Note 9 – Increased Use of Operating Leases

The Finance Director was recently reviewing Iberia's financial statements (the Spanish Airline now merged with British Airways). He noticed that Iberia had a large number of aircraft on operating leases. As a consequence the asset (the aircraft) and the associated liability (the lease payments) are not included in Iberia's statement of financial position.

As at 31 December 2010, Iberia had 112 aircraft of which 90 were held on operating leases.

Following is a summary of the Group's aircraft in service at 31 December 2010:

	Number of aircraft			
Fleet	**Under owned**	**Under finance lease**	**Under operating lease**	**Total**
A-319	–	–	23	23
A-320	3	6	26	35
A-321	–	4	15	19
A-340/300	6	1	11	18
A-340/600	–	2	15	17
	9	**13**	**90**	**112**

Of the 90 planes on operating leases the following are the expiry dates of the leases (the normal operating life of a plane is in excess of 20 years):

						Year						No. of
Fleet	**2011**	**2012**	**2013**	**2014**	**2015**	**2016**	**2017**	**2018**	**2019**	**2021**	**2022**	**Aircraft**
A-319	2	5	6	2	2	1	–	–	5	–	–	23
A-320	–	2	6	2	2	5			9	–		26
A-321	–	–	1	–	2	3	2	1	6	–	–	15
A-340/300	1	4	2	3	1	–	–	–	–	–	–	11
A-340/600	–	–	–	–	3	2	3	4	–	1	2	15
Total	**3**	**11**	**15**	**7**	**10**	**11**	**5**	**5**	**20**	**1**	**2**	**90**

In the year to 31 December 2010 Iberia spent €306 million on operating leases, all of which was expensed to the income statement. Under its operating leases it expects to pay the following amounts in future years (based on current agreements in place, these future amounts are not shown as liabilities in the statement of financial position):

€ million

Year	**31/12/2010**	**31/12/2009**
2011	278	242
2012	261	228
2013	205	177
2014	182	150
2015 and beyond	616	456
	1,542	**1,253**

The value of aircraft included in the Statement of Financial Position at 31 December 2010 is €821 million. This is the carrying value of the aircraft owned and held under finance leases (i.e. 22 aircraft).

The finance director believes that Iberia's approach to financing its operation is quite efficient. It removes from the statement of financial position a large portion of the potential assets and associated liabilities of a major element of operating an airline business. This, he believes, reduces the debt/equity ratio of the company which allows the company to access cheaper finance and provides a large amount of spare borrowing capacity giving it the flexibility to survive any downturns in its business. As a consequence, he has asked you to consider the implications of obtaining all future aircraft for Dove Air on operating leases.

Additional Note 10 – Offer of Employment

You have recently been approach by a recruitment company acting on behalf of another major airline. There is a senior financial accounting position available at this company. It offers much better career opportunities and a better remuneration package than your existing role.

You had been considering moving roles within Dove Air to broaden your experience but this appears to be a much more attractive proposition. You have decided to attend for interview.

You have not told your current employer of this approach or of your intention to apply for the position. You know that when individuals in sensitive positions in the company announce that they are leaving the company to take up employment with one of the company's competitors, they are asked to vacate the premises immediately and are paid out any notice periods in their contracts. You believe that you occupy such a sensitive position and your contract of employment has a two-month notice period.

You are also considering the implications of accepting a job offer with a rival company. Will you be permitted to bring the commercially sensitive information that you have in your possession to bear on your new position? This information has been acquired through experience (it is all in your head) over the past number of years – for example, you know the load factors on each Dove Air route which could be used by competitors to target the most profitable of Dove Air routes.

Requirements

(**Note:** Unless you are specifically required to consider deferred taxation, you can assume that it is not applicable.)

(a) Prepare the Consolidated Statement of Cash Flows for the year ended 31 December 2012.

(b) Draft a note to the finance director outlining the implications of making greater use of operating leases for Dove Air. Your note should include the positive and negative implications.

(c) Set out the ethical considerations of the approach made by the recruitment company and your subsequent role in the rival airline (assuming that you leave Dove Air).

Guidance Notes – Dove Air

Exam Technique

The usual advice applies here – manage your time carefully and make sure that you answer all sections rather than put all your effort into one or two sections.

The main technical element of this case study is the preparation of the Consolidated Statement of Cash Flows. The information is presented in a very familiar format – the consolidated financial statements are provided along with some additional information. You will have seen this style of questioning before so it should be a matter of applying techniques already practised to the information in the question.

There are a number of items in the additional information that are unique to the airline industry. It is unlikely that you will have seen these before. However, that should not get in the way of making a full attempt. Do not let yourself get psyched out – the key question that you should ask yourself is "what are the cash effects of this transaction?". If you can isolate the cash implications then you should be able to prepare the Consolidated Statement of Cash Flows.

Note that requirements two and three do not require detailed technical analysis; they require a discursive style answer. These can be answered out of sequence. This is worth considering as they may require less time to complete.

Answering the Case Study

Requirement (a) – Guidance

The requirement asks you to prepare a Consolidated Statement of Cash Flows. IAS 7, Appendix A, has an example of a Consolidated Statement of Cash Flows. The indirect method is the most common approach used in the ROI and the UK and is probably the method that you have used exclusively to date. This case study also requires the indirect method.

The illustrative example should act as a prompt; it will give you an indication of the line items that should appear in the Consolidated Statement of Cash Flows. It is not a comprehensive format and there will be additional line items in this case study that should be included.

It is important that you show in your workings how you have calculated each item in the Consolidated Statement of Cash Flows. Failure to do so could result in many marks being needlessly lost.

Ideally, you should have a well practised approach to preparing Consolidated Statements of Cash Flows. You should apply this approach as it will help you to focus. If you do not have an approach then the following might help.

Approach for Consolidated Statements of Cash Flows This approach is just a guide, it will not address all situations and does require judgement and common sense.

1. *Key Headings* Set out the key headings and line items in the Consolidated Statement of Cash Flows, leaving plenty of space for additional line items that will arise later.
2. *The Four PPE Figures* No matter how the information is presented you will always need to calculate the following items
   - depreciation on PPE;
   - cash payments to acquire PPE;
   - profit/loss on the disposal of PPE; and
   - proceeds from the sale of PPE.

These four items are all interconnected; they all relate to PPE. They appear at different stages in the consolidated statement of cash flows, e.g. depreciation is required as part of the 'cash flows from operating activities' calculation whereas payments to acquire PPE is found in 'cash flows from investing activities'. As a consequence, you may as well calculate all these items at the outset. Finally, these four figures are usually the most complex to calculate, therefore, they are likely to attract the most marks.

Often one or two of these figures will be provided (depreciation, in this instance, is provided) so this does make the task somewhat easier.

3. *Movement in Working Capital Items* Calculate the increase/decrease in the working capital items. This is a relatively straightforward calculation; just be aware of any acquisition or disposal of a subsidiary.
4. *Explain the Movement in the Statement of Financial Position* Can you explain how each item in the Statement of Financial Position has changed over the period? For each line item, you should set out the opening balance at the start of the year; include any charges to the income statement and the statement of changes in equity that affect the line item; and adjust for items in the additional information. If this does not give the closing balance, then a cash payment or cash receipt is a likely balancing item – you will need to use your judgement and common sense here.

   For example, take financial assets – equity instruments: before any calculation takes place, if there is a cash effect then it can really only occur if Dove Air buys or sells financial assets or receives a dividend/income from financial assets. The question that you need to ask yourself is: "Can I explain how financial assets – equity instruments have gone from €6,000,000 on 31 December 2011 to €6,180,000 on 31 December 2012?". To help you in this, you should consider related items in the income statement and the statement of changes in equity – in this instance 'other income' of €480,000 and 'gain on financial assets – equity instruments' of €180,000. Finally, scan through the additional information and you should notice that additional note 8 relates to financial assets – equity instrument.

   Additional note 8 says that dividend income is recognised as other income when received (as cash), any gains/losses due to share price movements are recognised in other comprehensive income. However, share price movements are non-cash items as cash is only received when the shares are sold. We also know that the increase in the value of shares was not due to the purchase or sale of shares as this is clearly stated in additional note 8.

	€
Opening balance	6,000,000
Included in the income statement	
as 'other income'	480,000
as 'gain'	180,000
Cash Received/Paid	Balancing figure
Closing balance	6,180,000

The balancing figure is −€480,000, this is the dividend that has been paid out on the shares. The figure is negative – is the amount cash received or cash paid? You should be able to reason that the amount is cash received as it relates to income. The last decision is to choose where this €480,000 of cash received should appear in the Consolidated Statement of Cash Flows – the illustrative example in IAS 7 may help; it includes this item as 'dividends received' under 'cash flows from investing activities'.

That was quite a long thought-process. With some practice, you should be able to eliminate a lot of the thinking. All you will need to show in your solution is the figures.

5. *The 'New' Items in the Consolidated Statement of Cash Flows* You will probably have prepared many Statements of Cash Flows as part of your previous studies. These will probably all have been single company Statements of Cash Flows. Don't forget the new items that appear in a Consolidated Statement of Cash Flows. Items such as (not an exhaustive list):
   - payments to acquire subsidiaries;
   - proceeds from the disposal of subsidiaries;
   - payments to acquire associates;
   - proceeds from the disposal of associates;
   - cash received from associates; and
   - payments of dividends to non-controlling interests.
6. *The Additional Information* In every Statement of Cash Flows case study there will be additional information. If you are having difficulty understanding the information just ask yourself the question "What is the cash implication of this?". This is probably especially true in additional note 7.

You should now make an attempt at the Consolidated Statement of Cash Flows, bearing in mind that marks are often awarded for the correct approach. It does not have to 'balance' to get a good mark so it is important to show your workings.

Requirement (b) – Guidance

This is a discursive question on the reporting around operating and finance leases. You can assume that Iberia has accounted for its leases correctly. The real issue is the impact that this is having on the financial statements of Iberia and, as a consequence, whether users of the financial statements of Iberia receive a complete picture of the business.

The next item to discuss is the impact that a change from finance to operating lease might have on Dove Air. The finance director believes that it will result in access to cheaper finance but is that really the case? Are there any other benefits to a move to operating leases? Finally, what are the practical risks of using operating leases over finance leases?

Requirement (c) – Guidance

This is a real dilemma faced by many accountants when they change position. It is very likely that you will have to deal with this in your future career. There is some guidance available but judgement is also required.

Take a look at the *Standards of Professional Conduct* and the *Code of Ethics* of Chartered Accountants Ireland. In particular, the section on Confidentiality, Section 140, paragraph 140.3, might also be of assistance. Also Part C: Professional Accountants in Business may provide some guidance. However, don't expect to find a conclusive answer here.

Recommended Reading

The above may also be referenced in *International Financial Accounting and Reporting*, 3rd Edition, by Ciaran Connolly (Chartered Accountants Ireland, 2011) and the relevant accounting standards as follows:

	Chapter	Chapter title	Chapter section	Standard
Requirement (a)	33	Statement of Cash Flows – Consolidated	33.1 – 33.3	IAS 7
Requirement (b)	8	Leases	8.2 – 8.4	IAS 17
Requirement (c)				Code of Ethics

Solution to Dove Air

Requirement (a)

This requirement can be laid out in a variety of different ways. In this solution, the approach outlined in the guidance given above will be followed.

1. Key Headings

- The 'key headings' is a template statement of cash flows to act as a prompt for the various line items. It is not reproduced here; a sample is provided in IAS 7 *Statement of Cash Flows*. The completed version is included in this solution.

2. The Four PPE Figures:

- depreciation on PPE: €1,500,000 (provided in additional note 1);
- cash payments to acquire PPE: €8,280,000 (see working 1, this is the most complicated calculation of this case study);
- profit/loss on the disposal of PPE: Loss of €1,680,000 (provided in the consolidated statement of comprehensive income); and
- proceeds from the sale of PPE: €3,000,000 (see working 2)

3. The Working Capital Movements:

- increase in inventory: €4,200,000 (see working 3);
- increase in receivables: €3,600,000 (see working 3); and
- increase in payables: €1,380,000 (see working 3).

Note: these increases were adjusted to take account for the additional amounts received on acquisition of the new subsidiary.

- Increase in deferred income: €80,000 (see working 3 and additional note 6)

Note: from Additional Note 6, Dove Air received €80,000 in additional cash which it has not recognised as part of revenue in 2012. This increases the cash from operations even though the service has not yet been provided.

4. The Consolidated Statement of Cash Flows

Dove Air Group

CONSOLIDATED STATEMENT OF CASH FLOWS

for the Year Ended 31 December 2012

	Refer to:	€000
Cash flows from operating activities		
Profit for the year	SOCI	10,030
Add tax expense	SOCI	2,820
Add loss on disposal of PPE	SOCI	1,680
Less profit on disposal of intangible asset	SOCI	(110)
Add goodwill impairment	SOCI	360
Add finance costs	SOCI/W17	860
Less other income	SOCI	(480)
Less share of profit of associate	SOCI	(840)
Add depreciation	W1	1,500
Less increase in inventory	W3	(4,200)
Less increase in receivables	W3	(3,600)
Add increase in deferred income	W3	80
Add: increase in payables	W3	1,380
Cash generated from operations		9,480
Tax	W4	(2,460)
Finance costs	W5	(960)
Net cash from operating activities		6,060
Cash flows from investing activities		
Proceeds from sale of PPE	W2	3,000
Purchases of PPE	W1	(8,280)
Purchases of landing rights/intangibles	W14	(50)
Proceeds from disposal of intangibles	W15	0
Cash paid to acquire subsidiary	W6	(1,620)
Cash received from associates	W9	240
Cash received from investments	W7	480
Net cash used in investing activities		(6,230)
Cash flows from financing activities		
Dividends paid to non-controlling interests	W8	(120)
Dividends paid	W10	(3,600)
Payments on finance leases	W16	(850)
Issue of share capital	W11	1,560
New borrowings	W12	960
Net cash used in financing activities		(2,050)
Net decrease in cash and cash equivalents		(2,220)
Cash and cash equivalents at beginning of year (Note 1 to the Consolidated Statement of Cash Flows)		3,840
Cash and cash equivalents at end of year (Note 1 to the Consolidated Statement of Cash Flows)		1,620

SOCI = Figure taken directly from Statement of Comprehensive Income

Dove Air Group
NOTES TO THE CONSOLIDATED STATEMENT OF CASH FLOWS
for the Year Ended 31 December 2012

Note 1. Cash and cash equivalents

	31/12/2012 €000	31/12/2011 €000
Cash (from Statement of Financial Position)	1,620	3,840

5. Workings to show the Movement in the Statement of Financial Position

The workings for the figures in the consolidated statement of cash flows appear below. In almost all instances, the procedure employed is to set out the opening and closing balance for a particular line item in the Statement of Financial Position. Then using the Statement of Comprehensive Income and the additional information, try to piece together the reason for the movement in the item from the start of the year to the end of the year. In many cases the missing figure will be a cash payment or receipt. This will require some practice, after a while you will get used to determining the reasons for the movement (often, they tend to repeat themselves).

The order in which the various line items are presented is largely irrelevant. However, it is probably a good strategy to start with the PPE related items. These are often the most difficult to arrive at and the results are required at different stages in the statement of cash flows. For that reason *working 1* and *working 2* are used to determine the four key PPE numbers:

- depreciation on PPE: €1,500,000 (provided in additional note 1);
- cash payments to acquire PPE: €8,280,000 (see *working 1*);
- profit/loss on the disposal of PPE: Loss of €1,680,000 (provided in the statement of comprehensive income); and
- proceeds from the sale of PPE: €3,000,000 (see *working 2*).

Then the movement in working capital adjustment is calculated in *working 3*. This is also a standard calculation that is required for every consolidated statement of cash flows that uses the indirect method. It is probably good practice to calculate it at this stage. Beyond that, *working 4* and forward do not follow any particular order.

Abbreviations Used:

SOFP 2011 – Statement of Financial Position as at 31 December 2011
SOFP 2012 – Statement of Financial Position as at 31 December 2012
Add note X – Additional note X
SOCI – Statement of Comprehensive Income
SOCE – Statement of Changes in Equity

Working 1 – PPE

	€000	Reference
Opening balance	46,400	(SOFP 2011)
Acquisition	1,560	(Add note 5)
Interest capitalised	100	(Add note 3)
Additions by finance leases	2,500	(Add note 4)
Transfer to non-current assets held for sale	(1,100)	(Add note 2)
Disposals	(4,680)	(Add note 1)
Revaluations	120	(Add note 1)
Depreciation	(1,500)	(Add note 1)
Additions for cash	8,280	(Balancing figure, includes €1m in advance)
Closing balance	51,680	(SOFP 2012)

Working 2 – Proceeds from Sale of PPE

	€000	Reference
Carrying value of PPE sold	€4,680	(Add note 1)
Loss on disposal	€1,680	SOCI
Cash received	€3,000	

Working 3 – Working Capital Movements

	Inventory €000	Receivables €000	Payables €000	Deferred income €000	Reference
Opening balance	2,400	7,200	2,160	€200	(SOFP 2011)
Acquisition	600	1,200	960	€0	(Add note 5)
	3,000	8,400	3,120	€200	
Closing balance	7,200	12,000	4,500	€280	(SOFP 2012)
Increase	4,200	3,600	1,380	€80	

Working 4 – Tax

	€000	€000	
Opening balance: Tax		1,836	(SOFP 2011)
Opening balance: Deferred tax		84	(SOFP 2011)
Acquisition		120	(Add note 5)
Income statement charge		2,820	(SOCI)
Cash paid		(2,460)	(Bal Fig)
Closing balance: Tax	2,304		(SOFP 2012)
Closing balance: Deferred tax	96	2,400	(SOFP 2012)

Working 5 – Finance Costs

	€000	
Opening balance	0	(SOFP 2011)
Income statement charge	860	(SOCI)
Interest capitalised	100	(Add note 3)
Cash paid	(960)	(Balancing figure)
Closing balance	0	(SOFP 2012)

Working 6 – Cash to Acquire Subsidiary

	€000	
Cost of subsidiary	(2,520)	(Add note 5)
Non-cash element	780	(Add note 5)
Cash paid	(1,740)	
Cash acquired	120	(Add note 5)
Net cash cost	(1,620)	

Working 7 – Financial Assets – Equity instruments

	€000	
Opening balance	6,000	(SOFP 2011)
Income in income statement	480	(SOCI)
Increase in fair value	180	(Add note 8)
Cash received	(480)	(Balancing figure)
Closing balance	6,180	(SOFP 2012)

Working 8: Non-controlling Interests

	€000	
Opening balance	3,480	(SOFP 2011)
Acquisitions	240	(10% of assets acquired)
Income in income statement	900	(SOCI)
Dividends paid	(120)	(Balancing figure)*
Closing balance	4,500	(SOFP 2012)

* These amounts were shown in the SOCE and are included here for completeness.

Working 9 – Associates

	€000	
Opening balance	7,800	(SOFP 2011)
Income recognised	840	(SOCI)
Cash dividends received	(240)	(Balancing figure)
Closing balance	8,400	(SOFP 2012)

Working 10 – Dividends Paid

	€000	
Opening dividends	0	(SOFP 2011)
Dividends incurred	3,600	(SOCE)
Cash paid	(3,600)	(Bal Fig)
Closing dividends	0	(SOFP 2012)

Working 11 – Issue of Shares

	€000	€000	
Opening issued shares		33,600	(SOFP 2011)
Opening share premium		840	(SOFP 2011)
Total opening balance		34,440	
Shares issued on acquisition		780	(Add note 5)
Shares issued for cash		1,560	(Balancing figure)
Closing issued shares	35,400		(SOFP 2012)
Closing share premium	1,380	36,780	(SOFP 2012)

Working 12 – Borrowings

	€000	
Opening borrowings	8,640	(SOFP 2011)
Acquisition	0	
Net new loans	960	(Balancing figure)
Closing borrowings	9,600	(SOFP 2012)

Working 13 – Non-current Assets Held for Sale

	€000	
Opening non-current assets held for sale	0	(SOFP 2011)
Transfers from PPE	1,100	(Add info 2)
Other transaction/cash	0	(Balancing figure)
Closing non-current assets held for sale	1,100	(SOFP 2012)

Working 14 – Intangible Assets/Landing Rights

	€000	
Opening balance	1,500	(SOFP 2011)
Additions – swap	150	(Add note 7)
Additions – cash	50	(Bal Fig/Add Info 7))
Disposals	(40)	(Add info 7)
Closing balance	1,660	(SOFP 2012)

Working 15 – Disposal of Intangibles

	€000	
Proceeds (deemed)	150	(Add note 7)
Cash proceeds	0	
	150	
Carrying value	(40)	(Add note 7)
Profit on disposal	110	

Working 16 – Payments on Finance Leases

	€000	€000	
Opening balance – current		750	(SOFP 2011)
Opening balance – non-current		4,250	(SOFP 2011)
		5,000	
New leases obtained		2,500	(Add note 4)
Cash paid		(850)	(Balancing figure)
Closing balance – current	800		(SOFP 2012)
Closing balance – non-current	5,850	6,650	(SOFP 2012)

Working 17 – Goodwill Movement

This working (W17) is a check to make sure that the goodwill figure can be fully reconciled. The amount of the goodwill impairment (€360,000) was disclosed separately in the Statement of Comprehensive Income. Hence, W17 (and W18) is not required in this instance and is shown for completeness only.

	€000	
Opening balance	4,500	(SOFP 2011)
Goodwill acquired (W18)	360	
Goodwill written off	(360)	(SOCI)
Cash/other movements	0*	
Closing balance	4,500	(SOFP 2012)

* As the cash effect is zero it is not necessary to calculate this figure, the calculation is included for completeness.

Working 18 – Goodwill Acquired

	€000	€000	
FV of consideration		2,520	(Add note 5)
FV of assets acquired	2,400		(Add note 5)
Group share (90%)	90%	2,160	(Add note 5)
Goodwill		360	

Requirement (b)

Note/Memo

To: FD Dove Air

From: A Financial Accountant

Re: Increased use of operating leases as a source of finance

Considering the financial statements of Iberia (financial year 31 December 2010), it is clear that the company makes extensive use of operating leases. The alternative for Iberia would be to utilise other sources of finance, e.g. finance leases, debt or more equity. For reasons that we can only speculate on, Iberia has chosen operating leases as a main source of its finance (it could be, e.g. that the tax regulations in Spain make operating leases an attractive/cheaper source of finance).

From a financial reporting perspective, the attribute of utilising operating leases over a more conventional source of finance is that the asset (i.e. the plane) and the associated finance do not appear on the statement of financial position of Iberia. The cost of the lease rentals appears on the statement of comprehensive income as an expense when incurred.

In the case of Iberia, it has 90 of its 112 aircraft on operating lease. The remaining 22 aircraft are either owned or on finance leases. The carrying value of the 22 owned and finance leased planes is €821 million. If all of the 90 aircraft that are on operating lease were to appear on the Iberia statement of financial position then the potential impact could be to increase PPE by €3,360 million and increase debt by €3,360 million. This is based on a crude calculation: (€821m/22 aircraft) × 90 aircraft = €3,360m (rounded). It does not take into account the age, size or condition of the aircraft.

If Dove Air were to finance its aircraft on a similar basis to Iberia, it would result in the removal of a large asset and associated liability from its statement of financial position. This would dramatically reduce the reporting gearing (Debt/(Debt + Equity)) of the company. Often this is presented as a 'benefit' of operating leases. In theory, as gearing falls the business should find it easier to access more and cheaper debt finance. This would be correct if gearing were decreasing legitimately. However, to assume that the providers of finance can be fooled this easily is a mistake. If Dove Air were to adopt this approach to finance then financiers to the company would adjust for the operating leases that do not appear on the statement of financial position. The end result is that Dove Air would probably not get access to any more finance or at a cheaper rate than it would have achieved under the current financing structures (i.e. without the use of operating leases).

In addition, it is possible that the use of operating leases could have the opposite effect – as investors (both debt and equity) become aware of large assets and liabilities not appearing on the balance sheet they grow suspicious of the company. This effect is often called 'information asymmetry', i.e. parties have access to differing amounts of information. As a result they begin to demand a premium for the increase in the risk that they perceive themselves to be taking. Therefore, instead of reducing the cost of finance, operating leases could increase the cost of finance.

If Dove Air were to utilise operating leases then it should be done for valid underlying reasons. There may be other, more genuine benefits to the use of operating leases. For example, there may be tax benefits (this will depend on the tax regulations that exist in a particular jurisdiction).

Operating leases tend to be for a shorter period than finance leases; this may provide a degree of flexibility that Dove Air believes is valuable. Should the airline industry enter recession, then Dove Air is left with valuable assets that it has no use for. However, if the company has a number of aircraft on operating lease, it may be able to return the aircraft and quickly downsize as appropriate. (If it cannot return the aircraft on operating lease, then it is likely that the term of the lease will soon be up and the company need not renegotiate the lease. Selling aircraft that are fully owned by the company may not be a palatable option under such circumstances as aircraft values usually fall in a recession.)

Some of the disadvantages of using operating leases include cost and 'roll-over' risk. The cost of operating leases tends to be more expensive than longer term sources of finance (finance leases or debt). This is because the financier needs to be compensated for the risk that the aircraft may be returned to them in the short term and they will need to find another airline to lease the aircraft to. Therefore, over time, Dove Air will incur a larger charge in the statement of comprehensive income than otherwise would be the case.

While operating leases provide Dove Air with flexibility, they also increase 'roll over' risk. When the shorter term of operating leases expire, Dove Air will need to renegotiate the agreement or obtain new planes from other lessors. This may be problematic, particularly if the lessors are unwilling to lease (i.e. lend) to Dove Air. Furthermore, Dove Air could be exposed to potential increases in rental charges. Where longer term sources of finance are employed there is a less significant risk.

In summation, obtaining finance is a matter of achieving a mix of various sources. To utilise operating leases almost exclusively would probably be a mistake for Dove Air. Perhaps, if Dove Air is considering expanding its fleet, it could consider financing some of the expansion through operating leases.

A final consideration is that the reporting regulation on leases (IAS 17 *Leases*) is undergoing a significant review. The outcome is that all leases that were previously accounted for as operating leases will now be treated more as finance leases with the asset and associated liability appearing on the statement of financial position. Consequently, in future periods one of the perceived 'benefits' of operating leases will no longer exist.

Requirement (c)

This is not an unusual situation for an accountant to find himself/herself in. There are two aspects to the issue as described:

- the non-disclosure to your current employer of the possibility of you leaving the company for a rival; and
- the use of commercially sensitive information gained with your current employer (Dove Air) to the benefit of your new employer.

Given the facts as described, you do not yet have an offer of employment with the rival airline. Currently, you are about to attend for interview. There is no guarantee that you will be successful at the interview. Therefore, there is little to convey to your current employer.

However, depending on the relationship that you have with your current boss and colleagues you may want to signal to them that you are looking for new challenges elsewhere or within Dove Air. Indeed, it is always better to be upfront with people than to spring surprises. Most superiors realise that people do not remain in the same organisation for extended periods, so news that you are considering your next career move should not be unusual. Their most common concern is likely to be how to replace you in the organisation, therefore a signal of your intention will allow them to think about these types of issues. A more forward-thinking boss may view your potential departure as an opportunity to consider how the finance function is operating and whether it may benefit from a more radical reorganisation.

The use of commercially sensitive information to the benefit of your new employer is a more difficult issue. There is some guidance in the Code of Ethics of Chartered Accountants Ireland. This solution refers to the *Standards of Professional Conduct, Code of Ethics*, however, the principles described in the code are not unique to accountants who are members of this particular institute. All of the other professional accounting institutes have their own codes of ethics. These codes are broadly similar. Therefore, the solution as presented does have a wider applicability. The *Code of Ethics* of Chartered Accountants Ireland is in compliance with the principles of the Code of Ethics of the International Federation of Accountants (IFAC) – an umbrella body of the professional accounting institutes. The core principles described within the code include 'integrity' and 'confidentiality'.

The *Code of Ethics* states that "The principle of integrity imposes an obligation on all professional accountants to be straightforward and honest in professional and business relationships. Integrity also implies fair dealing and truthfulness" (Code of Ethics 110.1). It would appear that the use of information in the manner proposed would contravene this principle.

The principle of confidentiality also supports the conclusion reached through the interpretation of the integrity principle. From the *Standards of Professional Conduct, Code of Ethics*, "The principle of confidentiality is not only to keep information confidential, but also to take all reasonable steps to preserve confidentiality … A safe and proper approach for professional accountants to adopt is to assume that all unpublished information about a client's or employer's affairs, however gained, is confidential" (Code of Ethics 140.0). This would indicate that the sensitive information gained while working with Dove Air cannot be used to the benefit of the new employer.

The *Code of Ethics* recognises that this is a common dilemma and does provide some specific guidance. It states that "The principle of confidentiality clearly does not prevent an employee from using the skills acquired while working with a former employer in undertaking a new role with a different organisation. Professional accountants should neither use nor appear to use special knowledge which could only have been acquired with access to confidential information" (Code of Ethics 140.3).

While this is a clear statement there may be judgement required to determine the distinction between skills acquired and knowledge gained, however, in this instance, the information on route statistics is closer to knowledge than skills. Therefore, using this commercially sensitive information would appear to be unethical. A complicating factor is that information on route statistics (and other potentially sensitive information) is in your head, it would be a significant challenge not to use this information as you cannot 'delete' what is in your head. (There is no evidence in the case study that you intend to deliberately collect information prior to possible departure – this would clearly be in breach of ethical principles.)

This stance may give rise to a difficult situation with your new employer, who may have hired you on the basis of your knowledge of their competitor. There are a number of means of dealing with this conflict:

- your new superior/boss is likely to be a professional accountant who should be subject to the same ethical requirements. It is also unethical to expect someone else to act unethically;
- the information that you possess is time specific, it will be out of date within a few months. There are other approaches to gathering this type of market intelligence using legitimate means. For example, you could send an employee to count the number of people queuing at the check-in desks for competitor airlines to get a sense of the busier routes. You could check the rival websites to get information on fares charged for various routes and times. The business development function in the organisation should have a system for obtaining market intelligence (legitimately);
- your new employer should respect the stance taken and the management of your new employer should have a strong commitment to ethical behaviour. The term 'what goes around, comes around' is appropriate in this context, when you eventually leave your new employer they can be confident that you will not disclose information that may be detrimental to them; and
- if the previous items do not convince your new employer then the *Standards of Professional Conduct, Code of Ethics*, does advise that you seek legal advice or contact the institute's ethics advisory service. (All of the professional institutes have facilities whereby members can seek direct advice on specific issues – do not expect answers, but a framework for analysing the problem may be presented.)

Case 9

Led Group

This case study is based on a company in the Pharmaceutical Industry. The company has both a manufacturing division and a research and development division. The accounting standards IAS 1, IAS 2, IAS 18, IAS 24, IAS 33, IAS 37, IAS 38, IAS 40, IFRS 3 and IFRS 10 are addressed in this case.

Background – The Led Group

You are the financial accountant for Led Plc (Led). Your job is hectic at the moment. The 2012 financial year has ended and you have just completed the first draft of the financial statements. There are a number of unresolved issues (see outstanding issues 1–4 and requirement (a)). In addition, the company is in a growth phase and has a number of investment options that the finance director is looking for help on (requirements (b)–(d)).

Led is in the pharmaceutical industry. It has a manufacturing plant in Clonmel but its research division operates from a state of the art facility in Dublin. The company has grown organically over the past 20 years and has been very successful. Up until recently, there has been a strong pipeline of new products coming from the research division. In an effort to generate greater scale and to move the business to the next level, the company has decided to embark on a process of growth by acquisition. It is hoped to float the company on an appropriate stock exchange in the next few years.

Year end is 31 December 2012.

Led Plc
DRAFT STATEMENT OF FINANCIAL POSITION
31 December 2012

	€000
Non-current Assets	
Property, plant and equipment	6,800
Financial assets – equity instruments	2,200
Intangible assets (all development expenditure)	11,000
	20,000
Current Assets	
Inventories	4,500
Trade receivables	2,000
Cash and cash equivalents	8,000
	14,500
Total Net Assets	**34,500**
Equity	
Ordinary share capital (€1 each)	5,000
Share premium	7,000
Retained earnings	12,000
Revaluation surplus	1,450
	25,450
Non-current Liabilities	
Bank loans	1,000
Bonds	2,500
Retirement benefit obligations	1,500
Deferred income	200
Deferred tax	500
	5,700
Current Liabilities	
Payables	2,800
Bank loans	300
Current tax	250
	3,350
Total Equity and Liabilities	**34,500**

Led Plc
DRAFT STATEMENT OF COMPREHENSIVE INCOME
For the Year Ended 31 December 2012

	€000
Revenue	**50,000**
Cost of sales	(32,000)
Gross Profit	**18,000**
Other operating income	500
Selling and distribution costs	(11,000)
Administration costs	(2,500)
Profit from Operations	**5,000**
Finance costs	(250)
Profit Before Tax	**4,750**
Taxation	(500)
Profit for the Year	**4,250**
Other Comprehensive Income	
Gain on property revaluation	250
	250
Total Comprehensive Income	**4,500**

Led Plc
DRAFT STATEMENT OF CHANGES IN EQUITY
For the Year Ended 31 December 2012

	Ordinary Share Capital	Share Premium	Retained Earnings	Revaluation Surplus	Total
	€000	€000	€000	€000	€000
Opening balance (at 1 January 2012)	5,000	7,000	7,750	1,200	20,950
Comprehensive income			4,250	250	4,500
Dividend			–		–
Closing balance (at 31 December 2012)	5,000	7,000	12,000	1,450	25,450

Outstanding Issues in Respect of Led Plc's Financial Statements

Outstanding Issue 1

The annual report of Led includes an accounting policy note for research and development. It states

> *"Internal research costs are charged against income as incurred. Internal development costs are capitalised as intangible assets only when there is an identifiable asset that will generate future economic benefits and the costs can be reliably measured."*

Led has a number of research projects in progress at the year-end including the following:

Project PR128

Project PR128 is a project to develop a new type of drug that will reduce the level of obesity in adults. The project commenced at the beginning of 2012. A company, unrelated to Led, carried out the initial research and Led purchased this research on 1 January 2012, along with certain patents that had been registered by the other company, for €1,950,000. Led capitalised these costs. Subsequent to the purchase, Led incurred and wrote-off €1,300,000 in further research costs and then decided to develop the product commercially. The development stage involves three phases of a number of regulated clinical trials. The drug cannot be sold commercially until all three phases are successfully completed. During 2012 the company successfully completed phase one of the trials and incurred €1,930,000 in development costs. These costs were all capitalised.

At 31 December 2012 Led estimated that it will cost another €8 million to complete the development process. It also anticipates that it could take another two years to successfully complete the clinical trials. The directors are uncertain if the project is commercially viable, however, they propose that, because the group are committed to the completion of this project, a provision for the entire €8 million should be made in the 2012 financial statements.

Project BLW11

Led is also developing a vaccine for HIV. The vaccine has successfully completed phase one and two of the clinical testing. The drug is in the late stages of phase three testing (the final stage) and an application has already been submitted for regulatory approval. The drug is similar to drugs the company has developed in the past, and management believes it will be favourably treated by the regulatory authorities. The costs for phase one and phase two and early phase three have been written off as research expenses to the statement of comprehensive income. The remaining costs, listed below, have been debited to a suspense account and included in trade receivables, as the company were unsure whether they should be treated as intangible assets or not.

These costs include:

	€
Materials and services	600,000
Cost of employee benefits	140,000
Registration and legal fees	60,000
Training cost *(operators)*	55,000
General administration overheads	35,000
Amortisation of patent	60,000
Borrowing costs *(specific)*	20,000
	970,000

Outstanding Issue 2

On 1 January 2012 Led entered into a contract with a larger pharmaceutical company to develop a new medical treatment for cancer. It is expected that the contract will take five years to complete. As part of the contract Led must periodically update its client on the development of the drug. The client has exclusive rights over any development results. The client made a €4 million up-front payment on signature which Led credited directly to revenue. Led will be paid five further annual payments of €2 million each, provided it demonstrates compliance with the development programme. The first of these payments was invoiced in December 2012 but payment was still outstanding at the year end. Led estimates that the total costs of the contract will be €12 million and by 31 December 2012 it had incurred costs of €5 million. These costs have been correctly entered into the financial statements.

Outstanding Issue 3

Led is also involved in the development of a drug that will have cholesterol lowering properties. This drug has not yet reached the stage where it is commercially viable and to date all of the costs have been written off as expenses. Ciaran O'Reilly, the operations director, believes there is a 45% chance that this drug will achieve regulatory approval in the near future. He has decided to manufacture a batch of this drug and store it in order to meet demand immediately after regulatory approval. At the year-end, 31 December 2012, the total cost of this inventory is €2.5 million and it is included in the total inventory figure in the draft financial statements.

If the drug does not achieve regulatory approval, there will be no other use for it.

Outstanding Issue 4

In February 2008 Led invested €2,750,000 in a site on the outskirts of Dublin. The land was zoned for agricultural use but there were positive indications, at that time, that rezoning would probably take place and the company could then build a second research facility on the site.

This land was revalued on 31 January 2010 to €4 million in line with an external valuation and Led's accounting policy. The valuation remained unchanged in the subsequent years. This is reflected in the financial statements above.

However, by the end of 2012, rezoning had not taken place. The company has been advised by a government official that rezoning is unlikely to happen any time in the foreseeable future. The value of this land has fallen to €1,400,000.

The directors have decided to abandon their plans for the second research facility. However, they are unsure what to do with the land. They could either sell the site immediately (incurring a large loss) or they could hold the land and lease it out for a couple of years. They have now agreed that leasing would be the best option. A brother of one of the directors owns a herd of cattle and has offered to lease the land from the company for a period of two years.

The land is currently included in property, plant and equipment. Led applies the fair value model permitted by IAS 40 *Investment Property* whenever it holds investment property.

Expansion Plans

Led has investigated a number of other businesses with the intention of making a bid to acquire them. One potential target is Advanced Pharmaceutical Research Ltd (APR). The finance director has provided you with a set of the most recent financial statements of APR. She is conducting most of the research and negotiations but is looking for your help with regard to a number of matters.

In particular, the finance director (FD) would like to know what impact the acquisition would have on the enlarged group's financial statements, gearing and EPS. However, there is considerable uncertainty over the price that will be paid as the negotiations have not yet begun.

The FD envisages two possible outcomes:

1. 80% of APR will be acquired for a combination of cash of €2.50 per share plus one share in Led per share acquired in APR. The cash element of the acquisition will be financed by debt. Any debt will be issued at 10% (ignore tax effects).
2. 100% of APR will be acquired with two shares in Led being offered for one share in APR.

Although unquoted, shares in Led have been valued at €3 each.

The finance director has provided you with a set of financial statements of APR. Her instruction to you was, for each of the two outcomes presented above:

- draw up the consolidated statement of financial position on 31 December 2012 on the assumption that APR is acquired on 31 December 2012; and
- calculate a projected profit after tax and a projected profit attributable to ordinary shareholders for the year ended 31 December 2013 using the data provided and assume no growth in sales and costs over the 2012 figures (save for the items specifically mentioned).

Use the adjusted financial statements of Led (i.e. your answer to requirement (a)) as the basis for your analysis.

While the FD does not have access to much detailed information (APR has not yet been approached so no due diligence has been carried out) she has ascertained the following:

- the fair value of the buildings of APR are worth €800,000 more than their book value. Led depreciates all buildings over 20 years. Depreciation on buildings is included as part of cost of sales;
- the accounting policies of APR and Led are the same; and
- the acquisition will generate cost savings in Led in distribution expenses of €2 million per annum (ignore tax effects).
- Led Plc has elected to measure non-controlling interests as their proportionate share of the net assets of the subsidiary.

APR Ltd
STATEMENT OF COMPREHENSIVE INCOME
for the Year Ended 31 December 2012

	€000
Revenue	**10,000**
Cost of sales	(5,500)
Gross Profit	**4,500**
Other income	250
Selling and distribution costs	(2,500)
Administration costs	(1,200)
Finance costs	(100)
Profit Before Tax	**950**
Taxation	(200)
Profit for the Year	**750**
Other Comprehensive Income	**0**
Total Comprehensive Income	**750**

APR Ltd
STATEMENT OF CHANGES IN EQUITY
for the Year Ended 31 December 2012

	Ordinary Share Capital	Retained Earnings	Total
	€000	€000	€000
Opening balance	1,000	2,250	3,250
Comprehensive income		750	750
Dividend		–	–
Closing Balance	1,000	3,000	4,000

APR Limited
STATEMENT OF FINANCIAL POSITION
as at 31 December 2012

	€000
Non-current Assets	
Property, plant and equipment	1,000
Financial assets – equity instruments	–
Intangible assets (all research and development)	5,000
	6,000
Current Assets	
Inventories	500
Trade receivables	750
Cash and cash equivalents	2,500
	3,750
Total Net Assets	9,750
Equity	
Ordinary share capital (€1 each)	1,000
Retained earnings	3,000
	4,000
Non-current Liabilities	
Bank loans	1,000
Bonds	2,500
Provisions	500
Retirement benefit obligations	200
Deferred income	200
Deferred tax	100
	4,500
Current Liabilities	
Payables	800
Bank loans	250
Current tax	200
	1,250
Total Equity and Liabilities	9,750

Requirements

(**Note:** Unless you are specifically required to consider deferred taxation, you can assume that it is not applicable.)

(a) You are required to set out the accounting entries for the outstanding issues 1–4 of Led Plc **and** redraft the statement of financial position at 31 December 2012.

Your answer should include detailed workings for each of the issues 1–4. You should justify your answers.

(45 marks)

(b) In accordance with the instructions of the finance director, for each of the potential outcomes prepare the consolidated statement of financial position at 31 December 2012 and calculate the projected profit after tax and profit attributable to the ordinary shareholders for the year to 31 December 2013 (you are **not** required to prepare a full consolidated statement of comprehensive income).

(35 marks)

(c) For each of the possible outcomes and for Led on its own, calculate:
  (i) the projected gearing ratio based on the consolidated statement of financial position at 31 December 2012 (gearing is defined as debt/(debt + equity). Led considers bank loans and bonds to be debt); and
  (ii) the projected EPS based on projected profits for 2013 (EPS is defined as per IAS 33).

(10 marks)

(d) Advise the financial director on the strategic direction of the business and on the outcome of your analysis.

(10 marks)
(100 marks)

Addendum

Try requirements (b) and (c) under the following circumstances[1]:

The FD has identified another possible scenario for the acquisition of APR (option 3):

100% of APR will be acquired for cash at €5 per share. This will be financed 60% by debt with 40% being raised by a rights issue; all existing shareholders will be offered one new share for five existing shares at a price of €2 per share. You can assume that all shareholders will exercise their rights fully.

[1] This addendum is included for practice only. A solution is provided.

Guidance Notes – Led Plc

Exam Technique

Read the case carefully and then read the requirements.

Requirement (a) of this case study is similar to the requirements of other case studies in this book. There are some problems with the financial statements of the parent company (issues 1–4). You are required to address these as part of requirement (a). The issues need to be resolved first and a revised statement of financial position produced. These issues are independent of each other. Consider each one in turn, decide on a course of action and move on to the next item.

In requirement (b), you are asked to complete a consolidated statement of financial position under two different financing alternatives. This has the potential to be very time-consuming but much of the basic information is the same for both alternatives. Furthermore, the 'additional information' is not overly complex – there are no intragroup transactions, for example; this makes the solution considerably more manageable. Note that the second part of the requirement does not ask you to prepare a statement of comprehensive income, it only asks you to calculate the profit after tax and profit attributable to the ordinary shareholders.

Requirement (c) is a follow-on analysis from requirement (b). You are asked to calculate the gearing ratio and the EPS for three different scenarios (Led on its own and the two financing alternatives), i.e. six calculations. You should not attempt this requirement before you have finalised requirement (b) as you will need the adjusted profit, the equity and debt figures to correctly calculate the EPS and gearing for the period.

Finally, requirement (d) is discursive. You will need to provide some advice based on your answers to the previous requirements. There are only 10 marks allocated so you are not expected to produce a lengthy answer.

As mentioned in all of the case studies, *manage your time*. You should establish, at the beginning, how much time you have and you should allocate the time accordingly. You will score better marks if you *attempt* all parts of the case rather than completing some sections and not answering others at all.

Answering the Case Study

Requirement (a)

Outstanding Issue 1 This issue examines the accounting treatment and presentation of research and development expenditure. IAS 38 *Intangible Assets* outlines the accounting guidance for intangible assets, including research and development.

In the case study, you are presented with two products currently under development, drug PR128 and drug BLW11. The drugs are at different stages of development.

The first thing you need to do is to classify each project into either *research* or *development*. To do this you must be familiar with the definitions as laid down in IAS 38, paragraph 8. The distinction between research and development is important as the accounting guidance differs considerably depending upon the classification. Further guidance on classification is given in IAS 38, paragraph 57(a)—(f). These paragraphs lay down the conditions that must be fulfilled before expenditure can be classified as development rather than research. (Remember the classification of the project will change over the course of its development. What is considered a research project in the current year may progress to a development project in later accounting periods.)

Once you have classified each project for the current reporting period, you must then consider how the expenditure should be presented in the financial statements. IAS 38, paragraphs 54–56, outlines the recommended accounting treatment for research expenditure and IAS 38, paragraphs 57–67, for development expenditure. If you consider that one (or both) projects are at an advanced stage of development, you will have to carefully consider how to account for the expenditure incurred. IAS 38, paragraphs 66–67, outlines what development costs are eligible for capitalisation and what costs should be expensed.

Finally, you need to comment on the proposed provision of €8 million for the completion of Project PR128. Do you consider it appropriate to make a provision for completion costs? Is the company truly *committed* to the completion cost, even in the event that the drug trials fail?

To answer this, have a look at IAS 37 *Provisions, Contingent Liabilities and Contingent Assets.* You should find your answer in paragraphs 14–26 of this standard.

Outstanding Issue 2 This contract involves the rendering of pharmaceutical development services to a third party. This service will generate significant revenue for the company over the next five years. You must decide how this contract should be presented in the financial statements. Should the revenue earned from this contract be recognised at the start of the contract, throughout the life of the contract or at the end of the contract period? How should the costs be presented? What profit should be recognised, and when should it be recognised?

To answer these questions you will need to consider the provisions of IAS 18 *Revenue.* IAS 18 is divided into three sections:

- The sale of goods (IAS 18, para 14–19);
- The rendering of services (IAS 18, para 20–28); and
- Interest, royalties and dividends (IAS 18, para 29–34).

The section of the standard that will be most relevant for this scenario is the section on the rendering of services. (**Note:** The provisions of IAS18 for the rendering of services are also outlined in IAS 11 *Construction Contracts*. IAS 11 applies to service contracts directly related to the construction industry while IAS 18 is applied to all other service contracts.)

Outstanding Issue 3 This issue tests your understanding of IAS 2 *Inventories* and, in particular, how inventory is measured. There are two points that you need to consider here. The first is whether this drug would constitute part of the stock-in-trade of a business. Remember, this product has not yet achieved regulatory approval. To answer this you need to be familiar with the definition of Inventory (IAS 2, para 6). Once you have established this you must then consider how these drugs should be measured in the financial statements. You are provided with the cost of these drugs – €2.5 million. Is this an appropriate measurement? IAS 2, paragraph 9, will give you the answer.

Outstanding Issue 4 Led invested funds in a plot of land in 2008. The directors' intention, at that time, was to build a second research facility on the site. The land is correctly included in PPE and measured at revalued amounts.

There has now been a change to the company's plans. The development has been abandoned and the company has decided to lease the land for a period of time, most likely to a brother of one of the company's directors. In addition the value of the land has fallen from €4 million to €1.4 million.

You must decide how to present this information in the financial statements. There are two relevant standards: IAS 40 *Investment Property* and IAS 24 *Related Party Disclosures*.

IAS 40, paragraph 8 includes a list of examples of what an investment property is. Have a look at this paragraph, in particular IAS 40, paragraph 8(b). If you decide that the land now fits the definition of an investment property, rather than owner occupied property, you will need to re-classify its presentation in the financial statements. You should refer to IAS 40, paragraphs 57–65 for this.

Finally, there is a related party issue. The land is to be leased to a brother of one of the directors. This transaction may constitute a *related party transaction* in accordance with IAS 24. IAS 24, paragraph 9 outlines who the related parties of an entity are. Take a look at this paragraph and consider what it says about the relationship of the entity to directors, and their close family members.

Once you have established the relationship, you then need to identify the appropriate disclosures for related party transactions. IAS 24, paragraphs13 and 24 will give you the relevant guidance.

Redraft of financial statements Once you have completed your deliberations on outstanding issues 1–4 you will be in a position to redraft the statement of financial position. This exercise should not take too long to do.

Requirement (b)

In this requirement you are required to draw up two statements of financial position (one for each of the potential outcomes). This is not as excessive as it sounds; the adjustments for the second scenario will largely be the same as for the first scenario.

Remember that the requirement is that the consolidated statement of financial position is prepared based on the individual statements of financial position as at 31 December 2012, i.e. the date of acquisition is the same as the year-end date so there are no post-acquisition retained earnings.

Follow the technique for the preparation of consolidated statements of financial position. The only real difference is that you will have to record the investment transaction first. So for each scenario:

- Preliminary step: Record the investment transaction;
- Step 1: Set out the group structure;
- Step 2: Deal with the 'additional information';
- Step 3: Prepare the consolidation table (i.e. calculate the goodwill, non-controlling interests and retained earnings figures). These are key figures in a consolidated statement of financial position and attract many marks; and
- Step 4: Bring step 2 and step 3 together by preparing the consolidated statement of financial position.

Preliminary Step: Record the investment transaction Under scenario one; this will involve determining the total cost of the investment in APR and then recording the investment in Led. Remember that the investment will be financed partially by issuing new shares and partially by obtaining/issuing new debt. Under scenario two, the cost of the investment in APR will have to be calculated again. This time the consideration is satisfied entirely by the issue of shares in Led to the original shareholders of APR.

Step 1 – Set out the group structure This is not contentious. For the first scenario APR is an 80% subsidiary and in the second scenario it is a 100% subsidiary.

Step 2 – Deal with the 'additional information' The additional information is found at the end of the case study; it is the information that the FD has ascertained (e.g. the fair value of the buildings is worth €800,000 more…).

Item 1: Fair values on acquisition At the time of the acquisition, you will need to consider the basis for valuing the assets acquired and the liabilities assumed. Is the carrying value appropriate or should fair value be used? IFRS 3, paragraph18, gives clear guidance here.

Once the adjustment to fair value is determined, you will then need to decide how to record the adjustment – is the other side of the adjustment to pre-acquisition retained earnings or post-acquisition retained earnings?

Reversal of Fair Value Adjustments Any adjustment made as part of the fair value process can have a knock on effect on the post-acquisition profits of the combined entity. However, in this requirement the reversal is not relevant as the date is 31 December 2012 and no time has elapsed to permit the reversal. The reversal will be important for the statement of comprehensive income.

Item 2: Accounting policies The accounting policies of Led and APR are the same – you will need to consider the implications of this.

Item 3: Synergies Many takeovers are justified on the basis of potential cost savings and this is no different. However, does the cost saving have any implication for this requirement (a statement of financial position as at 31 December 2012)?

You will need to consider the 'additional information' for each of the scenarios. How does the method of financing the acquisition impact upon these adjustments (i.e. will these adjustments be the same under each scenario)?

Step 3: Prepare the consolidation table Using the adjustments from step 2, you should now be in a position to calculate the goodwill on acquisition of APR, non-controlling interests and retained earnings – see any previous case study (e.g. Knightstown).

Step 4: Complete the statement of financial position This should be a relatively mechanical exercise as all the thinking has already been done. Take the revised financial statements of Led, include the investment transaction and the financial statements of APR. Then make sure that all the adjustments are correctly included.

Repeat the process described above for the other financing arrangement (this will not be as time-consuming as some of the transactions will be the same).

The second part of the requirement is to calculate the projected profit after tax and profit attributable to the ordinary shareholders for the newly expanded Led Group on the basis that APR is in the group for a full year.

As you are not asked to prepare the full statement of comprehensive income, the starting point should be the current profit after tax for Led and APR. Adjust these figures for the impact of the financing arrangement and the 'additional information' – determine the impact of the additional information on the annual profits of the entities in the group. Then remove any profit attributable to the non-controlling interests. Repeat this for each of the scenarios.

Requirement (c)

In this requirement, the most important matter to consider is the definition of EPS and Gearing. IAS 33 *Earnings per Share* provides clear guidance on calculating EPS, however, there is no similar standard on the calculation of the gearing ratio. Therefore, as long as a sensible approach is taken, it is difficult to incorrectly calculate the gearing ratio. The requirement gives some direction on the definition of debt that is employed by Led. It is a narrow definition of debt, just bank loans and bonds, but given the lack of a standard definition, this is acceptable.

In calculating EPS, be careful to include the correct number of outstanding shares in the denominator as it changes depending on the scenario.

Requirement (d)

This is a discursive requirement. Highlight the key findings of your analysis (i.e. requirements (b) and (c)). In addition, you should consider the reliability of the information that you have presented and the impact any transaction might have on ownership structures.

Recommended Reading

The above may also be referenced in *International Financial Accounting and Reporting,* 3rd Edition, by Ciaran Connolly (Chartered Accountants Ireland, 2011) and the relevant accounting standards as follows:

	Chapter	Chapter title	Chapter section	Standard
Requirement (a)				
Issue 1:	9	Intangible Assets	9.2	IAS 38
	14	Provisions, Contingent Liabilities and Contingent Assets	14.2 & 14.3	IAS 37
Issue 2	4	Revenue Recognition	4.2	IAS 18
Issue 3	11	Inventories	11.2	IAS 2
Issue 4	5	Investment Property	5.2	IAS 40
	22	Related Party Disclosures	22.2 – 22.5	IAS 24
Redraft Financials	2	Presentation of Financial Statements	2.3	IAS 1
Requirement (b)				
Consolidated Statement of financial position	26 27	Business Combinations and Consolidated Financial Statements Consolidated Statement of Financial Position	26.4 27.2 – 27.11	IFRS 3, IFRS 10
Requirement (c)				
EPS	23	Earnings Per Share	23.5 – 23.8	IAS 33
Requirement (d)				
Analysis	35	Analysis and Interpretation of Financial Information	35.2 – 35.3	

Solution to Led Plc

Requirement (a)

Outstanding Issue 1

"The recognition of an item as an intangible asset requires an entity to demonstrate that an item meets (a) the definition of an intangible asset *and* (b) the recognition criteria" (IAS 38, para 18).

The recognition criteria outlined in IAS 38, paragraph 57, require an entity to demonstrate that the technical and commercial viability of the asset has been established, that the entity intends (and can demonstrate an ability) to sell or use the asset and that the entity has the available resources to complete the development. Finally, the entity must demonstrate its ability to measure development expenditure reliably.

If the entity cannot satisfy **any one** of the above criteria, it will have failed to demonstrate that an intangible asset exists. In this situation the expenditure is recognised as an expense when it is incurred.

Project PR128 The expenditure incurred in 2012 should be treated as follows:

- The purchased research €1,950,000 can be capitalised. It is an acquired intangible. It is assumed that acquired intangibles meet the definition of an intangible asset and the recognition criteria. IAS 38, paragraph 25 states that "Normally, the price an entity pays to acquire separately an intangible asset will reflect expectations about the probability that the expected economic benefits embodied in the asset will flow to the entity. In other words the entity expects there to be an inflow of economic benefits...... Therefore the recognition critieria is always considered to be satisfied for separately acquired intangibles". This has been correctly treated in the financial statements. No adjustment is required.
- The completion of research costs €1,300,000 should be written off to profit or loss (IAS 38, para 54). This too has been correctly treated in the financial statements. No adjustment is required.
- The development costs of €1,930,000 requires some thought. As there is a requirement to successfully complete all three phases of the clinical trials before Led's product can be commercially launched, there would still be some doubt as to the **technical feasibility and commercial viability** of the drug at the end of 2012. Consequently the costs would fail the recognition criteria. This expenditure should be treated as on-going research costs and expensed.

In the draft financial statements these costs are presented as an asset. An adjustment will be required to write these costs off to profit or loss as follows:

	€000	€000
DR Expenses	1,930	
CR Intangible assets		1,930

- Finally, the completion costs. The directors propose making a provision in the financial statements for the costs of completing the project. The justification for this is that the company is 'committed' to completion. The reality may be somewhat different. The directors may be frontloading costs in order to smooth profits for the next two years. IAS 37 *Provisions, Contingent Liabilities and Contingent Assets* outlines the accounting treatment for provisions. IAS 37 is very clear on what a provision is and when one can be made. A provision should be recognised only when "an entity has a **present obligation** as a result of a **past** event" (IAS 37, para 14(a)).

In an effort to explain what 'obligation' means in the context of IAS 37, the standard uses terms such as "more likely than not" (IAS 37, para 15) and "probable" (IAS 37, para 14(b)) and "has no realistic alternative to settling the obligation" (IAS 37, para 17). In other words, a provision should be created only when the entity *knows* it will incur a liability at some point in the future and has no way to avoid it. (The uncertainty lies only around the timing or estimate but not the existence of the liability.)

This is not the situation for Led Plc. Led can avoid the remaining costs of the project. Led could choose to abandon the development work at any time *or* the remaining trials could fail. In either case the project would be discontinued and completion costs avoided.

So, at the present time, Led does not have an obligation, as defined by IAS 37. The €8 million are operating costs, to be incurred in the future, assuming the project is successful. Again the standard is clear "Financial Statements deal with the financial position of an entity at the end of its reporting period and not its possible position in the future. Therefore no provision is recognised for costs that need to be incurred to operate in the future…" (IAS 37, paragraph18).

Project BLW11 The costs of Phase I, II and early stage III have been correctly expensed to profit or loss as research expenditure. The question now is whether the remaining costs can be classified as development costs and included in intangible assets in the financial statements. IAS 38, paragraph 57, lays down the rules and they are outlined above.

There is no definitive starting point for the capitalisation of internal development costs. Management must use judgment, based on the facts and circumstances of each project. (**Note:** In the pharmaceutical industry a strong indication that the criteria have been met arises when an entity files a submission to the regulatory authority for final approval.)

As Led has already applied for regulatory approval, it can now capitalise the remaining internal development costs, because the project has fulfilled the criteria for recognition. However, only certain costs can be capitalised. The costs that may be included as an intangible asset are outlined in IAS 38, paragraphs 65–67, and comprise all directly attributable costs necessary to create, produce and prepare the asset to be capable of operating in the manner intended by management. The standard includes examples. For project BLW11 the following can be capitalised:

	€000	
Materials and services	600	Allowed (IAS 38, para 66(a))
Cost of employee benefits	140	Allowed (IAS 38, para 66(b))
Registration and legal fees	60	Allowed (IAS 38, para 66(c))
Training cost (*operators)*	0	Not allowed (IAS 38, para 67(c))
General administration overheads*	0	Not allowed (IAS 38, para 67(a))
Amortisation of patent	60	Allowed (IAS 38, para 66(d))
Borrowing costs (*specific)*	20	Allowed (IAS 38, para 66)
	880	

* The wording of this section states that selling, administrative and other general overhead expenditure unless this expenditure can be directly attributed to preparing the asset for use.

Currently €970,000 is included in trade receivables. An adjustment is required, €880,000 should be included in intangible assets while the remainder should be written off to profit or loss as follows:

	€000	€000
DR Intangible assets	880	
DR Expenses IS	90	
CR Trade receivables		970

Outstanding Issue 2

Note: The accounting treatment for the rendering of services over an agreed period of time is outlined in two accounting standards: IAS 18 *Revenue*, paragraphs 20–28 *and* IAS 11 *Construction Contracts*. IAS 11 is concerned with the rendering of services arising in the construction industry only while IAS 18 provides the accounting treatment for all other service contracts. This solution refers mainly to the provisions of IAS 18.

LED has entered into a contract that involves the rendering of pharmaceutical development services to a third party. This contract will generate significant revenue for the company for the next five years. IAS 18, paragraphs 20–28, permits entities to depart from the normal rules of revenue recognition by allowing revenue on service contracts to be recognised *throughout* the service period rather than when the service is complete. This is achieved by recognising revenue "… by reference to the stage of completion of the transaction at the end of the reporting period" (IAS 18, para 20). In the case study the contract between Led and the pharmaceutical company commenced in January 2012 and will last for a period of five years. Costs incurred on the contract in 2012, €5 million, have been properly treated in the financial statements, however, revenue has not. A total of €6 million has been included in revenue (€4 million upfront payment and the first of five €2 million instalments). This treatment is not in line with the stage of completion approach as outlined in IAS 18.

You will need to complete the accounting entries to bring the reporting in line with the provisions of IAS 18 paragraphs 20–28. To complete the entries you should follow four steps:

Step (1) Identify total revenue and total cost of the service contract
Step (2) Establish if the service contract is profit-making or loss-making[2]
Step (3) Identify the stage of completion at the reporting date *and*
Step (4) Complete the accounting entries in the financial statements.

- **Step 1 – The total revenue and total cost of the contract**

	€000	
Total revenue	14,000	(€4m + (5 × €2m))
Total costs	12,000	
Total profit	2,000	

- **Step 2 – Profit-making or loss-making contract**

The contract is profit-making so revenue and costs can be recognised by reference to the stage of completion at the end of the reporting period.

- **Step 3 – Identify the stage of completion of the contract**

IAS 18, paragraph 24, states that the stage of completion can be determined by a variety of methods including:
(a) Surveys of work performed;
(b) Services performed to date as a percentage of total services to be performed; or
(c) The proportion that costs incurred to date bear to the estimated total costs of the transaction.

The method that best suits the information provided in the case study is method (c). The stage of completion for the service contract is calculated as follows:

	€000
Costs that reflect services performed to date	5,000
Estimated total costs	12,000
	41.67%

As a substantial proportion of the total contract has been completed and the outcome of the contract is reasonably assured, revenue may be recognised in the period. Using the stage of completion basis, 41.67% of the total revenue of the contract may be recognised in the current period.

(**Note:** If the stage of completion at the end of the reporting period was very low it would imply that the contract was probably still in the early stages. In this case revenue would be recognised "only to the extent of the expenses recognised that are recoverable" (IAS18, para 26).)

[2] If the project is loss-making the accounting treatment would be different. IAS 11, paragraph 36, states that "when it is probable that total contract costs will exceed total revenue, the expected loss shall be recognised as an expense immediately".

- **Step 4: The entries to the financial statement should include:**

The Statement of Comprehensive Income

		€000
Revenue	41.67%	5,833
Cost of sales	41.67%	5,000
Profit		833

The statement of Financial Position IAS 18 does not refer to the presentation of service contracts in the Statement of Financial Position so we must revert to IAS 11 *Construction Contracts*. IAS 11, paragraph 42(a), states that an entity shall present "the gross amount due from customers for contract work as an asset". This will be made up of the net amount of (a) costs incurred plus recognised profits less (b) the sum of recognised losses and progress billings (IAS 11, paragraph 43).

The gross amount due at 31 December 2012 includes:

	€000
Costs incurred	5,000
Profit recognised	833
Recognised losses	0
Progress billings	(4,000)
	1,833

What is currently included in the financial statements for this contract is €6 million in revenue (€4 million initial payment plus first stage payment €2m), €4 million in cash and €2 million outstanding in trade receivables. These amounts must be adjusted. In accordance with IAS 18, €5.833 million revenue should be included and trade receivables should be stated at €1.833 million. To achieve this position the following adjustment is necessary:

	€000	€000
DR Revenue	167	
CR Trade receivables		167

Outstanding Issue 3

Inventories are assets that are (IAS 2, para. 6):

- held for sale in the ordinary course of business;
- in the process of production for such a sale; or
- in the form of materials or supplies to be consumed in the production process or in the rendering of services.

The batch of cholesterol lowering drugs would be classified as inventory of Led as the drugs are held for sale in the ordinary course of business.

Inventories should be measured at the lower of cost and net realisable value (NRV) (IAS 2, para 9). The practice of writing inventories down below cost to net realisable value is consistent with the view that assets should not be carried in excess of amounts expected to be realised from their sale or use (IAS 2, para. 28).

At 31 December 2012, the NRV of this inventory is **nil**. As the drug is still at the testing stage, it cannot be launched on the open market. It therefore has no value. In addition, if the drug trial fails there will be no use for this inventory and its value will also be nil.

An adjustment is required to reduce the value of this inventory, currently recorded at €2.5 million, to its NRV of nil:

	€000	**€000**
DR Cost of sales	2,500	
CR Inventory		2,500

Finally, it is important to mention that a new assessment will be made of the net realisable value of inventory in each subsequent period. IAS 2, paragraph 33, states "when the circumstances that previously caused inventories to be written down below cost no longer exist or when there is clear evidence of an increase in net realisable value because of changed economic circumstances, the amount of the write-down is reversed so that the new carrying value is the lower of the cost and the revised net realisable value".

Outstanding Issue 4

The land, on acquisition, was correctly included in PPE. The land was acquired for the company's own use rather than for investment purposes. The intention was to develop the site to extend the research capabilities of the group. The land was also properly revalued in January 2010, with a revaluation surplus of €1.25 million correctly credited to revaluation surplus.

By the end of 2012 the situation has changed. The land has fallen dramatically in value and the company's plans to develop the site have been abandoned.

The directors have decided to lease out the site. This constitutes a change in the use of the property. IAS 40, paragraph 57, states "transfers shall be made when, and only when there is a change in use, evidenced by: (among other examples) 'end of owner-occupation'."

The transfer process from owner-occupied property to investment property is clearly laid out in IAS 40, paragraph 61. This section states "If an owner-occupied property becomes an investment property that will be carried at fair value, an entity shall apply IAS 16 up to the date of the change in use" (i.e. 31 December 2012). If there is a difference between the carrying amount of the property and the fair value at the date of change of use, the difference shall be treated in accordance with the revaluation rules of IAS 16 *Property, Plant and Equipment* (IAS 40, para. 61). The revalued asset will then be transferred to investment property.

The journal entries to execute this change of use will be:

Journal entry 1	€000	€000
DR Revaluation Surplus	1,250	
DR Income Statement	1,350	
CR PPE		2,600
Journal entry 2		
DR Investment property	1,400	
CR PPE		1,400

The land is likely to be leased to a close family member of a company director. Close family members of key management of the entity are considered to be a related party in accordance with IAS 24 paragraph 9(a).

Certain disclosures must be made including the nature of the relationship as well as information about the transactions. These disclosures include:

- The amount of the transactions;
- The amount of outstanding balances including commitments;
- Provisions for doubtful debts relating to outstanding balances; and
- Expense recognised during the period in respect of bad or doubtful debts due for related parties.

IAS 24, paragraph 21, gives examples of transactions that should be disclosed if they are with a related party. IAS 24, paragraph 21(d), includes *leases.*

Summary of Adjustments

	Issue	PPE	Inv Prop	Intang. Assets	Inventory	Trade Rec.	Retained Earning	Reval. Surplus
		€000	€000	€000	€000	€000	€000	€000
Per draft		6,800	0	11,000	4,500	2,000	12,000	1,450
Project PR128	1			(1,930)			(1,930)	
Project BLW11	1			880		(970)	(90)	
Contract research	2					(167)	(167)	
Inventory – unapproved product	3				(2,500)		(2,500)	
PPE to investment property	4	(4,000)	1,400				(1,350)	(1,250)
Revised		2,800	1,400	9,950	2,000	863	5,963	200
Net change		(4,000)	1,400	(1,050)	(2,500)	(1,137)	(6,037)	(1,250)

Note: you are not required to prepare a summary of the adjustments – the requirement asks for a redrafted statement of financial position which follows.

Led Plc

REVISED STATEMENT OF FINANCIAL POSITION
as at 31 December 2012

	Original	Issue Number	Amount	Revised
Non-current Assets	**€000**			**€000**
Property, plant and equipment	6,800	4	(4,000)	2,800
Investment property	0	4	1,400	1,400
Financial assets – equity instruments	2,200			2,200
Intangible assets (all development expenditure)	11,000	1	(1,050)	9,950
	20,000			16,350
Current Assets				
Inventories	4,500	3	(2,500)	2,000
Trade receivables	2,000	1,2	(1,137)	863
Cash and cash equivalents	8,000			8,000
	14,500			10,863
Total Net Assets	**34,500**			**27,213**
Equity				
Ordinary share capital (€1 each)	5,000			5,000
Share premium	7,000			7,000
Retained earnings	12,000	1,2,3,4	(6,037)	5,963
Revaluation surplus	1,450	4	(1,250)	200
	25,450			18,163
Non-current Liabilities				
Bank loans	1,000			1,000
Bonds	2,500			2,500
Retirement benefit obligations	1,500			1,500
Deferred income	200			200
Deferred tax	500			500
	5,700			5,700
Current Liabilities				
Payables	2,800			2,800
Bank loans	300			300
Current tax	250			250
	3,350			3,350
Total Equity and Liabilities	**34,500**			**27,213**

Requirement (b)

Scenario 1

80% of APR will be acquired for combination of cash of €2.50 per share plus one share in Led per share acquired in APR.

Preliminary Step: Record the investment transaction Determine the cost of the acquisition and then record the investment in APR in the separate financial statements of Led.

Total number of shares in APR	1,000,000	
Number of shares acquired (80%)	800,000	
Number of shares to be issued in Led	800,000	(1 for 1)
Value of shares issued in Led (€3 each)	€2,400,000	
Value of cash/debt issued (€2.50 per share)	€2,000,000	
Total cost of investment in APR	€4,400,000	

To record the transaction:

	€000	€000
Debit/Increase Investment in APR	4,400	
Credit/Increase Bank loans		2,000
Credit/Increase Ordinary share capital		800
Credit/Increase share premium		1,600

Note: the issue of share capital at €3 each should to be split between nominal value (€1 per share) and share premium (€2 per share).

Step 1 – Set out the group structure

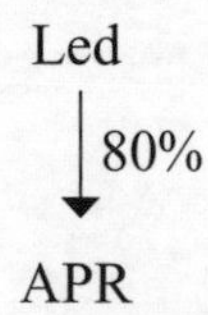

Step 2 – Deal with the 'additional information' On the date of acquisition the fair value of the buildings is €800,000 higher than their carrying value. Under IFRS 3, paragraph 18, the acquirer should measure all assets acquired at their fair value. As this increase in value took place prior to acquisition, the increase should be recognised in pre-acquisition retained earnings.

To record the adjustment:

	€000	€000
Debit/Increase PPE	800	
Credit/Increase Pre-acquisition retained earnings		800

(Non-controlling interests will need to be given their share of the increase in pre-acquisition retained earnings.)

There is no need to consider the reversal of the fair value adjustment as the statement of financial position is being prepared at the date of acquisition (31/12/2012) – this will be a matter for future financial statements: financial year 2013 and forward (see profit calculation for 2013).

The case study confirms that the accounting policies of the two entities are the same, hence no adjustment is required (IFRS 10, para B87).

The acquisition will generate synergies, however, these will not materialise until 2013 so they are not relevant for the statement of financial position as at 31 December 2012 (see profit calculation for 2013).

In conclusion, what may have appeared as a complex scenario has been reduced to two adjustments.

Step 3 – Prepare the consolidation table At this stage, the adjustments from the previous step are accumulated together. The goodwill, non-controlling interests and retained earnings figures are arrived at – these are the figures that attract the most marks in an examination scenario. At this point, the hard work has already been done in step 2 and it is a matter of following a process – this is why an approach similar to that set out in the consolidation table is beneficial.

CONSOLIDATION TABLE

	Goodwill €000	Non-controlling Interests €000	Retained Earnings €000	Revaluation Surplus €000
Investment in APR	4,400			
Ordinary share capital	800	200		
Retained earnings – pre-acquisition (3,000)	2,400	600		
Retained earnings – post-acquisition (0)		0	0	
Retained earnings – Led			5,963	
Revaluation surplus – APR				0
Revaluation surplus – Led				200
Fair Value Adjustment (€800,000)	640	160		
Total	560	960	5,963	200

Step 4 – Complete the statement of financial position This is an information management exercise. It is a matter of taking the revised statement of financial position of Led (answer to requirement (a)), the statement of financial position of APR along with the adjustments set out in step 2, and the final figures from the consolidation table and stitching them together into a consolidated statement of financial position.

Scenario 1: Led Group
STATEMENT OF FINANCIAL POSITION
as at 31 December 2012

Non-current Assets	Led €000	APR €000	Invest €000	FV Adj €000	Total €000	Notes
Property, plant and equipment	2,800	1,000		800	4,600	
Investment property	1,400				1,400	
Financial assets – equity instruments	2,200	0			2,200	
Goodwill	0		4,400		560	From table
Intangible assets (all development expenditure)	9,950	5,000			14,950	
	16,350	6,000			23,710	
Current Assets						
Inventories	2,000	500			2,500	
Trade receivables	863	750			1,613	
Cash and cash equivalents	8,000	2,500			10,500	
	10,863	3,750			14,613	
Total Net Assets	27,213	9,750			38,323	
Equity						
Ordinary share capital (€1 each)	5,000	1,000	800		5,800	Parent only
Share premium	7,000		1,600		8,600	Parent only
Retained earnings	5,963	3,000			5,963	From table
Revaluation surplus	200				200	From table
	18,163	4,000			20,563	
Non-controlling interests					960	From table
					21,523	

Non-current Liabilities				
Bank loans	1,000	1,000	2,000	4,000
Bonds	2,500	2,500		5,000
Provisions	0	500		500
Retirement benefit obligations	1,500	200		1,700
Deferred income	200	200		400
Deferred tax	500	100		600
	5,700	4,500		12,200
Current Liabilities				
Payables	2,800	800		3,600
Bank loans	300	250		550
Current tax	250	200		450
	3,350	1,250		4,600
Total Equity and Liabilities	27,213	9,750		38,323

Scenario 2

100% of APR will be acquired with two shares in Led being offered for one share in APR.

Much of the analysis carried out for Scenario 1 is reusable under Scenario 2 with some minor adjustment. The same approach will be used although this may be overly time-consuming.

Preliminary Step: Record the investment transaction Determine the cost of the acquisition and then record the investment in APR.

	000	
Total Number of shares in APR	1,000	
Number of shares acquired (100%)	1,000	
Number of shares to be issued in Led	2,000	(2 for 1)
Value of shares issued in Led (€3 each)	€6,000	
Value of cash/debt issued	€0	
Total cost of investment in APR	€6,000	

To record the transaction:

	€000	**€000**
Debit/Increase Investment in APR	6,000	
Credit/Increase Ordinary share capital		2,000
Credit/Increase Share premium		4,000

Note: the issue of ordinary shares at €3 each should be split between nominal value (€1 per share) and share premium (€2 per share).

Step 1 – Set out the group structure

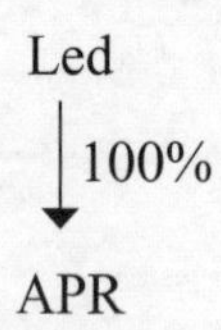

Step 2 – Deal with the 'additional information' This is the same irrespective of the nature of the investment transaction.

To record the increase in fair value of PPE:

	€000	€000
Debit/Increase PPE	800	
Credit/Increase Pre-acquisition retained earnings		800

(Non-controlling interests usually need to be given their share of the increase in pre-acquisition retained earnings, however, under this scenario there are no non-controlling interests.)

This was the only adjustment required under Scenario 1 and the same logic applies under Scenario 2, hence no further work is required.

Step 3 – Prepare the consolidation table At this stage, the adjustments from the previous step are accumulated together. The goodwill, non-controlling interests and retained earnings figures are arrived at – these are the figures that attract the most marks in an examination scenario. At this point, the hard work has already been done in step 2 and it is a matter of following a process – this is why an approach similar to that set out in the consolidation table is beneficial.

CONSOLIDATION TABLE

	Goodwill €000	Non-controlling Interests €000	Retained Earnings €000	Revaluation Surplus €000
Investment in APR	6,000			
Ordinary share capital	1,000	0		
Retained earnings – pre-acquisition (€3,000,000)	3,000	0		
Retained earnings – post-acquisition (€0)		0	0	
Retained earnings – Led			5,963	
Revaluation surplus – APR				0
Revaluation surplus – Led				200
Fair Value adjustment	800	0		
Total	1,200	0	5,963	200

Step 4 – Complete the statement of financial position This is an information management exercise. It is a matter of taking the revised statement of financial position of Led (answer to requirement (a)), the statement of financial position of APR along with the adjustments set out in step 2, and the final figures from the consolidation table and stitching them together into a consolidated statement of financial position.

Scenario 2: Led Group
STATEMENT OF FINANCIAL POSITION
as at 31 December 2012

	Led	APR	Finance	FV Adj	Total	Notes
	€000	€000	€000	€000	€000	
Non-current Assets						
Property, plant and equipment	2,800	1,000		800	4,600	
Investment property	1,400				1,400	
Financial assets – equity instruments	2,200	0			2,200	
Investment in APR/ goodwill	0		6,000		1,200	From table
Intangible assets (all development expenditure)	9,950	5,000			14,950	
	16,350	6,000			24,350	
Current Assets						
Inventories	2,000	500			2,500	
Trade receivables	863	750			1,613	
Cash and cash equivalents	8,000	2,500			10,500	
	10,863	3,750			14,613	
Total Net Assets	27,213	9,750			38,963	
Equity						
Ordinary share capital (€1 each)	5,000	1,000	2,000		7,000	Parent only
Share premium	7,000		4,000		11,000	Parent only

Retained earnings	5,963	3,000	5,963	From table
Revaluation surplus	200		200	From table
	18,163	4,000	24,163	
Non-controlling interests			0	
			24,163	
Non-current Liabilities				
Bank loans	1,000	1,000	2,000	
Bonds	2,500	2,500	5,000	
Provisions	0	500	500	
Retirement benefit obligations	1,500	200	1,700	
Deferred income	200	200	400	
Deferred tax	500	100	600	
	5,700	4,500	10,200	
Current Liabilities				
Payables	2,800	800	3,600	
Bank loans	300	250	550	
Current tax	250	200	450	
	3,350	1,250	4,600	
Total Equity and Liabilities	27,213	9,750	38,963	

The final element of requirement (b) is to calculate the projected profit of the enlarged group under each of the scenarios for the next financial year (year ended 31 December 2013).

The finance director has provided some guidance – assume no growth in sales and costs over the 2012 figures except for the items specifically mentioned. Therefore, the key complexity is the interpretation of the 'items specifically mentioned'; these include:

- any additional interest on loans obtained to finance the acquisition (scenario 1);
- additional depreciation as a result of the fair value adjustment; and
- any synergies arising from the acquisition.

- The additional interest on debt issued by Led to finance the transaction (scenario 1 only)
  - total debt issued is €2,000,000 at 10%, giving additional interest in Led of €200,000
- The additional depreciation as a result of the fair value adjustment
  - amount of fair value adjustment is €800,000. Buildings are depreciated over 20 years on a straight line basis. This gives an additional depreciation charge in APR of €40,000
- Synergies arising from the transaction all arise in Led and are €2,000,000.

Projected Profit for LED Group for the Year to 31 December 2013

Scenario 1

	Led	APR
	€000	€000
Profit for the year as originally stated	4,250	750
Adjustment – Outstanding issue 1 (–€1,930,000 – €90,000)	(2,020)	
Adjustment – Outstanding issue 2	(167)	
Adjustment – Outstanding issue 3	(2,500)	
Adjustment – Outstanding issue 4	(1,350)	
Revised profit/(loss) for the year	(1,787)	750
Additional interest	(200)	
Additional depreciation		(40)
Synergies	2,000	
Projected profit/(loss) for the year	13	710
Non-controlling interests		(142)
Projected profit/(loss) attributable to ordinary shareholders	13	568

Projected group profit for the year is €723,000 (€13,000 + €710,000).
Projected group profit for the year attributable to ordinary shareholders is €581,000 (€568,000 + €13,000).

Projected Profit for LED Group for the Year to 31 December 2013

Scenario 2

	Led	APR
	€000	€000
Profit for the year as originally stated	4,250	750
Adjustment – Outstanding issue 1 (– €1,930,000 – €90,000)	(2,020)	
Adjustment – Outstanding issue 2	(167)	
Adjustment – Outstanding issue 3	(2,500)	
Adjustment – Outstanding issue 4	(1,350)	
Revised profit/(loss) for the year	(1,787)	750
Additional interest	0	
Additional depreciation		(40)
Synergies	2,000	
Projected profit/(loss) for the year	213	710
Non-controlling interests		0
Projected profit/(loss) attributable to ordinary shareholders	213	710

Projected group profit for the year is €923,000 (€213,000 + €710,000).
Projected group profit for the year attributable to ordinary shareholders is €923,000 (€213,000 + €710,000).

Requirement (c)

Part (i): Projected EPS Calculation

IAS 33 *Earnings Per Share* gives clear guidance on the calculation of EPS. The numerator shall be the profit attributable to ordinary shareholders (IAS 33, para 12) while the denominator is the weighted average number of ordinary shares outstanding for the period (IAS 33, para 19).

The solution to the previous requirement gives the profit attributable to ordinary shareholders. The number of ordinary shares in issue will vary depending on the investment transaction (see various statements of financial position). However, the shares will be in existence for the full period (as the acquisition is assumed to have occurred on 31 December 2012). It is also assumed that no additional shares will be issued in 2013.

PROJECTED EPS 2013

	Led on Own	Scenario 1	Scenario 2
	000	**000**	**000**
Profit/(loss) attributable to ordinary shareholders	(€1,787)	€581	€923
Number of shares in issue	5,000	5,800	7,000
Projected EPS 2011	(€0.36)	€0.10	€0.13

Part (ii): Projected Gearing Calculation

There is no standard definition of gearing although some guidance is provided in the case study. Led defines gearing as debt/(debt + equity) and defines debt as bank loans and bonds.

PROJECTED GEARING RATIO 2013

	Led on own	Scenario 1	Scenario 2
	€000	**€000**	**€000**
Debt			
Non-current liabilities – bank loans	1,000	4,000	2,000
Non-current liabilities – bonds	2,500	5,000	5,000
Current liabilities – bank loans	300	550	550
Total debt	3,800	9,550	7,550
Equity	18,163	21,523	24,163
Debt + Equity	21,963	31,073	31,713
Gearing (Total Debt/(Debt + Equity)	17%	31%	24%

Requirement (d)

In this requirement you are asked to advise the finance director. There are many points that can be made here, what follows is a list of the more significant points. As there are only 10 marks allocated to this requirement, you would not be expected to write a lengthy answer.

In addition, the solution is presented as a narrative, this is usually more appropriate than a series of bullet points (although the narrative is effectively a series of bullet points stitched together).

Advice to the FD

A number of issues arise from the possible acquisition of APR. At the outset the analysis was prepared without much detailed information on APR, it would be a serious mistake to proceed with the acquisition without undertaking a full due diligence and more in-depth research.

The acquisition is expected to give rise to synergies (i.e. cost savings) of €2 million in Led, This would appear to be very optimistic as the value of the acquisition is €6 million (for a full paper transaction). This level of savings might prove difficult to realise given that selling and distribution costs are just €13.5 million (€11 million in Led and €2.5 million in APR). It is also unlikely that the shareholders of APR will be willing to sell their shares for €6 million so that Led can generate annual cost savings of €2 million. On the basis of the potential savings they would be arguing for a much higher price.

Under scenario 1 Led acquires just 80% of APR. This would need to be given some thought – 20% of the profits of APR will be going outside the group. In addition, any investment of management time and expertise of Led in APR will not fully benefit the shareholders of Led as there will be a leakage of 20% to the non-controlling interests.

A significant implication of scenario 2 is the number of shares in Led that will have to be issued. After the transaction Led will have 7 million shares in issue, of which 2 million will belong to the current shareholders of APR (29%). This will mean that the current shareholders of APR could have a large input into the expanded group. Serious consideration would need to be given to the dilutive impact of this bearing in mind the current shareholding structure of Led.

The acquisition of APR will result in the potential losses (of Led on its own) becoming profits (for the enlarged group). This is extremely positive from the group's perspective. Under scenario 1, losses of €1,787,000 become profits of €581,000, while under scenario 2 losses of €1,787,000 become profits of €923,000. Scenario 2 does result in a higher level of profitability, however, these profits need to be divided across an enlarged equity base.

Under scenario 2 (where the acquisition is financed by shares), the EPS is highest at €0.13 per share compared to €0.10 per share under scenario 1. This is because, although there are more shares in issue, the group has a lower cost base due to the absence of interest-bearing debt to finance the acquisition.

Scenario 2 also has a more attractive gearing ratio – 24% debt financed as opposed to 31% debt financed under scenario 1. This is because scenario 1 requires the group to issued additional debt to finance the transaction.

In conclusion, based on the limited information provided, as long as the increase in the issued share capital will not have a detrimental impact on the existing shareholders of Led, then scenario 2 would appear to be a more advantageous option.

Addendum to Requirement (b)

Scenario 3

100% of APR will be acquired for cash of €5 per share. This will be financed 60% by debt with 40% being raised by a rights issue – all existing shareholders will be offered one new share for five existing shares at a price of €2 per share. You can assume that all shareholders will exercise their rights fully.

Much of the analysis carried out for Scenario 1 is reusable under Scenario 3 with some minor adjustment. The same approach will be used although this may be overly time-consuming.

Preliminary Step – Record the investment transaction

Determine the cost of the acquisition and then record the investment in APR.

	000	
Total number of shares in APR	1,000	
Number of shares acquired (100%)	1,000	
Price paid per share (€5 per share)	€5,000	
Financed as follows:		
Value of debt issued	€3,000	
Value of equity issued	€2,000	
Number of shares to be issued in Led	1,000	(1 for 5)
Total cash raised (€2 by 1,000,000 shares)	€2,000	

To record the transaction:

	€000	€000
Debit/increase cash	5,000	
Credit/increase ordinary share capital		1,000
Credit/increase share premium		1,000
Credit/increase bank debt		3,000
Debit/increase investment in APR	5,000	
Credit/decrease cash		5,000

Note: the issue of share capital at €2 each should be split between nominal value (€1 per share) and share premium (€1 per share).

Step 1 – Set out the group structure

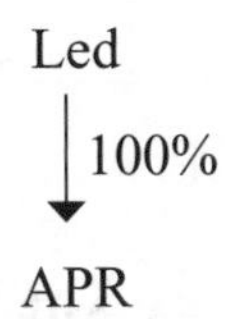

Step 2 – Deal with the 'additional information' This is the same irrespective of the nature of the investment transaction.

To record the increase in fair value of PPE:

	€000	€000
Debit/increase PPE	800	
Credit/increase pre-acquisition retained earnings		800

(Non-controlling interests usually need to be given their share of the increase in pre-acquisition retained earnings, however, under this scenario there are no non-controlling interests.)

Step 3 – Prepare the consolidation table At this stage, the adjustments from the previous step are accumulated together. The goodwill, non-controlling interests and retained earnings figures are arrived at – these are the figures that attract the most marks in an examination scenario. At this point, the hard work has been done (step 2) and it is a matter of following a process – this is why an approach similar to that set out in the consolidation table is beneficial.

CONSOLIDATION TABLE

	Goodwill €000	Non-controlling Interests €000	Retained Earnings €000	Revaluation Surplus €000
Investment in APR	5,000			
Ordinary share capital	1,000	0		
Retained earnings – pre-acquisition (€3,000,000)	3,000	0		
Retained earnings – post-acquisition (0)		0	0	
Retained earnings – Led			5,963	
Revaluation surplus – APR				0
Revaluation surplus – Led				200
Fair Value adjustment	800	0		
Total	200	0	5,963	200

Step 4 – Complete the statement of financial position This is an information management exercise. It is a matter of taking the revised statement of financial position of Led (answer to requirement (a)), the statement of financial position of APR along with the adjustments set out in step 2 and the final figures from the Consolidation Table and stitching them together into a consolidated statement of financial position.

Scenario 3: Led Group
STATEMENT OF FINANCIAL POSITION
as at 31 December 2012

	Led	APR	Invest	FV Adj	Total	Notes
	€000	€000	€000	€000	€000	
Non-current Assets						
Property, plant and equipment	2,800	1,000		800	4,600	
Investment property	1,400				1,400	
Financial assets – equity instruments	2,200	0			2,200	
Inv in APR/ goodwill			5,000		200	From table
Intangible assets (all development expenditure)	9,950	5,000			14,950	
	16,350	6,000			23,350	
Current Assets						
Inventories	2,000	500			2,500	
Trade receivables	863	750			1,613	
Cash and cash equivalents	8,000	2,500			10,500	
	10,863	3,750			14,613	
Total Net Assets	27,213	9,750			37,963	
Equity						
Ordinary share capital (€1 each)	5,000	1,000	1,000		6,000	Parent only
Share premium	7,000		1,000		8,000	Parent only
Retained earnings	5,963	3,000			5,963	From table
Revaluation surplus	200				200	From table
	18,163	4,000			20,163	

Non-current Liabilities				
Bank loans	1,000	1,000	3,000	5,000
Bonds	2,500	2,500		5,000
Provisions	0	500		500
Retirement benefit obligations	1,500	200		1,700
Deferred income	200	200		400
Deferred tax	500	100		600
	5,700	4,500		13,200
Current Liabilities				
Payables	2,800	800		3,600
Bank loans	300	250		550
Current tax	250	200		450
	3,350	1,250		4,600
Total Equity and Liabilities	27,213	9,750		37,963

The final element of requirement (b) is to calculate the projected profit of the enlarged group under scenario 3 for the next financial year (year ended 31/12/13).

Projected Profit for LED Group for the Year to 31 December 2013

Scenario 3	**Led**	**APR**
	€000	**€000**
Profit for the year as originally stated	4,250	750
Adjustment – Outstanding issue 1 (−€1,930,000 − €90,000)	(2,020)	
Adjustment – Outstanding issue 2	(167)	
Adjustment – Outstanding issue 3	(2,500)	
Adjustment – Outstanding issue 4	(1,350)	
Revised profit for the year	(1,787)	750
Additional interest	(300)	
Additional depreciation		(40)
Synergies	2,000	
Projected profit	(87)	710
Non-controlling interests		0
	(87)	710

Projected group profit for the year is €623,000 (€710,000 – €87,000).
Projected group profit for the year attributable to ordinary shareholders is €623,000 (€710,000 – €87,000).

Addendum – Requirement (c)

Part (i): Projected EPS Calculation

PROJECTED EPS 2013

	Led on own	Scenario 3
	000	000
Profit/(loss) attributable to ordinary shareholders	(€1,787)	€623
Number of shares in issue	5,000	6,000
EPS	(€0.36)	€0.10

Part (ii): Projected Gearing Calculation

PROJECTED GEARING RATIO 2013

	Led on own	Scenario 3
	€000	€000
Debt		
Non-current liabilities – bank loans	1,000	5,000
Non-current liabilities – bonds	2,500	5,000
Current liabilities – bank loans	300	550
Total debt	3,800	10,550
Equity	18,163	20,163
Debt + Equity	21,963	30,713
Gearing	17%	34%

Case 10

Elite Group

This case study is based on a diversified group of companies, Elite Group. The accounting standards addressed in this case include IAS 7, IAS 10, IAS 16, IAS 17, IAS 37, IFRS 5 and IFRS 7.

Background – Elite Group

Elite Group is a large conglomerate with activities spanning many different industries. You are located in the corporate headquarters where you work as a group reporting accountant. The group has a number of subsidiaries that were acquired over many years. Each subsidiary submits their financial statements and associated data and the group financial statements are prepared.

It is now early 2013 and the 2012 consolidated financial statements (statement of comprehensive income, statement of financial position, and statement of changes in equity) are nearly completed. The current draft is presented below.

A number of issues have come to light since the financial statements were prepared and it is your task to resolve those issues appropriately in the financial statements. Then you will need to complete the consolidated statement of cash flows. Finally, there are two additional matters relating to the disclosure of strategic decisions and risk management that the directors are looking for advice on. Details on the issues follow the draft consolidated financial statements.

The financial statements are scheduled to be authorised for issue in March 2013.

Draft Consolidated Financial Statements

Elite Group
CONSOLIDATED STATEMENT OF COMPREHENSIVE INCOME
For the Year Ended 31 December 2012

	€000
Revenue	11,900.0
Cost of sales	(5,460.0)
Gross Profit	6,440.0
Operating expenses	(2,765.0)
Gain on disposal of property (issue 1)	700.0
Loss on disposal of plant, property and equip	(91.0)
Profit from operations	4,284
Interest	(665.0)
Profit before Tax	3,619.0
Tax	(1,015.0)
Profit for the financial year	2,604.0
Other Comprehensive Income	
Property revaluation	87.5
Total Comprehensive Income	2,691.5
Profit for the Financial Year Attributable to	
Non-controlling interests	280.0
Equity shareholders	2,324.0
	2,604.0
Total Comprehensive Income Attributable to	
Non-controlling interests	280.0
Equity shareholders	2,411.5
	2,691.5

Elite Group
CONSOLIDATED STATEMENT OF CHANGES IN EQUITY
For the Year Ended 31 December 2012

	Share Capital €000	Share Premium €000	Retained Earnings €000	Revaluation Surplus €000	Total Equity €000	Non-cont Interests €000	Total €000
Opening balance	3,010.0	350.0	6,620.0	700	10,680.0	1,736.0	12,416.0
Share issue – purchase of subsidiary	175.0	87.5			262.5		262.5
NCI – purchase of subsidiary					0.0	420.0	420.0
Total comprehensive income			2,324.0	87.5	2,411.5	280.0	2,691.5
Dividends paid			(840.0)		(840.0)	(336.0)	(1,176.0)
Closing balance	3,185.0	437.5	8,104.0	787.5	12,514.0	2,100.0	14,614.0

Elite Group
CONSOLIDATED STATEMENT OF FINANCIAL POSITION
as at 31 December 2012 (and 31 December 2011)

	31/12/2012	31/12/2011
Non-current Assets	**€000**	**€000**
Plant, property and equipment	11,480.0	10,360.0
Financial asset (issue 1)	0.0	2,000.0
Intangible assets (goodwill)	224.0	0.0
	11,704.0	12,360.0
Current Assets		
Non-current asset held for sale (issue 1)	2,700.0	0.0
Inventory	4,270.0	4,480.0
Trade receivables	6,090.0	5,040.0
	13,060.0	9,520.0
Total Assets	24,764.0	21,880.0
Equity and Liabilities		
Equity		
Ordinary share capital	3,185.0	3,010.0
Share premium	437.5	350.0
Retained earnings	8,104.0	6,620.0
Revaluation surplus	787.5	700.0
	12,514.0	10,680.0
Non-controlling interests	2,100.0	1,736.0
Total Equity and Non-controlling Interests	14,614.0	12,416.0
Non-current Liabilities		
Finance leases payable	3,640.0	3,360.0
Deferred taxation	896.0	644.0
	4,536.0	4,004.0
Current Liabilities		
Bank overdraft	924.0	1,246.0
Payables	2,325.0	2,080.0
Provisions	300.0	300.0
Tax payable	665.0	574.0
Finance Leases Payable	1,400.0	1,260.0
	5,614.0	5,460.0
Total Equity and Liabilities	24,764.0	21,880.0

Outstanding Issue 1

Elite Plc acquired property in early 2012. The property was obtained as a result of a default on a loan agreement by a third party and was valued at €2 million at that date for accounting purposes, which exactly offset the defaulted loan. Although the property was in a state of disrepair, Elite was lacking office space and decided to occupy the premises on a temporary basis until a more suitable location could be secured for administration staff. Initially the property was classified as owner occupied. No depreciation was charged in 2012. Towards the end of 2012 Elite decided to sell the property. In order to secure a sale, significant remedial work was necessary. The repairs were carried out in January 2013. The property is expected to be sold for €2.7 million, after costs, by the end of March although no buyer has yet been secured.

The property is classified as 'held for sale' at the year-end under IFRS 5 *Non-current Assets Held for Sale and Discontinued Operations* at a value of €2.7 million and a gain for €700,000 has been recognised in the Consolidated Income Statement. Property is depreciated at 5% per annum on the straight line basis.

Outstanding Issue 2

Lease with TPR On 1 January 2012 Elite Plc leased land from a company, TPR Ltd. The beneficial and legal ownership of the land remains with TPR Ltd and in the event that the asset is required by them, the lease can be terminated immediately. The net present value of the total lease is €1 million and this was recognised in full, in administration expenses, in the 2012 statement of comprehensive income. A corresponding credit was made to trade payables. Lease payments are made annually in arrears. The lease term is five years. The NPV of the total lease payments was calculated using a discount rate of 10% (cumulative factor of 10% for five years is 3.79). The fair value of the land at the inception of the lease was €6 million.

The first rental payment is due, but will not be paid before the accounts are signed.

Lease with AK Arnold Ltd On 1 November 2012, Elite Plc disposed of some plant that had a carrying value of €3.5 million. The plant was sold to a finance company, AK Arnold Ltd, at fair value of €4 million and was immediately leased back by the group. The only entry made in the financial statements was to debit trade receivables and credit plant with the carrying amount of the asset. No cash had changed hands by the end of the period. The sale and leaseback arrangement involves a series of annual payments over five years of €480,000 per annum, payable in arrears.

There is general confusion over the appropriate accounting treatment for this arrangement. The confusion arises because the contract contains a clause which gives Elite an option to repurchase the plant at the end of the lease period. The plant may be repurchased at an amount equal to its fair value at the date of repurchase.

The financial director has proposed that this arrangement be treated as a sale and lease back arrangement in accordance with IAS 17 *Leases*. However, another director has disputed this approach. This director considers that, as the arrangement contains an option to repurchase, it should be treated as a financing arrangement and the 'disposal' proceeds treated as a long-term loan to the group.

The interest rate implicit in the agreement is 12%.

Outstanding Issue 3

The draft financial statements above do not include any adjustments to the provisions liability for 2012. You have extracted the following information about provisions for the period:

1. The opening provision is made up of the following:
   - €150,000 in legal costs – based on professional advice the company is likely to lose an important EU environmental case and be liable for damages in three years' time. The actual estimated liability has been discounted at 10% for three years, the undiscounted potential liability is €199,734
   - €80,000 to cover an onerous contract (not discounted, short-term provision)
   - €70,000 for sales returns and warranty costs.
2. During 2012, a further legal claim was made against the company and the costs of this claim are likely to be about €40,000. These will be due at the end of July 2013.
3. €20,000 worth of product, sold in 2012, was returned to the company in 2012 and repairs to damaged goods cost €28,000. No cash outlay has been made for these expenses. The amount due is included in trade payables. The provision for sales returns and warranty costs at the end of 2012 should be adjusted to 0.5% of revenue (before any returns in the period).
4. Finally, in December 2012 the company was released, without penalty, from the 2011 onerous contract.

The cost of capital of the company is 10% (discount factor at 10% for two years is 0.826, discount factor at 10% for three years is 0.751). Assume that any changes to the provisions liability affecting the statement of comprehensive income are charged/credited to opening expenses.

Additional Information – Consolidated Statement of Cash Flows

This additional information does not take into account any changes that may be processed as a result of the resolution of outstanding issues 1, 2 and 3.

1. In the current year Elite made one acquisition – Widney Limited. On 1 January 2012 Elite acquired 75% of the ordinary share capital of Widney Limited. The purchase was financed by €1,277,500 cash and the issue of 175,000 ordinary shares. On 1 January 2012 Elite shares had a market value of €1.50 each. The statement of financial position of Widney Limited on 1 January 2012 showed the following:

	€
Property, plant and equipment	1,470,000
Inventory	1,050,000
Receivables	840,000
Bank deposit	66,500

Bank overdraft	(962,500)
Trade payables	(560,000)
Tax payable	(224,000)
	1,680,000

2. At year end a review of goodwill was undertaken and it was found that the goodwill associated with the acquisition of Widney was partially impaired. The amount was written off to the statement of comprehensive income of Elite (included within operating expenses). Non-controlling interests is measured as the share in the net assets of the subsidiary (the traditional method).
3. Depreciation charged in the consolidated statement of comprehensive income of Elite for the year ended 31 December 2012 was €2,625,000.
4. The loss on disposal of property, plant and equipment (as stated in the consolidated statement of comprehensive income) relates to the scrapping of machinery during the year. The machinery had a net book value of €91,000. No proceeds were received.
5. Additions to Plant, Property and Equipment during the year include plant and machinery purchased under finance lease contracts which would have cost €1,680,000 if purchased outright. Property was revalued during the year, resulting in a revaluation upwards of €87,500. There was interest paid of €35,000, relating to the construction of a new factory which was capitalised.

Strategic Decision and Risk Management Disclosures

Strategic Decision The board of directors of the Elite Group is carrying out a strategic review of operations. The company intends to commence a restructuring programme in 2013. Restructuring will involve the disposal of two divisions of the parent company, both of which are loss-making. The board of directors is working on a final plan. They expect operations to continue in the beleaguered divisions until March 2014 after which they will be shut down. There will be significant job losses. The board is reluctant to make any announcement until the plans have been finalised. The plans will be finalised in November 2013. Restructuring should be complete by July 2014 and the property is likely to be sold in early 2015.

Initial estimates of the costs of restructuring include:

	2013	**2014**	
	€000	**€000**	
Redundancy		3,000	
Retraining and relocation		800	
Legal		250	
Operational losses	3,400	2,800	(three months)
Fair value adjustments for assets 'held for sale'		1,000	(loss)

Risk Management The group is considering its reporting of its cash and debt management practices.

Currently, the group does not permit any of its subsidiaries to borrow; all borrowing is done through the parent company, but at the moment the parent does not see the need to take out any borrowings.

As a result of this policy, the subsidiaries each operate an overdraft facility. All of the subsidiaries are currently in overdraft (all of the overdrafts add to €924,000). Each of the subsidiaries has agreed a committed limit with their respective banks – all of the limits added together result in a potential overdraft facility of €1,990,000. These limits are agreed on average for 18 months from the end of the current period, although this ranges from 6 months to 36 months. As long as the subsidiaries remain within the terms of the overdrafts, the bank is precluded from seeking repayment. Should the terms be broken, or at the end of the period agreed, the bank can demand payment within 30 days.

The weighted average interest rate on the overdrafts is 11%, ranging from 8% to 12%. One of the conditions of the overdrafts is that the account should be in credit for 30 days a year. Three of the subsidiaries did not achieve this during the current period, however, the banks concerned did not take any action but they did charge a penalty fee.

While the group has not exceeded the total of the overdraft limit during the current period, four subsidiaries did exceed their individual limits. The banks involved continued to honour any payments but charged a penalty fee. At year end two of the four subsidiaries were still operating above their approved limits.

Most of the overdrafts are unsecured, however, in the case of two subsidiaries security has been pledged to the bank. These are the two subsidiaries that have exceeded their limits at year end. The security is property (i.e. a factory), details are below:

Subsidiary	Agreed Limit	Actual Overdraft at 31 December 2012	Value of Security
	€	€	€
Poton	50,000	75,000	300,000
Fluton	25,000	28,000	200,000

Requirements

(**Note:** Unless you are specifically required to consider deferred taxation, you can assume that it is not applicable.)

(a) With regard to outstanding issues 1–3, set out the appropriate accounting treatment. Your answer should give a reasoned rationale for the appropriate treatment in each case. You should then redraft the financial statements.

(30 marks)

(b) Having regard to requirement (a) and the additional cash flow information specifically noted in the case study, prepare the consolidated statement of cash flows for the Elite Group.

(50 marks)

(c) Advise the directors on how they should disclose (no adjustments/figures are required):
(i) the 'planned' restructuring programme (if, indeed, they are required to disclose anything)
(ii) the management of financial risk (if, indeed, they are required to disclose anything).

(20 marks)

Elite Group – Guidance Note

Exam Technique

The usual advice applies here – manage your time carefully and make sure that you answer all sections rather than putting all your effort into one or two sections.

The main technical element of this case study is the preparation of the consolidated statement of cash flows. However, there is also a requirement to consider some outstanding reporting issues. You may have noticed that the issues described do not involve any transfer of cash therefore their impact on the consolidated statement of cash flows will be limited. These are stand-alone issues and can be considered independently of one another.

The information for the consolidated statement of cash flows is presented in a familiar format; see also the previous case study with a consolidated statement of cash flows – Dove Air. As is normal, the consolidated financial statements are provided along with some additional information. You will have seen this style of questioning before so it should be a matter of applying techniques already practised to the information in the case study.

There may be a number of items in the additional information that you may not be familiar with. However, that should not get in the way of making a full attempt – the key question that you should ask yourself is "what are the cash effects of this transaction?". If you can isolate the cash implications then you should be able to prepare the consolidated statement of cash flows.

In part (c) you need to consider the broader reporting implications but much of your answer should be based on the reporting standards with a little common sense added. This can be answered out of sequence. This approach may be worth considering as it may require less time to complete.

Answering the Case Study

Requirement (a) – Guidance

Outstanding Issue 1 This issue involves the presentation of a non-current asset that Elite intends to sell. The asset, a property, was obtained in a state of disrepair in early 2012. Remedial work, which has now been completed, was necessary before it could be sold. The company hopes to complete the sale by the end of March 2013. The asset is currently classified as a non-current asset held for sale and is measured at its fair value less costs to sell.

You must decide if this presentation is appropriate. You will need to review a couple of accounting standards to arrive at an appropriate answer to this issue: IFRS 5 *Non-current Assets Held for Sale and Discontinued Operations*, IAS 16 *Property, Plant and Equipment* and IAS 10 *Events after the Reporting Period.*

Outstanding Issue 2 *Lease with TPR* Elite has leased land from TPR Ltd. The lease period is five years. Lease contracts should be presented in the financial statements in accordance with IAS 17 *Leases.* IAS 17 classifies leases into finance leases and operating leases. You must decide on the appropriate classification for this lease. Have a look at paragraphs 7–19, in particular paragraphs 10(c) and 15A of the standard. Once you have classified the lease you should follow the measurement rules. The rules for finance leases (for lessees) are outlined in paragraphs 20–32 of the standard while operating leases are outlined in paragraphs 33–35.

Lease with AK Arnold Ltd The second lease *appears* to be a sale and leaseback agreement as it involves the disposal of an asset with an immediate leaseback from the new owner. However, there is some confusion over the presentation of the contract. The lease agreement permits Elite to repurchase the asset at the end of the lease period. One of the directors has recommended that the contract be treated as a long-term loan to the company rather than as a lease.

You must decide how to treat this transaction. IAS 17 *Leases*, IFRIC 4 *Determining whether an Arrangement contains a Lease* and SIC 27 *Evaluating the Substance of Transactions Involving the Legal Form of a Lease* will provide the appropriate guidance. If you consider the contract to be a leasing contract, you must then decide if it should it be presented as a finance lease or an operating lease. Paragraphs 7–19 of the standard will give you guidance on this matter.

Outstanding Issue 3 This issue relates to the movement of the provisions liability for the period. You are presented with the opening provision and a summary of changes during the period.

You must adjust the provisions liability. You should consider carefully the double-entry impact of each transaction. To complete this section you will need to be familiar with the guidance outlined in IAS 37 *Provisions, Contingent Liabilities and Contingent Assets.*

Requirement (b) – Guidance

The requirement asks you to prepare a consolidated statement of cash flows. IAS 7, Illustrative Example A, has an example of a statement of cash flows. The indirect method is the most common approach used in the ROI and the UK and is probably the method that you have used exclusively to date. This case study requires the indirect method to be used.

The illustrative example should act as a prompt; it will give you an indication of the line items that should appear in the consolidated statement of cash flows. It is not a comprehensive format and there will be additional line items that should be included in this case study.

It is important that you show in your workings how you have calculated each item in the consolidated statement of cash flows. Failure to do so could result in many marks being needlessly lost.

Ideally, the starting point for the consolidated statement of cash flows should incorporate the adjustments made in the previous section. However, if these adjustments are ignored (or incorrect), it should still be possible to complete the consolidated statement of cash flows and score very high marks for the attempt – although the solution will be incorrect. Clearly, the solution provided will follow the correct approach.

In completing the consolidated statement of cash flows you should have a well-practised approach to preparing consolidated statements of cash flows. You should apply this approach as it will help you to focus. If you do not have an approach then please refer to the approach outlined as part of the Dove Air guidance notes. Briefly:

1. **Key Headings** Set out the key headings and line items in the consolidated statement of cash flows, leaving plenty of space for additional line items that will arise later.
2. **The Four PPE Figures** No matter how the information is presented you will always need to calculate the following items
   (a) depreciation on PPE;
   (b) cash payments to acquire PPE;
   (c) profit/loss on the disposal of PPE; and
   (d) proceeds from the sale of PPE.
   Often one or two of these figures will be provided (depreciation in this instance is provided) which makes the task somewhat easier.
3. **Movement in Working Capital Items** Calculate the increase/decrease in the working capital items. This is a relatively straightforward calculation; just beware if there has been any acquisition or disposal of a subsidiary.
4. **Explain the movement in the Statement of Financial Position** Can you explain how each item in the statement of financial position has changed over the period? For each line item you should set out the opening balance at the start of the year. Include any charges to the statement of comprehensive income and the statement of changes in equity that affect the line item. Adjust for items in the additional information. If this does not give the closing balance, then a cash payment or cash receipt is a likely balancing item – you will need to use your judgement and common sense here.
5. **The 'New' Items in Consolidated Statement of Cash Flows** Items such as (not an exhaustive list):
   - payments to acquire subsidiaries;
   - proceeds from the disposal of subsidiaries;
   - payments to acquire associates;
   - proceeds from the disposal of associates;
   - cash received from associates; and
   - payments of dividends to non-controlling interests.
6. **The Additional Information** In every statement of cash flows case study there will be additional information. If you are having difficulty understanding the information just ask yourself the question – "what is the cash implication of this?".

Requirement (c) – Guidance

This is a discursive question on the reporting disclosures required for a 'planned' restructuring programme and the risk management practices of the group. There is no 'one size fits all' solution to these types of questions. Much will depend on the facts as presented, the guidance in the reporting standards and (most crucially) professional judgement.

The 'Planned' Restructuring Programme The disclosures required for the restructuring programme will hinge on the notion of 'planned' and how committed the group is to the restructuring. You will need to consider the following:

Should the divisions be classified as 'discontinuing/discontinued operations'? The impact of this is that the divisions should be presented separately in the statement of comprehensive income and in the statement of financial position. Take a look at IFRS 5 *Non-current Assets Held for Sale and Discontinued Operations*, paragraph 8A and paragraph 32.

Should a provision be set aside for the estimated costs of the restructuring? IAS 37 *Provisions, Contingent Liabilities and Contingent Assets,* paragraph 72, may help to resolve this issue.

The restructuring plans will be finalised in November 2013; does this constitute an event after the reporting period (IAS 10 *Events after the Reporting Period,* paragraph 7)? When is it likely that financial statements are authorised for issue for the year ended 31 December 2012, i.e. before or after November 2013?

The risk management disclosures IFRS 7 *Financial Instruments: Disclosures* will give the reporting requirements in this area. There is no absolutely correct answer to the scenario presented – IFRS 7, paragraph 7, states "an entity should disclose information that enables users of its financial statements to evaluate the significance of financial instruments for its financial position and performance". Clearly, a principles-based approach is applied to the disclosure of financial instruments although considerable guidance is provided. IFRS 7, paragraphs 31–42, will give further detail on what should be disclosed; you will need to discuss credit risk, market risk and liquidity risk, where appropriate.

If you are looking for practical guidance, take a look at the financial statements of any large company. Vodafone is a good example: their most recent financial statements will describe their processes, however, it might also be worth considering the financial statements of a company under cash flow pressure.

Finally, you are not asked to comment on the cash management processes of the group (which are not ideal) – any discussion of this will only waste time and will not attract any marks.

Recommended Reading

The above may also be referenced in *International Financial Accounting and Reporting*, 3rd Edition, by Ciaran Connolly (Chartered Accountants Ireland, 2011) and the relevant accounting standards as follows:

	Chapter	Chapter title	Chapter section	Standard
Requirement (a)				
Issue 1	20	Non-current Assets Held for Sale and Discontinued Operations	20.3	IFRS 5
	6	Property, Plant and Equipment	6.2	IAS 16
	15	Events after the Reporting Period	15.2	IAS 10

Issue 2	8	Leases	8.2–8.4	IAS 17
Issue 3	14	Provisions. Contingent Liabilities and Contingent Assets	14.2–14.3	IAS 2
Requirement (b)				
	33	Statement of Cash Flows – Consolidated	33.1–33.3	IAS 7
Requirement (c)				
Planned Restructuring	20	Non-current Assets Held for Sale and Discontinued Operations	20.4	IFRS 5
Risk Management Disclosures	25	Financial Instruments	25.4	IFRS 7

Solution to Elite Group

Requirement (a)

Outstanding Issue 1

This property is incorrectly classified as 'held for sale'.

Although the intention of the company, at the end of 2012, is to sell the property, IFRS 5, paragraph 7, states that, in order to qualify as held-for-sale, an asset must "**be available for immediate sale in its present condition**". As the necessary repairs were not carried out until after the year-end, this was clearly not the case at 31 December 2012.

Although the repairs were not completed by the end of the financial period, they were carried out before the financial statements were authorised. You should consider whether the timing of this event is relevant. IAS 10 *Events after the Reporting Period* will provide the relevant guidance. IAS 10, paragraph 3, classifies events that occur after the year-end as adjusting events or non-adjusting events. IAS 10, paragraph 3(a), defines adjusting events as "those that provide evidence of conditions that existed at the end of the reporting period".

At the end of December the property was still in a state of disrepair. It was not "available for immediate sale in its present condition" (IFRS 5, para 7). The property does not satisfy the requirements of IFRS 5 at the financial year-end. It should be classified as property, plant and equipment at 31 December 2012 and depreciation should be charged for the period. (Even if the repair work had been completed before the end of the financial year, the value at which the property was stated would still be incorrect. IFRS 5, paragraph 15, requires that non-current assets held for sale should be valued at the lower of their carrying value or fair value less costs to sell. The carrying value of the property at the period end is €1.9m (€2 million less one year's depreciation). This is lower than the fair value less costs to sell. The property would be valued at €1.9 million not €2.7 million.)

The sale of the asset after the year-end should be disclosed in the notes to the financial statements, if material, under the heading of 'non-adjusting events'. The nature of the event and an estimate of its financial effect should be disclosed.

The adjustments required to bring the accounting treatment in line with IFRS 5/IAS 16 include:

	€	€
DR PPE	2,000,000	
CR Non-current assets held for sale		2,700,000
DR Property Gain (SOCI)	700,000	
DR Operating expenses (depreciation charge, SOCI)	100,000	
CR PPE		100,000

Outstanding Issue 2

Lease with TRP Limited The issue here is the substance of the transaction. IAS 17 *Leases* classifies leases into finance leases and operating leases. A finance lease transfers substantially all of the "risks and rewards" of ownership to the lessee (IAS 17, para 8). An operating lease does not. The correct classification for this leasing contract is as an operating lease. This classification is appropriate for two reasons:

- TPR retains legal ownership of the asset and also retains the benefits of ownership. A lease is only classified as a finance lease if substantially all of the risks and rewards of ownership are transferred to the lessee (IAS 17, para 8). One of the indications that a lease is a finance lease is if, at the inception of the lease, the present value of the minimum lease payments amounts to at least substantially all of the fair value of the leased asset (IAS 17, para 10(d)). The present value of the minimum lease payments of the TPR lease amounts to only 16.67% of the fair value of the asset (€1m/€6m = 16.67%). Therefore this is not a finance lease.
- Another indicator of a finance lease is that the lease term is for the major part of the economic life of the asset even if title is not transferred (IAS 17, para 10(c)). Land normally has an indefinite economic life (IAS 16, para 58).

Therefore leases of land are normally classified as operating leases.

Lease payments on an operating lease should be recognised as an expense, on a straight line basis, unless another systematic basis is more representative of the time pattern of the user's benefit (IAS 17, para 33). There is no indication of another systematic basis in this instance, so the straight line basis is appropriate. Only one year's lease charge should be included in expenses in 2012, not the entire lease.

The annual rental is calculated as follows:

The present value of the lease payments is €1 million;
The lease period is 5 years;
The discount rate is 10%; and
The discount factor for 10% over 5 years is 3.79.

Annual cash flow, i.e. rental, is calculated as follows:

€1m/3.79 = €263,852

Currently a total charge of €1 million has been made to administration expenses. The correct charge should be one year's rental, i.e. €263,852. To correct this error we need to reduce administration expenses and trade payables by €736,148 (i.e. €1,000,000 − €263,852) as follows:

	€	€
DR Trade payables	736,148	
CR Operating expenses		736,148

Lease with AK Arnold Ltd This lease appears to be a sale and leaseback arrangement, although the inclusion of a repurchase option has caused confusion. In order to determine the true substance of this transaction (and therefore the accounting treatment) it is necessary to examine the detail of the repurchase clause. IAS 17 provides guidance on *how* to present a sale and leaseback arrangement in the financial statements. However, it does not give any indication whether a contract of this nature is actually a sale and leaseback arrangement, *or* some other form of financing agreement. Current best practice requires that where it is *almost certain* that a seller/lessee will reacquire the asset that is the subject of a sale and leaseback arrangement, in substance the arrangement may not involve a lease. In this case IAS 17 would not apply. (The transaction would probably be classified as a financing arrangement.) Where there is an option to reacquire, the exercise of which remains uncertain, IAS 17 will apply. The arrangement with AK Arnold involves an option (but not a requirement) to repurchase. There is no certainty of repurchase. Therefore IAS 17 *Leases* will apply. The arrangement will be classified as a lease and not, as is suggested by one of the directors, a loan to the group.

The lease now needs to be classified as a finance *or* operating lease. The normal rules of classification apply (IAS 17, para 7–19). A finance lease transfers "substantially all of the risks and rewards incidental to ownership" (IAS 17, para 8). An operating lease does not.

The leaseback arrangement is an operating leaseback as it does not transfer substantially all of the rewards of ownership to the lessee. This is determined as follows:

Present value of minimum lease payments (€480,000 × 3.6048[1])	= €1,730,304
Fair value of plant at inception of the lease	€4,000,000
Transfer % (PV of minimum lease payments)/(FV of Asset)	= 28.84%

IAS 17, paragraphs 58–66 outline the appropriate accounting treatment for sale and leaseback arrangements. Paragraph 62 states that "if the leaseback is an operating lease and the lease payments and the sale price are at fair value, there has, in effect, been a normal sale transaction and any profit or loss is recognised immediately."

The current accounting entries for this transaction are incomplete. The asset and trade receivable have been adjusted for the disposal of the plant at carrying value. No account has been taken of the profit on disposal. The adjustment would be:

	€	€
DR Trade receivables	500,000	
CR Profit on disposal		500,000

Finally, two months' rental is due at the end of the accounting period (€480,000 × 2/12). This will be incorporated as follows:

	€	€
DR Expenses	80,000	
CR Trade payables		80,000

[1] Cumulative discount factor of 12% for five years is 3.6048.

Outstanding Issue 3

The movement in provisions for the period will include:

	Legal claims (long-term)	Onerous obligations	Returns & warranties	Legal claims (short-term)	Total
	€	€	€	€	€
Balance 1/1/2012	150,000	80,000	70,000	0	300,000
Movements during the period					
Effect of discounting (note 1)	14,980				14,980
Provision charged to the SOCI				40,000	40,000
Current expenditures (note 2)			(48,000)		(48,000)
Effect of change in estimate charged to the SOCI (note 3)			37,500		37,500
Release of onerous contract (note 4)		(80,000)			(80,000)
Balance 31/12/2012	164,980	0	59,500	40,000	264,480

Note 1 IAS 37, paragraph 45, states that "where the effect of the time value of money is material, the amount of the provision shall be the present value of the expenditures expected to be required to settle the obligation." IAS 37, paragraph 60, states that, where discounting is used, the carrying amount of a provision increases in each period to reflect the passage of time. This is illustrated as follows.

In the case of Elite's long-term provision, the settlement date at the beginning of the period was in three years' time (therefore the provision was discounted by three years). By the end of the period this will be two.

	Undiscounted	Discount Factor	Discounted
	€		€
At 1 January 2012	199,734	0.751	150,000
At 31 December 2012	199,734	0.826	164,980
Change to reflect passage of time			14,980

(€150,000 × 10% = €15,000 is also acceptable)

The double entry for this transaction is to debit operating expenses and credit provisions with the movement. (**Note:** IAS 37, paragraph 60, states that "where discounting is used … the increase is recognized as borrowing coasts. However, for the purpose of simplicity, this case requires you to assume that all changes to provisions affecting the Statement of Comprehensive Income are charged/credited to operating expenses.")

Note 2 Current expenditure includes amounts spent on sales returns and repairs of goods under warranty. (The double entry for this transaction is to debit provisions and credit payables.)

Note 3 The provision for sales returns and warranties should be adjusted to 0.5% of revenue (i.e. 0.5% of €11.9m). (The double entry for this transaction should be to debit operating expenses and credit provisions with the adjusment.)

Note 4 In accordance with IAS 37, paragraph 59, if it is no longer probable that an outflow of resources will be required to settle the obligation, the obligation shall be reversed. (The double entry for this transaction is to debit provisions and credit operating expenses.)

Finally, an adjustment is required to reflect the changes to the provision liability. All of the changes to the provisions account will affect the statement of comprehensive income.

	€	€
DR Provisions	35,520	
CR Operating expenses		35,520

Summary of Adjustments

ADJUSTMENTS AFFECTING THE STATEMENT OF COMPREHENSIVE INCOME

		Property Gain €000	Operating Expenses €000
Per draft		700	(2,765)
Outstanding issue 1		(700)	(100)
Outstanding issue 2	Lease TRP		736
	Lease AK Arnold	500	(80)
Outstanding issue 3	Reduction of provision		36
Restated		500	(2,173)

ADJUSTMENTS AFFECTING THE STATEMENT OF FINANCIAL POSITION

	PPE	Assets Available for Sale	Trade Receivables	Payables	Provisions	Reserves
	€000	€000	€000	€000	€000	€000
Per draft	11,480	2,700	6,090	2,325	300	8,104
Outstanding issue 1	1,900	(2,700)				(800)
Outstanding issue 2 Lease TRP				(736)		736
Outstanding issue 2 Lease Arnold			500	80		420
Outstanding issue 3 Provision					(36)	36
Restated	13,380	0	6,590	1,669	264	8,496
Net change	1,900	(2,700)	500	(656)	(36)	392

All figures rounded to the nearest 000.

The revised financial statements are presented next.

Elite Group
CONSOLIDATED STATEMENT OF COMPREHENSIVE INCOME
for the Year Ended 31 December 2012

	Original	Outstanding Issue 1	Outstanding Issue 2	Outstanding Issue 3	Revised
	€000	€000	€000	€000	€000
Turnover	11,900				11,900
Cost of sales	(5,460)				(5,460)
Gross Profit	6,440				6,440
Operating expenses	(2,765)	(100)	656	36	(2,173)
Property gain	700	(700)	500		500
Loss on disposal of PPE	(91)				(91)
Interest	(665)				(665)
Profit before Tax	3,619				4,011
Tax	(1,015)				(1,015)
Profit for the Financial Year	2,604				2,996
Other Comprehensive Income					
Property revaluation	88				88
Total Comprehensive Income	2,692				3,083

Profit for the Financial Year Attributable to		
Non-controlling interests	280	280
Equity shareholders	2,324	2,716
	2,604	2,996
Total Comprehensive Income Attributable to		
Non-controlling interests	280	280
Equity shareholders	2,412	2,803
	2,692	3,083

Elite Group
CONSOLIDATED STATEMENT OF CHANGES IN EQUITY
for the Year Ended 31 December 2012

	Share Capital	Share Premium	Retained Earnings	Revaluation Surplus	Total Equity	Non-cont Interests	Total
	€000	€000	€000	€000	€000	€000	€000
Opening balance – original	3,010	350	6,620	700	10,680	1,736	12,416
Share issue	175	88			263		263
Purchase of subsidiary					0	420	420
Total comprehensive income			2,716	88	2,803	280	3,083
Dividends			(840)		(840)	(336)	(1,176)
Closing balance – revised	3,185	438	8,496	788	12,906	2,100	15,006

Elite Group
CONSOLIDATED STATEMENT OF FINANCIAL POSITION
as at 31 December 2012

	Original 31/12/2012 €000	Issue 1 €000	Issue 2 €000	Issue 3 €000	Revised 31/12/2012 €000
Non-current Assets					
Plant, Property and Equipment	11,480	1,900			13,380
Financial Asset	0				0
Intangible Non-current Assets (Goodwill)	224				224
	11,704				13,604
Current Assets					
Non-current Asset Held for Sale	2,700	(2,700)			0
Inventory	4,270				4,270
Receivables	6,090		500		6,590
	13,060				10,860
Total Assets	24,764				24,464
Equity and Liabilities					
Equity					
Ordinary Share Capital	3,185				3,185
Share Premium	438				438
Retained Earnings	8,104	(800)	1,156	36	8,496
Revaluation Surplus	788				788
	12,514				12,906
Non-controlling Interests	2,100				2,100
Total Equity and Non-controlling Interests	14,614				15,006
Non-current Liabilities					
Finance Leases Payable	3,640				3,640
Deferred Taxation	896				896
	4,536				4,536
Current Liabilities					
Bank Overdraft	924				924
Payables	2,325		(656)		1,669
Provisions and Deferred Income	300			(36)	264
Tax Payable	665				665
Finance Leases Payable	1,400				1,400
	5,614				4,922
Total Equity and Liabilities	24,764				24,464

Requirement (b)

1. The Four PPE Figures

The first step in the preparation of the consolidated statement of cash flows is to calculate the four, related, PPE figures.

1. Depreciation on PPE is €2,625,000 (provided in additional information item 3) and €100,000 (from outstanding issue 1);
2. Cash payments to acquire PPE are €4,064,000 (see working 1, this is the most complicated calculation of this case study);
3. Profit/loss on the disposal of PPE. There is a loss of €91,000 (provided in the statement of comprehensive income) and a gain of €500,000 on the sale or lease back transaction from outstanding issue 2 (also in the statement of comprehensive income); and
4. Proceeds from the sale of PPE are €0 (from additional information item 3) and the proceeds from the sale and leaseback transaction have not been received.

2. The Working Capital Movements

Before preparing the consolidated statement of cash flows, the movements in the components of working capital should be calculated.

Decrease in inventory is €1,260,000 (see working 2);
Decrease in receivables is €3,290,000 (see working 2);
Decrease in payables is €971,000 (see working 2); and
Decrease in provisions is €36,000 (see working 2).

Note: these decreases were adjusted to take account of the additional amounts received on acquisition of the new subsidiary. Also, the movement in receivables removes the 'capital' receivable, the proceeds of the sale and leaseback transaction. The effect of these entries is included under 'proceeds from the disposal of non-current assets'.

3. The Consolidated Statement of Cash Flows

Elite Group
CONSOLIDATED STATEMENT OF CASH FLOWS
for the Year Ended 31 December 2012

	Notes	€000
Operating Cash Flows		
Revised profit for the year	RSOCI	2,996
Add: Tax	RSOCI	1,015
Add: Interest	RSOCI	665
Add: Loss on disposal of plant	RSOCI	91
Less: Gain on disposal of property	RSOCI	(500)
Add: Depreciation	Add Info 3	2,625
Add: Depreciation on asset held for sale	Issue 1	100
Add: Decrease in inventory	W2	1,260
Add: Decrease in receivables	W2	3,290
Less: Decrease in payables	W2	(971)
Less: Decrease in provisions	W2	(36)
Add: Goodwill impairment	W3,W4	56
		10,591
Tax	W5	(896)
Interest	W6	(700)
		8,995
Investing Cash Flows		
Acquisition of Widney	W7	(2,174)
Proceeds from sale of PPE	Add Info 4	0
Proceeds from sale and leaseback	W13	0
Proceeds from disposal of financial asset	W11	0
Payments to acquire PPE	W1	(4,064)
Dividends to non-controlling interests	W8	(336)
		(6,573)

Finance Cash Flows		
Proceeds from issue of shares	W12	0
Dividends paid	W9	(840)
Fin Leases paid	W10	(1,260)
		(2,100)
Increase in Cash and Cash Equivalents (Note A)		322

Note A – Increase in Cash and Cash Equivalents	
Opening cash (bank overdraft)	(1,246)
Closing cash (bank overdraft)	(924)
Increase in cash and cash equivalents	322

Abbreviations Used:

SOFP 2011	Statement of Financial Position as at 31 December 2011
RSOFP 2012	Revised Statement of Financial Position as at 31 December 2012
Add Info X	Additional Information Item X (additional information for the Consolidated Statement of Cash Flows only)
Issue X	The impact of the changes made due to outstanding issue X (requirement (a))
RSOCI	Revised Statement of Comprehensive Income
RSOCE	Revised Statement of Changes in Equity
Bal Fig	Balancing Figure (this is usually the cash payment or receipt)

Workings The workings for the figures in the consolidated statement of cash flows appear below. In almost all instances, the procedure employed is to set out the opening and closing balance for a particular line item in the statement of financial position. Then, using the statement of comprehensive income and the additional information, try to piece together the reason for the movement in the item from the start of the year to the end of the year. In many cases the missing figure will be a cash payment or receipt. This will require some practice, after a while you will get used to determining the reasons for the movement (often, they tend to repeat themselves).

The order in which the various line items are presented is largely irrelevant. However, it is probably a good strategy to start with the PPE-related items. These are often the most difficult to arrive at and are set out in Working 1.

Next, the movement in working capital adjustment is calculated in Working 2. This is also a standard calculation that is required for every consolidated statement of cash flows that uses the indirect method. It is probably good practice to calculate it at this stage. Beyond that, Working 3 and forward do not follow any particular order.

Working 1: Payments to Acquire PPE

	€000	
Opening balance	10,360	SOFP 2009
Acquisitions: Widney	1,470	Add Info 1
Depreciation	(2,625)	Add Info 3
Disposals	(91)	Add Info 4
Additions: finance leases	1,680	Add Info 5
Additions: interest	35	Add Info 5
Revaluations	88	Add Info 5
Additions: Property in lieu of financial asset	2,000	Issue 1 – original entry
Transfer: Property transfer to non-current asset held for sale	(2,000)	Issue 1 – original entry
Additions: transfers	2,000	Issue 1 – correction entry
Depreciation on asset held for sale	(100)	Issue 1 – correction entry
Disposals	(3,500)	Issue 2
Additions: paid	4,064	Bal Fig
Closing balance	13,380	RSOFP 2010

Working 2: Working Capital Movements

	Inventory	Receivables	Payables	Provisions	
	€000	€000	€000	€000	
Opening balance	4,480	5,040	2,080	300	SOFP 2011
Acquired	1,050	840	560	0	Add Info 1
Increase/decrease	(1,260)	710	(971)	(36)	Bal Fig
Closing balance	4,270	6,590*	1,669	264	RSOFP 2012

* **Note:** The increase/decrease in receivables includes the €4,000,000 receivable on the sale and leaseback transaction. This is not an operating item. The effect of this item needs to be removed:

	€
Increase as stated above	710,000
Less increase due to capital transaction	(4,000,000)
Operating decrease in receivables	(3,290,000)

Working 3: Goodwill on Acquisition of Widney

	€000	€000	
Cash		1,278	Add Info 1
Shares (175,000 × €1.50)		263	Add Info 1
		1,540	
Assets	1,680		Add Info 1
Group	75%	1,260	Add Info 1
Goodwill		280	

Working 4: Goodwill Impairment

	€000	
Opening balance	0	SOFP 2011
Acquisitions	280	Working 3
Impairment	(56)	Bal Fig
Closing balance	224	RSOFP 2012

Working 5: Tax

	€000	€000	
Opening balance			
Deferred tax		644	SOFP 2011
Corporation tax		574	SOFP 2011
		1,218	
Incurred		1,015	RSOCI
Acquired – Widney		224	Add Info 1
Paid		(896)	Bal Fig
Closing balance			
Deferred tax	896		RSOFP 2012
Corporation tax	665	1,561	RSOFP 2012

Working 6: Interest

	€000	
Opening balance	0*	SOFP 2011
Incurred – statement of comprehensive income	665	RSOCI
Incurred – capitalised	35	Add Info 5
Paid	(700)	Bal Fig
Closing balance	0*	RSOFP 2012

* Since there is no interest payable or receivable shown on the statement of financial position these figures are assumed to be zero.

Working 7: Acquisition of Widney

	€000	
Cash paid	(1,278)	Add Info 1
Bank deposit acquired	67	Add Info 1
Bank overdraft acquired	(963)	Add Info 1
	(2,174)	

Working 8: Dividends to Non-controlling Interests

This can be taken directly from the statement of changes in equity since there was no dividend to non-controlling interests outstanding at the start or end of the year.

	€000	
Opening non-controlling interests	1,736	SOFP 2011
Profits to non-controlling interests	280	RSOCI
Acquisition (1,680 × 25%)	420	
Dividends paid	(336)	Bal Fig
Closing balance	2,100	RSOFP 2012

Working 9: Dividends

	€000	
Opening balance	0	SOFP 2011
Incurred	840	RSOCE
Paid	(840)	Bal Fig
Closing balance	0	RSOFP 2012

Working 10: Finance Leases

	€000	€000	
Opening balance			
Current	1,260		SOFP 2011
Non-current	3,360	4,620	SOFP 2011
Additions		1,680	Add Info 5
Paid		(1,260)	Bal Fig
Closing balance			
Current	1,400		RSOFP 2012
Non-current	3,640	5,040	RSOFP 2012

Working 11: Financial Asset

	€000	
Opening balance	2,000	SOFP 2011
Transfer to PPE	(2,000)	Issue 1
Cash received	0	Bal Fig
Closing balance	0	RSOFP 2012

Working 12: Share Issue

	Ordinary Share Capital	Share Premium	
	€000	€000	
Opening balance	3,010	350	SFOP 2011
Issue to acquire Widney	175	88	Add Info 1
Cash issue	0	0	Bal Fig
Closing balance	3,185	438	RSOFP 2012

Working 13: Proceeds from Sale and Leaseback Transaction

	€000	
Fair Value of Disposal	4,000	Issue 2
Cash received to date	0	Issue 2

Requirement (c)

1: Strategic Decision Disclosures

IFRS 5, paragraph 30 states that an entity shall "present and disclose information that enables users of the financial statements to evaluate the financial effects of discontinued operations and disposals of non-current assets (or disposal groups)".

Classification as discontinuing A discontinued operation is a component of an entity that either has been disposed of or is classified as held for sale, and:

(a) represents either a separate major line of business or a geographical area of operations, and
(b) is part of a single co-ordinated plan to dispose of a separate major line of business or geographical area of operations, or
(c) is a subsidiary acquired exclusively with a view to resale (IFRS 5, para 32).

Classification of the discontinued operations in 2012 In 2012 the directors are planning to restructure. The plans are internal, they have not been finalised and restructuring will not commence for another 12 months. The division is continuing to trade. Therefore the operation would not be classified as a discontinued operation in 2012 and IFRS 5 will not apply.

IAS 37 *Provisions, Contingent Liabilities and Contingent Assets* states that a provision for restructuring is recognised only when the general recognition criteria for provisions apply to the restructuring (IAS 37, para 71). This will be when a detailed formal plan is adopted and announced publicly (a board decision is not enough to show commitment) (IAS 37, para 72). The plans have not been finalised by the end of 2012, therefore no provision should be created.

IAS 10 *Events after the Reporting Period* includes the announcement of a plan to discontinue an operation after the reporting period as a non-adjusting item in the financial statements (IAS 10, para 22(b)). However the period to which IAS 10 refers is the period between the financial year-end and the date the accounts are signed. As the announcement of the restructuring will not be made until November 2013, IAS 10 will not apply (the financial statements are due to be authorised for issue in March 2013).

In conclusion, the restructuring will have no impact on the 2012 financial statements (see Appendix 1 of this case study for the implications for 2013 and 2014 – not asked for in the requirements).

2: Risk Management Disclosures

There is no absolutely correct answer to this requirement; what follows is just one possible wording. Much of the solution is a repackaging of the information as provided.

Under IFRS 7 *Financial Instruments: Disclosures* the group is obliged to disclose all information that will assist users to evaluate the significance of financial instruments on the financial position of the group and enable users to assess the nature and extent of the risks arising from the use of financial instruments. This is an onerous standard; it is focused on the user and therefore all pertinent information needs to be disclosed. In particular, the information on breaches of overdraft agreements should be provided. This is usually one of the most extensive notes to the financial statements of large companies – clearly they have taken the view that, if there is a doubt, more information should be provided. A sample disclosure note now follows.

Financial Risk Management of Elite Group The group does not operate a centralised treasury function; each subsidiary is responsible for its own cash management. However, individual subsidiaries are not permitted to borrow. At year-end the group had no outstanding borrowings (2011, nil).

Liquidity Risk Although subsidiaries are not permitted to borrow, each subsidiary has agreed an overdraft limit with its respective bank. The group has €1,990,000 of committed bank facilities, €1,066,000 of which was undrawn at year-end. These facilities have an average maturity of 30 June 2014, ranging from 30 June 2013 to 31 December 2015 (IFRS 7, para 39).

Lenders have the right, but not the obligation, to cancel their commitment with 30 days' notice should the conditions of the overdrafts be breached or at the end of the agreed period of the overdraft.

The conditions were breached in the following cases:

- four subsidiaries exceeded their agreed limits during the period;
- two of these subsidiaries continued to exceed their limits at period end; and
- three subsidiaries did not keep their account in credit for the agreed period (30 days per year) during the period.

In all of the above instances, the lenders involved did not take any action beyond charging a penalty. The amount of the overdrafts in breach and the penalties charged should be disclosed (IFRS 7, para 18 and 19).

Market Risk The weighted average rate of interest on the overdrafts is 11%, ranging from 8% to 12%. All of the overdrafts are on a variable interest rate basis. Elite should include a sensitivity analysis, showing, e.g. the impact on profits if interest rates increase by, say, 1%.

Credit Risk Not applicable.

Security The group has offered security in respect of two of the agreed overdrafts. The total value of the collateral offered is €500,000. In both cases the collateral offered is property. The overdrafts involved are currently in breach of their conditions, having exceeded their agreed limits of €75,000 in aggregate by €28,000 in aggregate. Under the terms of the overdrafts, the lender can now demand repayment within 30 days. Should the group be unable to repay, the lender can act on its security. To date, the lenders have neither demanded repayment nor sought their security. In the event of the lender demanding repayment, the group would be able to repay the overdraft using existing committed facilities from other subsidiaries thereby eliminating the liquidity risk (and subsequent foreclosure risk).

Appendix 1: Additional Disclosures for Planned Restructuring Applicable to the Financial Years 2013 and 2014

Note: This solution assumes that the process follows the restructuring schedule as outlined in the case study. The requirement did not ask that this detail be provided, however it is a useful exercise to follow the accounting implications of a restructuring from the planning stage to implementation.

2013 In November 2013, an announcement is made publicly although the actual restructuring does not commence. As a result of the public announcement (i.e. a firm commitment), the company may recognise a provision for restructuring costs in the 2013 financial statements.

IAS 37 is very specific about what costs may be included in this provision. Paragraph 80 states "a restructuring provision shall include only the direct expenditures arising from the restructuring which are those that are both (a) necessarily entailed by the restructuring *and* (b) not associated with the on-going activities of the entity." Paragraph 81 outlines what may not be included in this provision. This list includes:
(a) Retraining or relocating continuing staff;
(b) Marketing or
(c) Investment in new systems and distribution networks.

In addition, paragraph 82 states that " identifiable future operating losses up to the date of a restructuring are not included in the provision unless they relate to an onerous contract". There is no indication that this is the situation in 2013.

In the case study, the restructuring costs include redundancy costs, retraining and relocation and legal costs. In accordance with IAS 37 only the redundancy and the legal costs should be included in the provision. Relocation and training costs should not be included.

The effect of the costs on the 2013 financial statements will be a provision (and expense) of €3.25 million. In addition, IAS 37 requires the entity to give a brief description of the nature of the obligation and the expected timing of any resulting outflows of economic benefits (IAS 37, para 85(a)).

2014 The restructuring plans are implemented in 2014 and the divisions are closed down. The results for the discontinued activity will be presented in accordance with IFRS 5 *Non-current Assets Held for Sale and Discontinued Operations*, paragraphs 30–36(a).

Presentation of the Statement of Comprehensive Income IFRS 5, paragraph 33(a) explains that "the sum of the post-tax profit or loss of the discontinued operation and the post-tax gain or loss recognised on the measurement to fair value less cost to sell or fair value adjustments on the disposal of the assets (or disposal group) should be presented as a single amount on the face of the statement of comprehensive income". If the entity presents profit or loss in a separate statement of comprehensive income, a section identified as relating to discontinued operations is presented in that separate statement.

Detailed disclosure of revenue, expenses, pre-tax profit or loss and related income taxes is required either in the notes or in the statement of comprehensive income in a section distinct from continuing operations (IFRS 5, para. 33(b)). Such detailed disclosures must cover both the current and all prior periods presented in the financial statements (IFRS 5, para. 34).

An extract from the statement of comprehensive income might appear as follows:

EXTRACT FROM THE STATEMENT OF COMPREHENSIVE INCOME

	2014	**2013**
	€000	**€000**
Continuing Operations:		
Revenue	X	X
Cost of sales	X	X
Profit from continuing operations	X	X
Loss from discontinued operations (Note X)	(4,600)	(6,650)
Profit for the period	X	X

Note X: Profit from discontinued operations:

Discontinued Operations	**2014**	**2013**
	€000	**€000**
Operational profit/l (loss)	(2,800)	(3,400)
Restructuring costs	(4,050)	
Provision for redundancy costs	3,250	(3,250)
Operating profit	(3,600)	(6,650)
Impairment on assets held for sale (W1)	(1,000)	0
Loss on discontinued activities	(4,600)	(6,650)

W1: Profit on the measurement to fair value less cost to sell In 2014, the assets of the discontinued operation will be put up for sale. The assets (and liabilities) will be classified as held for sale and presented separately in the financial statements. In accordance with IFRS 5, paragraph 15 assets classified as held for sale shall be measured at the lower of carrying amount and fair value less costs to sell. For Elite the adjustment to fair value less costs to sell results in a loss of €1 million.

Case 11

IWTL

This case study is based on a company that has undergone a significant change in strategy in the most recent financial period. The accounting standards IAS 1, IAS 21, IAS 24, IAS 28, IAS 39, IFRS 3, IFRS 5, IFRS 7, IFRS 9 and IFRS 10 are addressed in this case.

Background – IWTL

It is now early January 2013. You are the financial accountant for International Warehousing Transport and Logistics Ltd (IWTL) and its related entities. In common with many other businesses, trading conditions have been difficult in recent years. As a result management decided to significantly change the strategy of the group, disposing of an Irish subsidiary and investing in a US business.

The Draft Financial Statements

The draft financial statements for the year ended 31 December 2012 are presented below.

STATEMENTS OF COMPREHENSIVE INCOME
for the Year Ended 31 December 2012

	IWTL	Kylemore	Rushmore
	€000	**€000**	**$000**
Revenue	14,000	3,750	6,000
Cost of sales	(12,400)	(825)	(1,500)
Gross Profit	1,600	2,925	4,500
Other income: profit on disposal	2,250		
Operating expenses	(5,500)	(1,275)	(3,000)
Operating Profit	(1,650)	1,650	1,500
Finance costs	(1,050)	(150)	(500)
Profit before tax	(2,700)	1,500	1,000
Taxation	425	(300)	(400)
Profit after tax	(2,275)	1,200	600
Other Comprehensive Income	0	0	0
Total Comprehensive Income	(2,275)	1,200	600

STATEMENTS OF FINANCIAL POSITION
as at 31 December 2012

	IWTL	Kylemore	Rushmore
Non-current Assets	**€000**	**€000**	**$000**
PPE	8,750	3,500	4,030
Investment in Kylemore	250		
Investment in Rushmore	3,000		
Financial asset	3,000		
Intangible assets	1,250	500	1,250
	16,250	4,000	5,280
Current Assets			
Inventories	4,900	1,200	800
Trade and other receivables	6,100	1,500	150
Cash and cash equivalents	500	1,200	450
	11,500	3,900	1,400
Total Assets	27,750	7,900	6,680
Equity			
Share capital	1,000	500	1,000
Share premium	500	0	0
Retained earnings	13,950	2,500	2,000
Revaluation surplus	1,150	0	0
	16,600	3,000	3,000
Non-current Liabilities			
Bank loans	1,000	2,000	1,500
Bonds	1,700	0	0
USD loans	3,000	0	0
Retirement benefit obligations	1,200	500	800
Deferred tax	500	450	250
Provisions	300	150	120
	7,700	3,100	2,670
Current Liabilities			
Trade and other payables	2,800	1,750	870
Tax liabilities	150	50	140
Bank loans	500	0	0
	3,450	1,800	1,010
Total Equity and Liabilities	27,750	7,900	6,680

IWTL
STATEMENT OF CHANGES IN EQUITY
for the Year Ended 31 December 2012

	Share Capital	Share Premium	Retained Earnings	Reval Surplus	Total
	€000	€000	€000	€000	€000
Opening balance	1,000	500	16,525	1,150	19,175
Comprehensive income			(2,275)	0	(2,275)
Dividends			(300)		(300)
Closing balance	1,000	500	13,950	1,150	16,600

Kylemore
STATEMENT OF CHANGES IN EQUITY
for the Year Ended 31 December 2012

	Share Capital	Retained Earnings	Total
	€000	€000	€000
Opening balance	500	1,300	1,800
Comprehensive income		1,200	1,200
Closing balance	500	2,500	3,000

Rushmore
STATEMENT OF CHANGES IN EQUITY
for the Year Ended 31 December 2012

	Share Capital	Retained Earnings	Total
	$000	$000	$000
Opening Balance	1,000	1,400	2,400
Comprehensive Income		600	600
Closing Balance	1,000	2,000	3,000

Additional Information

Kylemore Ltd

Original Purchase IWTL purchased 80% of Kylemore on 30 September 2006 for €1,000,000 when the ordinary share capital of Kylemore was €500,000 and its retained earnings were €300,000.

There was one fair value issue on acquisition. A building, with a remaining useful life of 25 years, had a fair value of €250,000 in excess of its carrying value. This adjustment was subsequently made in the records of Kylemore following the acquisition.

Disposal of Kylemore IWTL sold three-quarters (i.e. it sold 60% of the shares of Kylemore leaving it with a 20% interest in Kylemore) of its investment in Kylemore on 30 September 2012. IWTL still has one seat on the board of Kylemore to protect its interests and is considered to have significant influence over Kylemore.

IWTL had considerable difficulty locating a buyer for its shares in Kylemore and the shares were sold to the existing management of Kylemore for €3,000,000. However, the management of Kylemore were unable to raise finance so IWTL gave a loan to the management of Kylemore secured on the shares of Kylemore (with various restrictions on the sale of assets by Kylemore). The loan had an interest rate of 7% attached to it; this is indicative of underlying rates at the time. The loan is repayable in four years. The interest on the loan for the period to 31 December 2012 has been paid in full by the management of Kylemore (included in finance costs of IWTL as a credit).

IWTL accounted for the disposal of Kylemore as follows:

	€	€
DR Financial Asset	3,000,000	
CR Investment in Subsidiaries		750,000
CR Profit on Disposal		2,250,000

On the date of disposal, the ordinary share capital of Kylemore was €500,000 and its retained earnings were €2,200,000.

On the date of disposal, the fair value of the remaining 20% held by IWTL was €600,000 (removing the control premium).

There are no impairment issues with goodwill and no goodwill was written off over the course of the investment.

Rushmore Inc

On 30 September 2012, IWTL purchased 75% of the ordinary share capital of Rushmore Inc, a US company that reports in US dollars (USD). (USD is its functional currency.) The cost of the acquisition was $4,050,000 (paid in dollars). On that date the ordinary share capital of Rushmore was $1,000,000 and its retained earnings were $1,850,000.

Originally IWTL had hoped to use the proceeds of the disposal of Kylemore to fund the purchase of Rushmore, however, this was not possible (see previous section). Instead, on the date of the transaction, IWTL obtained a USD loan of $4,050,000. The interest rate on the loan was 5% which is indicative of the cost of borrowing in dollars. The principal amount is repayable in four years with the interest payable at the end of each quarter, assume that the effective interest rate on the loan is also 5%. The shares in Rushmore were given as security for the loan. All the interest outstanding on the loan had been paid, and correctly accounted for, by 31 December 2012.

IWTL did not specify a hedging relationship between the loan obtained and its investment in Rushmore.

IWTL accounted for the purchase as follows:

	€	€
DR Investment in Subsidiaries	3,000,000	
CR Bank		3,000,000
DR Bank ($4,050,000)	3,000,000	
CR USD Loan ($4,050,000)		3,000,000

Although the loan is denominated in USD, it is currently included in the statement of financial position of IWTL at €3,000,000.

On acquisition there was one fair value issue: a building, with a carrying value of $1,000,000 and a remaining life of 20 years, had a fair value of $1,240,000. While it is the intention of IWTL to get Rushmore to adjust the carrying value of the building, this had not occurred by year-end. Depreciation on buildings is charged to cost of sales.

The US business is operated on an independent basis. Rushmore is responsible for organising its own finance (except for equity finance), most of its operations are conducted in the USA and all of its major expenses are in USD. Consequently, the functional currency of Rushmore is USD (while the presentation currency of the group is Euro (EUR)).

The income and expenses of Rushmore arise evenly throughout the year.

RELEVANT EXCHANGE RATES

Spot rate on 30 September 2012	1 EUR = 1.35 USD
Spot rate on 31 December 2012	1 EUR = 1.30 USD
Average rate for 3 months to 31 December 2012	1 EUR = 1.32 USD

IWTL values non-controlling interests using the proportion of net assets method (i.e. the traditional method for the calculation of goodwill).

Requirements

(**Note:** Unless you are specifically required to consider deferred taxation, you can assume that it is not applicable.)

(a) Prepare the consolidated financial statements of the IWTL group. **(75 marks)**

(b) What would the effect be if IWTL had correctly specified a hedging relationship between the USD loan and the net investment in Rushmore (see IAS 21, paragraph 32 and IAS 39, paragraph 102)? **(10 marks)**

(c) The MD of IWTL would like to offset the loan payable on the purchase of Rushmore of €3 million with the loan receivable for €3 million from the new shareholders of Kylemore. He maintains that the group had intended to use the proceeds from the disposal of Kylemore to purchase the shares in Rushmore. In addition, both loans are for the same amount and have the same due date. Set out why the two loans cannot be offset. **(5 marks)**

(d) The transaction with the management of Kylemore is unusual. Set out the broad disclosures that IWTL should make (you are not required to draft the disclosure notes).

(10 marks)

Guidance Notes

Exam Technique

Read the case carefully then read the requirements.

This case study has a significant technical element (75% of the available marks). The technical aspects are mainly concerned with group accounting: a disposal of a subsidiary and an acquisition of a foreign subsidiary.

You should also notice that 25% of the available marks are allocated to requirements that are more discursive and less technical. In determining an approach to your solution, you will need to decide whether you should answer the requirements in sequence or if it would be more effective to answer some of the requirements out of order (i.e. concentrate more effort on the discursive questions)? If you feel you might be better able to answer any one of these three requirements (requirement (b)–(d)) then it might be sensible to begin here.

Finally, as with all of these case studies, you will need to manage your time. Make sure that you do not spend too much time on requirement (a) to the detriment of the other requirements.

Answering the Case Study

Requirement (a): Consolidated Financial Statements

This is a complex scenario and it will take some time to resolve. The requirement is to prepare the consolidated financial statements: the consolidated statement of financial position, the consolidated statement of comprehensive income and the consolidated statement of changes in equity. This is quite onerous; however, much of the analysis carried out for the consolidated statement of financial position can be reused for the other statements.

Translation of Foreign Currency Subsidiary The first step to deal with the foreign subsidiary is to resolve the fair value issue (in USD). See IFRS 3, paragraph 18, for justification of the approach. Then the resultant financial statements should be translated into Euro. See IAS 21, paragraphs 39 and 44–47. Remember, Rushmore was in the group for just three months.

Rushmore's functional currency is USD whereas its presentation currency is EUR. The next stage is to calculate any gains/losses on translation of Rushmore into EUR; this informationwill be required later. You will need to decide where any gains/losses on the translation of Rushmore should be recognised; should they be recognised in profit and loss (i.e. ultimately in retained earnings) or in other comprehensive income (i.e. in a separate reserve account and outside of 'normal' profits/losses); see IAS 21, para. 39.

As the subsidiary has only just joined the group, any foreign exchange gains or losses are fully recognised in the current period.

Consolidated Statement of Financial Position It is important to have a practised technique for the preparation of consolidated statements of financial position. The technique previously used in earlier cases studies can be relied on here again, although some alterations may be required given the complexity involved.

- Step 1: Set out the group structure;
- Step 2: Deal with the 'additional information';
- Step 3: Prepare the consolidation table (i.e. calculate the goodwill, non-controlling interests and retained earnings figures). These are key figures in a consolidated statement of financial position and attract many marks;
- Step 4: Finalise the foreign exchange gain/loss; and
- Step 5: Bring steps 2–4 together by preparing the consolidated statement of financial position.

Step 1: Group Structure In most of the previous case studies this was not contentious; however, you will need to decide on the nature of the relationship between Kylemore and IWTL.

Step 2: Additional Information

- **Kylemore** There is a lot of information provided on Kylemore. However, at this stage, it is the statement of financial position that is being prepared, so all that needs to be done is to ensure that the year-end position for Kylemore is correctly stated.

  Note that Kylemore is an associate at year end (see IAS 28, paras. 2 and 5). IAS 28, paragraph 10, gives guidance on the application of the equity method of accounting for associates. However, there is an issue with regard to the measurement of the initial cost of the investment – is it based on the original cost in 2006, (i.e. €250,000) or is it based on the fair value of the remainder of the original investment in 2012 (i.e. €600,000)? IFRS 10, paragraph B98(b), gives some direction on this. Remember that the group will be entitled to its share of the profits of Kylemore since it became an associate.

  The nature of the transaction (sale to the existing management) is not relevant at this point (but will be in later requirements). Also, the recognition of profits of Kylemore while it was a subsidiary is not an issue at this stage, this will be relevant when completing the statement of comprehensive income.

- **Rushmore** The accounting for Rushmore is more straightforward than the accounting for Kylemore.

  Beware that any goodwill arising is an asset of Rushmore and it too will need to be retranslated at the closing rate (IAS 21, para 47).

- **IWTL** Finally, the loan in USD that was obtained by IWTL will need to be considered. Should the loan (for $4,050,000) continue to be measured at €3,000,000 or should there be a retranslation using the year-end EUR/USD exchange rate? See IAS 21, paragraph 23, for guidance.

Step 3: Prepare the consolidation table Using the adjustments from step 2, you should now be in a position to calculate the goodwill on acquisition of Rushmore, non-controlling interests and retained earnings. For an example of a consolidation table, please see any previous case study, e.g. Knightstown. Do not forget to use the EUR figures for Rushmore, not the original USD figures.

Step 4: Finalise the foreign exchange gain/loss The foreign exchange gain on translation should have been calculated at the beginning as part of the translation exercise. At this stage it is a matter of adding the gain/loss on the translation of goodwill. The goodwill asset (from step 3) exists in the US as a US asset. It was calculated using an effective rate of 1.35 but the year end rate is 1.30. This is done to ensure consistency with the other assets and liabilities of Rushmore (see also IAS 21, paragraph 47).

Then determine the split between retained earnings and currency reserves. IAS 21, paragraph 39, states that gains/losses are recognised in other comprehensive income. The practice that has developed is that most companies distinguish between reserves that arise due to currency fluctuations and reserves that are retained earnings (non-currency related).

Step 5: Complete the Statement of Financial Position This should be a relatively mechanical exercise as all the thinking has already been done. Take the converted financial statements of Rushmore and combine them with the financial statements of IWTL, making sure that all the adjustments are correctly included.

Consolidated Statement of Comprehensive Income

1. *Translate Rushmore and calculate the foreign currency gain/loss* The statement of comprehensive income of Rushmore has already been translated into EUR (this was done at the beginning of this process as part of the consolidated statement of financial position). This also involved the calculation of the foreign currency gain (or loss). Therefore, a lot of the effort required to produce a consolidated income statement has been undertaken. Just remember, only three months of income and expenses of Rushmore will be included in the consolidated income statement as Rushmore joined the group on 30 September 2012.
2. *Account for the disposal of Kylemore* The next stage in the preparation of the consolidated statement of comprehensive income is to resolve the issue of the disposal of Kylemore. This requires calculating the gain (or loss) on disposal and recognising the income and expenses of Kylemore while it was a member of the group.

   To calculate the gain (or loss) on disposal: the proceeds should be compared with the carrying value of the group's share of the net assets disposed of, and the carrying value of the goodwill (IFRS 10, paragraph B98, provides guidance on how this should be done). The determination of the proceeds is an issue here – should the gain (or loss) be based on the proceeds of the proportion of the shareholding sold (60%) or should the proceeds be based on the full shareholding originally purchased (80%) with the additional 20% being valued at fair value? See IFRS 10, paragraph B98(b).

   The gain or loss on disposal along with the income and expenses of Kylemore for the first nine months of the period will need to be disclosed. IFRS 5, paragraph 33, gives the guidance here but an illustrative example in the implementation guidance on the standard (IFRS 5, IG Example 11) is more helpful – this illustrative example complies with the requirements of IFRS 5. Kylemore represents a discontinued operation, therefore, the income and expenses, and the gain on disposal should be disclosed separately with the detail provided by way of a note to the statement of comprehensive income.

3. *Deal with the additional information not already considered* (i.e. as part of item 1 or item 2, above). The only items that remain to be accounted for are the profits of Kylemore for the last three months of the period and the gain (or loss) on USD loan in IWTL.

   The group owned 20% of Kylemore for the last three months of the period. The profits that Kylemore generated in that period should be accounted for. As Kylemore is an associate, the regulations in IAS 28 *Investments in Associates* apply. IAS 28, paragraph 10, gives some guidance on the application of the equity method of consolidation; at this stage it is the implications for the statement of comprehensive income that are of interest not the valuation of the investment in associates (this was dealt with for the statement of financial position).

   The USD loan is included in the financial statements at €3,000,000. However, the actual amount due is $4,050,000. At year-end, because of the change in exchange rates, the amount owed in dollars does not equate to a liability of €3,000,000. First, should the amount be restated to reflect the year-end exchange rate (IAS 21, para 23 (a)) and then where should any gain or loss be recognised (IAS 21, para 28)?

The consolidated statement of comprehensive income should now be prepared. It will include:

- The income and expenses of IWTL (including the gain/loss on the USD loan);
- The translated income and expenses of Rushmore for three months;
- The group share of profits generated by Kylemore as an associate for three months; and
- The gain/loss on disposal of Kylemore and the income and expenses of Kylemore as a subsidiary for nine months shown as part of discontinued activities.

The final element is to calculate the profit attributable to the non-controlling interests. For the three months that Rushmore was part of the group, the non-controlling interests will be allocated 25% of the gains or losses and for the nine months that Kylemore was part of the group (as a subsidiary) the non-controlling interests will be allocated 20% of the gains or losses.

Consolidated Statement of Changes in Equity This is the final statement that you need to complete. The usual starting point is to begin with a blank template. This process has been used in earlier case studies and can be employed again in this instance.

Opening Balance This is the most difficult element of the statement of changes in equity. The opening balance for each component of equity needs to be calculated. Guidance on how to do this is set out below.

- Ordinary Share Capital: include the opening ordinary share capital of the parent company (IWTL) only;
- Share Premium: include the opening share premium of the parent company (IWTL) only;
- Retained Earnings: include the opening retained earnings of the parent company (IWTL) plus the group's share of the opening post-acquisition retained earnings of the subsidiary (Kylemore) at the start of the period; the opening balance for Rushmore is zero because at the start of the year it was not part of the group.
- Revaluation Surplus: include opening revaluation surplus of the parent company (IWTL); there is no revaluation surplus in any of the subsidiaries;

- Currency Reserve: zero opening balance as Rushmore, the foreign subsidiary, only joined the group during the year;
- Non-controlling Interests: 20% of opening net assets of Kylemore. (Rushmore did not become a part of the group until September of the current period.)

Of these items the retained earnings is where most of the complexity arises:

		€
Opening retained earnings of IWTL		X
Opening retained earnings of Kylemore	K	
Less pre-acquisition retained earnings	(Z)	
Less: fair value adjustment	(W)	
Opening post-acquisition retained earnings of Kylemore	Y	
Group Share at 80%		V
Consolidated opening retained earnings		V+X

Comprehensive Income The entries in this row are taken from the consolidated statement of comprehensive income. Some re-analysis will be required to correctly allocate the foreign exchange gain/loss. Only the foreign exchange gain/loss that arises from the translation of Rushmore will be included in the foreign currency reserve – IAS 21, paragraph 39(c).

Acquisition and Disposal of Non-controlling Interests When the shares in Rushmore were purchased, the group also acquired additional non-controlling interests. Likewise, on disposal of the shares in Kylemore, the group disposed of non-controlling interests. The value of non-controlling interests acquired or disposed of will depend on the appropriate percentage of the fair value of the net assets acquired and the appropriate percentage of the carrying value of the assets disposed of.

Dividend Include the dividend paid by the parent to the shareholders (and any dividend paid to the non-controlling interests – none in this case).

Requirement (b): The Hedging Relationship

This requirement addresses a complex area of financial reporting, therefore only a broad discussion of the issues is necessary. You should explain the following:

- explain the difficulty with the current situation (i.e. without a hedging relationship);
- outline the benefit of specifying a hedging relationship; and
- set out some of the broad conditions required for a hedge to be effective.

Much of the detail for this can be found in IAS 39, paragraphs 88 and 102 but it is extremely dense. In the first instance you should refer to *International Financial Accounting and Reporting*, 3rd Edition, (Chartered Accountants Ireland, 2011) pages 510–514.

Requirement (c): Offsetting Assets and Liabilities

The small number of marks (i.e. only five marks) allocated to this requirement should provide an indication of the level of difficulty and length of answer required here. IAS 1 *Presentation of Financial Statements*, paragraph 32, provides the general principle with further explanations and limited exceptions set out in paragraphs 33–35. Specific guidance on the offsetting of financial assets with financial liabilities can be found in IAS 32 *Financial Instruments: Presentation*, paragraph 42.

Requirement (d): Disposal of Kylemore

The financial reporting disclosure implications of the disposal of Kylemore can be categorised under a number of headings: IFRS 5 *Non-current Assets Held for Sale and Discontinued Operations*, IAS 24 *Related Party Disclosures*, IFRS 7 *Financial Instruments: Disclosures* and IFRS 10 *Consolidated Financial Statements*.

- Should the disposal of Kylemore be classified as a 'discontinued operation' (see IFRS 5, paragraphs 31 and 32)? If the disposal of Kylemore is a 'discontinued operation' then what information needs to be disclosed (IFRS 5, para 33)?
- Should the former management of Kylemore be considered a related party and should the nature of the transaction require further elaboration in the financial statements (see IAS 24, paragraph 9)? Could the management of Kylemore be considered a part of the 'key management personnel' of IWTL (see IAS 24, paragraph 9)?
- Referring to IFRS 7, how should the financial asset (the loan to the former management of Kylemore) be disclosed in the financial statements? Consider such matters as the valuation of the loan and the disclosure of credit risk and collateral. See IFRS 7, paragraphs 25 and 36.
- How should the loss of control of Kylemore be disclosed in the financial statements (see IFRS 10, paragraphs 25, B97–B99)?

Recommended Reading

The above issues may also be referenced in *International Financial Accounting and Reporting*, 3rd edition, by Ciaran Connolly (Chartered Accountants Ireland, 2011) and the relevant accounting standards as follows:

Chapter	Chapter title	Chapter section	Standard
Requirement (a)			
32	Disposal of Subsidiaries	32.5	IFRS 5, IFRS 10
29	Associates	29.3	IAS 28
31	Foreign Currency Transactions and Translation of Foreign Operations	31.3	IAS 21
27	Consolidated Statement of Financial Position	27.11	IFRS 3, IFRS 10
28	Consolidated Statement of Comprehensive Income	28.2	IFRS 3, IFRS 10
20	Non-current Assets Held for Sale and Discontinued Operations	20.4	IFRS 5

Requirement (b)

31	Foreign Currency Transactions and Translation of Foreign Operations	31.3	IAS 21
25	Financial Instruments	25.3	IAS 39

Requirement (c)

2	Presentation of Financial Statements	2.2	IAS 1
25	Financial Instruments	25.2	IAS 39

Requirement (d)

20	Non-current Assets Held for Sale and Discontinued Operations	20.4	IFRS 5
22	Related Party Disclosures	22.2, 22.5	IAS 24
32	Disposal of Subsidiaries	32.2	IFRS 10
25	Financial Instruments	25.4	IFRS 7

Solution to IWTL Group

Note: all figures in this solution have been rounded to the nearest thousand.

Requirement (a): Consolidated Financial Statements

Consolidated Statement of Financial Position

Preliminary Step: Convert Rushmore into EUR The first stage in the preparation of the consolidated statement of financial position is to convert the statement of financial position of Rushmore into EUR. As part of this process, the fair value adjustment should also be completed. Under IFRS 3, paragraph 18, the assets of Rushmore should be valued at fair value on acquisition. This will have the effect of increasing the value of PPE by $240,000, with a corresponding increase to pre-acquisition retained earnings. The follow-on effect of this is that the depreciation charge on the PPE of Rushmore will increase. Buildings are depreciated over 20 years but in the current period only three months' depreciation will apply as Rushmore was acquired on 30 September 2012. The entries for the fair value adjustment are set out below:

	$	$
Debit/Increase PPE	240,000	
Credit/Increase Pre-acquisition retained earnings		240,000
Fair value adjustment on acquisition of Rushmore		
Debit/Decrease Post-acquisition retained earnings	3,000	
Credit/Decrease PPE		3,000

The additional depreciation as a result of the fair value adjustment is $3,000, i.e. $240,000 spread over 20 years with just three months in the current period. The entry is booked to retained earnings in the statement of financial position; it flows through from cost of sales in the consolidated statement of comprehensive income.

Having completed the fair value adjustment, the financial statements of Rushmore should now be converted into EUR. The appropriate rate for the individual assets and liabilities is the closing rate (i.e. 1 EUR = 1.30 USD) as specified in IAS 21, paragraph 39(a). The only exception is that ordinary share capital and pre-acquisition retained earnings should be translated at the rate on the date of acquisition (i.e. 1 EUR = 1.35 USD) – the reason for the different rates is to permit the calculation of the foreign exchange gain or loss. Finally, if two different exchange rates are used to translate a USD statement of financial position, the resulting EUR statement of financial position will not balance. To ensure that the EUR statement of financial position balances, the post-acquisition retained earnings becomes the balancing figure.

Rushmore
STATEMENT OF FINANCIAL POSITION
(with Fair Value Adjustment and Converted to EUR)
as at 31 December 2012

	Rushmore	FV Adj	Rushmore	Rate	Rushmore
	$000	**$000**	**$000**		**€000**
Non-current Assets					
Property, plant and equipment	4,030	237	4,267	1.30	3,282
Intangible assets	1,250		1,250	1.30	962
	5,280		5,517		4,244
Current Assets					
Inventories	800		800	1.30	615
Trade and other receivables	150		150	1.30	115
Cash and cash equivalents	450		450	1.30	346
	1,400		1,400		1,077
Total Assets	6,680		6,917		5,321
Equity					
Share Capital	1,000		1,000	1.35	741
Retained Earnings – pre-acq	1,850	240	2,090	1.35	1,548
Retained Earnings – post-acq	150	(3)	147	bal fig	201
	3,000		3,237		2,490
Non-current Liabilities					
Bank Loans	1,500		1,500	1.30	1,154
Retirement Benefit Obligations	800		800	1.30	615
Deferred tax	250		250	1.30	192
Provisions	120		120	1.30	92
	2,670		2,670		2,054
Current Liabilities					
Trade and other payables	870		870	1.30	669
Tax liabilities	140		140	1.30	108
	1,010		1,010		777
Total Equity and Liabilities	6,680		6,917		5,321

At this stage, in order to calculate the foreign exchange gain or loss, the statement of comprehensive income of Rushmore will be converted into EUR. (It will be necessary to do this for the consolidated statement of comprehensive income so there is no additional work involved.) When translating the statement of comprehensive income, a number of issues need to be considered:

- Rushmore was only in the group for three months, hence only the income and expenses from 1 October 2012 to 31 December 2012 should be included in the consolidated financial statements. As the income and expenses of Rushmore arise evenly throughout the year, a simple time apportionment is justifiable.
- the effect of the fair value adjustment upon the statement of comprehensive income will need to be processed (i.e. the additional depreciation, through the cost of sales).
- finally, the USD amounts should be converted into EUR. IAS 21, paragraph 39(b), states that the rate on the date of the individual transactions should be used. However, this may not be very practical, and an average rate is permitted to be used where the exchange rate has been relatively stable (IAS 21, para 40).

Rushmore
STATEMENT OF COMPREHENSIVE INCOME
(With Fair Value Adjustment and Converted to EUR)
for the Year Ended 31 December 2012

	Rushmore	**Rushmore – 3 months**	**FV adj**	**Rushmore**	**Rate**	**Rushmore**
	$000	**$000**	**$000**	**$000**		**€000**
Turnover	6,000	1,500		1,500	1.32	1,136
Cost of sales	(1,500)	(375)	(3)	(378)	1.32	(286)
Gross Profit	4,500	1,125		1,122		850
Operating expenses	(3,000)	(750)		(750)	1.32	(568)
Operating Profit	1,500	375		372		282
Finance costs	(500)	(125)		(125)	1.32	(95)
Profit before Tax	1,000	250		247		187
Taxation	(400)	(100)		(100)	1.32	(76)
Profit after Tax	600	150		147		111
Other Comprehensive Income	0	0		0	1.32	0
Total Comp Income	600	150		147		111

The final stage of the translation of Rushmore into EUR is to calculate any foreign exchange gain or loss. The USD has strengthened over the period (one EUR buys less USD), hence the USD denominated net assets have increased in EUR value. Consequently, a foreign exchange gain is expected.

On acquisition, Rushmore had $3,090,000 (including the fair value adjustment) of net assets – this converts into €2,289,000 using 1 EUR to 1.35 USD. During the period, Rushmore generated $147,000 of income (including the fair value adjustment) – this converts to €111,000 using 1 EUR to 1.32 USD. At the end of the year, Rushmore had $3,237,000 (including the fair value adjustment) – this converts to €2,490,000 using 1 EUR to 1.30 USD. However, while the figures in USD all add correctly, the same items in EUR do not – the only reason for a difference is the effect of the change in exchange rates, i.e. the foreign exchange gain or loss.

Calculation of Exchange Gain/Loss on Translation of Net Assets (excluding Goodwill)

	$000	**Rate**	**€000**	
Net assets at acquisition	3,090	1.35	2,289	(includes FV adjustment)
Add profits since acquisition	147	1.32	111	(from statement of comprehensive income)
Exchange gain/loss		Bal Fig	90	(Gain, balancing figure)
Closing net assets	3,237	1.30	2,490	(from statement of financial position)

The movement in exchange rates has resulted in a gain of €90,000 for the group. This gain will be recognised in other comprehensive income (IAS 21, para 39(c)). This will be allocated between the equity shareholders and the non-controlling interests:

	€
Gain on foreign currency translation attributable to equity holders	67,000
Gain on foreign currency translation attributable to non-controlling interests	22,000
Total gain on foreign currency translation	90,000
(Any difference due to rounding.)	

When the €90,000 of the foreign exchange gain is added to the €111,000 of profits since acquisition, the total is €201,000; this is the total post-acquisition retained earnings of Rushmore in the translated statement of financial position.

The gain (or loss) on the translation of the goodwill asset in Rushmore will also have to be added to this. This will be calculated later as part of the consolidation process.

Now that Rushmore has been converted into EUR, the remainder of this requirement follows the process as before:

- Step 1: Set out the group structure;
- Step 2: Deal with the 'additional information';
- Step 3: Prepare the consolidation table (i.e. calculate the goodwill, non-controlling interests and retained earnings figures). These are key figures in a consolidated statement of financial position and attract many marks;
- Step 4: Finalise the foreign exchange gain/loss; and
- Step 5: Bring steps 2–4 together by preparing the consolidated statement of financial position.

Step 1: Set out the group structure The starting point for any consolidation question is to set out the group structure. At this stage, any relevant items of information should be noted; for example, when a company joined or left the group.

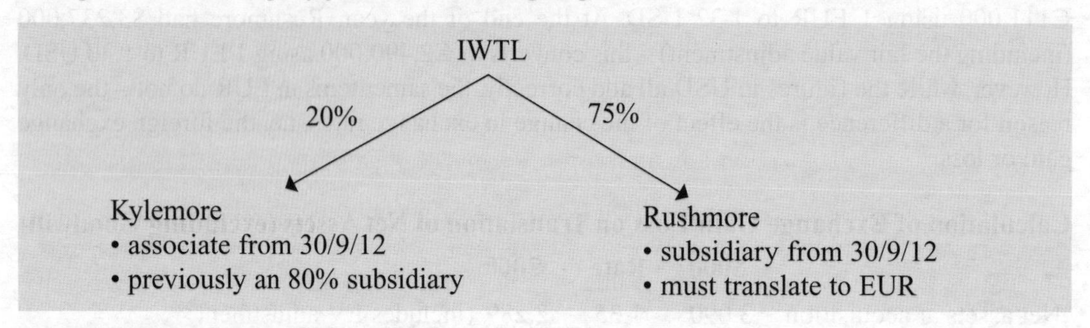

Step 2: The 'additional information'

- **Kylemore**

  At the year-end Kylemore is an associate. The 'investment in associate' needs to be properly recognised in the statement of financial position. The previous relationship with Kylemore (a subsidiary) is not relevant at this stage – this will be important for the consolidated statement of comprehensive income. There are two elements to the valuation of an investment in an associate (assuming no impairment issues). They are:
  - the cost of the investment; and
  - the investor's share of any profits or losses since acquisition.

  This is the equity method of accounting for associates as described in IAS 28, paragraph 10.

  There is a decision to be made regarding the measurement of the cost of the investment in Kylemore. Should the original cost of €250,000 be used? When Kylemore was originally purchased, an 80% interest cost €1,000,000. Therefore a 20% interest originally cost €250,000. Or should the fair value of the 20% on the date the relationship with Kylemore changed to an associate be used (i.e. €600,000)? IFRS 10, paragraph B98(b) (iii), clearly states that the retained investment is valued at fair value on the date the relationship changes.

  Since Kylemore became an associate, the retained earnings of Kylemore have increased from €2,200,000 to €2,500,000. This is a €300,000 increase; the group share of this is 20%, i.e. €60,000. As a consequence, the carrying value of the 'Investment in Associate' should be €660,000 (€600,000 being the fair value on acquisition and €60,000 of profits since acquisition). This compares with a current carrying value of €250,000. Therefore, an increase of €410,000 is required in the carrying value of the 'Investment in Associate', see below for the detail:

	€
Fair value on 1 October 2012	600,000
Group share of profits	60,000
Value of investment in Kylemore	660,000
Current carrying value	250,000
Increase required	410,000

Adjustment 1:

	€	€
Debit/Increase Investment in associate (Kylemore)	410,000	
Credit/Increase Retained earnings (IWTL group)		410,000

- **IWTL**

When the investment was made in Rushmore, IWTL obtained a USD loan of $4,050,000. At the time of the transaction, this translated into €3,000,000. The amount owed by IWTL is $4,050,000 (not €3,000,000); the liability in EUR is the USD liability translated into EUR using the exchange rate at the time the loan was received.

The functional currency of IWTL is EUR. At the year-end, since the loan is a monetary item owed by IWTL, it should be translated to EUR using the closing rate. This will result in a foreign exchange gain/loss as calculated below.

	€
Carrying value of loan ($4,050,000 @ 1.35)	3,000,000
Year-end value of loan ($4,050,000 @ 1.30)	3,115,000
Increase in loan (foreign exchange loss)	115,000

The loss on translation is recognised in profit (or loss) in the statement of comprehensive income (IAS 21, paragraph 28). The standard does not specify the expense heading that the amount should be allocated to – it could be included under operating expenses, interest/finance charges[1] or a separate expense (foreign exchange gain/loss). As there is no direction provided in the case study, an arbitrary decision was made to include this amount under operating expenses. Therefore the adjustment is:

Adjustment 2:

	€	€
Debit/Decrease Retained earnings	115,000	
Credit/Increase USD loan		115,000
(via operating expenses in the statement of comprehensive income)		

Step 3: The Consolidation Table

The consolidation table follows the same principles as in the previous case studies. The figures for Rushmore are taken from the translated statement of financial position:

	€	
Ordinary share capital	741,000	(split 75:25)
Retained earnings – pre-acquisition	1,548,000	(split 75:25)
Retained earnings – post-acquisition	201,000	(split 75:25)

[1]There is a theoretical logic to this – interest rate parity would suggest that the lower interest rate in USD is compensated for by the change in exchange rates.

These items are allocated to the various accounts as set out in the table below.

	Goodwill	Non-controlling Interests	Retained Earnings	Revaluation Surplus
	€000	€000	€000	€000
Cost of investment	3,000			
Ordinary share capital (Rushmore)	556	185		
Pre-acquisition retained earnings (Rushmore, €)	1,161	387		
Post-acquisition retained earnings (Rushmore, €)		50	151	
Retained earnings – Parent			13,950	
Revaluation surplus – Parent				1,150
Adj 1: Investment in Associates			410	
Adj 2: FX Loss on USD Loan			(115)	
Total	1,283	623	14,395	1,150
Exchange Gain on Goodwill (W1)	49		49	
Total	1,333	623	14,445	1,150

Currency reserve €117,000 | €14,328,000 Retained earnings

This split is explained later in the next section – Step 4: Finalise the Foreign Currency gain/loss

Step 4: Finalise the foreign exchange gain/loss

So far there have been a number of foreign exchange related issues:

- the foreign exchange gain of €90,000 on the translation of the net assets of Rushmore (this has been included in the translation of Rushmore into EUR);
- the foreign exchange loss of €115,000 on the translation of the USD loan into EUR; and
- finally, there is the foreign exchange gain (or loss) on the translation of the goodwill asset of Rushmore (this has yet to be determined – see below):
  - **Working 1 (W1): Exchange Gain on Goodwill**
    On completion of the first stage of the consolidation table goodwill is calculated at €1,283,000. However, goodwill represents an asset that has its basis in USD. The

goodwill of Rushmore (a company that operates mainly in a USD environment) is, consequently, a USD asset:

- Convert €1,283,000 into USD at the acquisition rate (i.e. 1 EUR = 1.35 USD) giving $1,733,000 (this is the USD value of the goodwill in Rushmore; this amount will not change in USD terms unless there is an impairment; however, it will fluctuate in EUR due to exchange rate movements);
- An asset with a value of $1,733,000 is worth €1,333,000 at the year-end (using the year-end rate (i.e. 1 EUR = 1.30 USD);
- Therefore the goodwill asset has increased in value from €1,283,000 (its acquisition valuation) to €1,333,000 (its year-end valuation) due to the movement in exchange rates. This gives a net gain of €49,000 (difference due to rounding);
- The impact of this is to increase the value of goodwill by €49,000 and the retained earnings of the group (through other comprehensive income) by €49,000. However, as this gain arises from the translation of an entity's financial statements from one currency (USD) into a different presentation currency (EUR), the gain is recognised in 'other comprehensive income'. Since goodwill is an asset that belongs in its entirety to the parent, all of the gain belongs to the group – this is because the group values non-controlling interests using the proportion of net assets method (i.e. the traditional method for the calculation of goodwill).

- **Summary of Foreign Exchange Items**

Currently retained earnings are €14,445,000 (see the retained earnings column in the consolidation table). This includes some items that relate to foreign exchange effects.

- The foreign exchange gain of €90,000 on the translation of the net assets of Rushmore is allocated to the group and the non-controlling interests.
  - €67,000, gain, is allocated to the group
  - €23,000, gain, is allocated to the non-controlling interests
- The foreign exchange gain of €49,000 on the translation of the goodwill of Rushmore is allocated in its entirety to the group.
  - €49,000, gain, is allocated to the group

Both of these items are recognised in other comprehensive income and can be shown as a separate reserve account (i.e. currency reserve). This is because these gains arise on the translation of the results and financial position of a company whose functional currency (USD) is different to its presentation currency (EUR).

	€
Opening balance of currency reserve	0
Gain on translation of net assets	67,000
Gain on translation of goodwill	49,000
Closing balance on currency reserve (difference due to rounding)	117,000

If €117,000 of a gain is transferred into a currency reserve, then this reduces the retained earnings from €14,445,000 by €117,000 to €14,328,000.

The loss on the USD loan of €115,000 is included in retained earnings as this is not arising on the translation of the results of a foreign entity into a different presentation currency.

Step 5: Prepare the Consolidated Statement of Financial Position

Bring steps 2–4 together by preparing the consolidated statement of financial position. Take the statement of financial position for IWTL and the translated statement of financial position for Rushmore. Combine these with the adjustments as set out (in this case there are only two adjustments). Include the figures for goodwill, non-controlling interests and retained earnings direct from the consolidation table (step 3) along with the details on the currency reserve.

IWTL
Consolidated Statement of Financial Position
as at 31 December 2012

	IWTL €000	Rushmore €000	Assoc Adj	Loan FX Adj	Group €000	
Non-current Assets						
Property, plant and equipment	8,750	3,282			12,032	
Investment in associates	250		410		660	
Goodwill	3,000				1,333	From table
Financial asset	3,000				3,000	
Intangible assets	1,250	962			2,212	
	16,250	4,244			19,237	
Current assets						
Inventories	4,900	615			5,515	
Trade and other receivables	6,100	115			6,215	
Cash and cash equivalents	500	346			846	
	11,500	1,077			12,577	
Total Assets	27,750	5,321			31,813	
Equity						
Share capital	1,000	741			1,000	Parent only
Share premium	500	0			500	Parent only
Retained earnings	13,950	1,749			14,328	From table
Currency reserve	0				117	From table
Revaluation surplus	1,150	0			1,150	
	16,600	2,490			17,095	
Non-controlling interests					623	From table
					17,717	

Non-current Liabilities				
Bank loans	1,000	1,154		2,154
Bonds	1,700	0		1,700
USD loans	3,000	0	115	3,115
Retirement benefit obligations	1,200	615		1,815
Deferred tax	500	192		692
Provisions	300	92		392
	7,700	2,054		9,869
Current Liabilities				
Trade and other payables	2,800	669		3,469
Tax liabilities	150	108		258
Lease creditor	0	0		0
Bank loans	500	0		500
	3,450	777		4,227
Total Equity and Liabilities	27,750	5,321		31,813

Consolidated Statement of Comprehensive Income This section of requirement (a) asks you to prepare the consolidated statement of comprehensive income. This involves a number of distinct elements:

- the translation of Rushmore and the calculation of the foreign currency gain/loss (already completed as part of the preparation of the consolidated statement of financial position);
- the disposal of Kylemore and the income and expenses of Kylemore prior to disposal; and
- the adjustments as a result of the additional information (not previously considered as part of the above two items).

Translation of Rushmore The translation of the statement of comprehensive income of Rushmore and the calculation of the foreign currency gain or loss has already been prepared as part of the consolidated statement of financial position. This is reproduced below.

Rushmore
STATEMENT OF COMPREHENSIVE INCOME
(with Fair Value Adjustment and Converted to EUR)
for the Year Ended 31 December 2012

	Rushmore	**Rushmore 3 months**	**FV adj**	**Rushmore**	**Rate**	**Rushmore**
	$000	**$000**	**$000**	**$000**		**€000**
Turnover	6,000	1,500		1,500	1.32	1,136
Cost of sales	(1,500)	(375)	(3)	(378)	1.32	(286)
Gross Profit	4,500	1,125		1,122		850
Operating expenses	(3,000)	(750)		(750)	1.32	(568)

Operating Profit	1,500	375	372		282
Finance costs	(500)	(125)	(125)	1.32	(95)
Profit before Tax	1,000	250	247		187
Taxation	(400)	(100)	(100)	1.32	(76)
Profit after Tax	600	150	147		111
Other Comprehensive Income	0	0	0	1.32	0
Total Comprehensive Income	600	150	147		111

The Disposal of Kylemore The gain (or loss) on the disposal of Kylemore needs to be calculated. This is done by comparing the proceeds (including the deemed proceeds of the fair value of the interest retained) with the carrying value of the group's share of the net assets disposed of and the carrying value of goodwill (IFRS 10, paragraph B98 provides the guidance on how this should be done, although interpretation of the paragraph is difficult).

	€	€
Actual proceeds		3,000,000
Deemed proceeds (FV of remaining interest)		600,000
		3,600,000
FV of the net assets of Kylemore on disposal date (30/9/2012)	2,700,000	
Group share	80%	
Group share of net assets	2,160,000	
Goodwill 'disposed of' (W2)	160,000	
Share of total assets disposed		(2,320,000)
Gain on disposal (see note 1 below)		1,280,000

The gain on disposal included in IWTL's financial statements (currently €2,250,000) needs to be removed and replaced with €1,280,000. This will be shown separately along with the income and expenses of Kylemore for nine months under discontinued operations (IFRS 5, paragraph 33).

- **Working 2 (W2): Goodwill Disposal**

	€	€
Original cost of investment		1,000,000
Net assets of Kylemore on date of acquisition	800,000	
Fair value adjustment	250,000	
	1,050,000	
Group's share	80%	(840,000)
Goodwill		160,000

- Note 1: **Gain on Disposal**

The gain on disposal arises from two sources, the gain on the actual shares sold (i.e. the 60%) and the gain on the re-measurement to fair value of the remaining shares (i.e. the 20%). It is not a proportionate split as the consideration received for the shares sold also includes a premium for control. The split is as follows:

	Total	Actual Shares Sold	Remaining Shares
	€000	€000	€000
Proceeds/deemed proceeds	3,600	3,000	600
Fair Value of Net Assets			
Group share of net assets	2,160	1,620	540
Goodwill 'disposed of'	160	120	40
Total net assets 'disposed of'	2,320	1,740	580
Gain on disposal	1,280	1,260	20

IFRS 5 is silent on how this split should be presented – in this solution the full amount is included as part of discontinued operations as the entity has lost control of the operation.

The Additional Information/Adjustments These items were analysed when the statement of financial position was prepared. At this stage, the impact on the statement of comprehensive income is under consideration.

- **Share of Profits of Associate**

By year-end Kylemore is an associate. The statement of comprehensive income should include the share of profits of the associate from 1 October 2012 to 31 December 2012. Since Kylemore became an associate, the retained earnings of Kylemore have increased from €2,200,000 to €2,500,000. This is an increase of €300,000; the group's share of this is 20%, i.e. €60,000.

Adjustment 1:

	€	€
Debit/Increase: Investments in associates (SOFP)*	60,000	
Credit/Increase: Share of profits of associate		60,000

* The debit side of this adjustment (to 'investments in associates' in the statement of financial position) was made when the statement of financial position was prepared.

- **Gain/Loss on Translation of Foreign Currency Loan**

When the investment was made in Rushmore, IWTL obtained a USD loan of $4,050,000. At the time of the transaction this translated into €3,000,000; however, the amount owed by IWTL is $4,050,000 (not €3,000,000), the liability in EUR is just the USD liability translated into EUR using the exchange rate at the time the loan was received.

The functional currency of IWTL is EUR. At year-end, as the loan is a monetary item owed by IWTL, it should be translated to EUR using the closing rate:

	€
Carrying value of loan ($4,050,000 @ 1.35)	3,000,000
Year-end value of loan ($4,050,000 @ 1.30)	3,115,000
Increase in loan (foreign exchange loss)	115,000

The loss on translation is recognised in profit (or loss) in the statement of comprehensive income (IAS 21, paragraph 28). The standard does not specify the expense heading that the amount should be allocated to: it could be included under operating expenses, interest/finance charges[2] or as a separate expense (foreign exchange gain/loss). As there is no direction provided in the case study, an arbitrary decision was made to include this amount under operating expenses. Therefore the adjustment is:

Adjustment 2:

	€	€
Debit/Increase: Operating expenses	115,000	
Credit/Increase: USD loan		115,000 (SOFP item)

SOFP = Statement of Financial Position, this item relates to the statement of financial position which has already been completed.

Now the statement of comprehensive income can be prepared:
- include the income and expenses of IWTL;
- include three months of the income and expenses of Rushmore. These should be included under continuing operations;
- include the income and expenses of Kylemore for the first nine months along with the gain on disposal. These are shown separately under discontinued activities. The income and expenses were calculated on a time-apportioned basis; and
- include the adjustments (the share of profit of the associate and the loss on translation of the USD loan).

[2] There is a theoretical logic to this – interest rate parity would suggest that the lower interest rate in USD is compensated for by the change in exchange rates.

IWTL
CONSOLIDATED STATEMENT OF COMPREHENSIVE INCOME
for the Year Ended 31 December 2012

	IWTL	Rushmore 3 months	Assoc Adj	Loan Adj	Group
	€000	€000			€000
Turnover	14,000	1,136			15,136
Cost of sales	(12,400)	(286)			(12,686)
Gross Profit	1,600	850			2,450
Share of profits of associate			60		60
Operating expenses	(5,500)	(568)		(115)	(6,183)
Operating Loss	(3,900)	282			(3,673)
Finance costs	(1,050)	(95)			(1,145)
Loss before Tax	(4,950)	187			(4,818)
Taxation	425	(76)			349
Loss after Tax	(4,525)	111			(4,469)
Discontinued activities (Note A)					2,180
Profit for the financial year					(2,289)
Other Comprehensive Income					
Foreign currency gains (W3)	49	90			139
Total Comprehensive Income	(4,476)	201			(2,150)
Profit/(Loss) for the Financial Year					
Attributable to ordinary shareholders					(2,496)
Attributable to non-controlling interests (W4a)					208
					(2,289)
Total Comprehensive Income/(Loss)					
Attributable to ordinary shareholders					(2,380)
Attributable to non-controlling interests (W4b)					230
					(2,150)

NOTE A: DISCONTINUED ACTIVITIES

On 30 September 2012 ITWL sold three-quarters of its investment in Kylemore. This was part of a strategic realignment of the group. ITWL still retains a 20% interest in Kylemore which, since 30 September 2012, is now accounted for as an investment in an associate.

The income and expenses of Kylemore from 1/1/12 to 30/9/12 are set out below:

	€000
Turnover	2,813
Cost of sales	(619)
Gross Profit	2,194
Operating expenses	(956)
Operating Profit	1,238
Finance costs	(113)
Profit before Tax	1,125
Taxation	(225)
Profit after Tax	900
Profit on Disposal (Note B)	1,280
Discontinued Activities	2,180

NOTE B: PROFIT ON DISPOSAL OF KYLEMORE

The gain on the disposal of Kylemore has been arrived at as follows:

	€
Actual proceeds	3,000,000
Deemed proceeds (FV of remaining interest)	600,000
	3,600,000
Carrying value of the net assets of Kylemore on disposal date (30/9/2012)	(2,320,000)
Gain on disposal	1,280,000

- **Working 3: Foreign Currency Gains**
  You recall from the statement of financial position workings there were three foreign currency items:
  - The foreign exchange gain of €90,000 on the translation of the net assets of Rushmore. This gain is not recognised in profit for the year, instead it is shown as part of other comprehensive income (IAS 21, para 39(c)). The gain is allocated to the group and non-controlling interests, this will be done when the non-controlling interests figure is calculated as part of working 4.
  - The foreign exchange gain of €49,000 on the translation of the goodwill of Rushmore. This gain is also recognised in other comprehensive income (IAS 21, para 39(c)). The gain is allocated in its entirety to the group, hence it is shown in the IWTL column so that it does not get included in the non-controlling interests calculation.
  - The loss on the USD loan of €115,000 is a loss arising on the translation of a monetary item to the functional currency of IWTL; hence it is included as part of profits (or losses) (IAS 21, para 28). This has already been done by including the loss as part of operating expenses.

- **Working 4a: Non-controlling Interests – Profit/(Loss) for the Financial Year**
  The loss for the financial year of €2,289,000 needs to be apportioned across the equity shareholders and the non-controlling interests. This is necessary because the group is only entitled to 75% of the €111,000 of profits made by Rushmore for the three months it was in the group and to 80% of the €900,000 of profits made by Kylemore when it was part of the group.

NON-CONTROLLING INTERESTS' SHARE OF PROFIT/LOSS AFTER TAX

	Kylemore	Rushmore	Total
	€000	€000	€000
Profit after tax	900	111	
Non-controlling interests' share	20%	25%	
Non-controlling interest	180	28	208

If €208,000 of profits out of a total loss of €2,289,000 belong to the non-controlling interests, then the position of the ordinary shareholders is even worse; their loss increases to €2,496,000. This is because the losses of IWTL are being offset by the profits of Kylemore and Rushmore. However, the ordinary shareholders are not entitled to all of the profits of Kylemore and Rushmore.

- **Working 4b: Non-controlling Interests – Total Comprehensive Income/(Loss)**
  To determine the split of the total comprehensive loss for the year, a similar approach is employed. The total comprehensive loss for the period is €2,150,000 but the group is only entitled to 75% of the €201,000 of total comprehensive profits contributed by Rushmore (i.e. €111,000 of 'profit for the financial year' and €49,000 of 'other comprehensive income') and 80% of the €900,000 of total comprehensive profits contributed by Kylemore (Kylemore had no 'other comprehensive income').

NON-CONTROLLING INTERESTS' SHARE OF TOTAL COMPREHENSIVE PROFIT/(LOSS)

	Kylemore	Rushmore	Total
	€000	€000	€000
Total comprehensive income	900	201	
Non-controlling interest share	20%	25%	
Non-controlling interest	180	50	230

If €230,000 of comprehensive income out of a total loss of €2,150,000 belongs to the non-controlling interests, then the position of the ordinary shareholders is even worse; their loss increases to €2,380,000.

Consolidated Statement of Changes in Equity Preparing the consolidated statement of changes in equity is a matter of setting out a blank template and filling in the various figures. Additional line items will be included for the disposal and acquisition of non-controlling interests. The most difficult element is determining the opening balances; the remainder of the statement is more straightforward as most of the figures have already been calculated.

The ending balances should correspond with the balances on the statement of financial position; if they do not, an error has occurred.

A solution is presented below; to arrive at the solution, follow the sequence of the workings.

- **Working 5 (W5): Opening Balances** To calculate the opening balances, it should be a matter of taking the previous year's closing balances. However, in an examination situation, you are not usually provided with the consolidated financial statements of the preceding period. As a consequence, the opening balances need to be derived.

  To calculate the opening balances you need to focus on the group situation at the start of the period. Most of the information for these calculations can be found in the opening balances of the individual statements of changes in equity.

  - *Ordinary Share Capital: Opening Balance* Include the ordinary share capital of the parent only. In the statement of changes in equity of IWTL this was €1,000,000. There was no issue of share capital during the period.
  - *Share Premium: Opening Balance* Include the share premium of the parent only. In the statement of changes in equity of IWTL this was €500,000. There was no issue of share capital which gives rise to a share premium during the period.
  - *Currency Reserves: Opening Balance* The opening position on this reserve is zero. This is because the foreign subsidiary joined the group during the period, hence at the start of the period there was no requirement for a reserve of this nature.
  - *Revaluation Surplus: Opening Balance* This is made considerably easier as the subsidiaries do not have a revaluation surplus. In the statement of changes in equity of IWTL this was €1,150,000 (and zero for Kylemore). There was no event during the period that resulted in a change to the revaluation surplus.
  - *Retained Earnings: Opening Balance* This is one of the more complex calculations. Include the opening retained earnings of the parent and the group share of opening post-acquisition retained earnings of the subsidiary. Remember, we are trying to determine the retained profits that the group's shareholders were entitled to at the start of the period.
    - in the statement of changes in equity of IWTL the opening retained earnings are €16,525,000;
    - in the statement of changes in equity of Kylemore the opening retained earnings were €1,300,000. However, the group is not entitled to all of these retained earnings – only the group's share of the post-acquisition retained earnings should be included. The fair value adjustment will also have to be taken into account; and
    - Rushmore can be ignored as it was not part of the group at the start of the current period.

IWTL Group
STATEMENT OF CHANGES IN EQUITY
for the Year Ended 31 December 2012

	Share Capital	Share Premium	Retained Earnings	Currency Surplus	Revaluation Surplus	Total	Non-controlling Interests	Total
	€000	**€000**	**€000**	**€000**	**€000**	**€000**	**€000**	**€000**
Opening balance (W5)	1,000	500	17,125	0	1,150	19,775	360	20,135
Comprehensive income (W6)			(2,496)	117		(2,380)	230	(2,150)
Acquisition of non-controlling interests (W7a)						0	572	572
Disposal of non-controlling interests (W7b)						0	(540)	(540)
Dividends (W8)			(300)			(300)		(300)
Closing balance	1,000	500	14,329	117	1,150	17,095	623	17,718

Opening Retained Earnings of the Group

	€000	€000
Opening retained earnings of IWTL		16,525
Opening retained earnings of Kylemore	1,300	
Less: pre-acquisition	(300)	
Less: fair value adjustment	(250)	
Generated since acquisition	750	
Group's share	80%	600
Opening group retained earnings		17,125

- *Non-controlling Interests: Opening Balance* On 1 January 2012, the value of the non-controlling interests' shareholding was equal to 20% of the net assets of Kylemore. From the statement of changes in equity of Kylemore, it is possible to determine the value of opening net assets of Kylemore – it is the opening total equity of Kylemore (opening ordinary share capital plus opening retained earnings).

Opening Non-controlling Interests

	€000
Opening ordinary share capital of Kylemore	500
Opening retained earnings of Kylemore	1,300
Total net assets of Kylemore on 1/1/12	1,800
Non-controlling interests @ 20%	360

- **Working 6 (W6): Comprehensive Income** For the comprehensive income line item, the figures are taken from the consolidated statement of comprehensive income which was prepared previously *but* a slight re-analysis is required:

- Into retained earnings, put the 'profit/(loss) for the financial year attributable to the ordinary shareholders'; this can be found in the consolidated income statement and is a loss of €2,496,000;
- Into non-controlling interests, put the 'total comprehensive income attributable to the non-controlling interests'; this can be found in the consolidated statement of comprehensive income and is an income of €230,000;
- Into currency reserve, put the group's share of the currency gains (or losses) that are recognised directly in reserves; these are the gains that relate to the translation of Rushmore:

	€
◦ Gain on translation of goodwill (all group)	49,000
◦ Gain on translation of net assets (75% of €90,000)	68,000
◦ Total currency gains of the group	117,000

Note: the remainder of the currency gains (i.e. 25% of €90,000) was allocated to the non-controlling interests. The non-controlling interests were allocated €208,000 of profits and €22,000 (i.e. 25% of €90,000) of currency gains to give a total amount of €230,000.

- **Working 7a (W7a): Acquisition of Non-controlling Interests** When the shares in Rushmore were purchased the group also 'acquired' additional non-controlling interests. The non-controlling interests effectively provide (perhaps unwittingly) finance to the group: to get control over a group of assets, the group need only purchase an interest to give it control (usually 50% plus one share). Therefore, to control a hypothetical group of assets of €100, the group has to spend at least €51 with the remaining €49 of finance provided by the non-controlling interests. It is at this point in the financial statements that the contribution of the non-controlling interests is accounted for.

  During the period the group took control of the net assets of Rushmore. At the time of the transaction these net assets had a fair value of $3,090,000. This converted into €2,289,000, using the exchange rate at the date of the acquisition (i.e. €1 = $1.35). However, IWTL did not have to buy all the shares in Rushmore to get control over its assets – it only purchased 75%. As the group values non-controlling interests using the proportional share of **net assets**, the non-controlling interests effectively contributed €572,000 (i.e. 25% of €2,289,000) worth of finance during the period. This is not 'free finance', the non-controlling interests do expect a return – when a dividend is paid by the subsidiary to the parent, the non-controlling interests will receive their share. See detailed calculation below:

THE VALUE OF THE NON-CONTROLLING INTERESTS IN RUSHMORE AT THE ACQUISITION DATE

	000
Ordinary share capital	$1,000
Retained earnings	$1,850
Fair value adjustment	$240
Total net assets in USD	$3,090
Convert to EUR (at 1.35)	€2,289
Non-controlling interests @ 25%	€572

- **Working 7b (W7b): Disposal of Non-controlling Interests** The same logic that was used for the acquisition of the non-controlling interests in Rushmore is applied, in reverse, to the disposal of non-controlling interests in Kylemore. When the shares in Kylemore were sold, the group also 'disposed' of non-controlling interests. The group sold 60% (leaving a 20% holding) of its holding in Kylemore, but it gave up control over 100% of the net assets of Kylemore. It is at this point that the movement in the non-controlling interests is accounted for.

  On the date of the disposal Kylemore had net assets of €2,700,000. Up to the date of disposal the non-controlling interests had provided the group with €540,000 (i.e. 20% of

€2,700,000) of effective finance. This is no longer the situation. See detailed calculation below:

THE VALUE OF THE NON-CONTROLLING INTERESTS IN
KYLEMORE AT THE DISPOSAL DATE

	€000
Ordinary share capital	500
Retained earnings	2,200
Total net assets	2,700
Non-controlling interests @ 20%	540

- **Working 8 (W8): Dividends** The only dividend that was paid during the period is that of the parent (IWTL) to the group's shareholders (this can be observed in the individual companies' statements of changes in equity – Rushmore and Kylemore did not pay any dividends). Therefore, the entire dividend of €300,000 was paid out of retained earnings.

  Note: paying a dividend from the currency reserve is not permitted as this is not a realised profit.

Conclusion The consolidated statement of changes in equity is the statement that links the consolidated statement of comprehensive income with the consolidated statement of financial position. The consolidated statement of changes in equity includes the profit (or loss) for the financial year from the consolidated statement of comprehensive income. The ending totals, the closing balances, should equal the balances that were calculated for the statement of financial position. This is the final check to ensure that (at least) the arithmetic has been performed correctly.

The completion of this requirement is quite time-consuming (much longer than that required for an examination). However, it is a comprehensive example of a complex consolidated style question/case study. None of the items on its own is difficult, but when the items are combined together, there is a lot of information to manage. This is one of the key skills in a case study – ensure that you have a system or process to fully resolve all the issues.

Requirement (b): The Hedging Relationship

This is a complex area in financial reporting. It involves the interaction between two of the more difficult reporting standards: IAS 21 *The Effects of Changes in Foreign Exchange Rates* and IAS 39 *Financial Instruments: Recognition and Measurement*. However, only a discussion of the broader issues is required.

The issue with the current situation is that the loss (or gain) on the translation of the USD loan taken out by IWTL is recognised as part of current profits but the gain (or loss) on the translation of the net assets that the loan was used to finance is recognised in 'other comprehensive income' (this is often called 'direct to equity'). The imbalance is that, while the two items are closely linked, the related gains and losses are treated differently. Ideally, the gains on one item (in this case, the net assets) should be matched by the losses on the other item (the loan).

While this may appear to be a minor issue, currencies have been know to fluctuate within wide bands and the resultant gains or losses can be large in the context of the profits of a company. Consequently, how the gains or losses are recognised can have a large impact on the reported profit after tax and the resultant perceptions of the market.

Take the example of Vodafone Group Plc. In the annual report for the year ended 31 March 2009, Vodafone reported a profit for the financial year of £3,080 million. This did not include currency gains on translation of £12,375 million (this was the correct treatment, following IAS 21). Had these gains been recognised in operating profits then Vodafone Group would have reported a profit for the financial year of £15,455 million – such a large reported profit would undoubtedly have had an impact on share price and market perceptions (this does depend on the efficiency of the market). See www.vodafone.com

In the current scenario, IWTL has booked a loss of €115,000 on the translation of the loan. This represents the increase in value of the loan in EUR due to the movement of the USD/EUR exchange rate. This loss is included as part of profit after tax of the IWTL group for the year. At the same time, while the liability to repay the loan has increased in EUR terms (resulting in a loss), so too have the assets that the loan was used to finance (resulting in a gain). The gain on the translation of the foreign subsidiary is €139,000. This gain is recognised in 'other comprehensive income'.

Had a hedging relationship been specified at the outset of the transaction, then 'hedge accounting' might apply. The broad principle of 'hedge accounting' is that there is a symmetrical basis for the recognition of profits and losses arising on the hedging instrument (the loan) and the hedged position (the investment in Rushmore). This will reduce some of the volatility that can arise, in the statement of comprehensive income, due to the movement in exchange rates.

The regulations governing the application of 'hedge accounting' are set out in IAS 39 and they are extensive. Companies elect to apply 'hedge accounting' if the circumstances warrant it. Since the criteria are so strict and time-consuming (and therefore costly), only larger companies have the expertise, systems and procedures to benefit from the provisions of IAS 39. The key criteria are (IAS 39, para 88):

- at the inception of the transactions there needs to be "formal designation and documentation" that sets out the company's strategy and reasons for establishing the hedge;
- the hedge should be "highly effective", i.e. the gains (or losses) on the hedge instrument should offset the losses (or gains) on the hedged position. The standard recognises that an exact match may not arise, so defines "highly effective" as a range between 80% and 125%. This is the ratio of the gain on the hedged item (the net assets of Rushmore) to the loss on the hedging instrument (the USD loan);
- the hedged instrument and position can be reliably measured (this is not an issue in this instance); and
- the hedge is assessed on an on-going basis to determine if it continues to be highly effective.

Once the criteria have been satisfied and the hedge is effective then the loss (or gain) on the translation of the USD loan can be set against the gain (or loss) on the translation of the net investment in Rushmore. This transaction is carried out within the currency reserve in 'other comprehensive income'. If there is not enough of a gain (or loss) in the current period in the currency reserve to absorb the loss (or gain) then any excess is recognised in the statement of comprehensive income. In the IWTL scenario the gain recognised in 'other comprehensive income' of €139,000 is more than the loss on the USD loan of €115,000.

In conclusion, had IWTL fulfilled the hedge accounting criteria then it could have set the €115,000 loss against the €139,000 gain in 'other comprehensive income'. This would have the effect of reducing the loss after tax by €115,000.

Requirement (c): Offsetting Assets and Liabilities

The basic principle with regard to offsetting assets and liabilities is described in IAS 1, paragraph 32. The regulation is quite clear: assets and liabilities cannot be offset unless permitted by another standard. In IAS 1, paragraph 33, there is an exception where offsetting assets with liabilities is permitted where it reflects the substance of the underlying transactions.

IAS 32, paragraph 42, provides specific guidance in relation to the offsetting of financial assets with financial liabilities (the loan receivable and the loan payable are examples of financial assets and financial liabilities, respectively). It states that unless there is a 'legally enforceable right' to offset the amounts and the company intends 'to settle on a net basis' then the offset option is not permitted.

In this instance, while the circumstances may be linked, these are two separate transactions, each with its own individual obligations. The repayment of the loan to purchase the investment in Rushmore is independent of the receivable from the new shareholders (i.e. the former management) of Kylemore. Therefore, there is no legal right of set-off; the bank that loaned the money to purchase the shares in Rushmore will have to be paid independently of the repayment of the loan to the former management of Kylemore.

The current treatment is correct and offsetting is not permitted.

Requirement (d): Disposal of Kylemore

The disposal of Kylemore gives rise to some extensive disclosures.

Under IFRS 5 *Non-current Assets Held for Sale and Discontinued Operations*, the disposal of Kylemore would be considered to be the disposal of a 'component' of ITWL that represents a major line of business (IFRS 5, para 32). It is evident that Kylemore's operations and cash flows can be clearly distinguished from the rest of the group's; this is how IFRS 5 defines 'component' (IFRS 5, Appendix A). The basic principle of the disclosure requirements of IFRS 5 is that users should be able to 'evaluate the financial effects of the discontinued operation' (IFRS 5, para 30). As a result, IWTL should disclose the following (IFRS 5, para 33):

- In the statement of comprehensive income, disclose Kylemore's (the discontinued operation's) profit (or loss) for the year as a single figure as well as the gain (or loss) on the disposal of Kylemore;
- The profit (or loss) for the year of Kylemore should be subsequently analysed into revenue, expense, tax and the profit (or loss) attributable to the parent (this can be presented in the notes to the financial statements);
- In the statement of cash flows, disclose the net cash flows under operating, financing and investing activities generated by Kylemore (this can be done in the notes to the financial statements);
- Prior period results should be presented so that all of the results of the discontinued operations are disclosed separately; and
- A description of the facts that led to the disposal.

Many of the disclosure items set out in the previous points, above, were presented as part of the consolidated statement of comprehensive income (see requirement (a)).
The circumstances surrounding the disposal of Kylemore are unusual. At the time of the disposal of Kylemore, the management of Kylemore could be considered to be part of the 'key management personnel' of ITWL. Professional judgement is necessary here – should the management of a subsidiary be considered to be 'key management personnel' within a group context? Notwithstanding this, the nature of the transaction is quite unusual and should be disclosed in the financial statements. This can be done within the 'related party' note to the financial statements or the note that describes the disposal of Kylemore. If the latter option is chosen (i.e. your view is that the management of Kylemore were not part of the 'key management personnel' of the IWTL Group) then enough information should be disclosed to permit users to evaluate the effect of the transaction.

Under IAS 24, paragraph 9, a related party includes the 'key management personnel'. This is significant because IAS 24 *Related Party Disclosures* describes certain disclosures that must be made where transactions are undertaken with related parties.

These include (IAS 24, para 18):

- The nature of the relationship between the parties;
- Information on the transaction (i.e. the disposal of Kylemore to its management);
- The amount of the transaction (€3 million);
- The amount of any outstanding balances (€3 million);
- The provision for bad or doubtful debts in relation to the transaction (€0); and
- Had any guarantees or commitments been provided or received these should be disclosed (the shares in Kylemore have been offered as security for the loan).

Finally, the receivable due to IWTL (€3 million) from the management of Kylemore is a financial asset of the group. Consequently, IFRS 7 *Financial Instruments: Disclosures* applies. This financial asset is now part of a collection of financial assets that the group holds (the group also holds cash and trade receivables, for example). Assuming that the financial asset is categorised as 'financial asset at amortised cost' (IFRS 9, para 4.1.2) and is correctly measured then, for that category, the following should be disclosed (only the significant disclosures and those that apply in the context of the €3 million receivable are set out):

- The carrying amount of the financial asset (IFRS 7, para 8);
- The net gain or loss on the financial asset and the total interest income (IFRS 7, para 20);
- The fair value of the each class of financial asset, how the fair value was arrived at and a comparison between the fair value and the carrying value (IFRS 7, para 25);
- The carrying amount of the assets pledged as collateral, in this case the investment in Rushmore has been offered as collateral for the loan; and
- The nature and extent of the risks arising from the financial asset. These risks should include:
  - Credit Risk (the risk of not being paid on time) (IFRS 7, para 36–38); and
  - Market Risk (e.g. the exposure of the receivable to changes in interest rates and exchange rates) (IFRS 7, para 40–42).

Since the interest rate on the €3 million receivable is indicative of underlying market rates, the fair value of the receivable is likely to be €3 million.

Case 12

The Rochfort Group

This case study is based on a food and confectionery business called the Rochfort Group. The accounting standards IAS 20, IAS 24, IAS 33, IAS 34, IAS 37 and IFRS 8 are addressed in this case. The case also addresses a financial review of the group.

Background – Rochfort Group

Paul Halligan looked up from his desk. He had not heard the first knock on the door. He had been engrossed in his working papers and had heard nothing. The second rap was louder and more urgent. He rose from the desk, stretched and walked over to open the office door. His assistant, Peter Piper, stood nervously at the door. He handed Paul a memo and turned away. It was 7pm on a Friday evening at the end of January 2013. Paul read the note. It was from the managing partner, Evelyn Keane. Evelyn wanted to meet with Paul, urgently, to discuss the latest draft of the 2012 financial statements of the Rochfort Group. The Rochfort Group is a large, prestigious, audit client of their practice, Ellis & Romney. Paul and Evelyn had already met several times in the past week to discuss the progress of the audit. The work was almost complete. Paul was reviewing the final draft of the financial statements when he had been disturbed. His plan, for the following Monday morning, was to begin completion of the outstanding disclosure notes. The accounts, prepared in accordance with International Accounting Standards, are due to be published on 12 March 2013.

Paul dialled the extension and spent the next 20 minutes in conversation with Evelyn. At the end of the conversation, Paul hung up the phone, turned off his computer and left his office for the weekend. He needed to think.

The Client

Rochfort Plc is a large publicly quoted company whose business interests are in food and confectionery. Rochfort was founded in 1920 by an entrepreneur named James Kelly. The business merged with a larger one in the 1950s to become Rochfort Ltd. In 1979, Rochfort was floated on the London Stock Exchange. Rochfort now employs 15,000 people in the ROI and overseas. Turnover for the group in 2012 was €1.2 billion.

Ellis & Romney were appointed auditors of the Rochfort Group in 2008 and have carried out all of the audit services for the group since then.

The reason for the urgent meeting on the Friday evening was that the CEO of The Rochfort Group, Sean O'Farrell, had contacted Evelyn Keane to inform her that a takeover bid had recently been made for the group by a US multinational company. The bidder, Shore Island Inc, has offered to buy a majority stake in Rochfort at a price of €2.65 per share. This represents a 75% premium on the current market price of the group's shares. The board of Rochfort has agreed to negotiate with the bidder and, on completion of a confidentiality agreement, has permitted Shore Island Inc access to the latest audited financial statements of the group.

Rochfort would now like the 2012 statements to be completed in the next seven days.

Completion of the Audit – The Financial Statements

On Monday morning Paul arrived at the office fresh and rested. He immediately opened the Rochfort audit file and set to work. He compiled a list of all outstanding tasks. It has now been agreed that a final draft of the financial statements, including all disclosure notes, will be presented to the directors of Rochfort Plc at the end of the current week. Paul needed to act fast.

Armed with a large mug of coffee and his favourite packet of biscuits, Paul set to work. The outstanding issues are detailed below.

The draft financial statements are included in Appendix (1).

Outstanding Issue 1 – Earnings Per Share

Paul extracted details of Rochfort's share capital from the audit file. The group has ordinary shares and preference shares in issue. The ordinary shares are class 'A' ordinary shares and qualify for full distribution rights. The preference shares are convertible instruments and are currently classified as equity in the financial statements of the group (you are asked to comment on this presentation later). The preference shares are cumulative. There were a number of changes to the group's share capital during the year. Paul summarised the changes as follows:

- On 1 February 2012 Rochfort issued two million ordinary shares at full market price. The share issue was fully subscribed and monies due were paid in full on application.
- As part of the group's repositioning programme, Rochfort acquired MB Limited on 1 March 2012. Rochfort issued eight million new ordinary shares at full market price in consideration of the acquisition. In addition to the eight million shares, the acquisition agreement states that, if MB Ltd earns profits in excess of €5 million by 31 December 2013, an additional 500,000 shares will be issued. Otherwise, no additional shares will be issued. By the 31 December 2012, MB Limited had earned profits of €800,000.
- On 1 April 2012 Rochfort Plc announced a rights issue. Shareholders were offered one new ordinary share for every three held at a price of €1.80 per share. The issue took place on 1 June 2012. The issue was underwritten by Eran Insurance Ltd. Paul noted that Rochfort's shares were trading at €2.40 on 1 April 2012 and at €1.95 on 1 June 2012.
- On 30 November 2012, Rochfort issued a further two million 5% convertible preference shares. These shares were sold in a private placing to an investment fund. These shares were issued at a premium. All of the issued preference shares are convertible into ordinary shares

on 1 January 2014, on the basis of one ordinary share for every two preference shares held *or* on 1 January 2015 on the basis of one ordinary share for every four preference shares held. The preference shares in issue on 1 January 2012 were originally issued on 1 January 2008.

The preference dividend of €508,333 (2011: €500,000) is included in the dividend charge and presented in the statement of changes in equity. You can assume there are no other charges on the preference shares.

- Finally, the company has a share option scheme. At 31 December 2012, there were 1.5 million outstanding share options in the group. These options were issued in 2009 and are exercisable in 2014 at €1.05 per share. The average market price of the company's shares in 2012 was €1.50. There was no change in the average fair value of the group's shares over the current or comparative period.
- The EPS figures reported in the 2011 financial statements were as follows:

	Continuing operations	Total profit
	€	€
Basic	0.61	0.68
Diluted	0.51	0.53

Paul is satisfied that the journal entries relating to the change in share capital have been correctly recorded in the financial statements.

Outstanding Issue 2 – Operating Segments

Next, Paul turned his attention to the requirements of IFRS 8 *Operating Segments.* He has already had preliminary discussions with the financial director, Anna Jones, about this matter. The following has been established:

1. The Group has four operating segments: Ingredients, Health Foods, Confectionery and Other Business. The ingredients segment manufacture and distribute specific ingredients across Europe while the health food segment manufactures and supplies branded foods to the Irish and European markets. Confectionery is distributed principally in the Irish market.
2. The operating segments identified align with the group's internal financial reporting system and the way in which the chief operating decision-maker assesses performance and allocates the group's resources. A segment manager is responsible for each segment and is directly accountable for the performance of that segment to the operating executive committee.
3. Inter-segment pricing is determined on an arm's length basis.
4. The chief operating decision-maker assesses the performance of the business based on the consolidated adjusted profit/ (loss) after tax of the group for the year.

5. Revenues from any single customer do not amount to 10% or more of the group's revenues.
6. Finally, following a repositioning of the group in 2012, the reportable segments and related information for 2011 have been restated in accordance with the revised group structure.

Paul summarised the segmental results for the current and restated comparative periods. These are as follows:

Segmental Results for the Rochfort Group
for the year Ending 31 December 2012

	Total Revenue €000	Internal Revenue €000	External Revenue €000	Operating Profits €000	Segment[1] Assets €000	Segment[2] Liabilities €000
Ingredients	765,790	76,579	689,211	85,495	435,958	145,761
Health food	305,434	30,543	274,891	35,623	181,649	60,734
Confectionery	111,111	21,111	90,000	14,249	72,660	24,294
Other	151,484	5,148	146,336	7,125	36,330	12,147
	1,333,819	133,381	1,200,438	142,491	726,596	242,935

Segmental Results for the Rochfort Group
for the year Ending 31 December 2011

	Total Revenue €000	Internal Revenue €000	External Revenue €000	Operating Profit €000	Segment Assets €000	Segment Liabilities €000
Ingredients	544,699	49,518	495,181	30,109	445,418	148,123
Health Food	198,072	18,007	180,066	4,301	44,542	45,576
Confectionery	78,265	16,206	62,059	6,452	55,677	22,788
Other	169,325	6,302	163,023	2,151	11,135	11,394
	990,362	90,033	900,329	43,013	556,772	227,882

(**Note:** The results from discontinued activities are included under the relevant segment headings.)

Paul also noted the following unallocated assets and liabilities:

	2012 €000	2011 €000
Unallocated assets	187,031	122,000
Unallocated liabilities	286,000	224,800

Unallocated assets include taxation, cash and cash equivalents and financial assets. Unallocated Liabilities include taxation, borrowings and derivatives.

---

[1] Excludes unallocated Assets.
[2] Excludes unallocated liabilities.

Finally, Paul noted the analysis of external revenue by geographical region as follows:

	2012	2011
	€000	€000
ROI	750,000	640,000
UK	290,000	200,100
Continental Europe	160,438	60,229
	1,200,438	900,329

Outstanding Issue 3 – Related Party Disclosures

Paul then moved on to related party disclosures. He reviewed the information he had gathered during the audit, which he considered might be necessary for completion of the related party disclosure note. The information includes the following:

1. The Board of Directors of the Rochfort Group includes the Chairman, Ken Browne, Chief Executive Officer, Sean O'Farrell and 14 other directors. Excluding the top two positions, 60% of the board are non-executive directors. During 2012 the remuneration paid to key management included salaries (2012: €2.003 million; 2011: €1.015 million), post-employment benefits (2012: €1.492 million; 2011: €0.580 million), and share-based payments (2012: €0.179 million; 2011: €0.088 million).
2. The Rochfort group owns three subsidiaries and has a significant interest in another company – Janus Ltd. Details of the investments and Rochfort's interests in them are as follows:

Investment	Shareholding	Influence
Caladonia Ltd	100%	Dominant
MB Ltd	100%	Dominant
Alexia	70%	Dominant
Janus Ltd	28%	Significant

Paul has already completed the necessary consolidation disclosures required by IFRS 12 *Disclosure of Interests in Other Entities,* IAS 28 *Investments in Associates* and IFRS 3 *Business Combinations.*

Transactions with these entities during 2012 included:

Related Party	Sales of Goods €000	Sales of Services €000	Purchases of Goods €000	Purchases of Services €000
Subsidiaries	80,029	53,352	35,000	14,790
Associates	878	994	1060	850

The 2011 transactions included:

Related Party	Sales of Goods €000	Sales of Services €000	Purchases of Goods €000	Purchases of Services €000
Subsidiaries	63,023	27,010	21,265	13,004
Associates	971	599	761	430

During the audit, Paul had carried out a sample check of transactions between Rochfort and these entities. He concluded that all related party transactions carried out during the period were carried out under normal commercial terms and conditions. The only year-end balance outstanding is an amount owed by Rochfort Plc to Caladonia Ltd of €600,000 (2011: €400,000).

3. Mr AL Kelly and Ms Janet O'Noone, non-executive directors of Rochfort, are also directors of another company, FreshCo Limited. FreshCo Limited is a fresh food distributor and, since 1 January 2012, has supplied Rochfort with fresh produce on a regular basis. Neither AL Kelly nor Ms Noone owns a substantial shareholding in either company. However AL Kelly is the operations director of FreshCo. Ms Noone does not hold a full-time position in either company. She serves on each board as a non-executive director for which she is paid a fee. Paul carried out a sample check of transactions that were made between FreshCo and Rochfort during the accounting period. The transactions were compared to open market prices for similar transactions. Paul has verified that transactions between Rochfort and FreshCo were made at the same price and terms as sales to third parties. Purchases from FreshCo during the year were €1,800,000. The amount outstanding at the period end was €475,000.
4. Finally, Paul reviewed details of a financing arrangement that was made during the year. A venture capitalist assisted the Rochfort Group in financing the acquisition of some plant. In addition to providing loan finance, the venture capitalist was offered a seat on the Board of Directors. The venture capitalist received director's fees, management fees and investment interest from Rochfort during 2012 amounting to €2 million.

Outstanding Issue 4 – Contingent Liabilities

A row has broken out amongst the directors. The row is about the disclosure or non-disclosure of information in the financial statements.

The background to this row is that, in 2012, a price-fixing allegation was made against Rochfort. The company was accused, by the European Competition Authority, of engaging in price-fixing practices over a period of five years between 2005 and 2010. The allegation came as a complete shock to the group. A legal case ensued and the case came to court in September 2012. Rochfort has vigorously denied the claim. Correspondence with the group's solicitors in January 2013 suggests that the outcome of the case remains unclear.

However, if Rochfort loses the case, the company could face legal costs and EU fines of up to €20 million.

The directors of Rochfort disagree over the best way to present this information in the 2012 financial statements. So far nothing has been included. Anna Jones wants to take a prudent approach and include a provision in the financial statements for the full €20 million. In addition, she would like to include a detailed note outlining the progress of the case to date. Paul Henry, another senior executive, is aghast at this idea. It is his opinion that nothing should be disclosed that might prejudice the company's defence. He believes that if a liability is recognised it may be viewed as an admission of guilt. He has proposed that nothing be mentioned in the financial statements about this case.

Outstanding Issue 5 – Memorandum to TJ Arnold

During the process of the audit, Anna Jones asked Paul Halligan if he would reply to a letter from a shareholder TJ Arnold.

TJ Arnold is a prominent and successful scientist who has accumulated significant personal wealth in recent times. In 2011 he invested some of his fortune into the share capital of Rochfort. The investment was substantial. Mr Arnold, although an avid contributor at shareholder meetings, does not have a lot of experience reading financial statements. He is in regular contact with Anna Jones querying the figures in the financial statements. This latest correspondence is lengthy. Anna has dealt with many of the queries herself but cannot dedicate any more time to this shareholder. She has asked Paul to complete the reply. Mr Arnold's latest queries are based on the 2011 audited financial statements. He is eagerly awaiting a copy of the 2012 annual report.

His outstanding queries include:

1. "There are Capital Grants included in the liabilities section of the statement of financial position. Why are these capital grants classified as liabilities? Rochfort does not have to repay these grants. I have already confirmed with Anna Jones that any conditions attached to the group's capital grants have already been fulfilled. Why would we continue to treat them as an obligation?"
2. "The earnings per share ratio reported in the financial director's review is significantly higher than the figure in the statement of comprehensive income. The review mentions an 'adjusted' EPS. What is this? Is this an error?"
3. "Finally, I would like to make a complaint about your auditors, Ellis & Romney. I received a copy of the 2012 Interim Financial Report on 10 August 2012. The interval between the reporting date and receipt of the report was inexcusably long. In addition, I do not believe the report was of a sufficiently high standard. The financial statements were much shorter than the 2011 year-end statements, many of the disclosure notes were omitted from the report and, worst of all, no audit report was included. This is a gross omission of the auditor's duties. I propose the auditors are removed from their position immediately and a formal complaint made about them to the appropriate regulatory body."

Requirements

(**Note:** Unless you are specifically required to consider deferred taxation, you can assume that it is not applicable.)

(a) (i) Based on the information presented in the case study complete the disclosure notes, as required by International Accounting Standards, for each of the outstanding issues 1–4 above. The notes should be prepared for both the current financial period (2012) *and* the comparative period where appropriate.

(ii) Comment on the current presentation of the convertible preference shares in the draft financial statements above.

(60 marks)

(b) In so far as the information in the case study permits, prepare a report that analyses the performance of the Rochfort Group for the financial period. You should use ratio analysis and the financial statements provided, along with the disclosure notes that were completed in requirement (a). You should assume that this report will form part of the group finance director's review.

(20 marks)

(c) Draft a suitable reply to TJ Arnold, clearly addressing the outstanding matters to which he refers in his letter.

(20 marks)

The draft financial statements are presented in Appendix 1.

Appendix 1

Rochfort Group
CONSOLIDATED INCOME
for the Year Ended 31 December 2012

	2012			2011		
	Continuing Operations	**Discontinued Operations**	**Total**	**Continuing Operations**	**Discontinued Operations**	**Total**
	€000	**€000**	**€000**	**€000**	**€000**	**€000**
Revenue	1,140,416	60022	1,200,438	855,313	45016	900,329
Cost of sales	(572,024)	(13001)	(585,025)	(460,533)	(19188)	(479,721)
Gross Profit	568,392	47,021	615,413	394,780	25,828	420,608
Administration expenses	(238,379)	(6621)	(245,000)	(205,052)	(10793)	(215,845)
Distribution expenses	(229,694)	(3428)	(233,122)	(156,297)	(6888)	(163,185)
Other gains	5,200		5,200	1,435		1,435

Operating Profit	105,519	36,972	142,491	34,866	8,147	43,013
Finance income	3,240	260	3,500	2,516	280	2,795
Finance costs	(14,696)	(3,674)	(18,370)	(12,808)	(1,746)	(14,554)
Profit Before Taxes and Associates	94,063	33,558	127,621	24,574	6,680	31,254
Share of results of associates	7,386		7,386	6,882		6,882
Income taxes	(26,696)	(2859)	(29,555)	(3,362)	(332)	(3,694)
Profit for the year	74,753	30,699	105,452	28,094	6,348	34,442
Attributable to:						
Non-controlling interests	2,109	3163	5,272	1,337	41	1,378
Equity holders of the parent	72,644	27,536	100,180	26,757	6,307	33,064

Rochfort Group

CONSOLIDATED STATEMENT OF COMPREHENSIVE INCOME for the Year Ended 31 December 2012

	2012 €000	**2011 €000**
Profit for the Year	105,452	34,442
Other Comprehensive Income/(Expense)		
Actuarial gain/(loss) – defined benefit	21,015	(25,312)
Foreign exchange translation gain	12,654	1,929
Fair value movements on cash-flow hedges	4,218	1,102
Other Comprehensive Income/Expense for the Period Net of Taxes	**37,887**	**(22,281)**
Total Comprehensive Income for the Year	143,339	12,161
Attributable to:		
Equity holders of the parent	138,067	10,783
Non-controlling interests	5,272	1,378

Rochfort Group
CONSOLIDATED STATEMENT OF FINANCIAL POSITION
as at 31 December 2012

	2012	2011
	€000	€000
Non-current Assets		
Plant, property and equipment	241,432	200,988
Intangible non-current assets (including goodwill)	203,992	179,000
Investments in associates	6,100	5,895
Financial assets	6,648	8,620
Deferred tax assets	4,091	7,800
	462,263	**402,303**
Current Assets		
Inventory	168,303	113,975
Cash and cash equivalents	102,178	37,904
Trade and other receivables	156,271	124,590
Assets held for sale	24,612	–
	451,364	**276,469**
Total Assets	**913,627**	**678,772**
Equity and Liabilities Equity		
Ordinary share capital (€1 shares)	80,000	50,000
Share premium	7,597	3,397
5% convertible preference shares (€1 shares)	12,000	10,000
Retained earnings	179,062	94,911
Other reserves	103,281	65,394
	381,940	**223,702**
Non-controlling interests	2,751	2,388
Total Equity and Non-controlling Interests	**384,691**	**226,090**
Non-current Liabilities		
Finance leases payable	12,153	7,422
Borrowings	308,717	256,733
Defined benefit scheme obligation	52,780	32,460
Deferred income (Capital grants)	17,593	8,115
	391,243	**304,730**

Current Liabilities		
Provisions for liabilities and charges	3,733	15,784
Trade and other payables	109,166	115,529
Taxation payable	1,222	1,870
Finance leases payable	15,311	14,769
Liabilities directly associated with assets held for sale	8,260	–
	137,692	**147,952**
Total Liabilities	**528,935**	**452,682**
Total Equity and Liabilities	**913,627**	**678,772**

Rochfort Group

Consolidated Statement of Changes in Equity
for the Year Ended 31 December 2012

	Total Share Capital €000	**Share Premium €000**	**Retained Earnings €000**	**Other Reserves €000**	**Total €000 (Controlling)**	**Non-controlling Interest €000**	**Total €000**
Equity as at 1 January 2012	**60,000**	**3,397**	**94,911**	**65,394**	**223,702**	**2,388**	**226,090**
Total comprehensive income			100,180		100,180	5,272	105,452
Currency translation differences				12,654	12,654		12,654
Fair value movement in cash flow hedges				4,218	4,218		4,218
Actuarial gain				21,015	21,015		21,015
Share issue	32,000	4,200			36,200		36,200
Dividends paid to shareholders (note)			(16,029)		(16,029)		(16,029)

Dividends paid to non-controlling interests						(4,909)	(4,909)
Equity as at 31 December 2012	92,000	7,597	179,062	103,281	381,941	2,751	384,691

Note 1: Total share capital includes both ordinary and preference share capital.
Note 2: The dividend declared on ordinary shares in 2012 is consistent with previous years.

Guidance Notes – The Rochfort Group

Exam Technique

This case study deals with disclosure notes. It is a departure from the style of requirement in the majority of case studies in this book. In this case study you are presented with a set of completed financial statements. All relevant adjustments have already been made. If you believe that additional adjustments are necessary you should just note the fact rather than redraft the financial statements. You are required, instead, to complete certain disclosure notes. Many of the notes relating to the financial statements have already been completed and are not mentioned in this case study. You are presented with information relating to **four disclosure notes** and you must complete the disclosure requirements in accordance with relevant International Accounting Standards. Comparative information is also given in some instances. You will need to consider how the comparative period is presented in the current financial statements.

This case study also requires some analytical work. You are asked, in requirement (b), to prepare a report analysing the performance of the group over the financial period. This report will involve the calculation of some ratios and a written review of the performance of the group over the accounting period. This is not particularly difficult but is an excellent test of your understanding of the elements of financial statements. You are to assume that this analysis will form a part of the financial director's review for the period.

You should ensure that requirement (a) is completed before you address the review. The EPS calculation and the operating segments note will give you useful information in assessing how the group has performed during the financial period.

The third requirement (c), involves the preparation of a letter. The letter will address some queries that were submitted to the group by an 'enthusiastic' shareholder. This shareholder has been in regular contact with the financial director. There is a suggestion that he is being a bit of a nuisance.

You must reply in an appropriately professional manner.

Finally, as we have mentioned in all of the previous case studies – manage your time and answer all sections. Do not spend too much time on any one section. Lay your work out clearly and professionally. Attempt all sections even if you do not complete them in the required time.

Answering the Case Study

Requirement (a) – Guidance

You are asked to prepare the disclosure notes for four different aspects of the financial statements. The four aspects are outlined in outstanding issues 1–4 of the case study. In preparing the disclosure notes, you will need to refer to the relevant guidance of the International Accounting Standards. You should also be mindful of comparative information and how this is presented. Guidance is offered as follows:

Outstanding Issue 1 – Earnings per share You are asked to prepare the necessary disclosure requirements for Earnings Per Share (EPS).

To complete this task you will need to review the contents of IAS 33 *Earnings per Share.* IAS 33 requires that entities present EPS on two levels: on the basis of ordinary shares in issue (basic EPS) and also on a basis that includes the effects of any other financial instrument that may entitle its holder to ordinary shares in the future (diluted EPS). The rules relating to basic EPS are outlined in IAS 33, paragraphs 9–29, while diluted EPS is covered in IAS 33, paragraphs 30–63. You should also bear in mind that there were discontinued operations during the period and these will also affect your EPS calculation.

In addition to completing the actual EPS ratio, you will also need to disclose details about how you arrived at your ratios. The disclosure requirements are outlined in IAS 33, paragraphs 70–73a of the standard. Finally you are required to comment on the current presentation of convertible preference shares. Would an alternative presentation be more appropriate? You should review the provisions of IAS 32 paragraphs 28–32. You are not required to make any adjustments on this matter.

Outstanding Issue 2 – Operating Segments Segmental reporting is the practice of disclosing, in a note, information about the various activities of an entity so that investors can evaluate the nature and financial effects of the business activities of the entity. In order to comply with this standard the entity must divide its activities into *operating segments* and present information about these segments in the financial statements. IFRS 8 *Operating Segments* outlines how this analysis should be carried out and what information should be disclosed in the financial statements. You should review this standard. IFRS 8, paragraphs 11–19, explain *how* to segment the activities of the entity for financial reporting purposes. IFRS 8, paragraphs 20–24, explains *what* segmental information should be disclosed and how it should be presented in the financial statements. Finally, a reconciliation is required to ensure that the total figures presented in the note agree with the financial statements. Guidance on this reconciliation is presented in paragraph 28 of the standard.

You should also consider that the group was repositioned during the year and this will have implications for the segmental note in 2012. The segments identified in the repositioned group will probably be different to the segments of comparative years. As a result, the 2011 segmental analysis will not be directly comparable with the current statements. You will have to consider if this is acceptable. IFRS 8, paragraphs 29–30, provides guidance as to how to present segmental information where there has been a "restatement of previously reported information".

Outstanding Issue 3 – Related Party Disclosures Related party disclosures are required to give stakeholders additional information about the existence of 'related parties' in an organisation *and* details of any transactions that take place between the entity and its related parties. This information is important as it gives stakeholders an added level of comfort that any transactions that take place between related parties, (who potentially have the opportunity to manipulate transaction values) are disclosed in full in the financial statements.

IAS 24 *Related Party Disclosures* gives the required guidance on this matter.

Before you answer this section you will need to establish exactly what a 'related party' is. IAS 24, paragraphs 9–12, will give you this information. The exact relationship must be disclosed in the financial statements. You will also need to determine what disclosures must be made about the relationships and about any transactions that take place between the related parties and the group. Paragraphs 13 to 24 of the standard will provide the answers.

Outstanding Issue 4 – Contingent Liabilities This issue requires you to comment on the most appropriate treatment for an action that has been taken against the Rochfort Group. At the end of the reporting period legal proceedings are on-going against Rochfort. The case is in court but no outcome is clear. You must consider how this action should be reported in the financial statements. You should bear in mind that this is a commercially sensitive issue and the facts must be considered carefully before the disclosures are made. An inappropriate level of disclosure may be hugely damaging for the entity. On the other hand, if it is likely that the case will go against Rochfort, the stakeholders must be informed.

To form an appropriate opinion you should consider the guidance of IAS 37 *Provisions, Continent Liabilities and Contingent Assets.* You will need to make a recommendation and you should be able to justify your recommendation. IAS 37 will provide you with the necessary guidance.

Requirement (b) – Guidance

Now that you have completed the disclosure notes, you are ready to carry out an analysis of the group's performance over the reporting period. You have plenty of material to work with including the financial statements for both the current and comparative financial periods, EPS ratios for both years *and* a breakdown of activity into reportable segments.

Your analysis should cover a number of aspects including profitability, liquidity, efficiency, growth and investment. You are not told *which* ratios to calculate so you will need to be reasonably familiar with what ratios will provide useful information about the performance of the business. Chapter 35 of *International Financial Accounting and Reporting*, 3rd Edition, by Ciaran Connolly (Chartered Accountants Ireland, 2011) provides an excellent overview of these ratios.

In order to give a comprehensive overview of performance, ratios need to be compared to some type of benchmark. This can either be to a comparative period or to average industry performance. You are provided with the comparative financial statements of Rochfort to help provide a more meaningful report on the performance of the group.

Requirement (c) – Guidance

In this final section of the case study you are asked to write a letter to a shareholder who has submitted a number of queries to the financial director about the 2011 financial statements. You are told that this shareholder is very enthusiastic but lacks experience in reading financial statements. You must bear this in mind when formatting your reply. The queries may appear simple but your answer should be equally so. Remember you are explaining some basic accounting fundamentals to this shareholder so you need to use language that is clear, precise and gets to the point without too much fuss. Otherwise Mr Arnold will be none the wiser. To answer his queries you will need to review the provisions of IAS 20 *Accounting for Government Grants and the Disclosure of Government Assistance,* IAS 33 *Earnings Per Share* and IAS 34 *Interim Financial Reporting.*

Recommended Reading

The above issues may also be referenced in *International Financial Accounting and Reporting*, 3rd edition, by Ciaran Connolly (Chartered Accountants Ireland, 2011) and the relevant accounting standards as follows:

	Chapter	Chapter title	Chapter section	Standard
Requirement (a)				
Issue 1	23	Earnings Per Share	23.5–23.8	IAS 33
Issue 2	24	Operating Segments	24.2–24.3	IFRS 8
Issue 3	22	Related Party Disclosures	22.2–22.5	IAS 24
Issue 4	14	Provisions, Contingent Liabilities and Contingent Assets	14.2–14.5	IAS 37
Requirement (b)				
	35	Analysis and Interpretation of Financial Information	35.2–35.6	n/a
Requirement (c)				
Query (1)	16	Accounting for Government Grants and Disclosure of Government Assistance	16.2	IAS 20
Query (2)	23	Earnings Per Share	23.5–23.8	IAS 33
Query (3)	34	Other Accounting Standards	34.2	IAS 34

Solution to the Rochfort Group

Requirement (a)

Outstanding Issue 1 – Earnings per Share

The first task is to complete the EPS ratio for the period. IAS 33 *Earnings per Share* lays out detailed rules for the calculation of EPS. The reason for the detailed guidance is that EPS is a an important global indicator of entity performance and is used widely by investors, analysts, stockbrokers and many other interested parties. It is important that the indicator is calculated consistently, across accounting periods and between entities, if it is to provide meaningful information. IAS 33 applies only to those entities or groups whose ordinary shares or potential ordinary shares are traded (or in the process of becoming such an entity) in a public market (IAS 33, para 2) – Rochfort is such an entity. IAS 33 requires entities to calculate and disclose EPS on two levels. The first is the basic EPS and the second level is the diluted EPS.

The presentation and disclosure for IAS 33 are summarised below. Detailed workings will follow.

ON THE FACE OF THE STATEMENT OF COMPREHENSIVE INCOME (IAS 33, PARA 66 AND 68)

	2012 (Continuing) €	**2012 (Discontinued) €**	**2012 (Total) €**	**2011 *restated* (Continuing) €**	**2011 (Discontinued) €**	**2011 *restated* (Total) €**
Basic EPS	1.02 (w1)	0.39 (w1)	1.41 (w1)	0.60 (w3)	0.07 (w3)	0.67 (w3)
Diluted EPS	0.95 (w2)	0.37 (w2)	1.32 (w2)	0.50 (w3)	0.02 (w3)	0.52 (w3)

IN THE NOTES TO THE FINANCIAL STATEMENTS
(for total profits only)

Basis of the numerator and denominator (IAS 33, Para 70(a) and (b))

Basic EPS
Basic EPS is calculated by dividing the profit attributable to the equity holders of the parent company by the weighted average shares in issue during the period

	2012 000	**2011 000**
Profit attributable to equity holders of the parent company	€99,672	
Weighted Average Shares in issue during the period	70,637	
	€1.41	€0.68 (*given*)

Diluted EPS
Diluted EPS is calculated by adjusting the weighted average shares outstanding to assume conversion of all potential dilutive ordinary shares

	2012 000	2011 000
Weighted average number of shares in issue	70,637	not given
Adjusted for options	450	not given
Adjusted for convertible preference shares	5,083	not given
Adjusted weighted shares	76,170	not given
Diluted EPS	€1.32	€0.53 *(given)*

Working 1: Basic EPS for 2012 Basic EPS is calculated by "dividing profit or loss attributable to ordinary equity holders of the parent entity (the numerator) by the weighted average number of ordinary shares outstanding (the denominator) during the period" (IAS 33, para 10). Where an entity has reported discontinued operations in the period, the ratio should be calculated on the basis of (1) total profit or loss attributable to the parent *and* (2) on profit or loss on continuing operations only (IAS 33, para 9). The entity should also disclose EPS from discontinued operations.

The basic EPS is calculated as follows:	Continuing Earnings €000	Discontinued €000	Total Earnings €000
Profit or loss attributable to equity shareholders of the parent entity (see below)	72,136	27,536	99,672
Weighted average shares (see below)	70,637	70,637	70,637
EPS	1.02	0.39	1.41

Profit or loss Profit or loss attributable to ordinary equity holders is calculated as "the profit or loss … attributable to the parent entity adjusted for the after-tax amounts of preference dividends, differences arising from the settlement of preference shares, and other similar effects of preference shares classified as equity" (IAS 33, para 12). Profit on continuing activities for the period is €72,644,000. Profit on total activities for the period is €100,180,000. For the purpose of calculating EPS for the period, the preference dividend (€508,333) is deducted from each profit figure. The preference dividend is calculated as 5% of preference shares in issue throughout the entire period €10 million plus one month's dividend on the two million preference shares issued on 1 November 2012.

Weighted average shares IAS 33, paragraph 20, states "… The weighted average number of ordinary shares outstanding during the period is the number of ordinary shares outstanding at the beginning of the period, adjusted by the number of ordinary shares bought back or issued during the period multiplied by a time weighting factor …"

Rochfort opened the financial period on 1 January 2012 with 50 million ordinary shares in issue. During the period the following changes were made:

Date of Change	Number of Shares	Type of Issue	Number of months outstanding at the period end
1 February 2011	2,000,000	Full market price	11 months
1 March 2011	8,000,000	Full market price	10 months
1 June 2011	20,000,000	Rights issue	7 months

Note: There are also an additional 500,000 contingent shares to consider. These have not been included in the above table. IAS 33, paragraph 24 states that contingently issuable shares are treated as outstanding and are included in basic EPS only from the date when all necessary conditions are satisfied. The relevant date in this scenario is 31 December 2013. Hence these shares have been excluded.

For shares that are issued at full market price the weighting is straightforward. It is calculated as "the number of days that the shares are outstanding as a proportion of the total number of days in the period. A reasonable approximation is adequate in many circumstances" (IAS 33, para 20). However, where ordinary shares are issued without a corresponding change in resources, the shares outstanding before the event occurred are adjusted proportionally as though the event had occurred at the beginning of the earliest period presented (IAS 33, para 28). Examples of this would include a capitalisation issue, a bonus issue and the bonus element of a rights issue. In a rights issue, the bonus element is treated as though it were in existence through-out the current and comparative financial periods.

In the case study a rights issue is made on 1 June 2012. A rights issue contains a bonus element as the shares are offered at a discount to their trading value.

The bonus element of a rights issue is calculated as the *cum-rights* price (market price immediately before the rights issue is made) divided by the *ex-rights* price (theoretical average price of each share immediately after the rights issue has taken place). In the case of the rights issue on 1 June 2012, the bonus element is €1.02 per share, calculated as follows:

Cum-rights price (price on 1 June 2012)			€1.95
Issue price (price shares are issued at in a rights issue)			€1.80
Ex-rights price			€1.91
Ex-rights price:			
3 shares	€1.95	€5.85	
1 share	€1.80	€1.80	
4 shares	=	€7.65	
Ex-rights	(7.65/4)	€1.91	
Bonus element of the rights issue (€1.95/€1.91)			1.02

This bonus factor should be applied to shares in issue before the rights issue takes place. This will adjust the shares prior to the rights issue as though these shares had been in issue throughout the period.

We are now in a position to calculate the weighted average number of shares. The calculation of the weighted average number of shares for the period is as follows:

Relevant dates	Type of Issue	(a) Shares 000	(b) Fraction of period b/f next change	(c) Bonus Factor	Weighted Shares (a) × (b) × (c)
1/1 to 31/1	Opening	50,000	1/12	1.02	4,250
1 February	New issue	2,000			
1/2 to 28/2		52,000	1/12	1.02	4,420
1 March	New issue	8,000			
1/3 to 31/5		60,000	3/12	1.02	15,300
1 June	Rights issue	20,000			
1/6 to 31/12		80,000	7/12	n/a	46,667
Weighted Average Number of Shares					**70,637**

Working 2: Diluted EPS for 2012 IAS 33, paragraph 30, states that an entity shall calculate diluted EPS. Paragraph 31 states "for the purpose of calculating diluted EPS an entity shall adjust profit or loss….and the weighted average number of shares outstanding for the effects of all dilutive potential ordinary shares". The adjustments that are required include:

Profit and loss Profit and loss is increased by the after-tax effect of dividends, interest recognised or other effects that would result from the conversion of the dilutive potential ordinary shares outstanding during the period (IAS 33, para 32(a)) (for example preference dividends would be saved if convertible preference shares are converted to ordinary shares).

Weighted Average Shares This will be the weighted average number of shares for the calculation of basic EPS plus the weighted average number of additional shares that would have been outstanding assuming the conversion of all dilutive effects of potential ordinary shares (IAS 33, para 32(b)). (Including the exercise of share options, conversion of convertible instruments and issue of contingent shares etc.)

Because of the potential variations that could result, the standard includes further guidance. The points that are relevant to this case study include:

1. Potential ordinary shares shall only be treated as dilutive when and only when their conversion to ordinary shares would decrease EPS from *continued operations* (IAS 33, para. 41).

(In other words, the starting point for determining diluted EPS is the basic EPS from continuing operations.)

2. In determining whether shares are dilutive or not, each issue of potential shares is considered separately. The sequence may affect dilution; therefore, in order to maximise dilution, each issue is considered in sequence "*from most dilutive to least dilutive* shares" (IAS 33, para 44). (We approach this by calculating the **incremental EPS** for each potential share issue first and then rank the issues in order from the lowest to the highest **incremental EPS**.)
3. "Dilutive potential ordinary shares shall be deemed to have been converted into ordinary shares at the beginning of the period or, if later, at the date of the issue of the potential shares" (IAS 33, para 36). (The share options and 10 million preference shares have been in issue for the entire period and will be deemed to be converted at the beginning of the period. two million additional preference shares issued on 30 November 2012 will be deemed to be converted from 30 November 2012.)
4. "… Contingently issuable ordinary shares are treated as outstanding and included in the calculation of both basic and diluted EPS if the conditions are satisfied.… If the conditions are not satisfied, the number of contingently issuable shares included in the diluted EPS calculation is based on the number of shares that would be issuable if the end of the period were the end of the contingency period" (IAS 33, para 52).

   (The earnings of MB limited at the end of 2012 were €800,000. Assuming this is the end of the contingency period the group would have failed to meet its target earnings on MB of €5 million. As a result no additional shares would be issued.)

In order to comply with the above rules, the calculation of diluted EPS should be carried out in two stages. The first stage is to identify and rank each potential issue. The second stage is to consider the cumulative effect of each dilutive instrument on the EPS. The most dilutive position is reported. This is illustrated below:

STAGE ONE: THE RANKING ORDER
(Ranking from most dilutive to least dilutive)

Instrument	Note	Earnings Effect	Potential Shares	Incremental EPS	Ranking	Dilutable (basic €1.02)
		€000	000			
Share Options	(1)	0	450	0	1st	Yes
Convertible Preference Shares:						
In issue for 12 months	(2)	500	5000	0.1	2nd	Yes
Issued 30 Nov 2011	(3)	8.3	83	0.1	2nd	Yes
Contingent shares	(4)	0	0	0	n/a	N/a

Note 1: Options and warrants have a dilutive effect only when the average market price of ordinary shares exceeds the exercise price of the option or warrant (IAS 33, para 47). The average market price for the period is €1.50 and the exercise price is €1.05. Therefore the option will have a dilutive effect.

The assumed proceeds are regarded as having been received from an issue at full market price. The difference between the number of shares issued and the number that would have been issued at average market price during the period shall be treated as an issue for nil consideration. This bonus element is considered to be the dilutable element of the option (IAS 33, para 45) (1.5m @ €1.05 = €1.575m. 1.5m – (€1.575m/€1.50) = 450,000 shares for nil consideration).

Note 2: Preference dividend saved on conversion to equity. Savings in preference dividend @ 5% p.a. 10 million preference shares in issue for 12 months (10m × 5% = 500,000).

Conversion is assumed to take place at the most favourable rate (IAS 33, para 39) (10 million preference shares converted to one ordinary share for every two preference shares held = 5 million shares).

Note 3: Diluted shares are deemed to have been converted at the beginning of the period or if later at the date of the issue of the potential shares (IAS 33, para 36).

Savings in preference dividend @ 5% p.a. Two million preference shares in issue for one month (2m × 5% × 1/12 = 83,000).

Conversion is assumed at the most favourable rate (IAS 33, para 39). (Two million preference shares converted one ordinary share for every two preference shares held for one month as additional shares issued 30 November 2012 = (2m/2 shares × 1/12 = 83,000).)

Note 4: There are no dilutive effects, as explained above.

STAGE TWO: DILUTED EPS IN ORDER FROM MOST DILUTIVE TO LEAST DILUTIVE
Calculation of Fully Diluted EPS

	Earning €000	**Shares 000**	**Diluted EPS**
Basic	72,136[3]	70,637	€1.02
Options	0	450	
	72,136	71,087	€1.01
Convertible Preference Shares	508	5,083	
	72,644	76,170	€0.95

[3] Potential ordinary shares shall be treated as dilutive only when their conversion to ordinary shares would decrease EPS (or decrease loss per share) from continuing operations (IAS 33, para 41).

Diluted EPS must also be disclosed based on total earnings (IAS 33, para 30):

	Earning €000	Shares 000	Diluted EPS
Basic	99,672	70,637	€1.41
Options	0	450	
Convertible preference	508	5,083	
	100,178	76,170	€1.32

Diluted EPS should also be disclosed based on discontinuing operations (IAS 33, para 68):

	Earning €000	Shares 000	Diluted EPS €
Basic	27,536	70,627	0.39
Options	0	450	
Convertible Preference Shares	508	5,083	
	28,044	76,170	0.37

Working 3: The Comparative Period Finally, the comparative period. IAS 33, paragraph 64 explains that if there has been a bonus issue, share split, or capitalisation issue in the current financial period the calculation of basic and diluted EPS of all periods should be adjusted *retrospectively*. This means that the bonus element attached to the June 2012 rights issue should be applied to the shares of the comparative period. This adjustment can be effected by multiplying the comparative period EPS by the factor of the ex-rights price/cum-rights price as follows:

	Continuing Operations €	Discontinued Operations	Total Operations €
Basic (as reported)	0.61		0.68
Restated for bonus element of rights issue in June 2012 (1.91/1.95)	0.60	0.07	0.67
Diluted (as reported)	0.51		0.53
Restated for bonus element of rights issue in June 2012 (1.91/1.95)	0.50	0.02	0.52

Presentation of Convertible Preference Shares in the Draft Financial Statements You are asked to comment on the presentation of convertible preference shares in the draft financial statements. They are currently presented as equity instruments. However the guidance in IAS 32 *Financial Instruments: Presentation,* paragraphs 28–32, may indicate that the presentation of the instrument should be quite different.

IAS 32, paragraph 15, states that "the issuer shall classify the instrument … as a financial liability, a financial asset or an equity instrument in accordance with the substance of the contractual arrangement and the definitions of a financial liability, a financial asset and an equity instrument." (The definitions of these terms are included in paragraph 11 of the standard.) The convertible preference shares of the Rochfort Group display features of both a financial liability and an equity instrument. Rochfort is obliged to pay fixed dividends each period to the preference shareholders. This is an indication of a financial liability as there is a "contractual obligation to deliver cash or another financial asset to another entity" (IAS 32, para 11(a(i))). However the shares also display features of an equity instrument as they "may be settled in the entity's own equity instruments" (IAS 32, para 11(b)).

A compound financial instrument is one that displays elements of both debt and equity. Rochfort's convertible preference shares will fall into this category. IAS 32, paragraphs 28–32, provides guidance on the presentation of compound financial instruments.

In accordance with IAS 32, paragraph 29, Rochfort should "recognise separately the components of the financial instrument". The debt element will be classified as a liability and the equity element will be included in the equity of the group. This split is determined on initial recognition.

The split process is outlined in IAS 32, paragraphs 31 and 32. The split is determined by first measuring the fair value of a similar liability that does not have an associated equity component. This will be the debt component of the instrument. The equity element is then determined by deducting the fair value of the financial liability from the fair value of the compound financial instrument as a whole. (You should assume a prevailing market rate for instruments without a conversion feature is 10%.) An illustration follows:

Step	Details	Preference shares in issue at 1/1/2012	Preference shares issued at 30/11/2012	Total
		€	€	€
(i)	Present value of principal payable at the end of 'n' years discounted at 10%			
	Existing shares: from 2008–2013 6 years			

(proceeds €10 million discounted at 10% for 6 years)	5,644,000		5,644,000
New shares: from 2013 to 2013 1 year (note) *(proceeds €2 million discounted at 10% for 1 year)*		1,818,000	1,818,000
(ii) Present value of interest payable for 'n' years			
Existing shares: 2008–2013 6 years *(500,000 discounted at 10% for each of 6 years)*	2,177,630		2,177,630
New shares: 2013–2013 1 year *(100,000 discounted at 10% for 1 year)*		90,900	90,900
Total liability component	7,821,630	1,908,900	9,730,530
Proceeds on issue	10,000,000	2,000,000	12,000,000
Residual – equity component	2,178,370	91,100	2,269,470

(**Note:** Assume 12 months rather than 13 for illustration.)

In the intervening years interest is charged to profit or loss at a rate of 10% on the debt instrument.

(The above table is adapted from "*Liability or Equity A practical guide to the classification of financial instruments under IAS 32*", Grant Thornton, July 2009)

Outstanding Issue 2 – Operating Segments

IFRS 8, paragraph 5, defines an *operating segment* as follows. "An operating segment is a component of an entity:

- that engages in business activities from which it may earn revenues and incur expenses (including revenues and expenses relating to transactions with other components of the same entity)

- whose operating results are reviewed regularly by the entity's chief operating decision-maker to make decisions about resources to be allocated to the segment and assess its performance and
- for which discrete financial information is available."

Reportable segments IFRS 8 requires an entity to separately report information about a segment that meets any of the following quantitative thresholds (IFRS 8, para 13):
- its reported revenue, from both external customers and intersegment sales or transfers, is 10% or more of the combined revenue, internal and external, of all operating segments; or
- the absolute measure of its reported profit or loss is 10% or more of the greater, in absolute amount, of (i) the combined reported profit of all operating segments that did not report a loss and (ii) the combined reported loss of all operating segments that reported a loss; or
- its assets are 10% or more of the combined assets of all operating segments.

If the total external revenue reported by operating segments constitutes less than 75% of the entity's revenue, additional operating segments must be identified as reportable segments (even if they do not meet the quantitative thresholds set out above) until at least 75% of the entity's revenue is included in reportable segments (IFRS 8, para 15).

In relation to Rochfort, we must initially identify the operating segments that are separately reportable. These can be identified by comparing the results of the group to the required thresholds:

STEP 1: IDENTIFICATION OF REPORTABLE SEGMENTS

	Revenue (Total)	Profit	Assets
Ingredients	57%	60%	60%
Health Food	23%	25%	25%
Confectionery	8%	10%	10%
Other (rounding)	12%	5%	5%
	100%	100%	100%

The Ingredients and Health food segments exceed the reportable thresholds for all three criteria and so each of them is a reportable entity.

The confectionery segment satisfies two of the three criteria and is therefore also a reportable segment. (Only one criterion needs to be satisfied.)

Finally, as the total combined revenue of the three reportable segments exceed the 75% reportable threshold, (i.e. 88%) no further breakdown is required of the remaining activities that are included in the segment 'Other Business'.

IFRS 8, paragraph 20, requires the following disclosures to be made about its reportable segments:

1. General information about how the entity has identified its operating segments and the types of products and services from which it derives its revenue (IFRS 8, para. 22);
2. Information about revenue, operating profits, segment assets and liabilities (IFRS 8, paras 21(b) and 23–27);
3. A reconciliation between the amounts provided in the note and the figures presented in the financial statements (IFRS8, para 21(b) and 28);
4. Some entity-wide disclosures that are required even when an entity has only one reportable segment, including information about each product and service or groups of products and services (IFRS 8, paras. 3–32);
5. Analyses of revenues and certain non-current assets by geographical area – with an expanded requirement to disclose revenues/assets by individual foreign country (if material), irrespective of the identification of operating segments (IFRS 8, para. 33); and
6. Information about transactions with major customers (IFRS 8, para. 34).

In relation to the comparative period, we are told that the segmental information for 2011 has been restated so that it is comparable with the revised composition of the business segments. IFRS 8, paragraph 29, requires that a restatement of comparative information be carried out where there have been changes to the structure of its internal organisation unless "the information is not available and the cost to develop it would be excessive". This is not an issue for Rochfort. The restatement has already been carried out.

The suggested note for Rochfort is as follows:

General information (IFRS 8, para 22): "The segments align with the Group's internal financial reporting system and the way in which the Chief Operating Decision Maker assesses performance and allocates the Group's resources. A segment manager is responsible for each segment and is directly accountable for the performance of that segment to the Operating Executive Committee. The operating segments of the group are Ingredients, Health Food, Confectionery, and Other Business.

Note: Normally the results of discontinued operations would be presented separately in the segment report. However, you are to assume, for the purpose of this case study, that these results are included in the relevant segment headings.

INFORMATION ABOUT REVENUE, OPERATING PROFIT, SEGMENT ASSETS AND LIABILITIES
for the Year Ended 31 December 2012
(IFRS 8, paras. 23–27)

	Ingredients	**Health**	**Confectionery**	**Other**	**Total**
	€000	**€000**	**€000**	**€000**	**€000**
Total gross segment revenue	765,790	305,434	111,111	151,484	1,333,819
Inter-segment revenue	76,579	30,543	21,111	5,148	133,381
Segment external revenue	689,211	274,891	90,000	146,336	1,200,438

Segment earnings before interest, tax and exceptional items	85,495	35,623	14,249	7,125	142,491

The segment assets and liabilities at 31 December 2012 and segment capital expenditure (none given) and acquisitions for the year then ended are as follows:

Segment assets	435,958	181,649	72,660	36,330	726,597
Segment liabilities	145,761	60,734	24,294	12,147	242,936

INFORMATION ABOUT REVENUE, OPERATING PROFIT, SEGMENT ASSETS AND LIABILITIES
for the Year Ended 31 December 2011
(IFRS 8, paras. 23–27)

	Ingredients €000	**Health €000**	**Confectionery €000**	**Other €000**	**Total €000**
Total gross segment revenue	544,699	198,072	78,265	169,325	990,361
Inter-segment revenue	49,518	18,007	16,206	6,302	90,033
Segment external revenue	495,181	180,066	62,059	163,023	900,329
Segment earnings before interest, tax and exceptional items	30,109	4,301	6,452	2,151	43,013

The segment assets and liabilities at 31 December 2011 and segment capital expenditure (none given) and acquisitions for the year then ended are as follows:

Segment assets	445,418	44,542	55,677	11,135	556,772
Segment liabilities	148,123	45,576	22,788	11,394	227,882

RECONCILIATION TO THE FINANCIAL STATEMENTS
(IFRS 8, para 21 and 28)

	2012	2011
	€000	€000
Total segment revenue	1,333,819	990,362
Inter-segment revenue	133,381	90,033
Reported external revenue	1,200,438	900,329
Segment asset	726,596	556,772
Unallocated assets	186468	122,000
Reported assets	913,064	678,772
Segment liabilities	242,935	227,882
Unallocated liabilities	286,000	224,800
Reported liabilities	528,935	452,682

ANALYSIS OF REVENUE BY GEOGRAPHICAL AREA
(IFRS 8, para 33)

	2012	2011
	€000	€000
ROI	750,000	640000
UK	290,000	200100
Continental Europe	160,438	60229
	1,200,438	900,329

INFORMATION ABOUT MAJOR CUSTOMERS
(IFRS 8, para. 34)

Revenues from any single customer do not amount to 10% or more of the group's revenue.

Outstanding Issue 3 – Related Party Disclosures.

We must first understand and identify who are the related parties of the Rochfort Group.

IAS 24, paragraph 9, provides this guidance: "A related party is a person or entity that is related to the entity that is preparing its financial statements." Related parties include:

1. A person (or a close member of that person's family) if that person has (i) control or joint control over the reporting entity; (ii) has significant influence over the reporting entity; or

(iii) is a member of the key management personnel of the reporting entity or of a parent of the reporting entity (IAS 24, para 9(a)). (In the case study this would include the key management of Rochfort.)

2. "The entity and the reporting entity are members of the *same group* (which means that each parent, subsidiary and fellow subsidiary is related to the others); (ii) if one entity is an *associate or joint venture* of the other entity (or an associate (iii) joint venture of a member of a group of which the other entity is a member); (iv) both entities *are joint* ventures of the same third party ..." (IAS 24, para 9(b)). (In the case study this would include Rochfort's subsidiaries Caladonia, MB Limited and Alexia. It would also include Rochfort's investment in Janus. Janus is an associate of the Rochfort group.)
3. Other indications of a related party relationship include a *post-employment defined benefit plan* for the benefit of employees of either the reporting entity or an entity related to the reporting entity (IAS 24, para 9(b)(v)).
4. Finally an entity is related to a reporting entity if the entity *is controlled* or *jointly controlled* by a person or a close member of that person's family who is identified in (1.) above; or if a person identified in (1.) above has significant influence over the entity or is a member of the key management personnel of the entity (or of a parent of the entity) identified in (1.) (IAS 24, para 9(b)(vi) and (vii)). (This may include FreshCo Limited.) We are told in the case study that two of the directors of Rochfort are also directors in FreshCo Limited. Common directorship, per se, does not make the entities related (IAS 24, para 11(a)). However, if either of these directors can assert influence on the relationship between the two entities (i.e. either the volume or price of goods sold to Rochfort), then both entities are deemed to be related parties. AL Kelly is the operations director of FreshCo. This is likely to give him influence over the relationship between FreshCo and Rochfort. The answer deems these two entities to be related.

IAS 24 also outlines what are deemed *not* related to the reporting entity (IAS 24, para 11). These include: two entities simply because they have a *director or key manager in common*, or *two venturers who share joint control* over a joint venture. *Providers of finance, trade unions, public utilities, and departments and agencies of a government* that do not control, jointly control or significantly influence the reporting entity, simply by virtue of their normal dealings with an entity (even though they may affect the freedom of action of an entity or participate in its decision-making process) are also not related. And finally, *a single customer, a supplier, franchisor, distributor, or general agent* with whom an entity transacts a significant volume of business merely by virtue of the resulting economic dependence are not considered to be related parties.

(Normally providers of finance are deemed not to be related to the entity. However if they are able to exert significant control over the operations of the entity then the relationship is altered. In the case study the venture capitalist has been offered a seat on the board of directors. We must make a judgement call on whether that gives him significant influence on Rochfort's operation. If you conclude that it does, the venture capitalist should be disclosed as a related party of the group. If you conclude otherwise, there will be no mention of this relationship in the related party disclosure note. The suggested solution concludes that the venture capitalist is not a related party. The basis for this decision is that, although he is a member of the board, he does not hold any equity finance and therefore the level of influence he can assert will be limited. You may argue the opposite.

In summary the related parties of Rochfort are:

Caladonia Ltd	subsidiary
MB Ltd	subsidiary
Alexia	subsidiary
Janus Ltd	associate
FreshCo	related through AL Kelly
Chairman, CEO and other directors	key management

The following disclosures must be made about related parties:

Relationships between parents and subsidiaries Regardless of whether there have been transactions between a parent and a subsidiary, an entity must disclose the name of its parent and, if different, the ultimate controlling party. If neither the entity's parent nor the ultimate controlling party produces financial statements available for public use, the name of the next most senior parent that does so must also be disclosed (IAS 24, para 13).

Management compensation Disclose key management personnel compensation in total and for each of the following categories (IAS 24, para 17):
- short-term employee benefits;
- post-employment benefits;
- other long-term benefits;
- termination benefits; and
- share-based payment benefits.

Related party transactions If there have been transactions between related parties, disclose the nature of the related party relationship as well as information about the transactions and outstanding balances necessary for an understanding of the potential effect of the relationship on the financial statements. These disclosures would be made separately for each category of related party and would include (IAS 24, para 18–19):
- the amount of the transactions;
- the amount of outstanding balances, including terms and conditions and guarantees;
- provisions for doubtful debts related to the amount of outstanding balances; and
- expenses recognised during the period in respect of bad or doubtful debts due from related parties.

The final note for Rochfort may appear as follows:

RELATED PARTY TRANSACTIONS

The related parties of the group include (IAS 24, para 13):

Subsidiaries:	Caladonia Ltd (100%), MB Ltd (100%), Alexia (70%)
Associate:	Janus Ltd (28%)
Other:	Key Management, FreshCo

FreshCo is a supplier to the Rochfort Group. Mr AL Kelly, non-executive director of the Rochfort Group, is the Operations Director of FreshCo Ltd.

Key Management Compensation (IAS 24, para 17)

	2012	2011
	€000	**€000**
Salaries*	2,003	1,015
Post-employment Benefits	1,492	580
Share-based Payments	179	88

* Salaries per individual would normally be disclosed.

The following transactions were carried out with the group and its related parties (IAS 24, para 18–19):

Sales of goods and services

	2012	2012	2011	2011
	Goods	**Services**	**Goods**	**Services**
	€000	**€000**	**€000**	**€000**
Subsidiaries	80,029	53,352	63,023	27,010
Associates	878	994	971	599

Sales to related parties were carried out under normal commercial terms and conditions.

Purchases of goods and services

	2012	2012	2011	2011
	Goods	**Services**	**Goods**	**Services**
	€000	**€000**	**€000**	**€000**
Subsidiaries	35,000	14,790	21,265	13,004
Associates	1,060	850	761	430
FreshCo	1,800			

Purchases from related parties were carried out under normal commercial terms and conditions.

Year-end Balances (IAS 24, para 18(b))

	2012	2011
	€000	**€000**
Subsidiaries	600	400
FreshCo	475	

Outstanding Issue 4 – Contingent Liabilities

The most appropriate treatment for this transaction depends on the likely outcome of the case. Anna Jones favours complete disclosure with the inclusion of a provision in the financial statements. Paul Henry would like to omit this information altogether until the outcome of the case is clear.

At the end of the reporting period, the outcome of this case remains uncertain. It could be argued that the Financial Director is being over-cautious in creating a provision. Payment may happen but it is by no means 'probable' at the end of 2012. The Rochfort Group may be liable.

A contingent liability is described in IAS 37, paragraph 10, as a "possible obligation that arises from past events and whose existence will be confirmed only by the occurrence or non-occurrence of one or more uncertain future events not wholly within the control of the entity". Contingencies are disclosed but not accrued.

A contingent liability is probably a fair presentation for this case. It will inform stakeholders of the progress of the case without admitting liability. The disclosures would include a brief description of the nature of the event and, where practicable, an estimate of its financial effect, and an indication of uncertainties relating to timing and the possibility of any re-imbursement.

There is, however, one exception to this. IAS 37, paragraph 92, explains that in extremely rare cases the information need not be disclosed if disclosure can be expected to seriously prejudice the position of the entity. In this situation, only information about the general nature of the case need be disclosed along with an explanation for the omission. An allegation of price fixing may have a very serious effect on the continued viability of the Armada group. It could be argued, therefore, that as this information is highly sensitive and prejudicial that they use paragraph 92 to excuse the group from making detailed disclosures about the case.

An appropriate level of disclosure would include:

CONTINGENT LIABILITIES

The Company is engaged in litigation arising in the ordinary course of its business. In 2012 a price-fixing allegation was made against the group. The group was accused, by the European Competition Authority, of engaging in price-fixing practices over a period of five years between 2005 and 2010. The group vigorously denies the claim. Legal proceedings have been underway since September 2012. Correspondence with the group's solicitors in January 2013 suggests that the outcome of the case remains unclear. However, we do not believe that any such litigation will change the group's ability to continue as a going concern.

Requirement (b)

TABLE OF RATIOS

	Ingredients		Health		Confectionery		Other		Total	
	2012	2011	2012	2011	2012	2011	2012	2011	2012	2011
Profitability										
Gross margin	n/a	n/a	n/a	n/a	n/a	n/a	n/a	n/a	51%	47%
External revenue as % of total sales	90%	91%	90%	91%	81%	79%	97%	96%	90%	91%
Total sales growth	41%	n/a	54%	n/a	42%	n/a	–11%	n/a	35%	n/a
External sales growth	39%	n/a	53%	n/a	45%	n/a	–10%	n/a	33%	n/a
Operating profit margin	12.4%	6%	13%	2%	15.8%	10.4%	5%	1%	12%	5%
ROSF (segment profit/segment net assets)	29%	10%	29%	–4%	29%	14%	29%	8%	37%	18%[4]
Asset Turnover										
Segment Asset Turnover (external revenue/segment assets)	1.58	1.11	1.51	4.04	1.24	1.11	4.03	14.64	1.31	1.33[5]
Shareholder Analysis (other)										
EPS of Group										
Basic (total) (per issue 1)									1.41	0.67
Diluted (total) (per issue 1)									1.32	0.52
P/E ratio (using an average share price of €1.50 and basic EPS)									1.06	2.23
Dividend per share (based on ordinary dividend)									19.40c	40.84c

(*continued over the page*)

[4] Total ROSF includes non-allocated net assets.
[5] Total Asset Turnover includes non-allocated assets.

Liquidity		
Current ratio	3.28	1.87
Acid test ratio	2.06	1.1
Cash to current liabilities	0.92	0.26
Receivable days	47.52	50.51
Payable days	68.11	87.90
Inventory days	105.01	86.72
Gearing Ratio		
Gearing ratio (excluding leases)	45%	53%
Interest cover ((operating profit + finance income)/finance costs)	7.95	3.15

The Analysis

The Rochfort Group delivered a strong performance in 2012 with strong growth experienced in all of the group's activites. The group delivered in 2012 in the following ways:

- Total revenue increased by 35% (33% external sales) over the previous period. Revenue improved in three out of four of the operating segments although the improvement varied between segments. Sales growth in the Health Food sector was particularly good at 54% (53% external). Other Business displayed disappointing results with revenue falling by 11% (10% external).
- Gross profit margin and operating profit margin increased in 2012. Total gross margin increased from 47% to 51% while the operating profit margin increased by 7 percentage points. Margins also improved across all operating segments with the Health Food sector again displaying the best performance in the period.
- The overall Return on Shareholder Funds was a healthy 37% for 2012. This compares favourably with the 2011 yield of 18%. ROSF again improved across all operating segments although, once again, the Health Food sector displayed the highest increase while the growth rate in the Confectionery market displayed disappointing results.
- Shareholder indicators are all positive. Earnings per Share (basic) increased by 107% while the return on shareholder funds improved by 19 percentage points.
- Dividends per share have fallen from 40.84c to 19.91c. This reduction is partially due to the increase in ordinary shares issued during 2012.
- The group has total committed debt facilities of €308.7 million at the end of 2012. Debt levels increased over the period from €256.7 million to €308.7 million although the overall gearing ratio has fallen from 53% to 45%. The improvement in interest cover is consistent with this reduction. Interest cover has more than doubled over the period.
- The group focused on the management of cash during the period and liquidity indicators testify to this improvement. All areas of liquidity, with the exception of inventory, show significant improvement over the period. Inventory turnover has slowed. Rochfort will be reviewing overall inventory control systems in 2013 as part of the normal review process.
- The group continues to supply to a wide range of customers. The group is not reliant on any one customer for its business. Indeed, revenue from any single customer does not amount to 10% or more of the Group's revenues.
- The group's share price did not change significantly over the financial year. The average price was €1.50. Although disappointing, this trend was consistent for all food businesses listed on the London Stock Exchange and reflects the challenging economic environment in which the group trades.

Requirement (c)

Dear Mr Arnold

Thank you for your recent correspondence. My name is Paul Halligan and I am an audit manager with Ellis & Romney, registered auditors. We are currently completing the audit of the Rochfort Group's 2012 financial statements. Anna Jacob, with whom you have been in contact, has asked me to write to you responding to the remaining queries that you have about the 2011 financial statements.

I have reviewed your letter. Your queries are valid and incisive. I will endeavour to respond as clearly as possible.

Capital Grants Capital grants are presented in the financial statements in accordance with IAS 20 *Accounting for Government Grants and Disclosure of Government Assistance.* Capital grants, which are grants relating to the acquisition of non-current assets, can be presented in the financial statements in two different ways. The approach adopted by the Rochfort Group is known as the *deferred income approach*. This means that, on receipt of the grant, the bank account is increased and a liability is created. It is this liability to which you refer in your letter. A portion of this liability is transferred to the statement of comprehensive income each period. This has the effect of reducing the liability and increasing reported profit. The standard requires that the grant is recognised as income *"on a systematic and rational basis over the useful life of the asset"* (IAS 20, para 26). The accounting standard does not refer to the period over which the conditions may be satisfied. For example, a grant received towards the acquisition of machinery, that has a useful life of 10 years, may be conditional on generating a certain number of jobs in a required period of time, say, three years. Under the current standard the grant will be transferred to the statement of comprehensive income over 10 years although, once the employment thresholds have been exceeded, there will be no obligation to repay the grant. This is not a desirable presentation. Indeed, the treatment of capital grants in IAS 20 conflicts with the treatment of grants in another accounting standard, IAS 41 *Agriculture.* Paragraph 35 of this standard states that *"If ... a grant is conditional, the entity recognises it as income only when the conditions have been met"* (IAS 41, para 35). The regulatory authority for accounting standards, the International Accounting Standards Board (IASB), is fully aware of this discrepancy. In fact, work commenced in 2004 on a project to revamp the accounting standard for government grants. However this has since been deferred pending completion of other projects that the IASB are currently engaged in.

Adjusted Earnings per Share First, let me put your mind at rest. There is no technical error in the financial director's review. The ratio is correct. You have, however, correctly observed that the ratio in the financial director's review is inconsistent with the figure in the Statement of Comprehensive Income. Let me explain.

EPS is often considered to be the single most important metric in assessing a company's profitability. The EPS ratio is also used to determine another very important ratio called the Price Earnings Ratio (P/E). These two ratios are used extensively by a wide range of stakeholders to assess financial performance. It is appropriate that there is regulation in place to govern how this ratio is calculated. IAS 33 *Earnings per Share* provides this regulation. IAS 33 lays down strict guidelines on how this ratio should be calculated.

However, the rules of IAS 33 are not employed in the wider financial industry. Investment analysts commonly publish alternative EPS ratios, described as headline (*or* adjusted *or* proforma) EPS. These alternative metrics often show results that are different to IAS 33 as a different version of earnings is used. Headline EPS omits exceptional items, among other things, from earnings.

IAS 33 recognises that there are many variations to the EPS ratio. In order to accommodate headline EPS ratios, the accounting standard permits inclusion of additional

EPS ratios in the annual report so long as "each ratio is disclosed with equal prominence" (IAS 33, para 73).

What you are reading in the financial director's review is the adjusted (headline) EPS, while the body of the financial statements reports the IAS 33 version. If you would like to reconcile the difference, you should refer to note x of the 2011 financial statements where a reconciliation of the figures is provided.

Note: If you want to broaden the discussion of adjusted EPS with your student group you could consider the questionable practice of highlighting the adjusted (and often better) EPS in financial statements. There is widespread criticism of this practice. The practice can be summed up in the following quote *"EEBS ratio: 'Earnings Excluding All the Bad Stuff.'"*[6]

Interim Financial Reporting I appreciate your comments about the 2012 interim report. However, as experienced auditors, we carry out our duties with the utmost care and adhere, at all times, to relevant laws and regulations. I think there may be some confusion, on your part, on what the purpose of an interim financial report is and what the report entails. Let me explain.

The purpose of an interim financial report is to report to shareholders, during the financial year, on the financial progress of the entity. 'Interim' can imply any period during the financial year but most commonly half year or quarter year. For Irish and UK publicly quoted companies, interim reports are prepared on a half-yearly basis.

The accounting standard IAS 34 *Interim Financial Reporting* provides guidance on what the report should contain. In accordance with this standard the report should contain either a complete or a condensed set of financial statements for an interim period (IAS 34, para 4). In addition to IAS 34 companies must also include in their interim report an interim management report and a responsibility statement. This is required as a result of EU Transparency Directive 2007. In practice, most companies choose the condensed option. A condensed set of financial statements should include the following:

- a condensed statement of financial position;
- either (a) a condensed statement of comprehensive income or (b) a condensed statement of comprehensive income and a condensed income statement;
- a condensed statement of changes in equity;
- a condensed statement of cash flows; and
- selected explanatory notes.

Rochfort's policy is to present condensed financial statements in their interim report. This will explain why the statements to which you refer are shorter than those presented in the final accounts.

On the matter of disclosure note omissions, paragraph 15 of IAS 34 states that "there is a presumption that anyone who reads an entity's interim report will also have access to its most recent annual report. Consequently, IAS 34 avoids repeating annual disclosures in interim condensed reports".

[6] Fox, 1998, cited in Johnson & Schwartz 2005, p. 919.

The date you received your interim report was 10 August 2011. This was 41 days after the half-year reporting date. This issue date is, in fact, ahead of the required deadline. IAS 34 encourages publicly-traded entities to have interim financial reports available not later than 60 days after the end of the interim period (IAS 34, para 1). You received your report 19 days ahead of this deadline.[7]

Finally, you mention the omission of an audit report. You do not need to worry; Ellis & Romney have not been negligent in their duty of care to their client. There is currently no legal requirement to have interim financial statements audited, although it is optional.

I hope this letter helps alleviate your concerns about the financial statements. If you have further queries, please do not hesitate to get back to me.

Regards

Paul Halligan BAA, FCA

[7] IAS 34 Para 1.

INDEX